The Merchant of Venice

THE MERCHANT OF VENICE

A Guide to the Play

VICKI K. JANIK

Greenwood Guides to Shakespeare

GREENWOOD PRESS
Westport, Connecticut • London

Library of Congress Cataloging-in-Publication Data

Janik, Vicki K.
 The merchant of Venice : a guide to the play / Vicki K. Janik.
  p. cm. — (Greenwood guides to Shakespeare)
 Includes bibliographical references and index.
 ISBN 0–313–30944–2 (alk. paper)
 1. Shakespeare, William, 1564–1616. Merchant of Venice. 2. Venice (Italy)—In
literature. 3. Shylock (Fictitious character) 4. Jews in literature. I. Title. II. Series.
PR2825.J36 2003
 822.3'3—dc21   2003045531

British Library Cataloguing in Publication Data is available.

Library of Congress Catalog Card Number: 2003045531
ISBN: 0–313–30944–2

First published in 2003

Greenwood Press, 88 Post Road West, Westport, CT 06881
An imprint of Greenwood Publishing Group, Inc.
www.greenwood.com

Printed in the United States of America

The paper used in this book complies with the
Permanent Paper Standard issued by the National
Information Standards Organization (Z39.48–1984).

10 9 8 7 6 5 4 3 2 1

CONTENTS

PREFACE

The Merchant of Venice embodies, and encourages, a multitude of contradictions. In its 400-year history, it has been the most popular comedy written by William Shakespeare, performed more often than any other play except *Hamlet;* yet many readers and viewers find it the least likable comedy in the canon. As a corollary, Shylock, the most famous character in all Shakespeare's comedies, is arguably the most troubling. Readers continue to ask whether Shakespeare intends for Shylock to expose the cruelty of the anti-Semitism surrounding him or to justify it. If the latter were true, the play itself would be anti-Semitic.

Indeed, the play has been mired in anti-Semitism. More completely and less distastefully, it is mired in money. Perhaps that explains some of its popularity. But like so many elements in the play, money has at least two faces: it is both the enemy of and the reward for virtue. In fact, *The Merchant of Venice* (*MV*) condemns much of what it condones—wealth, anti-Semitism, justice, possession, even some forms of love. The play guides us through a maze that continually leads to the dead end of paradox. Shylock is a villain and a scapegoat; Portia's wit, gently urging compassion, carries overtones of hardheartedness and arrogance; Antonio is as confident in his beneficence as in his bigotry; and Bassanio is devoted, most of the time. Themes in the play hold similar contrarieties. False seeming is both a trap—for Shylock—and a winning strategy—for Bassanio and Portia. A controlling paternal love helps Portia but alienates Jessica, and the riddling solutions at the center of the casket, bond, and ring plots imply clarity in language but demonstrate its opaqueness. And like a shiny, golden thread, money is woven through it all, through Antonio's reverence for the rules by which money is moved, through Bassanio's revelry in its pleasures, through Portia's awards of money to Lorenzo and Antonio in Belmont's moonlight. Perhaps if Shylock had been satisfied with Portia's proposed money settlement in the Venetian court, he too might have qualified to join that evening's moonlit celebration.

The paradoxes and questions in *MV* draw diverse critical responses and theatrical interpretations, which highlight what appears to be the play's flawed morality. The heroes are materialistic bigots, and the villain lives in suffering. This flaw troubles the audience, but it also mirrors real life, where lovers, like Portia and Bassanio, rarely offer or receive complete loyalty; and risk takers, like the merchant and the usurer, seek scapegoats to explain their failures. There are very good reasons for our fascination and dismay with a contradictory play like *MV.*

The purpose of this reference guide is to examine the complexities and the beauty of the play. In no way does the guide pretend to be exhaustive. In seven chapters, I present topics that have inspired book-length studies and hundreds of articles. For example, excellent texts and essays deal with Shylock, the history of anti-Semitism, usury, and love from a variety of critical perspectives. Thus I present an overview of scholarship, examine the dilemmas of the play, and identify sources for further study.

The guide is written so that each chapter stands alone as an individual overview, but the result of this is, of course, unavoidable redundancy. Some information and ideas must be repeated.

This guide is offered to new readers of the play as well as to those who are long familiar with its pleasures and perplexities. To clarify the play for the former group, I explain relevant terms throughout the text, but editorial and critical analyses of this play cannot be simplified.

Chapter 1 contains two discussions; the first concerns the probable date when Shakespeare wrote the play, and the second is an overview of the history of the text, beginning with descriptions of various versions of the texts that editors and printers have composed over 400 years. Problems with the text of *MV* are minor compared with those of other Shakespeare plays, but disagreements remain over the accuracy of the characters' names, the act and scene divisions, the stage directions, and some words in the script.

Chapter 2 examines contexts and sources for the play. Contextual topics—that is, relevant social and economic issues at the time Shakespeare wrote the play—include anti-Semitism and usury; and sources are the short stories, poems, debates, and plays that Shakespeare used in its composition. One story, contained in the collection titled *Il Pecorone* (*The Dunce*), by Giovanni Fiorentino, dominates as the source of the plot of *MV,* but others clearly contribute. The chapter describes these sources, their contribution to the play, and most important, the remarkable ways in which Shakespeare altered them.

Chapter 3 introduces dramatic structure and goes on to examine the plot, beginning with a review of comic plot structure applicable to the five acts of *MV.*

Chapter 4 discusses characters. It explores the origins, conventions, language, and actions of each main character and considers the often-paradoxical qualities each displays.

Chapter 5 investigates some of the themes suggested in the play. The themes comprise the implicit moral or philosophical questions the play raises about comic vision, Belmont and Venice, anti-Semitism, the differences between friendship and romantic love, and religion, justice, and mercy. These questions are embedded in the settings, plot structure, and characters and are by no means neatly delineated.

Chapter 6 surveys the literary criticism published about the play during the twentieth century. It includes brief explanations of major literary theories and describes their application to the play.

Chapter 7 is an overview of the 400-year performance history of *MV,* necessarily selective because of the play's popularity. It includes discussions of individuals who participated in these productions as well as the ways in which they reflect then current social and aesthetic values.

The text from which I quote the play is edited by M. M. Mahood (1987), an edition in the New Cambridge Shakespeare series. I have kept explanatory endnotes to a minimum in this text, using parenthetical notes to identify quotations from the play and other sources, and I include an annotated list of sources following the text.

I am fortunate to have worked with Dr. George Butler of Greenwood Press, whose gracious assistance, advice, and patience helped guide me through the difficulties inherent in completing a manuscript. I also am indebted to United University Professions, the professional union of the State University of New York, for granting me a Professional Development Award of a one-course release that provided me some time to work on the text. I thank my children, Victor, Tyra, Mary, and Carolyn, for their patience, support, and assistance. Finally, I remain deeply grateful for the source hunting, discussion, editing, proofreading, and love of my husband, Del, who regularly lives the inscription of the lead casket.

1

TEXTUAL HISTORY

DATING

William Shakespeare wrote *The Merchant of Venice (MV)* sometime between 1596 and 1598,[1] the *terminus a quo* and *terminus ad quem,* respectively. The later date is easier to fix than the earlier. On July 22, 1598, the play was listed in the Stationers' Register in London (described later in the chapter); and on September 7 of the same year, Frances Meres, who was very familiar with the contemporary theater, listed it in his treatise *Pallidis Tamia, Wits Treasury* among Shakespeare's (then) six comedies: "his *Gentlemen of Verona,* his *Errors,* his *Loue labours lost,* his *Loue labours wonne,* his *Midsummers night dreame,* & his *Merchant of Venice.*"[2] The first five are known to be early works; therefore, *MV,* placed last on the list, is logically the last written.[3]

The earliest date of authorship is generally agreed to be 1596, based on internal evidence from 1.1, when Salarino jokingly tells Antonio how he might fear for the safety of merchant ships at sea if they were his:

> I should not see the sandy hourglass run
> But I should think of shallows and of flats,
> And see my wealthy Andrew dock'd in sand
> Vailing her high top lower than her ribs
> To kiss her burial . . . (1.1.25–29)

In June 1596, English ships under the command of the Earl of Essex captured a Spanish galleon, the *San Andrés,* renamed the *Saint Andrew,* along with the *San Matias,* renamed the *Saint Matthew.* The two Spanish ships had run aground in Cadiz harbor. Although the *Saint Andrew* held a cargo worth only about 5,000 pounds, it was a large ship and became the largest ship in the Queen's navy. Londoners learned of the capture of these Spanish ships on July 30, 1596, and after that they regularly heard news that the *Saint Andrew* was in danger of capsizing in the sandy flats around England because of her great size. Later, Essex decided not to sail her through the Goodwin Sands off the coast of Kent, the location where, in *MV,* Salarino reports that one of Antonio's ships indeed was wrecked—in "the narrow seas . . . a very dangerous flat and fatal, where the carcasses of many a tall ship lie buried" (3.1.3–6). Thus modern editors, like Stanley Wells and Gary Taylor (119–20), M. M. Mahood (1), and Jay Halio (27–28), agree with John Russell Brown, who writes that the play's reference to the *Saint Andrew* is "reasonably certain" (xxvii).

Brown, Wells and Taylor, and Halio further establish the 1596 date, rather than an earlier one, with stylistic features. Brown claims that the play is reminiscent of the later comedies, *As You Like It* and *Twelfth Night,* rather than the five other earlier comedies named by Meres (76). Halio supports Wells and Taylor, who use the play's colloquialisms it verse figures, its metrical figures, and the Oras pause test[4] to place it before *King John,* before or after *Henry IV Part I,* and after *Henry IV Part II.* Halio further observes that the prose "looks forward to Falstaff's," and that Shylock's unwieldy dominance in the play guided Shakespeare to restrain himself in creating later comic villains, Don John and Malvolio (28–29). He also suggests that Portia has later reincarnations as Beatrice, Rosalind, and Viola, and Bassanio as Claudio and Orlando. Although much of this stylistic analysis presumes a subjectively determined evolution in Shakespeare's plays, it does support the *Saint Andrew* reference of 1596.[5]

TEXT HISTORY

The first edition of *MV* is a quarto edition,[6] named the Heyes-Roberts quarto after its publisher, Thomas Heyes, and its printer, James Roberts. Referred to as Q1, it was published in 1600, two to four years after Shakespeare wrote the play. The Heyes-Roberts quarto is the authoritative text and the basis for the second quarto in 1619 (Q2), the third quarto in 1637 (Q3), the First Folio edition in 1623 (F1),[7] and all modern editions. It is relatively free of errors and ambiguities; therefore, the probable manuscript or handwritten copy from which it was set was a fair copy, possibly written by Shakespeare himself.

Background

In Elizabethan London (1558–1603), the events leading to the publication of a play began when the playwright wrote the play for an acting company. Before it could be performed, the Queen's Master of the Revels, who for some 31 years (1579–1610) was Sir Edmund Tilney, licensed the play for acting.[8] W. W. Greg notes that such licensing was intended to "tighten [government] control over the stage" and involved scrutinizing and possibly reforming the text so that neither the heretical nor the seditious would appear on stage.[9] After performances began, when the company no longer found the play profitable in performance, or perhaps when the company needed funding, it sold the play to a potential publisher, who gained the license to print it from the printers and booksellers guild called the London Company of Stationers, formally incorporated in 1557 but active well before that. The Stationers' Guild had powers granted by the crown to control all publication except that done by the university presses of Oxford and Cambridge.

The potential publisher submitted to the Stationers' Guild an actual manuscript of a play in one of several forms, including the following:

- The author's "foul papers"—a rough draft often filled with erasures, alterations, and insertions.
- A "fair copy"—a recopied manuscript of the foul papers, which the author or a scribe would have completed for the acting company.
- The playbook, or "book of the play," today called the promptbook—usually a fair copy with additional stage directions in marginal notes that was used by an assistant to cue lines and action during the production of the play.

The playbook was generally presented to and approved by the Master of the Revels before performances began.

In Elizabethan London, a potential publisher, who was not necessarily the printer, took a manuscript to the Stationers' Hall for approval where either the upper Warden or the under Warden of the Company of Stationers, or both, granted approval for printing. With this approval, the title was included in the Stationers' Register,[10] a listing of about 70 percent of all books published in the city and its suburbs. This official acceptance for publication by the stationers served as a sort of self-censorship that discouraged further printing restrictions by existing government censors. Such censors were known as "correcters of the press," who, beginning in 1588, consisted of 12 clergymen under authority of the Privy Council, who had the right to determine a book heretical or seditious.

The Authoritative Text: The Heyes-Roberts Quarto (Q1)

The Merchant of Venice presents a somewhat unusual sequence of licensing and printing as recorded in the Stationers' Register. With the payment of a sixpence fee on July 22, 1598, James Roberts, a printer who held the privilege of printing "all manner of [play]billes" for London's theaters, gained the first of two entries for *MV* in the Stationers' Register. The listing reads as follows:

> xxij Iulij [1598]
>   Iames Robertes. / Entred for his copie vnder the hand*e*s of bothe
> the wardens, a booke of the Marchaunt of Venyce or otherwise called
> the Iewe of Venyce. / Prouided that yt bee not prynted by the said
> Iames Robert*e*s; or anye other whatsoeuer wthout lycence first had
> from the Right honorable the lord Chamberlen   vjd

Following Elizabethan practice, the name of the author is not included in the entry because the company itself owned the manuscript once the playwright turned it over to them. The listing gave no rights to the author or the acting company but rather established "the right of a stationer to the exclusive enjoyment of a copy which he had been the first to publish or had lawfully acquired from a former owner."[11] The 1598 entry for *MV,* however, did grant the acting company, the Lord Chamberlain's Men, or more specifically, the Lord Chamberlain himself, who served as the company's protector, the unusual right to stipulate if and when the play could be printed. Consequently, we can assume first, that in 1598 Roberts gained the manuscript legitimately because the entry included this protective clause, and second, that in 1598, the play was being profitably performed in the public theater by the Lord Chamberlain's Men, who wished to maintain exclusivity.

Also unusual, but by no means unprecedented, is the probability that the 1598 listing served not as a license to print but rather as an implicit "blocking" or "staying" entry. Such an entry effectively disallowed anyone else from printing the play. This theory was first proposed by Alfred W. Pollard,[12] and although he admits that evidence is clearly circumstantial, Greg supports the theory as follows:[13]

- As the printer of the acting company's playbills, Roberts was both familiar and dependable—the "obvious person" (121) to contact if the company in fact wished to have a staying entry for *MV.*

- Roberts entered similar staying entries for the Lord Chamberlain's Men five times in five years, when the company was known to have been protecting its repertory.

- In four of the five alleged staying entries, Roberts agreed not to publish without the license of the company.
- In two of the five entries, Roberts seems not to have had in his possession his own manuscript but rather a promptbook.[14]
- In three of the five entries, the company released the play after two years, but the publication was not completed by Roberts.
- Ten other plays of the Lord Chamberlain's Men were listed in the Stationers' Register by owners other than Roberts during this five-year period and were not stayed in this manner.

Greg concludes there is "at least some plausibility" to Pollard's theory that the 1598 entry served as a staying entry rather than as a license to publish (*Some Aspects* 121).

Roberts finally did print the play two years later in 1600, but he did not publish it. On October 28, 1600, he transferred the rights to Thomas Heyes, an action again recorded in the Stationers' Register. Probably both men went to the Stationers' Hall together, or Heyes submitted a written permission from Roberts, since Roberts's consent is noted in the following second entry in the Stationers' Register for the transfer of rights:

> 28 octobr' [1600]
> Tho. haies Entred for his copie vnder the hande*s* of the Wardens &
> by Consent of mr Robert*es*. A booke called the booke of the m'chant
> of Venyce   vjd

The reason for the transfer can only be conjectured. Mahood (168) suggests that Roberts may have had insufficient funds or time to publish the play in 1600 when the company finally granted permission. Notable is the odd redundancy in the title, "A booke called the booke," which suggests that Thomas Heyes brought a promptbook to the Stationers' Hall when this second listing was granted. Titles of promptbooks began with the phrase "the book of." This would further substantiate Roberts and Heyes's statement that the acting company, which owned the promptbook, had indeed granted the license required in the first entry of 1598, because the company had entrusted a copy of the play to the two men.

The printers in Roberts's office probably began work on *MV* in the autumn of 1600 and completed the text before the end of November, because December publications were usually given the date from the following year. They set a title page that identifies the play as a "history" rather than a "comedy" and includes a clever description that reads like one of

Roberts's playbills. Enticingly, it details Shylock's "crueltie" without disclosing whether the cruelty is successfully enacted or only attempted (see Figure 1).[15]

A first question about the printed text must concern its provenance. What sort of manuscript did the two compositors in Roberts's shop follow

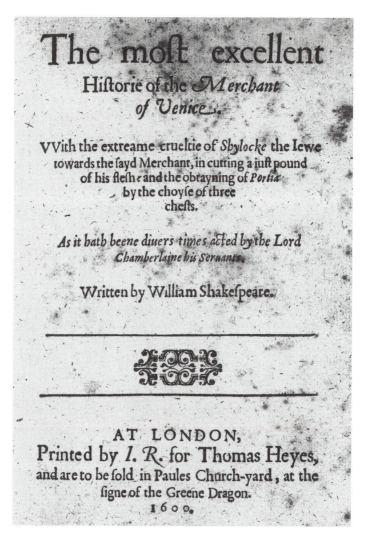

Title page of the Heyes-Roberts quarto, the first quarto edition (1600). By permission of the Folger Shakespeare Library.

in setting this first quarto edition of 1600: foul papers, fair papers, promptbook, or transcript of one? When Roberts gained the July 1598 Stationers' Register entry, "a booke of the Marchaunt of Venyce," he likely held foul or fair papers, but when Heyes and Roberts obtained the October 1600 Stationers' Register listing, they probably presented a promptbook, based on the redundancy in the title, as previously noted. The relative absence of errors in the quarto the compositors produced argues against foul papers, because the frequent corrections and alterations thought to be common to foul papers would result in a more confused, error-ridden print version.

In the first half of the twentieth century, Chambers and Greg contended that even though the promptbook was likely in Heyes's hands in October 1600,[16] internal evidence supports fair-copy provenance,[17] primarily because of the nature of the stage directions. Greg writes that a promptbook "would surely have straightened out the tangle of ambiguous prefixes," and stage directions are "on the whole rather scanty" (123), as practical promptbook stage directions could never afford to be.[18] Granted, a few are in the imperative mode of a promptbook—"*open the letter*" (3.2.234), "*play Musique*" (5.1.68)—but Shakespeare, as a theater professional, at times may have chosen the imperative mode himself.

The characteristics of the stage directions that support fair-copy rather than promptbook provenance fall into three groups:

1. Q1 has inconsistencies that would hamper theater prompting:
   - The names "Launce[let]" and "clowne" alternate in speech heads.
   - The names "Shy[locke]" and "Iew[e]" alternate in speech heads.
   - Confusion occurs in the speech heads among the names of the three "Sallies": Salarino, Solanio (sometimes spelled Salanio), and Salerio. This knotty problem is considered in greater detail in the discussion of Quarto 3 that follows. Several editors further argue that these three names refer to only two characters, whose names have inconsistent spellings.
   - Tubal has two entrances in one scene, at 3.1.60 and 3.1.62.

2. Q1 has vagueness that would lead to inconsistent performances:
   - The Q1 cues often read "*Sal.*", which could refer to any of the three Sallies and thus would be unworkable for a promptbook copy used during a production.
   - When Morocco enters, the stage direction calls for "three or four followers" (2.1.s.d.).
   - When Bassanio first talks with Lancelot, the stage direction calls for "a follower or two" (2.2.92.s.d.).
   - No stage direction is given for Portia's entrance in the street scene (4.2.1.s.d.).

3. Q1 has detailed literary description greater than that ordinarily included in promptbooks:

- The first casket scene begins, "enter Morocco, a tawny Moor all in white" (2.1.1.s.d.).

- The final casket test begins, "Bassanio comments on the caskets to himself" (3.2.62s.d.).

- Extra identification begins the first Belmont scene, "Her waiting woman *Nerissa*" (1.2.1.s.d.).

- Shylock's speech ends with an entrance by "*a man from* Antonio" (3.1.57.s.d.).

- Extra identification is included in the entrance that begins "The maskers, *Gratiano and* Salarino" (2.6.0.s.d.).

- Extra identification is included in the entrance that begins "Salerio, a messenger from Venice" (3.2.218.s.d.).

Most recent scholars agree on fair-copy provenance. Mahood states most strongly that "overall, there is a strong probability that every word in the copy for Q1 was Shakespeare's" (170), Halio writes that Q1 follows "very likely a fair copy" (86), and G. Blakemore Evans concludes that Q1 was set with "the use of some kind of authorial copy" (*Riverside Shakespeare* (1997) n. 283).

But in 1985, William B. Long effectively argued that presumptions of an orderly, highly annotated, consistent appearance in sixteenth-century manuscripts "are not valid" and that, unlike current theatrical practice, "authorial stage directions are very seldom changed in the theater" (122).[19] Thus postulates about the nature of promptbooks and fair and foul copies that ground arguments about provenance may be open to review.

If, however, we wish to assume fair-copy provenance, then the next question we may ask is whether that fair copy was written in Shakespeare's own hand. It is possible that Shakespeare, as the chief playwright of the company, could have had a fair copy produced by the playhouse scrivener (professional copyist), who himself might have left his own editorial fingerprints on the text. The compositors who worked in Roberts's shop also set *Hamlet* Q2 in 1604 or 1605 and, based on the 1594 quarto, *Titus Andronicus* Q2. They are known for their habit of following very carefully the idiosyncrasies of their sources, while many other printers created their own punctuation and format. This is evidenced from the idiosyncrasies Roberts's compositors reproduced from the 1594 *Titus* in their edition of 1600 and the varieties of punctuation they followed in plays by other dramatists. Named X and Y by Brown,[20] the two compositors each completed four or five large alternating sections of a text. Because the compositors of this very clear first quarto of *MV* also set the second quarto of *Hamlet,* which suffers from much textual confusion, some scholars conclude that the compositors worked from different types of manu-scripts: *MV* could have been set from a scribal copy, the *Hamlet* quarto from a holograph copy (written in the author's own hand).

Yet certain inconsistencies and awkward details, as well as similarities to other writings known to be Shakespeare's, suggest to Mahood that the copy used by the compositors was indeed in Shakespeare's hand.[21] Incon-sistency in Q1 begins in the first scene. It contains a repetition of Anto-nio's complaint of sadness, first to Solanio and Salarino (1.1.1*ff.*) and later to Gratiano, Bassanio, and Lorenzo (1.1.77*ff.*). Duplication occurs again, according to some readers, when 2.6 seems to have a double ending. At lines 60 and 61, Lorenzo speaks what sounds like a scene-concluding rhyming couplet, anticipating the planned masque:

> What, art thou come? On, gentleman, away!
> Our masquing mates by this time for us stay. (2.6.60–61)

But when Lorenzo and Jessica leave, Antonio enters, speaking briefly to Gra-tiano and telling him to hurry to the departing ship. Gratiano then responds with a second scene-concluding couplet at lines 69 and 70. Other irregulari-ties are the absence of a speech heading in 3.2 for the reader (Bassanio) of Antonio's letter and variations throughout the play in the form of the names of Solanio, Salarino, and Salerio, who is identified as "the messenger from Venice." For example, Solanio enters the first scene as Salanio, exits as Solanio, enters 2.4 as Salanio, and at line 61 is again Solanio.

While these irregularities do not serve as strong evidence that the au-thor's fair copy was the source, peculiarities in punctuation, capitaliza-tion, and spelling are more convincing. These peculiarities are similar to those in the other Shakespeare quartos previously mentioned as being set by the same careful compositors[22]—*Hamlet* Q2 and *Titus Andronicus* Q2. More important, the peculiarities in *MV* and *Hamlet* Q2 are similar to those in the handwritten additions to a play called *Sir Thomas More,* which most scholars agree were written by Shakespeare himself. These handwritten additions, known as Hand D, now serve as a unique model of manuscript idiosyncrasies characteristic to Shakespeare. Hand D uses nat-ural stops in conversation, as in the "Hath not a Jew eyes?" speech; the grammatically correct punctuation of set pieces, as in 5.1; and the overall light punctuation characteristic of the entire *MV* quarto.[23] Further support-ing the premise that Shakespeare used light punctuation, the Roberts com-positors used light punctuation in setting *Titus* Q2, although they included heavier punctuation in works by other authors.[24]

Another peculiarity of Q1 is that capital letters are used with decreasing frequency through the typesetting of the play. Wells and Taylor (324) as well as Halio (88) explain that this may be the result of insufficient capitals in the shop's type cases. But Mahood (173) argues that like the manuscript of Hand D (Shakespeare's presumed hand), the *MV* manuscript may have contained capitals only at the beginnings of lines following endstopped lines, and compositors X and Y may have increasingly followed this practice through the typesetting of *MV* Q1. Halio responds that if Shakespeare indeed did not capitalize first letters of certain verse lines, "it seems more likely that Shakespeare did not capitalize first letters of verse lines at all" (88).[25]

Spelling too in *MV* Q1, shows idiosyncrasies that are common to Hand D as well as to *Hamlet* Q2 but are absent from other work completed by compositors X and Y or from common use. The following chart describes these unique spellings based on information presented by Mahood (173):

MV (Q1)	*Hamlet* Q2	Hand D in *Sir Thomas More*	Contemporary Standard (set by compositors in non-Shakespearean manuscript)
-ewe	-ewe	-ewe	-ew
-owe	-owe	-owe	-ow
farwell	farwell	farwell	farewell
deare	deare	deare	deere
sayd	sayd	sayd	said
howre	howre	howre	houre
a leuen	a leauen	a leuenpence	eleuen (elevenpence)
how so	howsomeuer	[no sample]	howsoeuer

Although a mediating company scrivener may have maintained such orthographical variants, their survival is more likely if the compositors set the type directly from Shakespeare's holograph. Of the three plays listed in the chart, the clarity of Hand D and *MV* Q1 makes the inconsistencies of *Hamlet* Q2 the anomaly.[26] Still, the evidence is not conclusive for a handwritten manuscript. A careful scrivener employed by the Lord Chamberlain's Men could well have copied Shakespeare's unusual punctuation and spelling into a fair copy. Thus, although Mahood's premise is intriguing—that the manuscript "almost certainly came from Shakespeare's hand" (173)—Halio acknowledges that the evidence is only circumstantial and more accurately concludes that the copy was "possibly in Shakespeare's own hand" (86), while Wells and Taylor more specifically write that it was "either a reasonably fair copy in Shakespeare's own hand, or a very accurate transcript of such a document" (323).

The Pavier Quarto (Q2)

The second quarto edition of *MV,* Q2, is called the Pavier quarto of 1619. Its spurious printing is the result of Thomas Pavier's attempt to be the first publisher of Shakespeare's complete works after his death. Printing in the shop of William Jaggard and his son Isaac,[27] Pavier published 10 plays attributed to Shakespeare, the first 5 dated 1619. But on May 3, 1619, the Lord Chamberlain wrote the Stationers' Company to "take order for the stay" of further unapproved printing. After this, Pavier issued the other 5 plays with false dates, including *A Midsummer Night's Dream,* the doubtful quarto of *King Lear,* and *MV,* which were assigned original printing dates (1600 for *MV),* as if to pass them off as original quarto editions and gain some financial benefit from the unsavory affair.[28]

The *MV* title page in the Pavier quarto includes the imprint "Printed by *J. Roberts,* 1600," a misleading bit of information that, until the beginning of the twentieth century, had led editors to conclude that the Pavier edition was the first *MV* quarto printed. Because it has Roberts's name on the title page and not Heyes's name, it was thought to be the first printed version of the first manuscript that Roberts entered in the Stationers' Register in 1598. The Heyes-Roberts quarto of 1600 was therefore mistakenly thought to be printed from some other manuscript. Important editions of the play—including the *Variorum Edition of Shakespeare's Works,* edited by Horace Howard Furness and published in 1888, and the Cambridge editions of 1863 and 1891—followed the Pavier quarto.

In 1909, however, Greg, Pollard, and W. J. Neidig proved this conclusion to be inaccurate. The Q2 text shows evidence that Jaggard's compositors set the quarto from Q1: the presence of Q1 errors, the idiosyncratic printing of "G O D" (2.2.59) in full capitals with spaces between the letters (the practice of Roberts's compositors back in 1600), and the alteration of the word *coffer* in 4.1.350. The Heyes-Roberts quarto (Q1) has the word *coffer* printed with a broken piece of type on the second *f* so that the *ff* looks like an elongated *s* followed by a *t*. The word *coffer* thus looks like *coster,* which is the word printed in Q2. Quarto 2 is therefore a text derived from Q1 and has no textual authority.

Quarto 2 is further discredited on the basis of compositor determination, a study that identifies the individual compositors who set text. The compositors known as A and B set Shakespeare's First Folio in Jaggard's shop in 1623, and Compositor B may have also worked on Q2 of *MV.* Sections of text set by Compositor B have more errors, text alterations, and flawed solutions to compositorial problems, perhaps as a result of setting too many words from memory.[29] Thus Q2 contains such textual changes from Q1 as "husband's health" for Q1's "husband's welfare" (5.1.114), "twinkling of an eye" for Q1's "twinkling" (2.2.140), and the added word *O* to extend the prose line at 3.1.69 all the way to the right margin. Peter Blayney, however, argues that the compositors were not A and B but two other compositors whom he calls G and H. If so, he calculates that the sections set by compositors G and H contain 57 percent and 43 percent of the total number of errors in the text, respectively. Because the errors are divided between the compositors more equally, the failings of a single individual are considerably diminished.[30]

Granting the duplicity in the publication of Q2, Mahood argues that "we need to set aside our prejudices" (175) and acknowledge that in a few ways the study of compositor determination gives the text of Q2 some—but insufficient—authority. She notes several improvements in Q2 over Q1 and general changes that are a result of "intelligent and careful" (175) thinking. Among them are corrections of misprints in Q1. These include *e'en* for *in* at 3.5.17, the addition of necessary but missing stage directions, and the centering of stage directions that are squeezed to the right margin in Q1.[31] Halio also cites consistent capitalization at the beginnings of lines, improved punctuation, and modernized spellings (91).

Some alterations were the result of good intentions but poor theater, such as assigning the speeches of Salarino and Solanio according to their supposed personalities, one being quieter and one more talkative. Such speech assignments detract from the more amplified comic relationship between Gratiano and Lorenzo. As Mahood observes (179), the two Sallies who enter in 1.1 are undoubtedly not intended to be different from one another; according to the Heyes-Roberts quarto, Shakespeare seems to have intended that they be interchangeable. Quarto 2 also normalizes Shylock's unusual speech patterns, including his use of "moneys" and "a my shedding," and alters Lorenzo's teasing request to Jessica when they leave Venice. In Q1, Lorenzo cries, "on Gentleman," but in Q2 he says, "on gentlemen" (2.6.59). Some Q2 variants are included in Mahood's collation and in the collations of other editors, such as that of Wells and Taylor (324–28): *pearls* for Q1's *peales* (3.2.145), *misery* for Q1's *cruelty* (3.4.21), *apparreld* for Q1's *accoutered* (3.4.63), and *presently* for Q1's *instantly* (4.1.277). In any case, Mahood concludes that "Q2 is valuable for the evidence that Q2 affords of the way Q1 looked to a Jacobean" (177); but in many ways, this is a more accurate observation about the First Folio edition.

The First Folio Edition (F1)

The remarkable First Folio edition (F1) of 36 of Shakespeare's plays was published in 1623. As they had printed the second quarto of *MV* in 1619, William and Isaac Jaggard's printers composed the impressive volume, although John Heminges and Henry Condell supervised the entire project, gaining publishing rights, selecting copy texts, and overseeing its issuance. *The Merchant of Venice* is one of 18 plays included in the First Folio that had been previously published in separate quarto editions.

Two events motivating this achievement had occurred seven years earlier. In 1616, Shakespeare died, and Ben Jonson's *Complete Works* was published in a large folio edition, an unprecedented event given that never before had a dramatist's complete works been published in one large, comprehensive folio volume. It gave dramatic literature a new intellectual prestige, almost as if today, film were established as a category for a Nobel Prize. The publication of Jonson's *Works* together with Shakespeare's death undoubtedly served as an incentive to Heminges and Condell. But the two men also sought to memorialize the works of a man who had been their friend, at least since 1596 and 1598 when Heminges and Condell, respectively, were named as members of the Lord Chamberlain's (later, King's) Men. Shakespeare even listed them, along with Richard Burbage, as the only three Londoners in his will. In determining provenance for the plays to be included in the First Folio, Heminges and Condell enjoyed access within the company to accurate copies, whether in print or in manuscript. The project was huge, and printing alone lasted more than two and one-half years—from April 1621 to December 1623.[32]

Like the Pavier quarto (Q2), the First Folio of *MV* includes text that is based on Q1, but not the same copy of Q1 as the compositors used for Q2. Two states of Q1 existed: one had two incomplete lines (4.1.73–74), which the compositors probably noticed and corrected during the printing run, resulting in the second, emended state. The first of the two incomplete lines lacked three initial words, and the second, the first four words:

> . . . . well vse question with the Woolfe,
> . . . . the Ewe bleake for the Lambe (uncorrected Q1, 4.1.73–74).

The corrected version of Q1 was the copy used for Q2:

> [You may as] well vse question with the Woolfe,
> [Why he hath made] the Ewe bleake for the Lambe (corrected Q1, 4.1.73–74)

A copy from the earlier part of the run, with the missing words, served as the copy for the First Folio edition. Therefore, F1 provides a less-than-satisfactory completion of the two lines with the following improvisation:

> [Or euen as] well vse question with the Wolfe,
> The Ewe bleate for the Lambe: (F1, 4.1.73–74).

Some line changes result from differences between Elizabethan and Jacobean sensibilities.[33] For example, as a result of the 1606 act against stage profanity, the Q1 line, "Pray God grant," becomes F1's "wish" (1.2.90); and "no Gods my Iudge" in Q1 becomes "but well I know" in F1 (5.1.157). These changes may have been initiated in unrecorded theater performances. Similarly, Portia's Q1 uncomplimentary remark describing "the Scottish Lorde" transforms in F1 to "the other Lord" (1.2.63), a particularly prudent alteration at court performances for the Scottish king.

Indoor performances at the Blackfriars Theatre may have inspired the F1 division of *MV* into acts, because such performances included musical interludes inserted between acts.[34] The F1 copy of *MV* also contains two other theater-inspired additions: the notation of the prop (a letter) for Lancelot at 2.4.9 and seven notations for music not found in the quarto editions. These few additions in stage directions and text lead Greg to conclude that "recourse was certainly had to a theatrical authority of some kind, but there can have been no systematic collation of the text" (*Editorial Problem* 114).

Because of the nature of the changes that appear in the First Folio, Halio notes that it was "edited . . . to some extent by reference to a playhouse promptbook, as the evidence of additional stage directions specifying flourishes, music, properties, etc., shows" (92). Mahood suggests specifically that the number of uncorrected errors and missing stage directions make it likely that William Jaggard, someone in his employ, or possibly even a member of the acting company made additions to a Q1 copy, duplicating notes from an actual promptbook (178). F1 contains far fewer editorial corrections or changes than Q2, and unlike Q2, F1 maintains the confusion in the three Sallies' speech headings, using *Sal* and finally incorrectly distinguishing among them with *Salar*. Compositor B supposedly participated once again in setting the type, along with compositors C and D;[35] and a few of B's (presumably) memorial errors, resulting in word changes, are included in F1.[36] Because, as Mahood writes, F1 adds more errors than it deletes (178), F1 is not the authoritative copy used for modern editions. Wells and Taylor, however, note that some of F1's stage directions have authority, and the authors not only collate variations from the First Folio in the Textual Notes but also list rejected F1 variants.

Quarto 3 (Q3)

The third quarto (Q3) of 1637 was published by Thomas Heyes's son, Laurence, and is based on Q1 with the completed lines at 4.1.73–74. Although it adds errors and exchanges some words for their homonyms (*Ay* for the second *I* at 4.1.282 and *reine* for *raine* at 3.2.112), it contains only 40 substantive variants from Q1, while Q2 has 101 and F1 has 92 (Halio, 93). Editors agree that it lacks any textual authority; however, Q3 gains importance because it is the first to include "The Actors Names," the basis for the list of characters in modern editions.

This list of characters first included in Q3 highlights one of the editorial problems in the play—the three or possibly two gentlemen of Venice with similar names: Solanio, Salarino, and Salerio. Salerio is not included in Laurence Heyes's Q3 list, and when this character appears onstage in Act 3, the stage direction reads "Enter . . . *Salerio?* a messenger from Venice." Heyes's question mark highlights the possibility of a third Venetian. Such a third Sallie—Salerio—does indeed exist in the text of Q1. He is doubly introduced in Q1 both in the text with Gratiano's greeting and in the following stage direction:

> But who comes heere? *Lorenzo* and his infidell?
> what, and my old Venetian friend *Salerio*? (3.2.221–22)
> [Stage direction] Enter *Lorenzo, Iessica,* and *Salerio* a messenger
> from Venice (3.2.222.s.d.)[37]

The Pavier quarto (Q2) and the First Folio edition combine Salerio with Salanio so that only two Sallies—Salanio and Salarino—exist in the play. This practice was followed until Edward Capell (1767–1768) merged Salerio with Salarino, which maintained two Sallies, albeit differently. In the New Shakespeare edition of 1926, John Dover Wilson, who first nicknamed the characters the three Sallies,[38] agrees with Capell in concluding that Salarino and Salerio should be merged, but Wilson determined that the name should be Salerio because this name occurs in dialog five times and Salarino "could be a diminutive or corruption" (100) of Salerio. Wilson's name change from Salarino to Salerio in speech headings and stage directions was followed by Brown in the Arden edition (1955), and it became the standard until the New Cambridge Shakespeare edition (1987), in which Mahood introduced the messenger of 3.2, Salerio, as a third character. The following chart outlines major editorial name changes among the three characters:

Q1	No merging of characters = Solanio (or Salanio), Salarino, Salerio
Q2 and F1, and subsequent eds.	Salerio is merged with Salanio = Salanio and Salarino
Capell (1768)	Salerio is merged with Salarino = Salanio and Salarino
Wilson (1926), and subsequent eds..	Salerio is merged with Salarino = Salerio and Solanio
Mahood (1987), Halio (1993)	No merging of characters = Solanio, Salarino, Salerio

Mahood offers convincing arguments for three Sallies. A third character would have been no more expensive because the company used the practice of doubling (one actor playing two or more roles). The messenger of 3.2, Salerio, who is also the attendant ushering Shylock and Balthazar into court in 4.1, seems to be of another social class; he is more humble and reverential, less assured and witty. Third, Gratiano's greeting of Salerio in Belmont—"my old Venetian friend Salerio" (3.2.218)—would not be necessary to an audience that had seen him in four earlier scenes as either Salarino or Solanio. Finally, similar names among primary and secondary characters and among real and assumed identities in a Shakespeare play are not unusual: witness Grumio and Gremio, Tranio and Cambio in *The Taming of the Shrew*. Therefore, the New Cambridge Shakespeare (Mahood) and the Oxford Shakespeare (Halio), as well as other more recent complete editions of the plays and individual paperback editions, retain the three names included in the first quarto, which follows Shakespeare's manuscript copy, as discussed earlier.

Later Quarto and Folio Editions

The Second Folio edition of *MV,* published in 1632, and the Third Folio, published in 1663 and reprinted in 1664, included seven additional plays, only one of which, *Pericles, Prince of Tyre,* is now considered a part of the canon. The Fourth Folio of 1685 is based on the third. None of the seventeenth-century folios included *Sir Thomas More, The Two Noble Kinsmen,* and *Edward III*—three plays in which, modern scholars believe,

Shakespeare was at least a collaborator. Another quarto edition of *MV* appeared in 1637 and was reissued with a new title page in 1652. None of these five editions has any authority, and they are not significant in collations in the New Cambridge Shakespeare or current Oxford Shakespeare texts.

Eighteenth-Century Editions

Eighteenth-century editors developed a set of objectives for their editions, some of which are maintained by modern editors. Like modern editors, they sought to create texts that were readable; therefore, they modernized spelling, punctuation, and formatting for an ever-expanding audience and readership. Unlike twentieth-century editors, however, they wanted to purify the texts to satisfy the eighteenth-century aesthetic and literary ideals of classical order, attention to detail, and symmetry, rather than follow Shakespeare's original words. As a result, they made textual changes not in order to follow the earliest and most accurate text but rather to meet the standards of the eighteenth century.

The first important edition of the works of Shakespeare in the eighteenth century was completed in six volumes by Nicholas Rowe in 1709 and re-edited into eight volumes in 1714. Rowe, a poet and dramatist of excellent reputation whose plays are still published and read today, based his text on the most recent Fourth Folio of 1685. That edition contains modernizations as well as errors from earlier folio editions, which makes it, more than any other folio edition, least like Shakespeare's original text. Rowe took it further. Like most eighteenth-century editors, he wanted his critical edition to be accessible to the public. As a result, his edition offers modernized spelling, punctuation, grammar, and word substitutions. He also carefully added act and scene divisions according to eighteenth-century convention, using increasing detail through the edition so that all the plays follow the five-act convention of classical Roman drama, established by Seneca (4 B.C.E. to A.D. 65). Rowe also identified locations for scenes, sometimes describing them. For example, he begins 1.2, "Belmont. Three caskets are set out, one of Gold, another of Silver, and another of Lead. Enter Portia and Nerissa."[39] Scene designations were entirely unnecessary for the Elizabethan stage, however, because it had no proscenium arch and curtain and no interruptions at act changes, save musical interludes added for indoor performances. To make the plays easier to read, Rowe marked exits and entrances and added a *dramatis personae,* or list of characters, to the beginning of each play, as had been done in *MV* Q3.

A second eighteenth-century edition of the plays was completed by the great neoclassical poet Alexander Pope in 1725 and reprinted in 1728. He based his text on Rowe's and, with the same objectives, added annotations, more modernization, and even more act and scene divisions. Following classical or continental convention, he created scene changes whenever major characters enter or exit, thereby greatly increasing the number of scenes beyond those found in modern editions. He also completed Rowe's objective of scene designation, establishing a specific place for every scene. Most characteristic of Pope's edition, however, are his many significant text changes. Although he supposedly consulted 29 quartos and the First Folio, he did not use them to establish authenticity. Rather, he made major changes to conform to a classical ideal. He regularized the meter, removed anachronisms, and replaced whole sections because he considered them unworthy of Shakespeare. Art was intended to imitate nature—as the eighteenth century understood it—with consistent detail, classical design, and so-called realistic time and place relationships.

Other eighteenth-century editors of Shakespeare's plays followed. Lewis Theobald produced a seven-volume edition in 1733 that was reissued in 1740, 1752, 1772, and 1773. Even though he criticized Pope's edition, he used it as the basis for his own and was paid back when Pope named him the King of Dullness in *The Dunciad.* Bishop William Warburton further altered Pope's edition in 1747 and was said to have suffered the misfortune of hiring a cook who accidentally burned his large collection of Elizabethan quartos and manuscripts.

Samuel Johnson issued an eight-volume edition of the plays in 1765 that followed Warburton's text. Although Johnson's text is acknowledged as being error ridden, the edition is noted for its brilliant preface and textual commentary, in which Johnson further defines the eighteenth-century aesthetic as applied to Shakespeare.[40] He praises Shakespeare, saying that he is "above all writers, at least, above all modern writers, the poet of nature; the poet that holds up to his readers a faithful mirrour of manners and of life" (viii). But Johnson also justifies the heavy eighteenth-century editing, observing that Shakespeare is "so much more careful to please than to instruct, that he seems to write without any moral purpose. . . . This fault the barbarity of his age cannot extenuate, for it is always a writer's duty to make the words better. . . . In narration he affects a disproportionate pomp of diction and a wearisome train of circumlocution, and tells the incident imperfectly in many words" (xx, xxii).

Other important early editors include Edward Capell, who published a 10-volume edition in 1768. He was the first to base his edition on the First

Folio and in some cases on quarto editions, an unprecedented practice. While his selection of a control text was based on seemingly inconsistent standards, he was the first to recognize quartos as usually being Shakespeare's own text rather than as highly edited playbooks. In 1790, Edmund Malone issued another 10-volume edition. A scholar familiar with documents from the Elizabethan and Jacobean periods, including Henslowe's *Diary* and the Stationers' Register, Malone made his most important contribution to the editing of Shakespeare's works by granting authority only to the earliest printed versions of the texts. In the case of *MV,* this unfortunately meant that he granted authority to the falsely dated Pavier quarto (Q2). When Malone died, he left an incomplete variorum edition of the plays, which included all variants. It was completed in 1821 by James Boswell, son of Johnson's biographer, Thomas Boswell.

Nineteenth-Century Editions

Nineteenth-century editions of Shakespeare's works diverge into two types, representing popular social views of the period: first, that human society can overcome any difficult challenge, and second, that certain members of society require the care and protection of its stronger members. The first notion is reflected in the enormously complex variorum editions, which were intended to include all textual analyses and commentary for every line of every play; the second encouraged the bowdlerized editions that excised all lines that might offend the presumably delicate sensibilities of women and children. The first variorum edition was published in 1803 by Isaac Reed and was reprinted in 1813. More important was the third variorum edition, previously mentioned, based on the notes and earlier edition of Edmund Malone and completed by James Boswell. The most recent variorum edition was initiated in Philadelphia by Furness with the support of the Shakespeare Society. In 1871, the society published its first edition of *Romeo and Juliet.* More ambitious than any previous editions, the Furness variorum editions were to include portions of everything ever written about each play, every textual variant, and every potential source. Because of the immensity of this goal and the consequent time it requires, timeliness has been difficult to maintain in variorum editions, and the project begun by Furness is still not complete. The Furness variorum edition of *MV* was published in 1888 and remains invaluable.

The bowdlerized editions of the nineteenth century began in 1804 with a 4-volume *Family Shakespeare* developed by Reverend Thomas Bowdler, expanded to 10 volumes in 1818. Intended for a family audience, such editions were used in laundered readings of the plays and were far different from the original quarto or folio editions. For example, an edition of *MV* intended for high school students by W. J. Rolfe (first published in 1870) contains only 273 of the 329 lines in Act 5. Not surprisingly, all lines referring to "bed" or "Nerissa's ring" are counted among the missing.

Perhaps the most influential text of the nineteenth century is the non-bowdlerized one-volume Globe text of 1864. It became the standard text and, consequently, perhaps the most reprinted edition, especially for many student editions. Its scene divisions are still used today. It is based on the Cambridge Shakespeare, nine volumes edited by W. G. Clark, J. Glover, and W. A. Wright that were issued from 1863 through 1866. It was perhaps the most historically accurate text to date, based on the First Folio with a careful collation with the quarto collection in Trinity College, Cambridge, bequeathed by Edward Capell.

Editions Available Today

Twentieth-century editions show greater accuracy in following authoritative texts, primarily through the study of Elizabethan book production. Most credit for progress in this area of bibliographical studies goes to the New Bibliographers—Pollard, Greg, and Chambers, as well as J. Dover Wilson and R. B. McKerrow in the early part of the century. Their method of study examines the characteristics of promptbooks, playbooks, foul papers, fair papers, and printed copies. Watermarks, ornaments, typesetting, individual pieces of type, repetitions of text changes, deletions, creative alterations, and formatting in printing, as well as handwriting, punctuation, and spelling in manuscripts, become clues in the creation of accurate versions of the plays. This group of scholars belonged to the Malone Society at Cambridge, created in 1896, which was dedicated to the publication of scholarly reprints of Elizabethan plays and theatrical documents.

An available edition falls into one of two categories: a large single volume of the complete works, or individual volumes of each play published in a series over several years, with a different editor for each volume and a single person serving as the series editor. Both types of editions have genealogies; that is, one edition replaces another under a general name after several years. Among the series type is the Cambridge series of 1863–1866, replaced by the New Shakespeare editions begun in 1921 and completed in 1969 under the general editorship of John Dover Wilson and Sir Arthur Quiller-Couch, who died in the middle of the project. The New Cambridge Shakespeare series, under the general editorship of Philip Brockbank, and, after his death, Brian Gibbons, succeeds it.

The New Cambridge Shakespeare edition of *MV* (1987) is edited by M. M. Mahood and offers a newly edited text based on the authoritative Heyes-Roberts quarto (Q1), with both textual variants and notes at the foot of each page. The text is preceded by a 53-page introduction with 14 illustrations and emphases on "attitudes and assumptions behind the play" and a history of performance. The appendix contains a detailed textual study and a discussion of Shakespeare's use of the Bible in the play.

Another careful and thoroughly annotated series of individual plays in the twentieth century is the Arden Shakespeare series. The first series of 37 volumes appeared between 1899 and 1924 under the editorship of W. J. Craig (1899–1906) and R. H. Case (1909–1944). The New Arden series, begun in 1951 during the general editorship of Una M. Ellis-Fermor (1946–58) and continued after her death by Harold Jenkins and Harold F. Brooks, is even more dependent on the bibliographical method. The first Arden edition of *MV* was edited by Charles Knox Pooler, originally published in 1905, and reprinted five times. It was then revised and reset by John Russell Brown in the New Arden edition (1955, 1959). Like the Cambridge editions, this edition is based on Q1 and also offers textual variants from other texts, particularly from the First Folio. The New Arden books include notes at the foot of each page, but unlike the Cambridge editions, New Arden uses brackets within the text to clearly mark stage directions, act and scene divisions, and place locations not present in Q1. The 58-page introduction thoroughly covers standard scholarly topics, including text, dating, sources, stage history, and critical introduction. The five appendices each include a major source story or poem for the play. The most recent reprint (1997) is available in paperback; however, a third New Arden series is now progressing under the general editorship of Richard Proudfoot, Ann Thompson, and David Scott Kastan.

The most recent single-volume edition of the play is the Oxford Shakespeare, edited by Halio (1998) under the general editorship of Stanley Wells. Its well-documented 98-page general and textual introduction precedes the text. As in all twentieth-century editions, Q1 serves as the control text. It has collations at the foot of each page, and below these are notes and glosses. Following the text is a useful index of "points of more than routine interest" included in the text and in the introductions.

Other notable series of single-volume editions of Shakespeare's works are available in paper. The Bantam Classics series includes an edition of *MV* edited by David Bevington (1988). This edition has a description of the text, notes placed at the bottom of each page, a foreword by Joseph Papp, Bevington's introduction, and essays on performance and the playhouse. The text is followed by discussion of sources and a new translation of the main source of the play, *Il Pecorone,* by Kate and David Bevington.

The New Folger Library Shakespeare edition of *MV,* edited by Barbara A. Mowat and Paul Werstine (1992), replaces an original Folger edition in the Folger Library General Reader's Shakespeare series begun in the 1950s.[41] This edition, based on the authoritative Heyes-Roberts quarto, uses modernized spelling and punctuation, bracketed editorial additions, and regularized character names. Unlike other editions since that of John Dover Wilson (1926), this edition follows the practice of the New Cambridge Shakespeare edition (1987) and does not collapse Salarino, Solanio, and Salerio into two characters. Introductory material includes brief essays about the play and the accompanying text, and about Shakespeare's language, life, theater, and publications. Finally, the volume concludes with a critical essay by Alexander Leggatt, a list of textual notes, and a carefully annotated bibliography. The play itself is particularly readable, with the text printed on the right side of the page (recto), and notes, glosses, and a brief summary at the beginning of each scene on the facing side (verso).

The Signet Classic Shakespeare series, with Sylvan Barnet as general editor, includes an edition of *MV* edited by Kenneth Myrick (1965, 1998). Based on Q1, the text has glosses and paraphrases at the foot of each page and a brief two-page textual note at the end listing the several variants used in the text. Myrick adds a notably thorough 81-page introduction, and, following the text, 64 pages of representative critical essays by readers from Nicholas Rowe (1709) to Sylvan Barnet (1987), who writes about stage and screen performances. A usefully categorized annotated bibliography completes the volume.

Several complete editions of Shakespeare's works are currently in print. Such volumes include not only the works but also lengthy and highly informative general introductions to the study of Shakespeare. G. Blakemore Evans is the textual editor of *The Riverside Shakespeare* (1997), a handsome volume with both black-and-white and color illustrations. The 1974 edition contains a 56-page general introduction written by Harry Levin focusing on the general characteristics of the plays, texts of the works themselves, a chronology, a table of sources, and facsimiles of 19 pages from the beginning of the First Folio. The 1997 edition adds a valuable 22-page discussion of trends in Shakespearean criticism by Heather Dubrow, explaining literary and critical movements in Europe and North America from the eighteenth century to the present. Following the texts are three appendices describing performance history, a broad range of records and documents, allusions to Shakespeare and his works, and annals. *MV*, like the other plays in the volume, is printed in two-column pages, with notes at the foot of each page and textual endnotes. A critical introduction by Anne Barton appears as well. Although the First Folio (1623) categorizes the plays as comedies, histories, and tragedies and lists *MV* 9th among 14 comedies, the Riverside edition places it 6th in a chronology of 13 comedies, with all the works arranged in Evans's suggested categories of comedies, histories, tragedies, romances, and poems.

Stanley Wells and Gary Taylor serve as editors of the three-volume *The Complete Oxford Shakespeare* (1987), originally published in one 1,432-page volume in 1986 titled *William Shakespeare: The Complete Works*. These volumes should not be confused with individual editions such as Halio's. Histories, comedies, and tragedies compose three separate volumes published in modern spelling. *The Comical History of the Merchant of Venice, or Otherwise Called the Jew of Venice* is listed 7th among 20 play titles in the second volume entitled *Comedies* (601–30) and is preceded by a one-page introduction. The editors have chosen to follow "the more theatrical version" of each play, that which "comes closest to the 'final' version of the play," and which may have lines deleted because Shakespeare "and his company found that the play's overall structure and pace were better without them" (xxx–xxxi). Such deleted lines are printed as "Additional Passages" at the conclusion of each play. Neither notes nor glosses accompany the texts. For reprints of "precise directions of the original text" the introduction invites readers to see Wells and Taylor's 671-page, single-volume textual analysis of the plays, *William Shakespeare: A Textual Companion* (1987), which is intended to accompany the one-volume *Complete Works* edition. The former's six-page description of the text of *MV* (323–28) explains the quarto and folio history and provides textual notes and collations, rejected folio variants not included in the collations, and a listing of quarto stage directions.

David Bevington is the editor of *The Complete Works of Shakespeare* (1997), another beautiful volume with color illustrations of historical paintings and modern performance photographs. After a 108-page introduction, the works are presented in five groupings: comedies, histories, tragedies, romances, and poems. Three appendices, maps, textual notes, a bibliography, and an index conclude the volume. The text of *MV*, following the Heyes-Roberts quarto (1600) is listed 6th in a proposed chronological arrangement among 13 comedies. It is introduced with a critical essay and glossed at the bottom of each two-column page. Textual variants are given at the end of the entire volume.

In 1997, W. W. Norton published *The Norton Shakespeare* based on the Oxford edition, with Stephen Greenblatt as general editor. The pages are smaller than those of other editions, and the text contains 3,420 characteristically thin pages. According to the 76-page general introduction, the purpose of the *Norton Shakespeare* is "to present the modern-spelling Oxford Complete Works in a way that would make the text more accessible to modern readers." That means the edition provides introductions, textual notes, and brief bibliographies for each work as well as marginal word glosses and footnotes interpreting lengthier passages. It brackets stage directions and other additions to editions published after the 1623 First Folio. Norton also has published *The Norton Facsimile of The First Folio* (1968) based on copies prepared by Charles Hinman of the First Folio in the Folger Library, and Yale has produced a facsimile edition of the First Folio (1954) owned by the Elizabethan Club of Yale University.

NOTES

1. For complete discussions of the dating of *MV,* see John Russell Brown, *The Merchant of Venice,* New Arden Shakespeare (1955; repr., Cambridge: Harvard University Press, 1959), xxi–xxvii; M. M. Mahood, *The Merchant of Venice,* New Cambridge Shakespeare (Cambridge: Cambridge University Press, 1987), 1–2; and Jay Halio, *The Merchant of Venice,* Oxford Shakespeare (Oxford: Clarendon Press, 1993), 27–29.

2. D. C. Allen, ed., *Frances Meres's Treatise "Poetrie"* (Urbana: University of Illinois Press, 1933), 76.

3. E. K. Chambers suggests another *terminus a quem* of 1596, citing a letter from the autumn of 1596, written by Francis Davison. In the letter, Davison twice mocks an unnamed but politically powerful, hunchbacked man by calling him "St. Gobbo" ('who can only be the hunch-backed Robert Cecil'), seemingly after the clown character in the play. But this reference is unlikely because the word *Gobbo* means "crook-backt," according to a 1598 Italian dictionary, and Davison had traveled to Italy. See Chambers, *William Shakespeare: A Study of Facts and Problems* (Oxford: Clarendon Press, 1930), vol. I, 372, and Brown, xxii.

4. The Oras pause test measures the distribution of pauses within verse lines. For a full discussion and table of results of this test in dating the plays of Shakespeare and his contemporaries, see Stanley Wells and Gary Taylor, *William Shakespeare: A Textual Companion* (Oxford: Clarendon Press, 1987), 107–8.

5. An earlier *terminus a quo* is 1594, a date based on the June 1594 execution of Roderigo (Ruy) Lopez, Queen Elizabeth's Jewish physician. Shakespeare may have written *MV* at the height of this notorious affair, and the play probably contains references to it. But even if the Lopez references are accurate, they do not disprove the 1596 *terminus a quo*, because Lopez was infamous throughout the remainder of the century. In fact, in 1596, three years after Christopher Marlowe had been killed and two years after Lopez had been executed, Marlowe's play about the Jew Barabas, *The Jew of Malta,* was produced eight times by the Lord

Admiral's Men, the acting company rivaling Shakespeare's company, the Lord Chamberlain's Men. The Lopez affair and Marlowe's play are included in a discussion of anti-Semitism in London in Chapter 2 of this guide.

6. Printers in Tudor and Stuart London typically followed one of two formats: quarto or folio. A quarto edition of a book is printed on sheets about 13-1/2 inches by 8-1/4 inches, folded twice, and then cut. This makes four rather small leaves or eight pages, groups of which are bound together. The pages of a folio edition are twice the size of quarto edition pages. It is printed on sheets of the same size, folded only once, and then cut, producing two leaves or four pages, groups of which are bound together. Books were also printed in octavo formats, cut 8 from the sheet and first noted in 1582, and duodecimo formats, cut 12 from the sheet and first noted in 1658. Eighteenth-century editions of Shakespeare's plays often had these formats.

7. Roberts's quarto edition has 11 gatherings of four leaves, with each gathering labeled alphabetically from *A* through *K*. Each is cut from two foldings of one large sheet and printed on both sides, yielding eight sides, or pages, for a total of 44 sheets, or 88 pages, and paginated A1, A2, A3, A4, B1, B2, B3, B4, and so forth. Each side has half the following header running across the top of two pages: "The comicall Historie of [page break] the Merchant of Venice."

8. In 1606, the Master of the Revels also was granted the power to license publications.

9. W. W. Greg, *Some Aspects and Problems of London Publishing Between 1550 and 1650* (Oxford: Clarendon Press, 1956), 104. Greg, Chambers, and A. W. Pollard were key figures in a small group of scholars known as the New Bibliographers, textual scholars of the early twentieth century who made significant discoveries in the analysis of early modern texts, such as those of *MV.*

10. See Greg, *Some Aspects,* 25–38, concerning the method by which the Company of Stationers compiled this register.

11. See Greg, *Some Aspects,* 63, 112–22. Other valuable studies of the text history of this play and other plays are Alfred W. Pollard, *Shakespeare's Folios and Quartos* (London: Methuen and Company, 1909); W. W. Greg, *The Shakespeare First Folio* (Oxford: Clarendon Press, 1955); and Peter Blayney, "Compositor B and the Pavier Quartos: Problems of Identification and Their Implications," *The Library,* 5th series, 27 (1972): 179–206.

12. See Pollard, *Shakespeare's Folios and Quartos,* 66, and *Shakespeare's Fight with the Pirates* (London: A. Moring, 1917), 43.

13. Greg devotes the final section in *Some Aspects* (112–22) to blocking entries, in which he examines the five so-called blocking or staying entries James Roberts made between July 22, 1598, and February 7, 1603, for five plays performed by the Lord Chamberlain's Men, the first of which is the 1598 entry of *MV.*

14. Greg's point here seems unrelated to *MV.* It is more likely that Roberts had a manuscript for the 1598 listing and that Heyes (accompanied or not by Roberts) brought the promptbook when he gained the second listing (1600) in the Station-

ers' Register, which gave publishing rights to Heyes.

15. The title page shown in Figure 1 is a copy of a Q1 edition owned by the Folger Library.

16. Roberts could have obtained Shakespeare's own manuscript when he gained the 1598 Stationers' listing. This could have been during a production run, when the actors needed the promptbook, and therefore it would have been unavailable. Roberts may have then kept that manuscript on the condition that it not be printed until the Chamberlain's Men (called the King's Men after 1603) gave permission. When that happened two years later, he and Heyes transferred the listing, using a borrowed promptbook as evidence that they had indeed received license to print from the Lord Chamberlain's Men. See Mahood, 170–71; and Greg, *The Editorial Problem in Shakespeare,* 2nd ed. (Oxford, Clarendon Press, 1951), 123–24.

17. See Brown, xiv–viii; Halio, 86; Chambers, I: 370; and Greg, *Shakespeare First Folio,* 256.

18. See Brown, xiv; and Mahood, 169–71.

19. See William B. Long, Stage-Directions: A Misinterpreted Factor in Determining Textual Provenance," *TEXT* 2 (1985): 121–37, for a full discussion questioning presumptions about sixteenth-century promptbooks.

20. See John Russell Brown, "The Compositors of *Hamlet* Q2 and *The Merchant of Venice,*" *Shakespeare Bulletin* VII (1955): 17–40.

21. Other editors do not entirely support Mahood's position that the manuscript was a fair copy written in Shakespeare's hand. Halio concludes that it was "possibly in Shakespeare's own hand," (86) while Brown somewhat ambiguously says that the manuscript "was very close to Shakespeare's own" (*New Arden MV* xiv).

22. See Wells and Taylor, 323, for a chart of the alternating sections completed by each compositor, X and Y, and Halio, 88–90, for a full discussion of the printing of the first quarto.

23. See Wells and Taylor (11), for a facsimile of "the most legible of the pages" from *The Booke of Sir Thomas Moore*. These editors describe Hand D as using "virtually no punctuation at the end of verse lines and little medial punctuation" (10).

24. Another of what Wells and Taylor call "two particularly striking peculiarities" in the typesetting of Q1 is the use of question marks in place of other ending punctuation in certain sheets, possibly because of missing stops and commas from the type case of one of the compositors (324).

25. Wells and Taylor note that the first edition of *MV* is "the sole erratic exception" to the otherwise universal practice of capitalizing initial letters in verse lines in the printing of Shakespeare's plays (10).

26. The second quarto edition of *Hamlet* Q2 contains many errors; as a result, textual scholars agree that it was set from the author's foul papers, the confusions of which contribute to errors in the quarto. Like *MV* and the *Titus Andronicus* Q2, it was set by Roberts's printers, who are known to have followed manuscripts assiduously, even in matters of spelling and punctuation. To conclude that the pre-

sumed confusion in the *Hamlet* Q2 foul papers argues against *MV*'s authorial manuscript is to presume that an author always produces the same kind of manuscript.

27. Mahood writes that Q2 was "produced in Isaac Jaggard's printing shop" (174); while Greg, *Editorial Problem*, 131; Brown, *New Arden MV,* xviii; and Halio, 90, say that it was printed by Isaac's father, William Jaggard.

28. See Greg, *Editorial Problem*, 131–34, for a description of the history of the publication of Shakespeare's canon as well as the accompanying editorial problems.

29. See Mahood, 174; Halio, 91–92; D. F. McKenzie, "Compositor B's Role in *The Merchant of Venice* Q2 1619," *Shakespeare Bulletin* XII (1959), 75–90. McKenzie argues that Compositor B set the entire text of Q2, which explains its alterations and errors.

30. For a more detailed discussion, see McKenzie, 75–90; and Blayney, 79–206. Blayney further notes that Compositor B's work is similar to that of Compositor G.

31. See Mahood, 175–77, for an extensive discussion of variants in the Pavier quarto.

32. See Charlton Hinman, *The Printing and Proof-Reading of the First Folio of Shakespeare,* 2 vols. (Oxford: Clarendon Press, 1963), for further information on the First Folio.

33. Queen Elizabeth died in 1603 after having named her nephew, King James VI of Scotland, as her successor. James encouraged a more traditionally religious government, including of the passage of a 1606 act against profanity on the stage.

34. Eleven of the 36 plays in the First Folio are similarly divided into acts; 18 are divided into acts and scenes; *Hamlet* is divided into scenes through Act 2; and 6 have with no divisions at all.

35. See Wells and Taylor, 149–154, concerning attributions to compositors of the First Folio edition of *MV*. The line numbering used in this chart, called through line numbering (TLN), follows Charlton Hinman, *The Norton Facsimile First Folio of Shakespeare* (New York: Norton, 1968).

36. Further information is available in Greg, *Shakespeare First Folio,* and Christopher Spencer, "Shakespeare's *Merchant of Venice* in Sixty-three Editions," *Shakespeare Bulletin* XXV (1972): 89–106.

37. These lines follow Q1, as printed in *The Merchant of Venice: 1600 Hayes Quarto,* Shakespeare Quarto Facsimiles No. 2 (1957; repr., Oxford: Clarendon Press, 1963).

38. See *The Merchant of Venice,* eds. Sir Arthur Quiller-Couch and John Dover Wilson, New Shakespeare edition (1926; rev., Cambridge: Cambridge University Press, 1953), 100–104; also, Halio, 87; Mahood, 179–83.

39. For this edition of the play, see Nicholas Rowe, *Works of Shakespeare,* vol. 2 (1709; repr., New York: AMS Press, 1969).

40. See Samuel Johnson, *The Plays of William Shakespeare,* 18 vols. (1765; repr., New York: AMS Press, 1968).

41. These volumes are associated with the Folger Shakespeare Library in Washington, D.C., a research library founded in 1932 by the book collector Henry Clay Folger. More successful than any other book collector, Folger gathered more than 75 of the approximately 230 extant copies of the First Folio, numerous fragments and quarto editions, and many later folio editions, all of which are held in the Folger Shakespeare Library.

2

CONTEXTS AND SOURCES

The excitement of increasing wealth was permeating London when Shakespeare wrote *The Merchant of Venice* in the mid-1590s. Entrepreneurial Londoners, absorbed in growing rich, needed credit and funding; they sought loans from investment bankers, mortgage holders, or anyone who could give them financing to enlarge their businesses, accelerate foreign trade, and explore other continents. Still, Christian London condemned usury as a sin. The resulting double standard, the conflict between the "outward shows" (3.2.73) of piety about money and the need for expensive credit, nourished an ongoing tension in London life. Add to this London's chronic anti-Semitism, heightened in 1594 with the sensational execution of the Queen's Jewish physician, and we must admire how shrewdly Shakespeare timed his play about the Jew—the alien whose manic desire for violence is finally made to serve the goals of Christian capitalism, the moneylender whom everyone needed but no one liked. Shylock is almost a metaphor of the moral confusion created by England's newly invited and newly invading capitalism. Harley Granville-Barker famously contended that *MV* is "a fairy tale,"[1] but it is far more than that; it carries the plutocratic and xenophobic burdens of the emerging modern world.

Even though Shylock and the mercantilism of Venice are the most well-known elements of *MV*, the other characters and their story lines quantitatively dominate the plot: Portia has the most lines; Antonio, the merchant, is the play's namesake; and the four love unions of Portia and Bassanio, Jessica and Lorenzo, Nerissa and Gratiano, and Antonio and Bassanio compose most of the action. For these plots, Shakespeare drew on source stories, as he and his contemporaries regularly did in writing plays for immediate production. They used historical chronicles, short fiction, and even older plays, any of which might be mythic, anonymous, or directly attributable to others. But Shakespeare intermingled sources, juxtaposing and enriching themes and characters, so they evolve, sometimes paradoxically; and he added new plot action, raising questions that fetch only incomplete answers. This chapter examines two of the play's contexts, usury and anti-Semitism in sixteenth-century mercantile London, as well as the literary sources of the flesh-bond, casket-selection, and runaway-daughter plots.

CONTEXTS

Usury

In *MV*, Shylock informs us in his first aside that he practices "usance" (1.3.37), lending for an interest charge, which remained illegal in sixteenth-century England until the statute of 1571 allowed individuals to gain 10 percent interest on loans.[2] Usury was practiced during Shakespeare's lifetime by both Catholics and Protestants yet they condemned it as sinful and associated it with Jews. Jews were not, however, the money-lenders in Elizabethan England; rich merchants and bankers were. Peter Berek suggests that Elizabethans rationalized the divide between the ethics and practice of usury by falsely identifying it with Jews—the most convenient Others of the world—thereby shifting usury as far away from the English as possible (145).[3]

Clerics and lay writers of the time often harshly condemned usury and Jewish usurers. In *A Discourse Upon Usury* (1572), Sir Thomas Wilson, a Doctor of Civil Laws and Master of the Queen's Court of Requests, creates a fictional dinner conversation about usury among four men: a preacher, a doctor of law, another lawyer, and a merchant. In the preface, Wilson writes of the "ouglie, detestable and hurtefull synne of usurie . . . amongst all other offenses next to Idolatrie, and the renouncing of god . . . , there is none more heynous, none more offensive, and none more hurtfull to anye well governed common weale."[4] In the ensuing conversation, Wilson emphasizes the relationship between Jews and usury. The doctor condemns "the Iewe, that hath used thys horrible sinne most above all others . . . [and] hath so robbed the christians wheresoever hee came, that his evill lyvinge seene, hee is banished out of the most places in christendome, and worthely." Of usurers, he disdainfully says, "And no better do I call them then Iewes, yea, worse than any infidel, that wittingly lyve by the onely gayne of their money" (283). He says usurers are idle and the principal cause of bankruptcies to men whose borrowing dearly "hath wholie eaten them upp and undonne them forever" (284). Usurers are worse than thieves because a thief harms only one person at a time, but a usurer harms many and worse, "beareth the countenaune of an honest man, and is commonly taken to bee the best man in his paryshe"; thus "hee undoeth as many as hee dealeth with all, under the coloure of amitie and lawe" (285). Once under the net of the usurer, a borrower has little hope for escape. All this is done with the false appearance of good. The usurer is a "devouring caterpillar" or an *Aspis* whose "poyson goeth by a lyttle and a little through all the partes of the body . . . [and the borrower] dieth in pleasure" (285). Toward the end of the fictional conversation, the preacher laments that the English are using the ways of the Jews. In the 47th year of the reign of Henry III, 500 Jews were slain in a riot because of usury; "one Iew would have forced a Christyan man to have geeven unto him more than twoo pence for the usurye of twenty shillings by the weke"; now "these Iewes are gone. Would god the Christyans remayninge and our country men at this time dyd not use theire fashyons" (378). Thus the mythic image of the evil Jewish usurer was widely known and accepted in Tudor England.

But condemnation gradually softened because of the needs of the growing economy. Thirty years after *MV* was written, Sir Francis Bacon wrote a short essay titled "On Usury" (1625).[5] In it, he tempers the blanket disapproval of usury Wilson had written before the mercantile economy of England mushroomed. Bacon notes the harms and benefits of usury, first dismissing the religious arguments against it: that nature does not allow money to beget money; that usury gains profit on the Sabbath; that usurers should wear orange hats because they "judaize"; and that usury is a tithe to the devil. Then, admitting usury to be "a lazy trade," Bacon more practically recognizes it as a revenue drain on farming and merchandising and as a limitation on the distribution of wealth since the usurer gains back more than the borrower receives. Yet usury is a necessity because the young cannot begin businesses without it: it is a gradual solution to financial exigency, and it is the only assistance available to the needy, since interest-free charity from the wealthy is a vain wish. Thus, Bacon concludes, a controlled credit market is the most practical compromise for the inevitability of usury. Shakespeare wrote *MV* three decades earlier, however, and the moral condemnation and contemporary practice of usury had not yet reached Bacon's compromise position.

John Gross writes that at the end of the sixteenth century, usury was a common source of funding for agriculture, manufacturing, and domestic and foreign trade.[6] Although the church proclaimed that usury breaks the

Laws of God, nature, and nations,[7] the practice was common even among the most famous and powerful in Tudor England. These included Sir Philip Sidney; the earls of Essex, Leicester, and Southampton; Shakespeare's acting company, the Lord Chamberlain's Men; and Queen Elizabeth, who had borrowed from European bankers. Even Shakespeare's father, John, lent money at interest and, in fact, was prosecuted twice and fined once for charging excessive rates, 20 and 25 percent.[8]

Gross speculates about Shakespeare's practice of usury, because several documents prove that he indeed lent money. Many of his associates in London borrowed money, particularly those in the theater, who needed large sums of money to produce plays. James Burbage, who built the first public theater in London in 1576, is recorded as borrowing hundreds of pounds. Shakespeare made many large investments himself, all of which seem highly unlikely without his gaining credit, although whether he paid interest is not known. He invested in the Globe Theater, in the second largest house in the town of Stratford, in 120 acres outside the town, in half interest in the tithes of three hamlets, in a house in London, and in malt (Gross 61). Thus, although Shakespeare did not identify with Shylock, he was not so impractical in his own life as to observe Antonio's lofty prohibitions against lending (or borrowing) barren money. In the real world of the 1590s, where money was being exchanged in other than the abrupt and non-work-related ways depicted in the play, credit was becoming a necessity for the poor to survive, the middle class to prosper, and the wealthy to maintain control.

Nevertheless, popular literature followed religious dicta condemning usury. Two of the possible source or analogue stories for the play, Antony Munday's romance *Zelauto, or The Fountain of Fame* (1580) and the anonymous ballad *Gernutus* both present villains who are usurers.[9] The nature of the evil is the same; it is an almost blasphemous propagation of the inanimate that destroys the soul of the lender and the body of the borrower. In *MV,* Antonio speaks metaphorically that profit gained from interest is unnatural breeding; it is reproduction of that which is naturally barren; but in a more practical sense, usury can never be offered to a friend because it is destructive:

> . . . lend it not
> As to thy friends, for when did friendship take
> A breed for [of] barren metal of his friend? (1.3.124–26)

The conventional representation of the usurer in drama is far more exaggerated than even Shylock. Although Shylock is merely tricky and ungenerous to his servant, and selectively cruel, the conventional moneylender, not necessarily Jewish, is repulsive looking, diseased, stingy, pervasively cruel, and overtly worshipful of money.

According to Gross, although moneylenders on the stage were not necessarily Jews and were rarely so in real life, in the minds of people in Tudor England and all over Europe, "'Jew' and 'usurer' were virtually synonymous" (54). Jews had been barred from most trades in those European nations where they were allowed to live, so the few who came to money lending did so by default in spite of rabbinical scholars who had condemned usury as early as the eleventh century. Still, Christians' identification of Jews with money lending was ubiquitous. Christian Germans who lent money were called "Christian Jews"; the French called a moneylender "Juif," a deeply insulting name even though Jews were nearly nonexistent in France; and the English generally agreed with invective like that of Henry Smith, a preacher who in 1591 railed that "there be no such usurers on earth as the Jews" (Gross 54–55). Jewish lending was likened to prostitution; Samuel Purchas warned "not to be a lover of filthy lucre, from filthy stews, from filthy Jews" (Shapiro 99). In England, monstrous imagined Jewish lending practices conveniently distracted people from the reality of Christian usury. Bias against usury thus became bias against Jews. Still, England, like other Christian economies in Europe, was dependent on money lending, although not necessarily by Jews.

Ironically, in *MV,* the practice of usury does not occur; it only serves to condemn Shylock, the self-proclaimed usurer. Shylock does not lend the 3,000 ducats at interest; he only demands a forfeit or penalty if Antonio does not return the principal within the term of the bond. Forfeits were far more acceptable to the Christian ideology of the time; yet, as the play demonstrates, their effects could be equally devastating.

Anti-Semitism

The anti-Semitism of London in the 1590s was more intense than that in many other European cities where Jews lived openly. No Jews officially resided in London, because they had been exiled from England presumably in 1290 by Edward I and were not to return officially until 366 years later in 1656. The largest concentration of Jews resided far away in the Iberian Peninsula. They lived there either openly as Jews, as sincerely converted Christians, or as Conversos or New Christians—covert Jews but avowed Christians (the disparaging term *Marrano,* or *pig,* was a popular name for these people). Always unwelcome, Jews were finally expelled from Spain by Ferdinand and Isabella in 1492 and forced to convert to Christianity in Portugal in 1497. Some migrated to the Low Countries, particularly Antwerp, and during the reign of Henry VIII (1509–1547) perhaps one hundred Portuguese New Christians came to London, where they lived successfully as traders with Portugal and Spain after making "counterfeit professions" of Christianity.[10] Decades later, in the reign of Elizabeth, they were joined by another colony of about one hundred more Marranos (Gross 31–32). Additionally a group of non-Marrano Jewish musicians came to London from Italy, but they had been recruited by the music-loving Henry VIII to improve the musicianship of the court. Their families and they were gradually assimilated into Christian society in London through public conversion and marriage. Among the most notable were the members of the Bassano family, who performed at court and whom Shakespeare may well have known (Gross 34).

Unlike the few Jews in England, Jews in other countries could live openly, although they were not well received.[11] Berek records that Marranos in Turkey at the end of the century were very important to commerce, techniques of warfare, and printing; yet Muslims placed them beneath Christians, requiring them to become Christians as a necessary step before they could convert to Islam. Ironically, English travelers to other countries write of the Jews they encountered in relatively benign terms. Like the Frenchman Nicholas Nicholay (1585), the English traveler William Davies (1614) records the hatred shown to New Christians by the Turks. Samuel Purchas acknowledges that since biblical times, when the Jews were dispersed over the world, they have wandered as travelers, sometimes expelled, never accepted, and subjected to "'cruell and unkind hospitalitie'" that, Purchas anticipates, will end with their eventual acceptance of Christ (Berek 141). In 1581, a less biased English traveler, Lawrence Aldersey, respectfully describes a Jewish Saturday religious service in Venice, although he compares it to papist ritual. Sir Edwin Sandys (1610) has a mixed assessment of Jews. They are honorable and holy, he says, but they are also despised, scattered, and wretched. Travelers to Palestine write similar reports: even in their ostensible homeland, Jews are outsiders and are mistreated and beaten. Berek observes that travelers to countries where Jews lived openly generalize about Jews much as they generalize about other people from foreign lands and do not judge them as monstrous villains. He proposes that this is because "these Jews abroad posed no challenging questions about what it meant to be English" and therefore were no threat to the concept of English nationalism (144).

Yet a long and vile mythology supported bias against Jews in Elizabethan England. James Shapiro explains that the breadth of so-called Jewish crime extends far beyond the economic crime of charging exorbitant interest on loans to include ritual murder (89–111). Myths of such crimes were popular in Elizabethan England but extend back at least to the twelfth century and forward into the twentieth century. Raphael Holinshed chronicles the crucifixion of a child by Jews in Norwich in 1144. In fact, in Greece, obscure tales of Jews committing ritual murder predate the birth of Christ. In Elizabethan England, Jews were widely spoken of as ritual murderers who kidnapped, circumcised, crucified, and ate Christian children; used human blood in Passover cooking; and poisoned wells, a practice which it was believed had caused the Black Plague that killed one-third of Europe. In the context of such beliefs, to accuse Jews of exploitative lending was no stretch for the imagination.

As a consequence, Berek argues, Jews had to maintain multiple identities: as Christians, as Jews, as Englishmen, as Portuguese, and as Spanish. This encouraged a way of life, he says, that "was plural and unstable," and as a result "the most important quality of Jewishness in Elizabethan England" was "life lived in perpetual pretense, where names, nationalities, past history, and religious beliefs are all masks or appearances put on for some particular purpose"; in which "nothing can be assumed to be what it appears" (132–34). To the English, then, Jews seemed socially and economically successful but disturbingly mysterious because of the roles they were forced to play. This created, Berek proposes, mixed feelings toward upwardly mobile but chameleon-like Jews, feelings of "allure and anxiety" (135).

Berek further suggests that this image—of the individual who was forced to change continually on the outside in order to remain the same within—was the inspiration for Christopher Marlowe in his creation of the character Barabas in *The Jew of Malta*. Marlowe's hero is evil because he is a Jew, and inherent in that is his delight in refashioning himself, being loyal to no one, and seeking to adapt for self-interest. This Marlovian anti-Semitic image and not the reality of Jews within the society, Berek contends, is the model for other stage Jews like Shylock. The "hostile representation of Jews is profoundly shaped by Marlowe's peculiar vision" (138). The Jew, then, became a dramatic and frightening symbol of social change. The English were far more anxious about the change symbolized by Jews than they were about individual Jews themselves. Marlowe had handed his fellow Englishmen an easy-to-use symbol for their fears. Thus the dramatic image of Jewish moneylenders developed, although such individuals were virtually nonexistent in Elizabethan England.

In London, a few of the one or two hundred Jews rose to prominence. Most influential was Hector Nunes, a physician and associate of Lord

Burghley and Sir Francis Walsingham, advisor to the Queen. Most infamous, however, was Roderigo (Ruy) Lopez, physician to the Queen and sometime international intriguer and double agent against Spain. Serving as an interpreter in London for the Portuguese pretender, Don Antonio, in 1593, he was charged with plotting to poison the Queen for King Philip of Spain, England's enemy. He did indeed receive a gift of a diamond and ruby ring from Philip, but he gave it to Elizabeth, who wore it at her waist until she died. When the young favorite of Elizabeth, the Earl of Essex, sought war with Spain, he turned against Lopez, who, along with his co-conspirators, was tortured into a confession. On June 7, 1594, Lopez was hanged, drawn, and quartered at Tyburn, where the Queen's assent was not required for execution. Interestingly, the Calendar of State Papers Domestic for 1591–1594 includes some ninety pages describing this affair, yet references to Lopez's Jewishness occur on only four. In London, however, the always-lingering anti-Semitism exploded into public statements. The prosecutor, Edward Coke, wrote that Lopez was "worse than Judas himself"; and the crowd jeered him at his execution when he claimed allegiance to the Queen. Anti-Semitism dominated the atmosphere. Taking advantage of this, the Admiral's Men, the rival acting company of Shakespeare's Lord Chamberlain's Men, very successfully revived Marlowe's *The Jew of Malta* during the trial and later in 1594 and 1596, after Marlowe had been killed.

In 1880, Sidney Lee suggested that Shakespeare was encouraged to write *MV* because of the sensationalism brought on by the trial. The play may indeed contain two references to Lopez. First, the name of the character Antonio may derive from the name of the Portuguese Pretender, although the antecedent is doubtful because the name Antonio occurs in several of Shakespeare's plays. Second, as H. H. Furness points out, in the trial scene, Gratiano splenetically compares Shylock's "currish spirit" to that which "governed a wolf, who—hanged for human slaughter— / Even from the gallows did his fell soul fleet"(4.1.133–34). John Dover Wilson adds that *wolf* translates into the Latin *lupus,* similar to Lopez (in Brown xxiii). But wolves were commonly compared to particularly vicious humans, so this theory remains speculation.

Surely the events of 1593–1594 inflamed a vivid anti-Semitism, which the Admirals' Men's revival shrewdly turned into financial gain. This anti-Semitism may even have encouraged Shakespeare to create *MV* from its Italian sources. Or perhaps, as Berek contends, Marlowe's Barabas directly stimulated Shakespeare to produce his even more popular Jew. But to whatever extent anti-Semitism or Marlowe's Barabas is responsible,

Shakespeare rode the wave of popular culture with *MV;* and whether the play characterizes, condemns, or condones anti-Semitism, it contributes to the most recent 400 years of anti-Semitism's infamy.

SOURCES

The Flesh-Bond Plot

The plot of *MV* is related to at least eight sources and analogues, the first group of which concerns the flesh-bond story.[12] Records reveal flesh-bond stories in many cultures—from India to Rome and from Israel to Western Europe.[13] Arguably, these may include any story of an agreement to sacrifice human life in order to save or reward others, either human or animal. Such tales occur in the Hindu epic the *Mahabharata,* the Hebrew Talmud, and medieval story collections such as a thirteenth-century version of the *Gesta Romanorum* and the *Cursor Mundi.* Analogues to *MV* (similar or parallel stories) that are more contemporary with the play include an undated song called "The Ballad of Gernutus," describing a Jewish usurer in Venice;[14] "Declamation 95 / Of a Jew, who would for his debt have a pound of the flesh / of a Christian," published in *The Orator* in 1596 in London and written in French by Alexander Silvayn and translated into English possibly by Lazarus Liot; and *Zelauto, or The Fountain of Fame,* Book III, by Antony Munday (1580).[15]

Il Pecorone

By far the most important source of the play is a story by Ser Giovanni Fiorentino (of Florence), the first story of the fourth day in a series of tales called *Il Pecorone* (which can be translated as "The Big Sheep," "The Dumb Ox," or "The Dunce") written in the late fourteenth century and published in Milan in 1558.[16] Ser Giovanni's story contains the three main plot elements of *MV:* the bond between the merchant and the Jew, a (very different) wooing test for the hand of the lady of Belmont, and the ring plot following the courtroom scene. It lacks the casket-selection process, the Jessica subplot, the Nerissa-Gratiano marriage in the parallel plot, and the clown episodes. Because there is no known contemporary translation into English, we may assume that Shakespeare either read the Italian version or had seen or read a now lost intermediary source.

Some literary critics hypothesize that such an intermediary source is an anonymous lost play called *The Jew.* Its existence is verified only because the less-than-successful, rigidly conservative actor Stephen Gosson mentions it in his *Schoole of Abuse* (1579). Critical of the theater, Gosson writes that *The Jew* is one of only two plays (the other is named *Ptolome*) performed at the Red Bull that do not belong among the generally corrupt dramas of the time. He describes *The Jew* as "representing the greedinesse of worldly chusers, and bloodly mindes of Usurers . . . neither [play] with amorous gesture wounding the eye: nor with slouenly talke hurting the eare of the chast hearer."[17] If we accept the premise that "the greediness of worldly chusers" refers to the choosers in the casket-selection plot and "bloody mindes of Usurers" means Shylock, the flesh-seeking lender, then *The Jew* would predate *MV* in the linking of the flesh-bond plot and the casket-selection plot, which replaces *Il Pecorone*'s less lofty wooing test of suitors in Belmont. But Gosson's words are hardly sufficient to describe an ur-*Merchant,* particularly when no other external evidence exists. Other arguments weaken the ur-*Merchant* premise:

- Gosson's two descriptions may refer to a single plot about a worldly chooser who is also a bloody usurer.
- Combining two Italian plots was not yet an English practice.
- Amorous gestures do indeed occur in this story, especially in the casket-selection plot.

Evidence exists in *MV* that Shakespeare himself was the first to combine the casket-selection and flesh-bond plots, because nonfunctional, fossilized bits of *Il Pecorone*'s plot survive in *MV* as unexplained detritus. For example, in the play, Portia and Bassanio have already met before Bassanio arrives in Belmont in Act 2, an event narrated in *Il Pecorone* but unaccounted for in *MV*. Next, when Bassanio (the character parallel to the source's Giannetto) asks Antonio for money in *MV,* he argues that he needs these extra funds because he has already spent other now lost money and must recoup his losses. He says that as a boy, he shot a second or third arrow "The self-same way with more advised watch / To find the other forth" (1.1.149–50). The source story tells of Giannetto spending money in the same manner three times in a row. Such spending is implicit in Bassanio's speech, but it is not portrayed in the play. Finally, in *MV,* Portia travels to and from Venice by land more quickly than Bassanio does by sea. The play does not explain why this is true, but in Ser Giovanni's story, the lady of Belmonte instructs Giannetto, "Take a horse at once, and go by land, for it is quicker than by sea" (Bullough 471).

More interesting than the fossilized remains of the source in *MV,* which deny an intermediary play, are Shakespeare's alterations to *Il Pecorone* and

its reassuringly ordered world of romance. His deletions and additions reshape and enlarge elements of the story, producing dimension, ambiguity,
and beauty. *Il Pecorone* begins well before *MV.* Young Giannetto is the third
and youngest son of a wealthy merchant in Florence who, after his father's
death, goes to live in Venice with his childless and loving godfather,
Ansaldo.[18] With unprecedented generosity, he gives Giannetto access to all
his wealth, urging him to "get the goodwill of everyone" in Venice, a task
that the charming young man easily accomplishes.

Neither Ansaldo nor Giannetto shows the ambiguity of Shakespeare's
characters. Ansaldo is a consistently virtuous, forgiving, paternal figure,
reminiscent of the biblical father in the parable of the prodigal son,
while Antonio is less easily labeled. He gives Bassanio loyal friendship
even to the death; but he is also mysteriously depressed when Bassanio's
potential marriage looms, explicitly biased against the Jewish moneylender, and stubbornly unwilling to question the Venetian civil law that
condemns him.

Soon two of Giannetto's new friends ask him to outfit a ship and sail to
Alexandria with them in the spring. Incidental to the plot, these characters
never become distinctive figures like Bassanio's comrades. With
Ansaldo's blessing, Giannetto accepts their offer, and the older man out-
fits a fine ship for his godson. Out at sea, Giannetto sees a harbor in Belmonte that, the captain warns him, belongs to a rich widow who demands
that anyone who lands there must sleep with her. If he is unable to "enjoy"
her during the night, he must forfeit all his goods and leave. If he succeeds, he becomes the lord of the seaport, the country, and the lady herself. This test for winning the lady is far different from Shakespeare's
borrowed casket test. It diminishes the lady's virtue, making her far more
acquisitive. She is a widow—by convention, more lascivious than the virginal and dutiful Portia, who obeys her dead but loving father. The lady of
Belmonte serves as a sexual temptress to the hero, and unlike Portia, she
offers no contrast to the Venetians; she covets wealth as actively as they
do. As a result, the atmosphere of Belmonte is not set apart from that of
Venice; it holds the tension of sexual and worldly lust and encourages lust
in its visitors, unlike risk-taking love, which the lord of Belmont implicitly advocates in the casket test in *MV.*

Giannetto ignores the captain's warning that he who lands in Belmonte
and fails to consummate a sexual union with the lady of Belmonte forfeits
his ship and leaves immediately. He secretly orders that his ship steal
away from the other two and dock in Belmonte. When he lands, the lady
entertains him grandly, and the people are very pleased with him. Finally,
at night, the lady leads him to her chamber and offers him sweetmeats and

wine, which, as she always ensures, is drugged. Giannetto eats, drinks, and falls into bed, sleeping until the following morning. Thus he fails; he is asked to rise and leave, with only a horse and enough money to ride back to Venice.

When he finally returns to Venice, in his embarrassment, he lies, saying that he has been shipwrecked, but Ansaldo is grateful that Giannetto has not been killed. The following spring, this entire adventure occurs again, but this time Giannetto agrees to accompany his friends because he feels that he must return to the lady to marry her or else die. Thus unlike Bassanio, who had similarly met Portia before the play begins, Ansaldo proclaims no self-serving financial motives; he is enraptured by the lady and goes to Belmonte motivated by love. Unfortunately, he loses his ship a second time, which reduces his godfather to very modest circumstances, unlike Antonio, who is cash poor because of his own risky business ventures.

Even though Ansaldo is reluctant, Giannetto makes a third voyage to regain the wealth he has lost, partially because he is "ashamed to live in this way." This is the point in Ser Giovanni's story where *MV* begins. Since the old man does not have enough money to outfit another trading ship, he is forced to borrow 10,000 ducats from a Jew of Mestri, who lends the money on condition that if it is not returned by St. John's Day the next June, he can take a pound of flesh from whatever part of Ansaldo's body he chooses. Ansaldo asks only to see Giannetto if he should be forced to die because of the bond.

Once at sea, Giannetto eludes his companions and sails into the harbor at Belmonte. A third time he goes to the lady's chamber at the end of the day, but one of the lady's maids feels compassion for Giannetto and whispers to him, "Pretend to drink but do not drink tonight." He follows her advice, remains awake, and finally gives "the satisfaction of wedlock." The lady is "highly pleased" and announces the next morning that Giannetto will be the lord of Belmonte. Without question, in establishing the character of the lady, Ser Giovanni's marriage test is far different from Shakespeare's. But the tale also presents a hero of charm, sexuality, and perseverance, while Shakespeare's Bassanio possesses wit, courtesy, and growing virtue. In 1.3, Bassanio had shrewdly mistrusted Shylock's offer of the bond in Venice; later he selects the correct casket in Belmont, praises Portia in highly stylized courtly verse, and immediately postpones the pleasures of the marriage bed to rescue his friend. The unconsummated marriage between Portia and Bassanio also contrasts to the marriage of Giannetto and the lady in *Il Pecorone,* who marry and live together until the next June on St. John's Day when Giannetto suddenly remembers Ansaldo's bargain. He tells his wife of the desperate situation and rides by horse to Venice with 100,000 ducats she has given him to bring Ansaldo safely back to Belmonte.

Meanwhile, back in Venice, Ser Giovanni's Jew of Mestri insists on the pound of flesh, but in a far less dramatic fashion than Shylock's "I will have my bond" repetitions when Antonio is held in a Venetian jail in 3.3. The Jew grants Ansaldo a few more days of life so he can see Giannetto one last time. There will be no mercy from the terms of the bond because the Jew wishes "to commit this murder so that he could say that he had killed the greatest of the Christian merchants." As in Shakespeare's Venice, the city is "a place where the law [is] enforced," and the Jew has his rights because the bond is delinquent. When Giannetto arrives in Venice with his 20 followers, he knows that he must seek mercy and offers 20, 30, 40, 50, 100,000 ducats; but the Jew, sounding like Shylock, refuses, saying, "Understand this: if you were to offer more ducats than this city is worth, it would not satisfy me: I would rather have what the bond says is mine."

Unknown to Giannetto, the lady of Belmonte, without any waiting-woman, has secretly traveled to Venice herself, disguised as a lawyer from Bologna, and as such she offers to settle any disputes in the city, especially the one concerning "the base Jew." Because of her offer, the Jew, uncharacteristically, and Giannetto agree to come before the Bolognese lawyer and the judge. When the judge reads the bond, and the Jew once again refuses to take the 100,000 ducats, the disguised lady warns, "It will be better for you." But the Jew is adamant, and, as he takes a razor to make a first cut, she suddenly warns him that if he takes more or less than a pound, he will lose his own head; and if he spills any blood, he will die himself. So "if you are wise," she cautions, "you will take great care what you do." Finally, the Jew understands and asks for the 100,000 ducats. He is refused, as he is at his requests for 90, 80, 50, and even the original 10,000 ducats. The people cry mockingly, "He who thought to ensnare others, is caught himself." With that, the Jew tears the bond into pieces in a great fury.

Although the overall situation and outcome are similar, Shakespeare makes significant changes to this scene (*MV* 4.1). Portia/Balthazar appears in a somewhat more reasonable circumstance, not as a lawyer cum judge for hire but rather as a substitute consultant from Rome recommended by the learned but "very sick" Bellario, to whom the Duke had sent a letter concerning the case. More important, Portia offers a cleverly constructed argument that ensnares Shylock far more completely than that presented by Ser Giovanni's lady of Belmonte. Portia asks for mercy from

Shylock, offers him generous sums of money, requests the presence of a surgeon, and finally condemns him with three, not two, conditions placed on the bond. The first two, taken from the tale—that he cut only bloodless and perfectly measured flesh from Antonio's body—allow Shylock the opportunity to refuse and so escape any additional punishment from the court. Shakespeare, however, adds a third, more cruel and inescapable condition based on Shylock's status as a Jew. He has no power to evade punishment after Portia informs him that "If it be proved against an alien, / That by direct or indirect attempts / He seek the life of any citizen" (3.2.345–47) of Venice, the alien is guilty. Without the merciful intervention of the Duke, Shylock, presumed guilty, would be condemned to death and the loss of his estate. Antonio further condemns him to a Christian conversion. Unlike the Jew of Mestri, he is destroyed and leaves the scene not in anger but in despair. That Shakespeare increases Shylock's suffering and makes it contingent on his alien status clouds the virtue of the heroes with their biased, self-righteous arrogance of class.

Later in *Il Pecorone,* acknowledging the high cost of good counsel, Giannetto offers his disguised lady 100,000 ducats as payment for the courtroom victory. But she refuses, instead asking for the young man's wedding ring. With great reluctance, Giannetto offers it, saying, my lady "will think I have given it to some other woman and so be angry with me and think I love another—and yet I love her better than I love my self." In Shakespeare's play, Bassanio relinquishes the ring at Antonio's insistence, raising earlier questions about the relationship he has enjoyed with Bassanio and about Bassanio's own independence.

Finally, the last scene in Belmonte holds the plot's conclusions, which, again, Shakespeare enlarges. After both Giannetto and the lady return to Belmonte separately, the lady feigns anger at him for having had dalliances with former mistresses in Venice. Then, noticing the missing ring, she increases her accusations. Giannetto bursts into tears, and the lady embraces him and tells him the true story, which makes him very happy. Giannetto gives to Ansaldo in marriage the maid who had warned him of the drugged wine, and they all live on in happiness. That Shakespeare leaves Antonio alone at the end, sufficiently pleased that he has regained his fortune, limits our happiness with and for him and sets up arguable parallels between him and Shylock. He remains an enigma, neither hideous nor harmonious. Earlier, in 5.1 of *MV,* Lorenzo had reflected on the concord among the celestial spheres, which humans can imagine but cannot hear because they are closed in by their "muddy vestures of decay." Lorenzo's lines suggest the limitations placed on human potential in a comic world like this one, inhabited by imperfect characters. But this comic world is not sustained evenly throughout the play. The suffering inflicted on the alien Shylock and the violence he longs to commit—both of which Shakespeare expands in the play, intertwined with the newly added themes of filial ingratitude, murderous revenge, and greed-based prejudice—are neither ridiculous (Aristotle's description of the comic) nor resolvable and hint at the pain of tragedy.

The story elements missing from *Il Pecorone* but present in *MV* reveal the substance of Shakespeare's invention. First, he emphasizes financial transactions. Shylock claims to borrow money from Tubal and lends it to Antonio, who lends it to Bassanio, who spends it on the lavish show of wealth and thereby wins a dowry of more money—money that Portia inherits from her dead father. Additionally, Jessica and Lorenzo steal money from Shylock and later are promised a large inheritance. Even the clown Lancelot leaves one job for another with more perquisites. Finally, before the play began, Antonio had invested money in trading ships, and presumably after the play ends, he will receive a substantial profit as a return on that investment as well as on the half of Shylock's money that he will manage as a trustee for Lorenzo.

Shakespeare also creates far more complex relationships in both Belmont and Venice: each setting in *MV* has a father, a marriageable daughter, and her suitor, while Venice also includes the ambiguous friendship/love between Antonio and Bassanio, far less straightforward than the father-son relationship of *Il Pecorone*. Shylock, who appears in only five scenes, gains dimension because he is a father and a husband as well as a usurer and a vengeful killer. And although the moneylenders in both stories are arguably bloodthirsty, seemingly because they are Jews, the Jew of Mestri is a solitary figure, while Shylock responds with emotion to a family— Jessica and his dead wife, Leah—which raises questions about the pervasiveness of his villainy. Similarly, the melancholy mercantilist, Antonio, denies us conventional classification, unlike Ansaldo, the always-doting godfather. Portia, no longer a conventionally wily, avaricious widow, is likewise ambiguous. From a distance, she is a chaste and obedient virgin; but close up, she is witty and assertive, sometimes a wily, unbending barrister and other times a pampered daughter who grudgingly submits to a de facto arranged marriage. Bassanio too is no longer the naively inquisitive and, later, love-struck young Giannetto but is rather a perhaps overly engaging debtor whose love for Portia is often less than convincing. Other elements of the play increase the comic tone: distinctive but flighty young men befriend Bassanio in Venice; a Christian clown is a servant to both Jew and Christian; and the husband-wife ring plot is doubled by stock comic characters: the wily waiting woman Nerissa and the braggart friend

Gratiano. Shakespeare's alterations and expansions of the characters' relationships in the source create in *MV* exquisite explorations of love and virtue as well as lurking prejudice.

The Casket-Selection Plot

The most important story element of *MV* not found in *Il Pecorone* is the casket-selection process, which Shakespeare grafts onto the wooing and winning of the lady in Belmont, replacing *Il Pecorone*'s bed test. Recorded stories of high-stakes casket selection are common and varied in western literature from at least the ninth century. Stories include between two and four caskets; some stories have identical caskets, and others have caskets of varied appearance. In the former stories, correct selection depends on the friendliness of Fortune or the grace of God; in the latter stories, correct selection is based on the virtue or wisdom of the chooser.

In the ninth century, a Greek monk named Joannes Damascenus wrote the earliest known version of a casket plot in the story of Barlaam the hermit. Translated into Latin before the thirteenth century, this moral tale tells of a wise king and his nobles. They complain that he spends too much time conversing with the poor people of the land. In response, the king orders that four caskets be made, two of gold and filled with human bones, and two covered with pitch and filled with jewels. Then the king commands that the nobles select between the two sets. Predictably, they choose the gold caskets. The king then observes that they err in the same way as they do when they judge people; they "look with the eyes of sense" rather than "with the eyes of the mind" (Bullough 458).[19]

Casket-selection stories are also included in the *Speculum Historiale* (Lib. XV, Cap. x, 1290) by Vincent de Beauvais; in Boccaccio's *Decameron* (Day X, Story 1); and in two stories in Book Five of the *Confessio Amantis* by John Gower. Boccaccio's tale illustrates a different moral—that what one receives is controlled by quixotic Fortune, not the goodness of others or one's own wisdom.

Gesta Romanorum, Tale LXVI

The source tale in the *Gesta Romanorum* suggests in contrast that the identity of the winner of the prize casket depends not on personal wisdom, God's grace, or Fortune's whim but rather on the winner's humility and faith in the goodness of God. The *Gesta Romanorum* is a collection of medieval tales; a selected English translation was published in London in 1577 and again in a revised version in 1595. Most scholars consider Tale

LXVI of Ancelmus the Emperor in the latter version a probable source for the casket test in *MV* because, unlike the earlier text, it contains the word *insculpt* (engraved), the same word Shakespeare gives to Morocco but includes in no other work. The dark-skinned prince recalls an English coin "Stamped in gold; but that's insculpted upon" (2.7.57).

The short tale describes the creation of peace between the King of Naples and the Emperor of Rome through the marriage of their children. The last third of the story tells of the final trial or marriage test given to the King of Naples's daughter, who has been sent by her father to marry the son of the Emperor Ancelmus of Rome. On her sea journey to Rome she is shipwrecked and swallowed by a whale, which she mortally wounds from within its stomach with a knife. As the dying animal seeks land, an earl named Pirius and his men smite it, rescuing the princess and taking her to the Emperor. The Emperor is pleased by her survival but requires that she pass a test similar to the casket test taken by Bassanio, although the princess will receive no penalty if she chooses incorrectly. The first of the three vessels, or caskets, is "made of pure Gold well beesette with precious stones without and within, full of dead mens bones" and bearing a superscription, "*Who so chooseth mee shall finde that he deserueth.*" The second is of "Fyne siluer, fylled with earth and wormes" and bearing a superscription, "*Who so chooseth me shall finde that his nature desireth.*" The last is lead, "full within of precious stones, and therevpon was insculpt this posey. *Who so chooseth mee, shall finde that God hath disposed for him.*" The maid prays for God's grace to help her choose the correct casket, selects the correct lead vessel based on the premise that God never disposes evil, marries the prince, and together "with great solempnitie, & much honour," they live "to theyr liues ende."[20]

Several of these story elements are included in the casket test in *MV.* The contest serves as an eligibility test for marriage; as previously noted, the source's unusual term *insculpt* is repeated; the father of one of the marriage partners is the creator of the test; and the appearance, contents, and inscriptions (although switched) on two of the caskets are similar. But Shakespeare altered key elements of the story to blend them into and deepen the plot of *Il Pecorone.* The genders of the marriage prize and the wooer are necessarily switched; the potential bride and not her father actively manages the contest with the help of her waiting woman; and the bride's presence, participation, and partiality are major plot elements. These changes highlight and develop Portia as the dutiful and loving heroine of a comic romance. But during the casket scenes, she also proves to be opinionated, petulant, witty, shrewd, fearless, and sufficiently discriminating to desire as a husband the one man who proves to be worthy of her.

Shakespeare's alterations of the terms of the contest are also significant. First, the Lord of Belmont, who controls the contest from the grave, has placed a penalty on those contestants who select incorrectly. As evidence, Shakespeare adds two other contestants, Morocco and Arragon, who precede Bassanio as unsuccessful wooers, doomed to remain without legal heirs. Their penalties also highlight their specious reasoning: Morocco reasons that all men desire "the fair Portia," who logically must be encased in fair gold. He follows two mistaken premises: that something that is fair outside will also be fair inside, and that desire and desirability are sufficient reason for marriage—or that a trophy wife is a worthy goal. Arragon is foolish enough to believe that his own human judgment can determine what he justly deserves and that a wife may serve as a worldly reward for excellence.

Second, the inscription on the lead casket is changed from the source's overt dependence on God to the dictum that the chooser "must give and hazard all he hath." This offers a double message. First, it describes the qualities that the Lord of Belmont seeks in his daughter's husband—a willingness to risk everything for the wife that he will love. Second, it describes Bassanio himself, who has indeed gambled everything he has, even the life of his dear friend, to select the casket. Further, the reasoning Bassanio uses to select the casket is much like the moral described in Damascenus's tale—that outward appearances do not necessarily reflect inner virtue. These plot changes foretell a virtue and a constancy emerging later in both the wooer and his would-be bride.

The Runaway Daughter

Analogues for the third plot element in *MV*, the Jessica-Lorenzo-Shylock action, occur in medieval and early modern literature. The love story between Rodolfo and Brisana in *Zelauto* is such an analogue, as well as the adventures of Giuffredi Saccano and Carmosina in Masuccio's *Il Novellino,* written in the fifteenth century but untranslated into English during Shakespeare's lifetime.[21] Most well known, however, is Christopher Marlowe's play *The Jew of Malta.*[22]

The Jew of Malta

Marlowe probably wrote this play sometime between December 1588 and February 1592, when William Henslowe recorded its performance.[23]

It was presented by the Lord Strange's Men, probably by the Admiral's Men, and by other acting companies at least 36 times during the four-year period ending in June 1596. Midway during this period, in 1594, the intensified anti-Semitism achieved with the execution of Roderigo Lopez made additional performances financially profitable. While the play has no known source, it does refer to the Turks' siege on Malta in 1565, which, unlike the fictionalized siege in the play, was unsuccessful.

The play begins with a 43-line prologue delivered by a character named Machevill who tells the London audience that while the world thought that Machevill was dead, it is not true; rather, he [the speaker] "is come from France / To view this land, and frolic with his friends" (1.1.3–4) and "to present the tragedy of a Jew / Who smiles to see how full his bags are cramm'd" (1.1.30–32). This Jew, a very wealthy merchant named Barabas, lives prosperously on Malta with his lovely and devoted daughter, Abigail. His argosies go around the world, increasing his wealth, "Bags of fiery opals, sapphires, amethysts, / Jacinths, hard topaz, grass-green emeralds, / Beauteous rubies, sparkling diamonds" (1.1.25–27). In a soliloquy, Barabas claims that he is among those Jews who have "More wealth by far than those that brag of faith" (1.1.121). But the Christian government of Malta confiscates his money to fight the Turks, a terrible blow to Barabas because wealth is the stuff from which he gains freedom and power. So he fights back. His acquisitiveness turns to treachery, his greed to violence, and like other Marlovian heroes, he descends into increasingly more reprehensible deeds, finally planning to sabotage both the government of Malta and the Turkish invaders. He murders people more and more indiscriminately: the son of the governor who is Abigail's beloved, two monks, a convent of nuns, and even Abigail herself. In the end, he is caught in one of his own traps when he slips into a cauldron of boiling oil and dies, an unmistakable image of his descent to hell.

Literary critics regularly compare and contrast Shylock to this more extravagantly violent prototype. Geoffrey Bullough, writing in 1957, finds Barabas "a real person as well as a figure of horror" in the first two acts. He believes that Shakespeare's Shylock, a "villain with a point of view, not just a monster, owes much to Marlowe's Jew" (454); and "for much of the atmosphere of his Jewish theme, Shakespeare was thus indebted to Marlowe" (356).[24] In the New Arden edition of *MV* (1959), John Russell Brown observes that Shakespeare "was probably influenced by *The Jew of Malta* because, in addition to obvious verbal parallels and the presence of a lovely daughter, "the villain Barabas coloured Shakespeare's conception of a Jew." But "more intangible" an influence, he suggests, "may be real Jews living in contemporary London" (xxxi). Anne Barton describes

Barabas as a figure of "fantastic evil" who is "half Machiavel, half vice, a brilliant caricature more than a credible human being," while Shylock "is a closely observed human being" (250-51). M. M. Mahood calls *The Jew of Malta* "a persistent presence, which Shakespeare manipulates with confident skill." She says that echoes from Marlowe's play may be heard in *MV,* but *MV* "is a different kind of play and the product of a different kind of imagination." Marlowe's play is a "powerful and grotesque tragedy" that Shakespeare is "holding at bay" rather than mimicking (7–8). Berek maintains, as noted earlier, that Barabas indeed establishes the frightening image of the stage Jew, including Shylock. Most recently, Harold Bloom argues that Barabas, a villain both "farcical and scary," is outdone by Shylock. Barabas is "a ferocious Machiavel" and a "cartoon," antithetical to Shylock, who is a "grim Puritan" and a "realistic mimesis" (*Shakespeare: The Invention of the Human* 171, 173).

Even though *The Jew of Malta* is a tragedy, it would be difficult to deny its value as an influence on Shakespeare when he wrote the "comicall History" of *MV* some 4 to 10 years later.[25] First, *MV* contains verbal echoes of Marlowe's play. Second, although *The Jew of Malta* was performed as a revival, both plays responded to popular interest in Jews encouraged by the Lopez affair of 1594. And third, one of the most important changes Shakespeare made to his source story, *Il Pecorone,* is the character development of the nameless Jewish moneylender from Mestri, who in *Il Pecorone* hopes to boast that he has killed the wealthiest of the Christian merchants. Shakespeare enlarges Ser Giovanni's moneylender with a personal life similar to that of Barabas. Both Shylock and Barabas have wealth and a daughter over whom they wield obsessive control; yet they themselves are beset by society's ugly biases.

But differences between the plays are vast. Barabas is a merchant, not a moneylender, and more important, is a far flatter character than Shylock. His actions are unpredictable only in the depth of their hideousness. For this reason, he seems like a caricature or an exaggeration and therefore not believably tragic. Furthermore, he exists in the center of the awful world of Mediterranean intrigue, so he fits in well as he boisterously commits ever more monstrous murders and revels in the trappings of wealth and power. The action swirls in a downward spiral of increasing evil as Barabas soliloquizes a Machiavellian, self-serving morality that requires only that he maintain self-control. Indeed, in the prologue to the play, Machevill disdains religion and finds weakness and ignorance the only sins, observing that Barabas has acquired wealth "not got without my means." Granted, Shakespeare was spurred on by *The Jew of Malta,* but the play's genre and tone, its overall structure, and its Jewish villain differ significantly from *MV.*

Perhaps, however, *The Jew of Malta* is a more balanced play, admittedly at a far less complex level than *MV.* Medieval and Renaissance Christian Europe associated the Jew-as-devil-follower with a vicious and exciting violence both in the real world and in art. Such unthinking fury saturates the whole world of *The Jew of Malta.* It is a world of horror—hardly tragic in a classic sense because disorder seems destined to prevail. On the other hand, the more courteous and self-assured affluence of Venice and Belmont in *MV* is less obviously evil, so Shylock's intended violence threatens to throw off the balance of the play, to weigh down the action in Venice so that Belmont's story pales. In his creation of Shylock, Shakespeare begins with only the outline of the Jew of Mestri from *Il Pecorone.* But he amplifies that Jew with an imaginative refashioning of Marlowe's prototype, who possesses a daughter, wealth, and a dearth of comrades. As a result, Shylock the moneylender carries the vigor of Barabas in a tortured soul, and his presence dominates the Venetian action so that balance with the Belmont action is elusive, almost like the piece of Antonio's flesh Shylock wishes to place on his courtroom scales.

NOTES

1. Harley Granville-Barker, *"The Merchant of Venice,"* in *Prefaces to Shakespeare,* Vol. 4. 1946. (Princeton: Princeton UP, 1965), 88–119.

2. In 1624, the House of Commons finally struck out the passage in the usury statute ruling that "all usury was against the law of God, leaving it to be determined by divines." See James Shapiro, *Shakespeare and the Jews* (New York: Columbia University Press, 1996), 98–100.

3. See Peter Berek, "The Jew as Renaissance Man," *Renaissance Quarterly* 51 (1998): 128–62.

4. See Thomas Wilson, *A Discourse Upon Usury,* ed. R. H. Tawney (New York: Frank Cass, 1963), 177. (Orig. pub. 1572.)

5. See Francis Bacon, "On Usury," in *Essays, Civil and Moral in 'The New Atlantis' by Francis Bacon; 'Areopagitica' and 'Tractate on Education' by John Milton;'Religio Medici' by Sir Thomas Browne,* ed. Charles W. Eliot (New York: P. F. Collier, 1909), 106–9.

6. See John Gross, *Shylock: A Legend and Its Legacy* (New York: Simon and Schuster, 1992), 48.

7. Richard Hooker (1553 or 1554 to 1600) wrote extensively of these ideas in *Of the Laws of Ecclesiastical Polity* (New York: E. P. Dutton, 1907).

8. See Shapiro, *Shakespeare and the Jews,* n. 256, for a detailed discussion of usury and anti-Semitism in Tudor England.

9. Geoffrey Bullough writes that this story is "probably pre-Shakespearean" and may derive from the plot of the old play *The Jew.* See Geoffrey Bullough, ed., *Narrative and Dramatic Sources of Shakespeare* (London: Routledge, 1957), I:

445–514.

10. Much of the information about the history of Jews in London is in D. M. Cohen, "The Jew and Shylock," *Shakespeare Quarterly* 31 (1980): 53–63. Cohen argues that the play is anti-Semitic and that even though Shakespeare clearly understood the humanity of Jews, he was willing to use a sensational stereotype—a "profoundly troubling" conclusion about Shakespeare. See also Gross, *Shylock: A Legend*, and Shapiro, *Shakespeare and the Jews.*

11. See Berek, "The Jew as Renaissance Man," for a detailed comparison between English attitudes toward Jews in other countries and their far more biased opinions of Jews living in England.

12. Flesh-bond stories are described in Hermann Sinsheimer, *Shylock: The History of a Character* (1947; repr., New York: Benjamin Blom, 1963), 71–82.

13. See Bullough, *Narrative and Dramatic Sources,* I: 445–514, for full translations or original English versions of eight sources and analogues for *MV* as well as Bullough's thorough introduction. A less comprehensive source study is Kenneth Muir, *Shakespeare's Sources,* vol. I (1957; repr., London: Methuen, 1961). The New Arden edition of the play, edited by John Russell Brown (Cambridge: Harvard University Press, 1959) also includes the texts of five sources and analogues in the appendices following the text, 140–73.

14. See the introduction and Appendix II in *The New Arden Shakespeare*, xxxi and 153–56, for a discussion and reprint of "The Ballad of Gernutus." The poem may have been entered into the Stationers' Register under the title "ballad called the vsurers rewarde" on June 19, 1594.

15. Both the "Declamation" and *Zelauto* are included in Bullough, 482–90.

16. For complete translations of this story, see Bullough, 463–76; *The New Arden Shakespeare,* 140–53; T. J. B. Spencer, ed., *Elizabethan Love Stories* (Baltimore: Penguin Books, 1968), 177–96; and a new translation of *MV* published by Bantam Classics and edited by David Bevington (New York: Bantam, 1988).

17. This quotation is excerpted in Bullough, 446, and M. M. Mahood, *The Merchant of Venice,* New Cambridge Shakespeare (Cambridge: Cambridge University Press, 1987), 5.

18. Quotations from the story are taken from the translation included in Appendix I of *The New Arden Shakespeare,* 140–53.

19. Bullough discusses this tale (458) and includes full text versions of other casket-selection stories more contemporary with and similar to *MV.*

20. See Brown, 172–74 for the full translation of this tale from which these excerpts are taken.

21. See Bullough, 486–90, 497–505.

22. Although Bullough calls *The Jew of Malta* "one of Shakespeare's major sources" (454) in his introduction and identifies it as a "source" preceding the excerpts he includes, I agree with Mahood, who finds the play "a strong theatrical influence" (New York: Riverhead Books, 1998; xxxi); Brown, who says it "probably influenced" Shakespeare (181); and Harold Bloom, who calls Barabas a

"stimulus" (*Shakespeare: The Invention of the Human*). Thus it is more accurately an analogue.

23. See Christopher Marlowe, *The Jew of Malta,* in *Complete Plays and Poems,* ed. E. D. Pendry (London: Everyman, 1976, 1997), 327–91. Quotations from the play are taken from this edition.

24. The relationship between Barabas and Shylock is a long-popular topic in the literary criticism of both plays, and Bullough discusses it in at least two separate passages.

25. In the Quarto 1 of 1600, the title page calls the play a "Historie," while the running heads label it a "Comicall History." In 1698, Frances Meres listed it among six comedies by Shakespeare; similarly, in 1623, Heminges and Condell included it among the comedies in the First Folio edition.

3

DRAMATIC STRUCTURE

To examine the dramatic structure of this comedy—its plot, characters, and language—first we must keep in mind the contributions of the sources. The dramatic structure silhouettes the playwright's alterations to those sources, which make *The Merchant of Venice* witty, ironic, and most of all, enigmatic. Second, we need to recognize that like all art, *MV* imitates the complexity of human experience. It offers no conclusions about characters or plot; yet as art, the play has formal design—a series of scenes offering exposition, conflict, and denouement, woven into unity. Consequently, we respond to the design of its form, which serves as a template that orders but never disentangles the complexity of its content. The superimposition of design over content contributes to the tension of Shakespeare's art. The result is that metaphorically, the play offers elegantly framed questions, never their answers.

Finally, we should admit to our wavering responses as we read or watch the play. Our approval of Venice and Belmont ebbs and flows; our satisfaction with events is incomplete; and we cannot maintain an unfailing respect for any single character. And this does not even touch on Shylock. Walter Cohen writes, "No other Shakespearean comedy before *All's Well That Ends Well* (1602) and *Measure for Measure* (1604), perhaps no other Shakespearean comedy at all, has excited comparable controversy."[1] Certainly *MV* is the first of Shakespeare's so-called problem plays, "as much a 'problem'," W. H. Auden concludes, "as one by Ibsen or Shaw."[2] It reminds us that a tidy neatness in themes and explanations do not represent the human condition; such order exists only in the narrow fantasies of single individuals. As in life, nothing is static in the play, particularly the attitudes of the audience. Cohen suggests that the audience ought not to

seek interpretations at all, because the play "requires us not so much to interpret as to discover the sources of our difficulty in interpreting" (47).

Indeed, the investigation of dramatic structure does not lead to a neat
exegesis. Still, attempting to delineate a structural symmetry, critics often
simplify the play's genre and action as romantic comedy with a double
plot—bond and casket, which are associated with Venice and Belmont, respectively.[3] Venice is money and Belmont is love, except for the startling
outsider, Shylock. Graham Holderness notes that these settings have been
identified with "different moral systems . . . [and] have been interpreted in
the light of ethical oppositions between Law and Love, Justice and
Mercy."[4] But such analysis ignores the play's paradoxes. Nor can the
characters be easily categorized. Readers again use geography to group
them, as if place accords to its residents a given value system. On the contrary, characters share an ambiguity that makes absolute moral judgments
foolhardy. The play's several plots and characters are too tightly intertwined, fused with parallel themes and action, and saturated with irony to
be assigned mutual exclusivity. What appears to be true on the surface is
not necessarily so when we look more carefully. Finally, the language is
remarkably varied compared with that of Shakespeare's then-existing
plays—from the highly ornamented, conventional Petrarchan love language of Bassanio to the earthy dialectic, painful lamentation, and comic
repetition of Shylock. The juxtaposition of such verbal variety is illustrated in the final scene: the play concludes in what some critics describe
as the harmonious and loving world of Belmont,[5] but the last words, delivered by the self-nominated fool, Gratiano, is a bawdy and ambiguous
pun.

PLOT

The Folio Edition of 1623 separates *The Merchant of Venice* into five
acts, following the conventional English five-act comic plot formula of
the late sixteenth and early seventeenth centuries. This convention, a set
of standards accepted by contemporary dramatists and their audiences, allows that characters face problems that become increasingly more complex before being resolved with a happy ending and little real damage to
any of the protagonists. Such an ending mirrors the observation of Aristotle, who noted in the latter half of the fourth century B.C.E., that while
comedy dramatizes a fable and is an imitation of lower types, it does not
include "the full range of badness."[6] Thus life-threatening danger may
exist, but it does not succeed.[7] Roman New Comedy, exemplified in the
plays of Plautus (250–184 B.C.E.) and the more decorous dramas of Ter-

ence (186–159 B.C.E.), formalized this comic plot into the five-act structure revived in the Italian theater and continued in the English comedy.
The conventional pattern includes an Act 1 protasis, or exposition, which
lays out the situation; an Act 2 and Act 3 epitasis, or conflict, which develops the increasing complications logically; an Act 4 catastasis, or
recognition scene, which often involves a disguise; and an Act 5 catastrophe (really anastrophe, or turning up of the plot), which clarifies the plot's
remaining mysteries and includes the denouement or unraveling.

But the first printed copy of *MV,* the Heyes-Roberts quarto of 1600,
which likely followed Shakespeare's manuscript, has no act divisions. It is
a series of scenes set apart from one another only by the exeunt of all the
characters from the stage and the entrance of others. As a result, the unit of
action is the scene. This ongoing flow of scenes, then, governs the order of
the action in *MV.* The play's plots—the flesh-bond plot, the casket-selection plot, the runaway-daughter plot, and, to a lesser degree, the clown
plot, the ring plot, and the vagaries in the career of the merchant—surge
forward like a series of overlapping waves. Each has it own exposition,
conflict, climax, and denouement; and scenes from each plot alternate,
juxtaposing the streets of Venice with the lavish halls and gardens of Belmont. Sometimes plots are spliced with portmanteau scenes, which present action belonging to two or more plots, and always the plots are
dependent on one another for resolution.

If we examine the organization of the play into what most editors since
Nicholas Rowe (1709) have separated into about 20 scenes, we can identify this arrangement of cascading plots.[8] The exposition of the bond plot
is introduced in 1.1 and fully established in 1.3 with the introduction of
Shylock. It swells into the tension of its conflict in 3.1 and 3.3; extends
beyond the casket plot to reach a climax and resolution in the 4.1 courtroom scene; and has its denouement in 4.2, perhaps with a coda appended
in 5.1. Shortly after the bond plot is under way, the casket plot begins with
an exposition in 1.2; continues with the conflict in 2.1, 2.7, and 2.9; seems
to climax with Bassanio's correct casket selection in 3.2; and closes with
the denouement of the young people's declarations of love in the same
scene. Development of the love bond between Portia and Bassanio, however, reaches a far more believable resolution at the conclusion of the play.
The runaway-daughter plot is the third to begin. Jessica enters the play in
2.3 when she confides her plans to Lancelot. This plot moves forward in a
rush of three subsequent scenes, and in 2.8, Solanio and Salarino recall the
departure of the lovers from Venice. The lovers reappear married but un-
settled in 3.2, 3.4, and 3.5 and finally settle as a financially stable couple
at the end of 5.1, the final scene.

Even the minor plot elements follow the three-part order: the exposition of the ring plot begins at the betrothal of Portia and Bassanio in 3.2, gains complications in 4.2, and resolves in 5.1. Another miniature plot, resolved almost immediately, concerns Lancelot Gobbo's wish in 2.2 to leave the employ of Shylock and serve Bassanio. Finally, overarching the entire play is the increasing financial and physical danger facing the title character, the merchant of Venice. The first scene presents the exposition describing his despondency and risky sea trade. At intervals in the play (1.3, 3.1, 3.2, 3.3, 4.1), his troubles intensify, and they are almost providentially resolved with Portia's miraculous news of Antonio's returned ships loaded with wealth in the final scene.

A variety of dramatic devices hold together these several coexistent plots. The portmanteau scenes juxtapose action: for example, the key 3.1 scene opens with Solanio and Salarino's lament over the loss of one of the ships owned by "the good Antonio, the honest Antonio." Then, at the entrance of Shylock, a contrasting mockery quickly evolves: yes, they tell him, we knew all about the impending flight of your daughter with her Christian lover, and we applaud it because she is far superior to you. But when Salarino asks Shylock of further news of Antonio's fortunes, he responds with disgust over his money-losing deal with a bankrupt debtor and justifies revenge with the "Hath not a Jew eyes?" speech. Later, after hearing from Tubal more details of both Jessica and Antonio, he comments with alternating grief and glee as he begins to contrive a revenge plan with Tubal. Several other scenes splice plots: the 1.3 expository scene, when Bassanio's pilgrimage to Belmont—the casket plot—becomes possible because of Shylock's and Antonio's bond; the 3.4 conflict scene, when Portia, the casket prize, plots to travel to Venice and eliminate Antonio's bondage; and the 4.2 denouement and conflict scene, when Bassanio's gift to Portia/Balthazar concludes the bond plot but intensifies the ring plot. Finally, the plots contain parallel actions and themes. Three plots center on parent-child bonds, three sets of lovers marry, and two older wealthy Venetians seek success in the marketplace. Parallel themes of wealth, risk, bias, and time exist in both the Venice and Belmont plots, highlighting contrasts between them or, viewed ironically, similarities.

Thus, while classical and archetypal models shed light on the plot of *MV*, we can be neither limited nor distracted by the notion of a single plot infrastructure. Each plot begins separately; rises in tension, often through essential links with other plots; and resolves, in most cases, with the promise to the protagonists of financial fortune. An overarching five-act plot summary does not entirely explain the contrapuntal waves within the overall action, each beginning and ending separately but harmonizing with one another, building toward what are aesthetic resolutions but not complete repose. We must examine this construction and those variants from the conventional five-act formula that make *MV* a masterful but contradictory play.

ACT 1

Scene 1.

More lengthy than that of the classical model, the exposition of *MV*, containing explanations of the play's various plots, extends through 2.3 when Jessica appears for the first time. The five expository scenes answer the traditional questions of *who, what, where, when, why, how*, and *which* and introduce interrelationships among the plots and parallel themes. They contain the tension of wrong order, typical of a story's exposition, and forge into the conflict made dangerous by the risks the protagonists accept: Antonio's investment in uncharted trading ships and his agreement to a life-threatening but nonusurous bond, Portia's passive participation in the casket test, Lancelot's efforts to escape Shylock, Bassanio's dangerously funded and potentially heir-destroying quest for a wealthy wife, and Jessica's escape with her Christian lover and her father's ducats. Over all this, like a thick fog, hangs wealth, suffocating the worlds of Venice and Belmont. Almost as if they are infused with the noxious values enveloping them, nearly all the characters seek risk because of wealth, attack others because of wealth, and accept the man-made measurement of property and time as indisputable truths because of wealth. Amid such weighty material pressures, love must survive, and in Act 5, happily it is still breathing.

The first 56 lines of the first scene establish themes of financial gain and risk in an atmosphere of ennui and, in Antonio's case, despondency.[9] Scene 1 begins in the middle of a conversation, as Shakespeare's plays often do. Antonio, the wealthy and respected Venetian merchant, apparently responding to a previous observation, agrees with his acquaintances Salarino and Solanio that he is indeed unaccountably sad. Salarino and Solanio respond that Antonio could have two reasons for such melancholy: money and love. For 32 lines (1.1.8–40), they imagine money as the problem and compare Antonio's argosies to rich citizens and to elaborate pageants in the sea. In life's smallest events, they find reminders of Antonio's risky sea ventures: a moving blade of grass and breath blowing on hot soup suggest a storm at sea, sand in an hourglass hints of shallows and flats, the stones of the church walls seem to be "dangerous rocks." Characteristic of the play, Salarino's and Solanio's comments are scattered with images of mercantilism and wealth. Karen Newman observes that such imagery, which both characterizes speakers and emphasizes themes, represents the "exchange of goods," whether merchandise or women (117). But Antonio denies such fear for his argosies, assuring the pair that his "whole estate" has not been gambled "Upon the fortune of this present year" (1.1.43–44), although he later confesses otherwise to Bassanio. This elicits Solanio's one-line conclusion: "Why then you are in love" (1.1.46), an idea no one pursues and Antonio dismisses. The proportion of 32 lines to 1, weighting commerce so heavily over love, is the first evidence of Venice's obsession.

Soon Gratiano, Lorenzo, and Bassanio enter, with Gratiano's similar observation that Antonio is "marvelously changed" (1.1.76). When Antonio again complains of his "sad part" in this world, Gratiano's advice holds more language of commerce: people seeking life's joy "lose it that do *buy* it with much care" (1.1.75).

Finally Antonio and Bassanio are alone, and Antonio can ask for details of the lady to whom Bassanio has sworn a pilgrimage. The language of wealth continues as Bassanio begins with explanations about his own profligate lifestyle, which has left him in debt, most of all to Antonio. He tries to convince Antonio to lend him money once again, so he might repay it plus his original debt—a plan, he claims, is as sensible as if Antonio were to shoot a second arrow in the direction in which he had just lost a first in order to regain both. Antonio, always but ambiguously loving, scorns Bassanio's attempts at persuasion: "you do me now more wrong / In making question of my uttermost" (1.1.154–55). Bassanio tells of the prize, a treasure who is Portia, a lady wealthy, fair, and virtuous. She is "richly left"; all know of her "worth," many "renowned suitors"—"Jasons"—woo her, and he himself would woo her also, had he sufficient means. Portia, with hair "like a golden fleece" (1.1.160–75), can be his. Bassanio predicts:

> I have a mind presages me such thrift,
> That I should questionless be fortunate. (1.1.174–75)

Antonio responds with regret that "all my fortunes are at sea" (1.1.176), but he offers to join Bassanio in finding a loan, which Antonio will secure with his own credit.

Thus enriched with language of wealth and commerce, the exposition initiates interdependence between the two major plots and what will become parallel action: the casket test will depend on the flesh-bond because, as this scene establishes, the pursuit of a bride requires money. Further, the pursuits of treasure from sea trade and of wealth from marriage become parallel risks. Antonio pursues credit to finance his friend's potentially lucrative courtship, even as all his wealth is sailing in dangerous waters. Similarly, Bassanio pursues Portia to pay his debts, risking future wealth and even progeny, with borrowed money to mask his poverty.

Scene 2.

Echoing Antonio's confession of sadness, Portia and Nerissa's first scene is spoken in prose, like other important sections of the play. Theirs is a euphuistic prose style,[10] contrasting with the less elaborate prose of so-called lower characters—typically, tradespeople, clowns, or villains.[11] Commentators offer a variety of principles that Shakespeare may have followed in arranging his verse with his prose, but as Jonas Barish concludes, the surfeit of theories is "mainly a highly charged impressionism combined with a spurious classificationism" ("Shakespeare's Prose," qtd. in Rabkin, n. 262).

In any case, like Antonio, Portia begins with a complaint: "my little body is aweary of this great world" (1.2.1). Nerissa, Portia's waiting woman, disparages her lament, observing that it would be valid "if your miseries were in the same abundance as your good fortunes are" (1.2.3–4). Portia next protests the selection of her eventual husband according to the will of her dead father. Nerissa responds that his casket test is inspired; after all, her father was "ever virtuous; and holy men at their death have good inspirations"(1.2.23–24). Nerissa then catalogs the six visiting "princely suitors" (1.2.28) who are in Belmont, and Portia explains why each should be purged, mocking men as she later does in Act 3 when she tells Nerissa of her planned male masquerade in Venice. Ethnic and gender stereotyping monopolize her reasons: the Neapolitan loves only horses, the frowning County Palatine is gloomy; the Frenchman Monsieur LeBon is a fatuous fool and a slave to style; the Englishman is silent, provincial, and unfashionable; the Scotsman is miserly; and the German is a drunk. But both Nerissa and Portia agree that the Venetian soldier and scholar who once visited Belmont long ago, Bassanio, was "the best deserving a fair lady" (1.2.97). Soon word arrives that the just-evaluated undesirables are departing, but the Prince of Morocco will soon arrive. Portia denounces him too because of his presumed dark skin, "the complexion of a devil" (1.2.107). Ironically, then, the theme of bigotry is introduced not in Venice but in Belmont, foreshadowing the prejudice permeating Venice in the next scene. In fact, Belmont bigotry is the stuff of Belmont wit. And in Belmont, wealth is as weighty a burden as it is in

Venice; it imbalances the disposition and occupies the mind with the responsibilities and risks attendant on its proper maintenance.

Scene 3.

The third expository scene introduces Shylock as he negotiates with Bassanio and then Antonio over the terms of the bond, enabling Bassanio to go to Belmont and Shylock to ensnare Antonio's life. Again, the scene begins in the middle of a conversation in which Bassanio tells Shylock the terms of the proposed bond—3,000 ducats for three months lent to Antonio. Again, it is prose. Shylock as a bargainer focuses narrowly on the terms of the bond, repeating details, emphasizing the financial risk of lending money to a cash-poor man who can promise profit only when his ships return from various dangerous journeys to Tripolis, the Indies, Mexico, and England.

It may be argued that Shylock's use of tedious repetition makes him appear simpleminded and, consequently, less dangerous. The ploy misleads Bassanio into a false sense of control:

> SHYLOCK. I think I may take his bond.
>
> BASSANIO. Be assured you may.
>
> SHYLOCK.   I will be assured I may: and that I may be assured, I will bethink me—may I speak to Antonio? (1.3.23–25)

Initially, then, Shylock seems somewhat less than quick-witted, perhaps because he is feigning dullness, as a skillful villain might. And the lines just quoted, while repetitious and seemingly superfluous, hold within them his stipulation to "be assured," his eventually murderous trap for Antonio.

Shylock refuses Bassanio's invitation to dine with the Christians, which his faith cannot abide, when Antonio enters, and in a rare verse aside, Shylock makes clear his hatred for Antonio. He confides that, first, the man is a Christian; second, he brings down the lending rate in Venice; and finally, he publicly chastises Shylock for lending money at interest. When Shylock reenters the conversation with Antonio and Bassanio, his words contradict his aside, establishing his disingenuousness. He claims that he is out of cash and must himself borrow money from Tubal, "a wealthy Hebrew of my tribe," to lend Antonio (1.3.49)—a condition contradicted later that evening when Jessica collects so much ready wealth around the house that one small jewel is worth 2,000 ducats. Finally, Shylock again claims to have forgotten the length of the term of the loan, a somewhat odd lapse since Shylock forgets little, not even the destinations of Antonio's ships.

Antonio and Shylock share an intense hatred of one another, but not its expression. The alien Shylock whispers his venomous thoughts outside Antonio's earshot and then smiles deferentially to his face, while the more powerful upper-class Antonio—"Signior Antonio" to Shylock—self-righteously hurtles his feelings at Shylock, whom he regularly calls "Jew." Antonio promises to spit on Shylock, spurn him, and call him "dog" again. He asks for terms of a loan appropriate to an enemy. But Shylock will not respond in kind; he denies hate, claims to seek friendship, and finally offers the "merry sport" of a notarized bond. If this bond is forfeited, Shylock jests, Antonio must pay with an equal pound of his fair flesh, "In what part of your body pleaseth me" (1.3.144). Perceptively, Bassanio sees beyond appearances and warns, "I like not fair terms and a villain's mind" (1.3.172); but Antonio, confidently overruling him, foreshadows the play's outcome in his observation, "The Hebrew will turn Christian, he grows kind" (1.3.171). Ironically, the agreement also serves as a metaphoric exchange of hearts: Antonio agrees to risk his own heart as collateral for Bassanio to win the heart of another, Portia, as a prize. Conveniently enough, the present market value in Venice of each is the same: 3,000 ducats, plus risk.

Finally, in addition to wealth, this scene introduces another unifying theme: the Venetian desire to control time. In Venice, time moves forward in regimental fashion, seemingly ordered by society's clocks and calendars. This is a mixed blessing: it overlooks the present but offers the promise of a bountiful future, a condition, by the way, not shared in Belmont. Antonio places his confidence in the future with his final couplet: "Come on, in this there can be no dismay, / My ships come home a month before the day" (1.3.173–74). To most of the Venetians, including Shylock, time shines its most brilliant light on the future, threatening and often darkly shadowing the present. Such a perception nearly dooms Antonio because he makes decisions based on his expectation of wealth three months' hence, rather than on his present cashless condition. He agrees to Shylock's time-bound bond and is trapped, not by the money, but rather by the time limits. In Act 4, Shylock is similarly caught. His hoped-for Venetian justice, generated with the passage of three months' time, turns out to be as ephemeral as the future itself. Venice's near obsession with the clock and the calendar places a golden light on an illusory future and consigns to darkness the joy of the here and now.

ACT 2

Scene 1.

Following the classic model, Act 2 begins the conflicts. In Belmont, the theme of bigotry continues from the previous two scenes. When the Prince of Morocco arrives, he asks Portia, "Mislike me not for my complexion," since, he assures her, his blood is as red, his nature as valiant, and his woo-

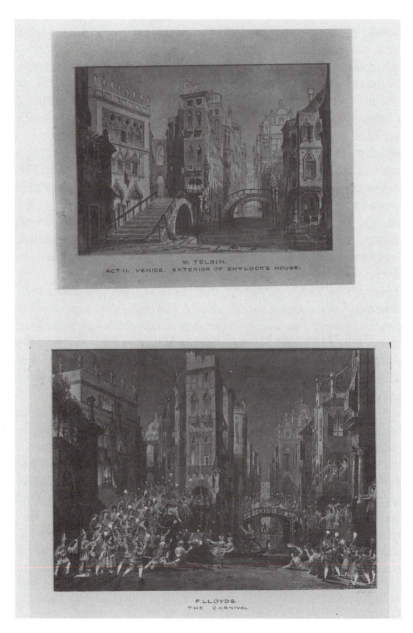

Act 2. The Exterior of Shylock's House. Later that Evening. The Carnival Outside Shylock's House. Paintings of Charles Kean's settings from his production at the Princess's Theatre (1858). By permission of the Folger Shakespeare Library.

ing as effective as any man "northward born" (2.1.1, 4). With dramatic irony, Portia dryly promises that he stands "as fair / As any comer I have looked on yet" (2.1.20–21) and restates the awful risk of failing the casket test: "swear before you choose, if you choose wrong, / Never to speak to lady afterward / in way of marriage." (2.1.40–42).

Scene 2.

Making his entrance alone, the clown, Lancelot Gobbo, is a character more important in the original productions than we might assume. First, he was undoubtedly played by one of the Lord Chamberlain's Men's most famous actors, the comic Will Kempe. But more important, clowns and fools regularly play critical roles in the art of most world cultures. They seem different from others, perhaps oddly out of focus, refusing to express the accepted wisdom of the ordered community. On the contrary, they "explode, invert, blur, or establish anew order, balance, and harmony" (Janik 2).[12] The clown represents and encourages the loosening of order, the humble acceptance of humanity's imperfections, and the absence of permanent understanding. They expose foolishness with humor, thereby helping others realize the futility of an orderly quest for truth or control of fate. If clowns' visions are not ordered and peaceful, it follows that their language cannot be a beautiful design imitating nature—one explanation for why the clown Lancelot, along with his father, uses the convention of prose speech rather than blank verse.

Further, 2.2 is significant because it mirrors the theme of risk taking for material gain. It also foreshadows other dramatic action: most apparently, Jessica's parallel departure from Shylock, and the reasoning process in which a character must weigh alternatives and arrive at a serviceable conclusion. In his opening speech, Lancelot contemplates whether to leave the service of Shylock and seek a position with Bassanio. Parodying Everyman, the morality play hero, Lancelot soliloquizes in prose that he is tempted by the fiend at his elbow to leave Shylock and is chastened by God's representative, conscience, "hanging about the neck" of his heart (2.2.10), to remain loyal. Wavering, he decides to seek Bassanio's service because the fiend "gives the more friendly counsel" (2.2.23). Later we hear his more mundane but probably more powerful motives: Bassanio will feed him more generously, and he "gives rare new liveries" (2.2.89).

Like Lancelot's decisions, others are similarly reached with inconclusive evidence: Antonio must decide to accept the bond; Morocco, Arragon, and Bassanio must select a casket; the duke must rule on Antonio's fate. Indeed, even the audience must make decisions. Is Portia indeed wise and virtuous, or is she biased, materialistic, and vindictive? Is Shylock a fiend or a sadly doomed victim of a hateful world? Do Antonio and Bassanio enjoy an idealistic friendship or a loving romance? Like Lancelot, the audience evaluates the evidence and draws conclusions. And their decisions, like those of Lancelot, risk hinging on the superficial attractiveness and power of the individuals being assessed. The audience must be careful not to side with Bassanio, Portia, and their friends for the same reason Lancelot does—because their clothes are better.

The scene moves to an exchange between Lancelot and his sand-blind father, old Gobbo, who enters seeking his son. Again, this parallels the parent-child relationships that dominate both the casket and runaway-daughter plots. For a moment, Lancelot lies to Gobbo, saying that Lancelot is dead, but he quickly reneges, kneeling to seek his father's blessing. Although this parodies the story in Genesis 29 when Jacob falsely gains his father's blessing, it also parallels Jessica's trickery of her father followed by Portia's submission to her father's casket test. The clown, in miniature, prefigures both the runaway-daughter and casket plots, moving from the filial disloyalty of the first to the obedience of the second. Finally, Bassanio enters and agrees to employ Lancelot, who departs happily at the promise of new clothes.

Again, time's relentless order controls Venice. Like Antonio, Bassanio notes its passage both when he enters and when he exits. The pleasure of the party the Venetians have planned for the evening is tempered by time's constraints, and he orders, "let it be so hasted that supper be ready at the farthest by five of the clock" (2.2.93–94). Then when he exits, he seems impatient with the present and hurries to the future, telling Gratiano, "I have some business" (2.2.175) before the planned merriment of the evening. Like other Venetians, Bassanio finds more reality in the future than in the present.

Scene 3.

Scene 3 is the exposition introducing the runaway-daughter story, the third story line, which tells of a less-than-serene filial relationship. Jessica asks Lancelot to carry a note secretly to Lorenzo explaining her plans for their escape from Venice, which must be arranged quickly since it must take place that night. She calls her house "hell," and Lancelot names her a "most sweet Jew" (2.3.10–11); yet she does not allow her implicit victimhood and personal virtue to limit her will to "Become a Christian and [Lorenzo's] loving wife" (2.3.19–20). If we are to believe her words, the scene increases our estimate of Shylock's oppression of others and introduces yet another variation on the themes of risk, wealth, and the urgency of Venetian time.

Scenes 4 through 6.

Scenes three through six were joined into one scene by eighteenth-century editors because they all occur in Venice, flowing together and rushing forward with the clearly noted passing hours. The young men further their plans for departure as Lancelot arrives with Jessica's note. Lorenzo confides to Gratiano that he will escape with Jessica disguised as his torchbearer, and Bassanio reminds the group, " 'Tis now but four o'clock" (2.4.8), an hour before the planned dinner festivities.

After four o'clock, Shylock receives Bassanio's invitation to dinner, probably delivered by Lancelot. He recognizes an ill omen in his earlier dream of money bags, and presumes that in going to the feast he is walking into some "ill a-brewing" (2.5.17). Shylock disdains the celebratory recreation of the Venetians—their music, their masks and disguises, their "shallow foppery" (2.5.34)—as beneath both him and his daughter and orders her to keep the sounds of the Christian fools from his "sober house" (2.5.35). After Shylock leaves for the feast, in a closing couplet Jessica derides him, "if my fortune be not crossed, / I have a father, you a daughter, lost" (2.5.55). Her goal, then, is an end to filial attachment, the opposite from Portia's continuation of filial duty even after her father's death—both of which were, of course, foreshadowed in Lancelot's earlier encounter with his father.

Finally the oppression of Venice's clock and the seductiveness of wealth become nearly unbearable. At nine o'clock, an ideal dark moment for escape, Lorenzo arrives late because of his "affairs" (2.6.23), meets his waiting friends below Jessica's window, and beckons her to come down. She appears above in the clothes of a page, the first androgynously dressed female character, with a casket filled with her father's treasure that will finance the couple's gondola voyage from Venice to more pleasurable destinations.

Scene 7.

With a break in the continuing events of Venice, the story returns to Belmont, where the conflict of the casket plot heightens with Morocco's ill-fated selection of the gold casket. The motif of flawed evaluation—that appearance determines reality and wealth determines humanity—having been introduced in 1.3, takes on new dimension. Morocco makes his wrong choice of the gold casket to "'gain what many men desire'" (2.7.37), by valuing possession—golden wealth and golden girl—and by meshing images of money and maiden, losing the distinctions between them:

> . . . They have in England
> A coin that bears the figure of an angel
> Stampd in gold; but that's insculpt upon:
> But here an angel in a golden bed
> Lies all within. (2.7.55–59)

Seeking to gain what others desire is an empty goal. Furthermore, a corollary motif of the play is that gaining possession, any possession, is a false reality; it is an illusion in Venice and downright foolishness in Belmont. Morocco learns "what many men desire" is not a suitable goal for marriage when he opens the gold casket to find a skull and scroll with and a note telling him that "Gilded tombs do worms infold" (2.7.69).

In the casket source story in the *Gesta Romanorum,* only one contestant, the heroine, has the opportunity to select a casket, so readers do not discover any written contents in the gold and silver caskets, which have external inscriptions much like those in *MV.* The failure of this suitor and the next dramatizes the risk Bassanio will finally assume. Finally, Portia's comments on Morocco's dark, departing image argue against the dichotomous simplification of Venice as mercantile and Belmont as paradisiacal. As Morocco leaves, cruelly condemned to an unmarried life, Portia says, "A gentle riddance! Draw the curtains, go. / Let all of his complexion choose me so" (2.7.78–79).

Scene 8.

Scene 8 serves as a review of the offstage misfortunes of Shylock and Antonio. First, Salarino and Solanio explain how Bassanio and Gratiano have left Venice together, but Lorenzo and Jessica apparently have slipped away in their own gondola. Shylock has been crying throughout the city over his double loss, his two precious stones and his daughter, a cry that was mocked even by the boys in the street. Meanwhile, Salarino tells of Antonio's loss, a trading vessel in the English Channel. Solanio responds that he may be in danger; since Shylock seeks revenge for his daughter's absence, Antonio must "keep his day, / Or he shall pay for this" (2.8.24–25). Besides, Antonio has shed tears over Bassanio's departure, even though he puts up a brave front. Solanio concludes that because of the absence of Bassanio, they must go to cheer Antonio, who "only loves the world for him" (2.8.60).

Scene 9.

The final scene of Act 2 is yet another suitor's loss of future paternity and family as he selects the other cursed casket in Belmont. If we were to assume that Portia wished him to win, we might believe that she offers him a clue in her remark to him, "Everyone doth swear / That comes to hazard for my worthless self" (2.9.17). The foolish arrogance of Arragon, however, leads him to dismiss the lead casket, because Portia would need to be far fairer, he thinks, if he were to hazard all for her. He then eliminates the gold because he does not wish to be among *hoi polloi,* all of whom desire Portia. So he settles on silver, the casket that will "get him as much as he deserves" (2.9.58) and so, offers him a blinking idiot's head. After Arragon's exit, a messenger announces a young visitor who heralds the arrival of his lord. This young Venetian, undoubtedly Gratiano, comes, according to the messenger, as a "forespurrer, . . . a day in April never came so sweet / To show how costly summer was at hand" (2.9.92–94). We now anticipate the fairy tale climax, when Bassanio will select the correct casket and Antonio's original investments for Bassanio not only will be returned but will yield dividends to the younger man for life.

ACT 3

Scene 1.

The portmanteau scene in Venice presents the turning point in the bond plot, when Shylock decides to seek his murderous vengeance on Antonio. The moment when he reaches this conclusion is debatable: when he lashes out at Solanio and Salarino, when he hears news of Jessica and Antonio from Tubal, or in the final lines when he asks Tubal to meet him at the synagogue for further discussion. In any case, the scene is a turning point for Shylock; it leaves him consumed with only a single goal. When Shylock enters, we are moved to pity him because of Solanio and Salarino's taunts. Their ridicule rises as Solanio likens Shylock to the devil, "here he comes in the likeness of a Jew" (3.1.18). They mock his loss of Jessica, jeering that he is as opposite from his daughter as jet is from ivory. Shylock also rues the bond with the prodigal, bankrupt Antonio and threatens to use it for vengeance.

One of Shakespeare's most famous speeches is centered in this pivotal scene, placed in the same position in the play as the "To be or not to be" speech in *Hamlet* and the death of Mercutio in *Romeo and Juliet.* In three prose sections, Shylock explains why he wants Antonio's flesh—if only for fishbait to feed his revenge—each with its own parallel syntax. First, he lists eight ways in which Antonio has harmed him, four of which are financial, and all because Shylock is a Jew. Second, he presents three increasingly lengthy questions beginning with "Hath not a Jew eyes?" that identify 13 sensate qualities Jews share with Christians. Finally, he uses six if-then rhetorical questions that further align the humanity of Jews and Christians, beginning with "If you prick us do we not bleed?" and concluding with their shared instinct for revenge. The Jew is as vengeful as the Christian, Shylock threatens, only more so. "The villainy you teach me I will execute, and it shall go hard but I will better the instruction" (3.1.56–57).

As Salarino and Solario exit, Tubal enters and provides the straight lines, the bits of information he has gained in Genoa about Jessica and Antonio, for Shylock's responses. He passes from joy over yet another of Antonio's losses—this time in Tripolis—to despair and rage over the loss of Jessica and the financial expense of finding her "—would she were hearsed at my foot, and the ducats in her coffin" (3.1.70–71). Shylock continues, "No news of them, why so? And I know not what's spent in the search. Why thou loss upon loss" (3.1.71–73). The pendulum of our compassion moves as close as it ever comes to Shylock when Tubal next tells him that in trade for a monkey, Jessica has given up a turquoise ring in Genoa. Shylock laments the loss of the ring, a gift long ago from Leah, before she was his wife: "I would not have given it for a wilderness of monkeys" (3.1.96–97). Then he is overcome by hatred for Antonio and by greed: "I will have the heart of him if he forfeit, for were he out of Venice I can make what merchandise I will"(3.1.100–102). And from that time, he remains viciously hateful until his courtroom defeat. His plan may not yet have crystallized, but his point of view will not change.

Scene 2.

Back in Belmont, the plot escalates beyond both Morocco and Arragon to Bassanio's climactic casket selection, again a portmanteau scene. The stage direction notes that he and Portia enter with "all their trains" in great splendor. Bassanio apparently has indeed been lavish in purchasing liveries for his men with the borrowed money, just as Lancelot had presumed. Portia declares her love for Bassanio, telling him that she is "though yours, not yours" (3.2.20). She wishes at the very least to retard time, if not entirely to stop it. He and Portia use images of torture to describe their love; he "lives upon the rack" (3.2.25); and if he fails, she promises that her "eye shall be the stream / And watery deathbed for him" (3.2.46–47).

Interestingly, this scene holds much of the play's rhymed verse. Each of the caskets contains a rhymed message locked within it; Bassanio's casket selection and Portia's lines preceding it end in couplets; the song accompanying Bassanio's selection is composed of tercets and couplets; Portia's excited whispers to herself over Bassanio's correct selection are three couplets with one line stretching into a 12-syllable alexandrine; the message within the casket is eight tetrameter lines with two sets of four rhyming lines; and Bassanio's joyful reaction to the message is five iambic couplets. So much highly stylized language, filled with artifice, suggests that this scene is intended to be different from the others. Because it is the climax of the casket plot—a plot of love—the stylized language of romance indicates a most highly designed and ornamented reflection of nature. Catherine Belsey suggests that "in his triumph Bassanio displays all the symptoms of passion: he is bereft of words" ("Love in Venice" 143). She identifies this as a symptom of his desire, always a dangerous condition. On the other hand, noticeably increased artifice suggests control, uncharacteristic of passion but typical when two young people are strongly attracted to one another yet still uneasy in their talk and dependent on conventional forms to say the right thing.

Belsey also explains that the caskets' riddles hold the danger of words. Riddles "are traditionally dangerous because they exploit the duplicity of the signifier, the secret alterity that subsists in meaning" (143).[13] They offer proof that words are not transparent, not neatly limited in meaning. To believe otherwise is a dangerous assumption, especially to those who naively assume that their own interpretations of words are shared by everyone. Belsey notes, "Riddles are posed by the wise to isolate the foolish," and that not until the Enlightenment's insistence on the transparency of language were riddles discredited as mere child's games (144). Sometimes in fables and myths, as in *MV*, the hero must solve a riddle to win the hand of the desirable princess. In such cases, the danger of the riddle with its hidden solution and maddening obfuscations inform the nature of desire—also a frustrating, agonizing, and enigmatic obsession that leads to risky and dangerous action.

In *MV*, Bassanio must decide whether the contents of the selected casket will be a prize that is universally desired, one that is uniquely deserved, or one that must be won at great risk. The first two riddles may *turn out* to be true, but the last *is* true right then and there before it is opened, as Bassanio's choice proves. A riddle solved is like desire gratified, Belsey continues. Both have an end that creates a feeling of finality. This implies that Bassanio's correct choice could be a conclusion were his feelings only desire. But the play is about love, which, through use, flourishes and grows, holding ever-new enigmas, like language itself.

The scene highlights the theme of false appearance. Portia asks that musicians play and sing as Bassanio makes his choice, surely an encouragement of romance that is harmonious with nature. Significantly, the lyrics are a request for a death knell to fancy, the superficial vision of the eye alone. Bassanio's evaluations of the caskets then begin, almost as a response to the

The Merchant of Venice

thought in the song, "So may the outward shows be least themselves" (3.2.73). Like characters in many other Shakespearean plays, including *Hamlet* and *Twelfth Night,* the hero observes that vice is universally masked by outward hints of virtue. Bassanio observes, "There is no vice so simple but assumes / Some mark of virtue on his outward parts (3.2.81–82). Ornament is "purchased by the weight"; it is a "guild shore / To a most dangerous sea" or, in a more ethnic metaphor, "a beauteous scarf / Veiling an Indian beauty"; and "the dowry of a second head, / The skull that bred them in the sepulchre" (3.2.89–98). Gold, Bassanio concludes, is "food for Midas," and silver, "a pale and common drudge"; but the paleness of lead "moves me more than eloquence" (3.2.101, 103, 106). In a closing couplet, he selects the lead casket, without ever reading the inscriptions.

When he opens the casket and finds Portia's likeness, however, he ironically reverts to ornamented Petrarchan verse to express his joy,[14] perhaps suggesting that, like Portia, he is better as an instructor than as a follower of his own wise words about ornament, or perhaps that the present moment holds especially golden but self-conscious romance.

In her excitement, Portia gives him all her possessions symbolically with her ring. The bestowal of this gift, then, becomes the exposition of the ring plot, the final plot to be introduced. Portia explains the conditions attached to the ring, just as the bond and the casket test were made risky with conditions. Immediately, the more comic and often earthy secondary set of lovers, Gratiano and Nerissa, announce that they too will marry, and Gratiano proposes a wager of one thousand ducats on who will have the first son.

But the emphasis turns abruptly away from Bassanio the lover to Bassanio the self-absorbed, careless friend. Along with Jessica and Lorenzo, Salerio suddenly arrives from Venice with news that all Antonio's merchant vessels have been lost—"From Tripolis, from Mexico, and England, / From Lisbon, Barbary, and India" (3.2.267–68), and since the three-month bond is past due back in Venice, Shylock demands the pound of flesh. We again sense the disparity in time between Venice and Belmont.[15] Three months have passed in Venice since Bassanio left at the end of 2.6. But no such length of time has passed in Belmont. Bassanio's arrival in Belmont occurs at the end of 2.9, and the casket selection of this scene follows immediately. We may deduce that the trip itself is short, because Portia and Nerissa later depart from Belmont for Venice in the evening (4.2) and arrive before sunrise, while Bassanio and his company arrive soon after. If Shakespeare had not intended this disparity, then he would not have alternated scenes so insistently throughout the first two acts. In Belmont the emphasis on present time contrasts the always-moving time in Venice, passing with clock-and-calendar regularity into the future.

Act 3 Scene 2. A Room In Portia's House. Bassanio, Portia, and Attendants, with One Casket Opened. Engraving by Geo. Noble and painting by R. H. Westall (June 4, 1796). By permission of the Folger Shakespeare Library.

In the ensuing conversation, Jessica accuses Shylock of even greater malice. She explains that Shylock had planned early on to refuse any delinquent payment, since before she left, her father had told his friends, Chus and Tubal, that he preferred Antonio's flesh to 20 times the principal. Obviously ignoring Jessica, Portia offers 12 and then exactly 20 times the bond to save Antonio, and Bassanio promises to leave quickly for Venice with Gratiano after a speedy wedding. Portia's final vow that Nerissa and she "will live as maids and widows" (3.2.309) is hardly more true on its surface than Shylock's promise in 1.3 of kindness and merry sport.

Scene 3

Scene 3 recalls the overarching circumstance of the plot begun in 1.1—the risks and fortunes controlling the Venetian merchant. In Venice, the imprisoned Antonio addresses Shylock very differently now, as "good Shylock," but Shylock interrupts, warning him that he will not relent and will have his bond. When Shylock departs, Antonio acknowledges his doom to Solanio, explaining why Shylock hates him: he compassionately has saved debtors from Shylock by paying their forfeitures. He understands that the duke cannot alter Venetian law because that would "impeach the justice of the state" (3.3.29). In many ways, then, the scene foreshadows the courtroom scene: Shylock behaves with compulsive malevolence while Antonio establishes his compassion and humility, and all the while, justice must be served. At first, the scene seems to highlight the differences between the two men, but ironically, it also points out their shared belief in law that must, in the end, serve commerce and ownership.

Scenes 4 and 5

Like the previous scene in Venice, these scenes in Belmont prepare for the climactic trial scene with further hints and only partial explanations. Portia and Lorenzo praise Antonio, whose goodness has just been dramatized. Portia sets the stage for her intercession at the trial in Venice, although no one, not even the audience, knows of her intentions. With a control of the situation only gradually revealed to the audience, guilefully she requests that Lorenzo and Jessica direct the affairs of Belmont during (now Lord) Bassanio's absence, and Nerissa and she will live at a convent two miles away, praying until the return of their husbands—a falsehood that the audience will recognize in a moment. She then sends Balthazar, her servant, on an errand to bring clothes and notes from her learned cousin, Doctor Bellario of Padua, and meet her at the ferry dock to Venice. Finally alone with Nerissa, Jessica reveals her plan that they dress as young men, fooling the world about their gender with clever lies, manly strides, and boasts of frays and fine ladies scorned. She promises to continue relating her plan to Nerissa offstage, where the audience can no longer hear.

Scene 5 carries out the plan for Jessica and Lorenzo's oversight of Belmont. Theirs is a playful governance. The first two-thirds of the short scene is witty conversation among Lancelot, Jessica, and Lorenzo. Jessica and Lancelot speculate on her limited chances of ending up in heaven, considering her Jewish parentage; and he also doubts the desirability of her being a Christian as it will only raise the demand for pork. Lorenzo enters, chiding Lancelot that he is overly attentive to his wife and that "the Moor is with child by you" (3.5.31). With Lancelot's punning answer, Lorenzo observes, "How every fool can play upon the word!" (3.5.360). Like Lancelot's language in 2.2, the unlimited meanings in speech and the often earthy disorder they create are emblemized by the clown. In *The Praise of Folly* (1509), Erasmus's narrator Stultitia or Folly argues that human survival would end if she, Folly, did not encourage the sometimes bawdy and sometimes silly language of love, which dissolves superegos and thus allows "romance, lust, and love to thrive and give birth to the next generation" (Janik 2). This scene not only contrasts Portia and Bassanio's earlier earnestness in love and the nearly violent subsequent trial scene, but it also rings in a necessary lightheartedness in Belmont, the necessary prelude for love and fecundity.

ACT 4

Scene 1

The climax of the bond plot in the Venetian courtroom finally brings the major characters together for the one and only time. Portia and Shylock deliver some of the play's most memorable speeches, and Antonio, Bassanio, and the brash Gratiano are singularly ineffective. The courtroom is not neutral. The Duke begins by calling Shylock an "inhuman wretch" (4.1.3), even before he enters. Then tactfully, if falsely, the Duke suggests to Shylock's face that his "apparent cruelty" to the "poor merchant" (4.1.21, 23) must certainly be a ruse; therefore, he punningly and impotently concludes, "We all expect a gentle answer, Jew" (4.1.34). Following his usual rhythmic, repetitive, verb-heavy pattern, Shylock responds that, unfortunately, his "humour" (4.1.43) dictates his behavior; affection "Masters oft passion, sways it to the mood / Of what it likes or loathes" (4.1.50–51). The lines are fascinating psychology. Shylock even provides a catalog of uncontrolled behavior: seeing pork on the table, seeing a cat, or hearing bagpipes all can cause physical responses of revulsion. And seeing Antonio similarly affects

Shylock, thus with his "lodged hate and certain loathing," seeking Antonio's death is as natural as killing a serpent that has attacked.

After Antonio's far less effective response, the Duke warns Shylock that his lack of mercy may someday be returned to him. He responds that he needs no mercy and adds that Venetian society is based on property rights, which include ownership of slaves. It is these property rights that allow him to possess Antonio's flesh.

Then, just as the Duke is about dismiss the court because his legal expert, Dr. Bellario, has not arrived, Nerissa enters with a letter from Bellario, introducing the brilliant young Balthazar. We may question how the Duke happened to expect Portia's cousin Bellario at this opportune moment. We can speculate that Portia had asked her cousin to volunteer his expertise, that the Duke agreed, and that Portia herself then appeared. In any case, when she enters dressed as the brilliant young man Balthazar, she first asks the identity of the merchant and the Jew. This may suggest her supposed objectivity, a visual change in Antonio's circumstance, or a similarity between the two men. She continues, noting that Venetian law allows the bond, and asks Shylock for mercy. To his question of why, she responds with her famous 23-line "quality of mercy" speech. Many readers believe that in this speech she presents a Christian position, the New Law, as opposed to the Old Law of unyielding justice represented by Shylock. Others, however, note that this speech is highly ironic because only several dozen lines later, Portia herself shows no mercy whatsoever to Shylock.[16] Out of context, the speech effectively espouses mercy, a response not unique to Christianity. In context, however, Portia's words are a set piece, not always representative of her own behavior.

When Shylock refuses to be merciful, she then offers him three times the amount of the debt. Clearly, she realizes that the likelihood he will agree is nil, based on Jessica's and the messenger Solanio's testimony in 3.2. With his scales ready, Shylock anticipates cutting the flesh from Antonio's breast, and Portia makes her third plea, this time for a surgeon to stop the wounds. Again Shylock refuses. Antonio delivers his supposed last words—that he is grateful for his quick end rather than a painful continuation of life in poverty, surely an especially hellish state in mercantile Venice, and that Bassanio remember him to Portia as another lover. Overcome, Bassanio makes his hyperbolic declaration that

> . . . life itself, my wife, and all the world,
> Are not with me esteemed above thy life.
> I would lose all, ay sacrifice them all
> Here to this devil, to deliver you (4.1.280–83)

Portia responds that if his wife were there, she would "give you little thanks" (4.1.284). And after Gratiano makes a similar offer, Shylock marvels that "these be the Christian husbands!"(4.1.291). We too may question whether Bassanio's offer is mere exaggeration or if it is sincere and therefore foolishly wrong. But we must also recall the inscription on the lead casket: "Who chooseth me, must give and hazard all he hath"—a behavior required of Bassanio for him to have participated in the casket test and to have become the Lord of Belmont. Unquestionably, Bassanio again hazards all with this offer.

Finally, Portia reaches the climax of her argument. After she notes that the court must award Shylock the pound of flesh, she clarifies the two nouns; *flesh* and *pound.* First, he may only take flesh; if any blood is let, all Shylock's goods will be confiscated by the state. Stunned, Shylock agrees to the earlier offer of three times the bond. But Portia refuses because justice demands exactness, not compromise. She adds her next frightening qualification: Shylock's cut must be an exact pound, not the "estimation of a hair" more or less than a pound. If he fails, not only must his goods go to the state, but Shylock must die.

The perfect balance of justice, symbolized in the scales of Lady Justice, requires absolute wisdom. There can be no errors at all if the scales are to remain balanced. When the goal of perfect balance is not achieved, then justice is not achieved, and compassion and compromise become necessary to make up for mistakes, to reconfigure, to yield, to settle. The two legal considerations cited by Portia—taking illegal possession (of blood) and using inaccurate measures (of flesh)—are injustices; they are not contrived or petty; therefore, a court must consider them. They highlight the omniscient wisdom and skill required to achieve true justice. They also imply that on earth, in flawed, human hands, justice can never be perfect. Consequently, it must be tempered by mercy.

These two considerations are included in *Il Pecorone,* but Shakespeare adds one more troubling element to Shylock's fate. Because he is an "alien," a Jew, and has "by direct or indirect attempts" (4.1.345–346) sought the life of a citizen, Portia advises that, according to Venetian law, Shylock must lose his goods, and his life is at the mercy of the Duke. The overtly biased Gratiano disdainfully mocks Shylock, telling him that he would do well to hang himself except that he now has no money to buy the rope.

So far, Shakespeare has swung our sympathies far away from Shylock, but now with this, Portia's third and final decree, along with Gratiano's almost cackling glee, our judgments are not so clear. The Duke immediately offers clemency, "the difference of our spirit" (4.1.364), that underscores the difference between Shylock's attempted murderous violence and the

"THE MERCHANT OF VENICE" AT THE LYCEUM THEATRE—THE TRIAL SCENE
"*Portia*: Tarry a little : there is something else.—This bond doth give thee here no jot of blood."—ACT IV., SCENE I. *Graphic* 1879

Four Scene 1. The Trial Scene. Graphic of Henry Irving (Shylock) and Ellen Terry (Portia) at the Lyceum Theatre (1879). By permission of the Folger Shakespeare Library.

Christians' more subtle and successful legal violence. Finally, in response to Portia's request, Antonio arranges the financial settlement: he will manage half of Shylock's wealth to be held in trust for Lorenzo and Jessica, and Shylock will convert to Christianity and bequeath the remaining half of his assets to Lorenzo and Jessica upon his death. Some argue that a sixteenth-century Christian audience might think the conversion a blessing, Shylock's only opportunity to reach heaven; but embedded as the central in a series of three apparent punishments, it is hardly so. Shylock makes a final exit, ill, poorer, defeated, and, as a Christian who is unable to lend money at interest, without a livelihood.

Immediately, the remaining characters carry on with humor and happiness. The Duke, Bassanio, and Antonio try to offer Portia/Balthazar a reward, but she adamantly insists that she wants Bassanio's wedding ring, the symbol of his wedding vows. Furthering the ring plot, Bassanio hesitates to give up the ring, but after Balthazar exits, Antonio urges his friend to give up the ring because of the wise young man's "deservings and my love withal" (4.1.446); so Gratiano is sent to deliver the ring.

Scene 2

In the final scene in Venice, the turning point in the ring plot and denouement of the bond plot, Gratiano catches up to Portia and Nerissa, and hands over the ring. Portia responds, unruffled, "His ring I do accept most thankfully, /And so I pray you tell him" (4.2.9–10), and encourages Nerissa likewise to retrieve the ring that she has given Gratiano. Is this the abandonment of a love bond? Has Portia here proven that the two men are untrustworthy? Clearly, the tone is happy, and Portia knows, as we must also, that in this ring trick, a metallic symbol of love is being measured against love itself. Once again, mere appearance is being valued against all-powerful reality. Because we have already been well schooled in this lesson, we are finally permitted to laugh at it.

ACT 5

Scene 1

The final act, a single scene, serves as both the climax of the ring plot and the final resolution of the casket plot—a moment of tension and unraveling that suggests a probable future for the characters, except Shylock. Night has fallen in Belmont, and Jessica and Lorenzo comment on its beauty, cataloging other mythic lovers who engaged in lovemaking "in such a night as this" (5.1.1). But this is comedy, and irony pervades the lines. All the lovers listed—Troilus and Cressida, Pyramus and Thisbe, Dido and Aeneas, Jason and Medea—have tragic ends and sadness in the moonlight, as Jessica and Lorenzo well know. The fifth and final example of the night's great lovers is, they mockingly conclude, themselves. Love and sexuality, as Desiderius Erasmus writes, require the loosening agents of humor and laughter, and since this final scene serves almost as a paean to the many dimensions of imperfect human love, the humor in these lovers' words is an appropriate overture. This, along with the entrance of the clown Lancelot and the natural harmony of the scene's music, sets the comic tone for the return of Portia and Nerissa; the entrance of Bassanio, Gratiano, Antonio, and their followers; and their all-too-human reconciliations.

But no sooner has Portia welcomed Antonio to the house than Gratiano is heard defending himself over his missing wedding ring. Bassanio is moved to mutter, "Why I were best to cut my left hand off / And swear I lost the ring defending it" (5.1.177–78). The audience knows all this to be a trick and without life-threatening consequence. Thus, for nearly the first time in the play, we are not swayed to change sympathy, and we are confident that all will be resolved easily.

The action, then, throughout the final three acts expands the meanings in the ring—from an emblem of Bassanio's marital chastity in 3.2, to an emblem of his respect for Balthazar/Portia's wisdom in 4.2, to the source for Gratiano's eventual sexual punning or equivocation in 5.1, because the term *ring* can also refer to the cervix. Bassanio would have been wrong minded indeed to have held back the ring from young Balthazar, since agreeing to the exchange demonstrates that base metal can in no way equal the human life of Antonio, a premise supported in the Duke's court.

Commentators recognize other meanings in the ring. Belsey suggests that the multiple meanings in the ring in 5.1 address the question "what . . . does it mean to be a wife? . . . The solution to the riddle of the rings is thus a utopian vision of the new possibilities of marriage" ("Love in Venice" 149). Portia becomes a "fellow-warrior, partner and friend"; as a result, "the term *wife* absorbs the meaning of 'friend'" (149–50). This was a "disruptive" notion, Belsey explains, at "the cultural moment" at the end of the sixteenth century, when the patriarchal order was being challenged with redefinition of the wife's role. Sigurd Burckhardt contends that the meaning of the ring extends even to the plot itself, which is shaped as a ring; the bond of Venice is transformed into the gentle bond of Belmont, renewed when Bassanio regains the ring, a moment, Burckhardt says, when "the circle closes," showing that poetry is "equivocal—public and private, common and gentle, useful and beautiful" (236).

The ring, then, remains equivocal; it is the plot itself, a love pledge, an embrace, an icon of love within the community, an emblem of the mystery of words, a sexual pun, a simple prop. Neither it nor the meaning of any word can be entirely pinpointed. As a symbol of expanding love, it is an admixture of desire and respect. Desire is controlled by the ring, respect cannot be contained by it.

Portia further adds to the general joy in the conclusion when she advises Antonio that three of his argosies have returned filled with treasure and informs Lorenzo that he will inherit Shylock's money. Antonio tells Portia, "you have given me life and living" (5.1.286), an ambiguous expression of gratitude contrasting Shylock's Act 4 precisely defined despair: "you take my life / When you do take the means whereby I live"

(4.1.372–73). Lorenzo calls his financial good news "manna in the way / Of starved people" (5.1.293–94).

The play ends with increasing sexual wordplay,[17] and the three closing couplets spoken by Gratiano are direct references to lovemaking as he speaks of Nerissa:

> Whether till the next night she had rather stay,
> Or go to bed now, being two hours to day.
> But were the day come, I should wish it dark,

THE FIFTH ACT.

SCENE THE FIRST.—BELMONT. *A Grove before Portia's House.*

Act 5 Scene 1. A Grove before Portia's House with Jessica and Lorenzo. Illustration from *The Merchant of Venice: A New Adaptation to the Stage.* With notes, original and selected, and introductory articles by Henry L. Hinton (1867). By permission of the Folger Shakespeare Library.

> Till I were couching with the doctor's clerk.
> Well, while I live I'll fear no other thing
> So sore as keeping safe Nerissa's ring. (5.1.302–7)

One might accuse Shakespeare of ending the play trivially, after Lorenzo's earlier philosophical musings, almost as if the sexual were replacing the spiritual. But like the mathematical concepts of zero and one, the absence of something (zero) implies its presence (one), just as its presence always holds its absence.[18] Gratiano's closing lines are the ground on which we understand human order exists—some shifting combination of spirituality and "muddy vesture of decay." Gratiano, the self-appointed fool, appropriately emblemizes human imperfection and its joyful acceptance. The final rhyme on the punning word *ring* echoes the rich linguistic and thematic tension of the play itself.

At the beginning of the play, Nerissa implied that Belmont is no less absorbed in wealth than Venice. But in this final ring scene, Portia parodies the prideful Venetian assumption that wealth confers wisdom to mete out justice and control destiny. The ring conflict lasts only a moment and ends in the chaos of laughter at a pun. This does not deny the reality of the hegemony of wealth, or even the inevitable risk in love. But it does imply that ferry rides from Venice to Belmont lead to freedom for lingering in present pleasure and happy hope.

NOTES

1. See Walter Cohen, "*The Merchant of Venice* and the Possibilities of Historical Criticism," in *ELH* 49 (1982), 765–89.

2. See W. H. Auden, "The Dyer's Hand," in *The Dyer's Hand and Other Essays* (1948; repr. New York: Vintage, 1968), 218–237.

3. Lawrence Danson's *The Harmonies of* The Merchant of Venice (New Haven, Conn.: Yale University Press, 1978) is most thorough in presenting an interpretation of the play as a romantic comic structure that ends in a harmonious unity of earlier disorder. Such a structural perspective on comedy is offered in Northrop Frye's *A Natural Perspective: The Development of Shakespearean Comedy and Romance* (New York: Harcourt, 1965).

4. See Graham Holderness, introduction to the New Penguin edition of *The Merchant of Venice* (London, New York: Penguin, 1993).

5. See, for example, Sigurd Burckhardt, *Shakespearean Meanings* (Princeton, N.J.: Princeton University Press, 1968); and Harold Goddard, *The Meaning of Shakespeare,* vol. 1 (Chicago: University of Chicago Press, 1951).

6. See Aristotle, *Poetics,* ed. L. J. Potts (Cambridge: Cambridge University Press, 1953), 23, for Aristotle's brief, extant description of comedy.

7. In the mid-twentieth century, Northrop Frye imposed a simple structural pattern on these comedies. He suggests that the three-part archetypal form of ritual is mirrored in the plots of myths and fables and in the plots of Roman, Italian, and English comedies. Such plots begin with characters living under a wrong order, which forces sterility and an absence of loving sexuality imposed by the entire society, its laws, or perhaps its powerful older people. In *MV*, such blocking agents are the laws of Venice, or the city's controlling passion for wealth, or perhaps even Portia's father's casket test. Next comes the central section of the play, a period of confusion or license and frequently lost identity. Act 2 begins this central section with Lancelot's brief disguised foolery with his father, foreshadowing the other disguises—Jessica's costumed departure from Venice, Bassanio's falsely wealthy entourage that travels to Belmont and gains a victory in both money and love, and the Act 4 courtroom triumph by the two disguised females, as well as their trickery in gaining their husbands' rings. The three-part archetypal plot form concludes with a renewal of right order marked by a festive celebration, a revel, or *konoms,* from which comedy may have received its name. In *MV*, Act 5 brings a new and enlightened society where the young man and woman are betrothed or married amid festivity and the promise of loving sexuality. See Frye, *A Natural Perspective* 72, for a full discussion of this topic.

8. See Nicholas Rowe, *The Works of Mr. William Shakespear,* vol. 2 (1709; repr. New York: AMS Press, 1969). Rowe's scene divisions were based on classical principles and were adapted to a stage with a proscenium arch. They serve as a model for modern editions save in the fewer scene divisions in Act 2.

9. All references to line numbers in this discussion are taken from M. M. Mahood, *The Merchant of Venice,* New Cambridge Shakespeare (Cambridge: Cambridge University Press 1987).

10. The euphuistic prose style, taking its name from the style of John Lyly's *Euphues: The Anatomy of Wit* (1579), includes colloquial proverbs, balanced antitheses and parallelism, wordplay, repetition, classical references, and logical organization.

11. The supposed convention of Renaissance drama, regularly disregarded by dramatists, is that so-called lower characters speak prose while higher, more noble characters usually use poetry.

12. See the introduction to Vicki Janik, *Fools and Jesters in Literature, Art, and History* (Westport, Conn.: Greenwood Press, 1998), 1–22, which provides a description of the traits of the fool and clown as they exist and have existed in the cultures of the world.

13. In her essay "Love in Venice" [in Shakespeare and Gender: A History, eds. Deborah E. Barker and Ivo Kamps (London: Verso, 1995), 196–213], Catherine Belsey describes the "sexual politics" of *MV* and Venice's unfortunate effects on literary lovers through those of Erica Jong in *Serenissima* and Jeannette Winterson in *The Passion* in the twentieth century.

14. Such verse is called Petrarchan because it follows the style of the fourteenth-century Italian poet Petrarch. Among its conventions are elaborate com-

parisons embellishing descriptions of the beauty and virtue of the beloved.

15. A discussion following the text in the Variorum edition of the play (1888) describes the variations in the passage of time between Venice and Belmont.

16. This position is held, for example, by Goddard, Derek Traversi, and Burckhardt.

17. The sexual references in 5.1 increase toward the scene's close, as demonstrated in the following lines:

> PORTIA. I will become as liberal as you;
>   I'll not deny him anything I have,
>   No, not my body, nor my husband's bed:
>   Know him I shall, I am well sure of it."
>   Lie not a night from home. Watch me like Argus.
>   If you do not, if I be left alone,
>   Now by mine honour which is yet mine own,
>   I'll have that doctor for my bedfellow. (5.1.226–33)

> GRATIANO. Let not me take him then,
>   For if I do, I'll mar the young clerk's pen.
>   (5.1.236–37)

> PORTIA. . . . Pardon me Bassanio,
>   For by this ring the doctor lay with me.
>   (5.1.258–59)

> NERISSA. . . . my gentle Gratiano
>   For that same scrubbed boy the doctor's clerk,
>   In lieu of this, last night did lie with me.
>   (5.1.260–62)

> GRATIANO. What, are we cuckolds ere we have deserved it?
>   . . . .
>   Were you the clerk that is to make me cuckold?
>   (5.1.265, 281)

> BASSANIO. Sweet doctor, you shall be my bedfellow;
>   When I am absent, then lie with my wife.
>   (5.1.286–87)

18. See R. A. Zimbardo, "The King and the Fool: *King Lear* as Self-Deconstructing Text" *Criticism* 32 (Winter 1990): 1–29, for a discussion of the fool's role in establishing order.

4

CHARACTERS

Characters in comedies often have their origins as conventions; that is, comic types who fulfill certain dramatic expectations for the audience, who, in turn, watch with what William Wordsworth famously called "a willing suspension of disbelief." Thus a comedy like *The Merchant of Venice* generally revolves around an ingenue (Portia), a beautiful, young, and virtuous heroine; and a juvenile lead (Bassanio), a good-hearted, brave, strong, and potentially virtuous young male. Both of them face a senex, or older male blocking figure (Shylock, or perhaps Portia's dead father) who keeps the young lovers from uniting. This character may also be something of a malcontent, disdainful of and excluded from society. The lovers are often assisted by a wily nurse (the waiting-gentlewoman Nerissa), who is loyal to the ingenue and serves as her foil, contrasting the ingenue's loveliness. The juvenile lead may be contrasted by his sidekick (Gratiano), whose foolish arrogance is more thoughtless than pernicious. Additionally, comedies regularly include a clown (Lancelot Gobbo), who is either a natural or artificial fool, that is, naturally simple or clever and witty. He is a conventional character whose straightforward, zestful self-interest allows him no direct stake in the love alliances of the plot but who supplies clever wordplay and insight into events. Characters in *MV*, including the second set of lovers, Jessica and Lorenzo, clearly fit these categories, while Antonio, neither malcontent nor hero, remains further from any comic convention.

Although these characters in *MV* are associated with comic types, they contain far greater dimension. Their behavior is unpredictable, contradictory, and evolving. They change as they meet different characters and as the action progresses; and if we have the opportunity to hear them in soliloquy, we may discover yet another, supposedly truer side to their natures. They may be inconsistent, hypocritical, developing; they are certainly not carelessly drawn. As we puzzle through their paradoxical actions, we derive only fragile interpretations, apt to fall apart at our next reading. This is the excitement of Shakespeare—we continue to rearrange pieces, find new ones, and create yet more puzzles. In his essay "Meaning and Shakespeare," Norman Rabkin chooses *MV* as his "test case" to explore meaning in art and observes, "The essence of our experience is our haunting sense of what doesn't fit the thesis we are tempted at every moment to derive; in fact, the ultimate irreducibility to a schema may be the hallmark of the work of art and the source of its power" (in Wheeler 118).

In other words, Shakespearean characters at first seem highly malleable to theoretical constructions, and this includes the characters in *MV.* But variations in their behaviors allow them to support an assortment of interpretations; but never, as Rabkin points out, does one thesis suffice. Portia may be a coldhearted, hypocritical bigot or the source of wise counsel who saves everyone, even Shylock, for a heavenly afterlife. And Shylock suffers as a victim of bigotry, but he is also presented as a cruel and only minimally human villain, motivated by passionate self-interest, greed, and a thirst for blood. Bassanio may be a charming but irresponsible materialist, spoiled by the love of his friend; but sometimes he is a self-absorbed arrogant bigot or, conversely, a young man growing into wisdom. Antonio wins praise as a loving friend and ethical merchant rescuing Shylock's "victims," but his disgust for Shylock often seems inspired by bias. And the nature of Antonio and Bassanio's relationship implies romance but only to some readers. Shakespeare draws enigmatic characters. He is, as Samuel Johnson elegized, "the poet of nature; the poet that holds up to readers a faithful mirrour of manners and of life"; and his designs contain the order and density of art. Rabkin reminds us, however, that "pattern is not art" and that if the play is like life, as Johnson says, then our response to it is also "quintessentially like life, characterized by process, tension, resistance, and an ineffable sense of integrity" (118).

PORTIA

As the heroine of the play, Portia is, as Harold Bloom notes, "the play's center" (*Shakespeare: The Invention* 177). She is not a comically conventional, two-dimensional, good-girl ingenue, nor is she the trickster widow of dubious virtue from the source story, *Il Pecorone,* who becomes a loving wife after a satisfying night in bed with the hero. Catherine Belsey writes, "Portia has more than one identity" (in Coyle 148).[1]

For example, she plays a distinct and always-key role in the three trial scenes, each based in divine and secular law; and she achieves success in all of them. In the casket plot, she is, by her father's decree, a commodity to be possessed in marriage; in the bond plot with Shylock, she argues as a quasi-barrister; and finally, in the ring plot, she determines the law itself. But her success derives from her accommodation to each situation; she embraces rather than rebels against its limitations, and she is thrice victorious. In her marriage, she rises above its restrictions by becoming both the bestower and the bestowed, gift and giver. In court, she defeats Shylock's demand for justice by showing that humans, like Shylock, are insufficiently wise to discover perfect justice; and back in Belmont she transforms the lost wedding ring into a celebration of her husband's and her own imperfect humanity, the acknowledgment of which is the precondition for mercy.

Before examining these actions more closely, however, first we must understand Portia's wit, which is only inconsistently a virtue. Although she enjoys the traditional ingenue attributes—virtue, beauty, and wealth—these do not hide imperfections that derive from her wit—her biased cynicism, guile, and willfulness. These imperfections, the dark side of her obvious strengths, still provide benefits, serving her both as weapons and as reminders of her own need for mercy. Her wit first explodes in 1.2, with her scathing catalog of ethnic stereotypes that deflates her six current suitors—all of whom fortunately leave without taking the risk of trying to gain her hand. When she is informed that the Prince of Morocco is soon to arrive, she says that even if he is a saint, if he has "the complexion of a devil," she would prefer that he "shrive" her rather than "wive" her (1.2.107–8).

Her wit supports her guile as well. When she greets Morocco, she disingenuously tells him that even if the lottery had not been arranged, he stands "as fair / As any comer I have looked on yet / For my affection" (2.1.20–22). More important, after Bassanio wins the casket test in Act 3, Portia vows to him that her "gentle spirit / Commits itself to yours to be directed / As from her lord, her governor, her king" (3.2.163–65). Yet by scene's end, she is secretly plotting to go to Venice, while explaining to Bassanio, Lorenzo, and assorted others that she will remain in a convent in Belmont.[2] Expectedly, her wit grounds her willful resentment of her entrapment in an arranged marriage, particularly when the arranger, her father, is dead and the selection process is based on a riddle.[3] The entrapment turns more frustrating when Bassanio arrives in Belmont, her memory of him as a scholar and soldier from Venice evolves into infatuation and love, and she candidly confesses her feelings to him.

During his casket selection, she sheds her passive role, requesting that a song be sung—a metaphor of harmony[4] or perhaps a puzzle containing clues to the correct casket. Leslie Fiedler argues that Portia offers clues to Bassanio, thus giving him an advantage. As "witch as well as bewitched," Portia offers "the spell of the music" (in Bloom, *MV* 75), and the words of the song she has sung to him offer a warning against seduction by appearance or fancy:

> It is engend'red in the eye
> With gazing fed, and fancy dies
> in the cradle where it lies. (3.2.67–69)

Additionally, the song's first three lines all end on rhymes with the word *lead:*[5]

> Tell me where is fancy bred,
> Or in the heart or in the head?
> How begot, how nourishd? (3.2.63–65)

But Portia's wit has an even stronger benefit; it is her means to self-awareness. Portia is not blind to her own imperfections. When Nerissa observes that Portia is flawed by self-indulgence—suffering from a surfeit of "good fortunes"—Portia admits that she is right. She confesses, "I can easier teach twenty what were good to be done, than be one of the twenty to follow mine own teaching"(1.2.13–15). She knows that, like anyone else, she preaches virtues that she herself does not follow. Portia recognizes the limitations of her own merits, the necessary precondition to requesting and rendering mercy.

Next we may examine her role in the three key plots. In her essay "Portia's Unruly Ring," Karen Newman finds strength in Portia's wit and will in the casket plot. Newman sees the caskets as devices to be used for an arranged marriage, a contract legalizing one of society's most powerful methods of exchange: "marriage is the most fundamental form of gift exchange. Such an exchange system existed in early modern England where marriage, among the elite at least, was primarily a commercial transaction determined by questions of dowry, familial alliances, land ownership, and inheritance"(118, 120–22).[6] The play emphasizes this male-male relationship, with women serving as the commodity for exchange, because the "exchange of Portia from her father via the caskets to Bassanio is the ur-exchange upon which the 'main' bond plot is based" (120).

Gift giving gains meaning, Newman explains, because it bestows power on the giver and establishes a hierarchy between the giver and the receiver.[7] In the casket scene, Portia reveals the identity of the giver—not her dead father after all, but rather herself. After Bassanio selects the winning casket, Portia offers herself to him with love and self-deprecation but also the sudden objectivity of the third person:

> . . . But the full sum of me
> Is sum of something: which to term in gross
> Is an unlessoned girl, unschooled, unpractised;
> Happy in this, she is not yet so old
> But she may learn; happier than this,
> She is not bred so dull but she can learn;
> Happiest of all, is that her gentle spirit
> Commits itself to yours to be directed
> As from her lord, her governor, her king; (3.2.157–65)

She ends her speech with the terms of her marriage bond to Bassanio:

> . . . and even now, but now,
> This house, these servants, and this same myself
> Are yours, my lord. I give them with this ring,
> Which when you part from, lose, or give away,
> Let it presage the ruin of your love,
> And be my vantage to exclaim on you. (3.2.169–74)

Newman observes that this bond "shifts the speech from her personal commitment to a more formal bond marked by the giving of her ring, and that move is signaled by the shift to the third person" (123). The ring "here represents the codified, hierarchical relation of men and women in the Elizabethan sex/gender system" (124). Newman concludes that because Portia's gift is too great for Bassanio to reciprocate, she gains the advantage in the marriage.

More unusual, however, are, first, that the bride gives her possessions and herself in marriage, and, second, that only the bride offers a ring, bidding her husband to wear it always or risk losing everything. With these unusual qualifications, she becomes at once the commodity and its possessor. She is not a mute, powerless "gift," transferred from father to husband; rather, she controls her fate, voluntarily offering herself to her lover under carefully stated conditions. She demands that her love be returned, a demand that Bassanio eagerly accepts:

> . . . But when this ring
> Parts from this finger, then parts life from hence:
> O then be bold to say Bassanio's dead! (3.2.183–85)

Portia thus enters the play lamenting the unacceptable premise that she is a commodity of legal exchange. But with her wit and her love, she goes on to arrange the terms of the exchange herself: her love leads her to a worthy and loving partner, and her wit creates a marriage bond that gives her an escape clause.

In the bond test of Act 4, she once again successfully adapts to the situation, embracing the terms of the bond and using them to gain victory. She tells the Duke, "I am informd throughly of the cause" (4.1.169). Her opening requests for mercy are sincere because earlier she admitted weakness to Nerissa and Bassanio.[8] We must grant mercy, she says, because

> . . . in the course of justice, none of us
> Should see salvation. We do pray for mercy,
> And that same prayer doth teach us all to render
> The deeds of mercy (195–98).

But mercy is not a requirement of justice in Venice's law. After Shylock refuses to be merciful three times, she begins her three-part argument within the framework of the bond's law. The first two parts are conditions Shakespeare borrowed from *Il Pecorone,* but the third (without a known source) traps Shylock, leaving him no escape. Her lessons from the casket scenes support her arguments in court. In the course of the casket test, Portia has learned that desire is as undirected and uncontrollable as the flow of blood when the flesh in cut, and that the exact quantification of what one "deserves" is the goal of only a blinking idiot. Thus Shylock could neither have flesh without blood nor quantify an exact pound. Both would be impossible. But Portia's third condition is the worst because it damns Shylock for a deed he has already committed. He has sought to harm a Venetian citizen—a capital crime in Venice—and he must now be punished. He is guilty and has no recourse.

Some readers ask why Portia fails to show Shylock the sort of mercy she has rhapsodized over only a few lines earlier. In fact, the Duke and Antonio seem more generous to Shylock than she is. First, we must remember that Portia has no power; she is a barrister or perhaps merely a consultant in the court. Neither role would give her the power to offer mercy; she can only inspire it. And although Shylock did not heed her words about the quality of mercy, apparently the Duke and Antonio were listening. She effectively encourages mercy from the Duke and Antonio, telling Shylock, "Down therefore, and beg mercy of the Duke" (4.1.359) and then prods Antonio, "What mercy can you render him, Antonio?" (4.1.374). As a result, neither the Duke nor Antonio entirely destroys Shylock, the would-be destroyer.

Finally, Act 4 ends in a continuation of the ring plot, with Portia's demand for Bassanio's ring. Bassanio can do nothing that will *not* be wrong. Portia places him in a no-win predicament so that he is forced to lose and later ask for forgiveness. He would seem petty if he denied Balthazar the ring. At first, with embarrassment, he refuses to give the ring; but Antonio, who is more sentimental, urges him:

> My lord Bassanio, let him have the ring.
> Let his deservings and my love withal
> Be valued 'gainst your wife's commandement. (5.1.445–47)

Bassanio finally gives the gift, but Portia/Balthazar still holds the upper hand in gift giving, because she has just bestowed an even more precious gift: the life of Bassanio's friend. Thus Bassanio's second trial poses as unwinnable a victory as Venetian law does for Shylock. Both demand mercy. Bassanio either must ignore Balthazar's rescue of Antonio's life or ignore the value of the marriage symbol. He is checkmated by Portia's wit. Portia must win and he must lose. Thus, in Belmont, he must call for mercy:

> Pardon this fault, and by my soul I swear
> I nevermore will break an oath with thee. (5.1.247–48)

After this, Bassanio follows Portia's lesson that praying for mercy teaches us to render the deeds of mercy when he forgives Portia for creating such a test in the first place:

> Sweet doctor, you shall be my bedfellow;
> When I am absent, then with my wife. (5.1.284–85)

Both lovers request and render mercy, a necessary circular activity between flawed human beings. Portia creates a requirement for marriage: mercy—forgiveness—must continually flow between the lovers. What begins as a humiliation for Bassanio, then, ends as a promise of continued love and mercy between Portia and him. With wit and virtue, Portia instructs others not so much to overcome their own mortal weaknesses as to acknowledge them, ask mercy for their ill effects, and thereby learn to offer mercy or forgiveness to others.

BASSANIO

Bassanio, the juvenile lead, evolves somewhat like the main character in a *Bildungsroman,* the story of the maturation of a young man. Harley

Granville-Barker suggests that in production, Bassanio is the embodiment of "the magnificent young man" of Venice (in Wilders 70)—an extravagant, confident, and careless youngster who depends on others for his livelihood, and who, so his social set has convinced him, cannot court wealthy Portia without the trappings of money. His maturation requires that he abandon his easy life to hazard all he has, reorder his values from material to human, and replace his youthful self-importance with a more modest sense of himself. In sum, he must exchange self-absorption for self-sacrifice.

Bassanio has greater dimension than Giannetto, the parallel character from *Il Pecorone*. At the beginning of the play, Bassanio is a more careless and clever youth, and at the end he is a wiser and more loving adult than Giannetto. In Scene 1 he seems to be a flamboyant and superficial gold digger who sees in Portia a convenient and attractive route to financial security. He has, David Bevington writes, lost his previous fortune through unnamed "amiable faults of reckless generosity and a lack of concern for financial prudence" (178). Like Giannetto, Bassanio has met the lady of Belmont before, knows her to be "richly left," beautiful, and virtuous— qualities we may hope he is cataloging in ascending order. He knows he must take some risk to possess her, but he has an almost unquestioning faith that he will be successful in Belmont, if only he can fund the trip. As it happened when he was a child, his second arrow, he predicts, will land very close to his first. He will succeed in whatever challenge Belmont presents, even though he has lost before.

But like Portia, Bassanio is perceptive from the beginning. He is clever enough to know that he must see beyond appearances. For example, when Antonio considers Shylock's offer of the bond in 1.3, an agreement friendly on the surface and poison at its core, Bassanio warns him, "I like not fair terms and a villain's mind" (1.3.172). Such perception serves as evidence that Bassanio has the wit to win the casket test. Although he can recognize potential danger, Bassanio cannot shed his self-centered goals and refuse Shylock's offer because it endangers Antonio.

Once he has the money in hand, Bassanio begins, characteristically, to spend it. Among his purchases are the new livery for Lancelot and all the other splendid clothes worn by Bassanio's retinue, the gifts he brings to Belmont, and even the going-away festivities to which Shylock is ironically invited. Bassanio unquestioningly continues his usual spendthrift ways, his youthful enthusiasm stifling any prudence he might consider.

The casket test in 3.2, however, is a turning point for Bassanio. First, in selecting the winning casket he proves his wit, and then, after receiving Antonio's letter, he shows self-awareness, admitting his thoughtlessness.

Although Portia may have offered assistance, Bassanio selects the correct casket because he concludes "the world is still deceived with ornament" (3.2.74). Rene Girard suggests that Bassanio, the only participant in the casket test who is a Venetian, makes the correct selection because "Venice is a world in which appearances and reality do not match"; therefore, Bassanio alone "knows how deceptive a splendid exterior can be" (in Bloom, *William Shakespeare's* The Merchant of Venice 93). But Marc Shell finds irony in Bassanio's judgment because "he himself uses and has used words and gold to purchase 'valor's excrement'" (in Bloom 114). False seeming—wearing a pleasant appearance over a black heart—is a popular theme in Shakespeare's plays. Hamlet warns that "The devil hath power / T' assuming a pleasing shape"; Lady Macbeth urges Macbeth to "Look like th' innocent flower / But be the serpent under 't"; just as Bassanio warns Antonio of Shylock's "fair terms" and "villain's mind" and comments during the casket test:

> There is no vice so simple but assumes
> Some mark of virtue on his outward parts. (3.2.81–82)

Using a variety of similes and metaphors, Bassanio continues contrasting inner realities with appearances. The hearts of cowards are as false as "stayers of sand" and their livers are "white as milk"; but outwardly they have "beards of Hercules and frowning Mars," "valor's excrement [excrescence]" (3.2.82–87). Bassanio observes that beauty too is false; it is "purchased by the weight which therein works a miracle in nature, / Making them lightest that wear most of it" (3.2.89, 91). Using macabre images, he implies that "crisped, snaky golden locks" could be counterfeit—a wig, hair from a "skull that bred them in the sepulchre" (3.2.92, 96). His similes and metaphors grow more florid and frequent:

> Thus ornament is but the guild shore
> To a most dangerous sea; the beauteous scarf
> Veiling an Indian beauty; in a word,
> The seeming truth which cunning times put on
> To entrap the wisest. (3.2.97–101)

Concluding, he dismisses gold, the "hard food for Midas," and silver, the "pale and common drudge / Tween man and man" (3.2.102–4), and selects lead because it is plain, honest, and not eloquent.

But like Portia, Bassanio speaks more wisely than he acts. His attraction to beautiful and rich Portia and his extravagant preparations to court her belie his lofty ideas about false seeming. He fails to follow his own wise words, both in his own speech and in the ornament and trappings of the entourage he felt obliged to bring to Belmont, paid for with Antonio's life-threatening loan. He does not recognize the dissonance between his own precepts and his actions.

Finally, the inscription on the lead casket itself offers clues to Bassanio's success. The lord of Belmont intended for the casket test to be a test of love. Love indeed breeds desire, but more important, desire impels risk taking. The casket test measures such risk taking or hazarding for love. Catherine Belsey writes, "Only Bassanio is motivated by desire and knows that lovers give and hazard all they have" (143).[9] Anyone standing before the caskets who is aware of what he is doing in the present moment—that is, risking any other future marriage as well as legal progeny—*must* select the correct casket: "'Who chooseth me, must give and hazard all he hath'" (2.9.20). Besides his future, Bassanio is risking all he has ever had, including his dearest friend. The lead casket demands everything right now—Bassanio "*must* give and hazard all he hath," not "*shall* gain what many men desire" or "*shall* get as much as he deserves." Love demands. Bassanio is sufficiently self-aware to know that *at the moment* he is indeed risking everything for love.

Because he is a risk taker, Bassanio is made worthy in the world of the play. Shakespeare introduces hazarding as the only activity named among the casket inscriptions that is not borrowed from the source story in the *Gesta Romanorum*. It is the required, laudable means to a praiseworthy goal. If we are unsure of the virtue of Bassanio's goals and, by extension, of Antonio's goals, we cannot be unsure of the two men's courage in accepting hazard as the means.

Bassanio's successful selection of the casket and Portia's eager agreement ensure their marriage; yet his development as a man worthy of so desirable a bride is still unproven. Immediately after his victory in 3.2, Bassanio expresses his passion with sometimes odd hyperbolic verse, but he still must succeed in tests in the world outside Belmont. This opportunity arrives with Salerio's message, reminding Bassanio of Antonio's fate. Unlike the source story in which Giannetto forgets his godfather's bond with the Jew of Mestri, Bassanio has no reason to think that Antonio has forfeited the bond, because several ships were expected to arrive laden with wealth. Bassanio can barely believe the news:

> . . . . But is it true, Salerio?
> Hath all his ventures failed? What, not one hit? (3.2.265–66).

Exhibiting a new courage to confess his own false seeming, Bassanio admits to Portia his financial debt to Antonio, describing his respect for his friend and his haste to return and help him. He promises fidelity as he leaves. But when he returns to Venice, he is unable to give Antonio relief and can only make his ineffective offers for Antonio's life, the last of which is "life itself, wife, and all the world" (3.2.280). It is a cavalier generosity that only elicits Shylock's mockery, "These be the Christian husbands!" (4.1.291). Whether this offer inspires Portia's later no-win demand for Bassanio's ring remains conjecture. Bassanio does not distinguish himself in Venice's court or in responding to Portia's demand for the ring. He does, however, demonstrate once again his willingness to take intemperate risks for love.

Act 5 completes Bassanio's development.[10] His offer to give and hazard everything for the life of Antonio further proves that he is the man described on the lead casket; he can be trusted to take risks for those he loves. Refusing to hand over the ring would not have shown him to be a truer husband, because no one could entirely win the ring test. A ring is, after all, not the beloved, and Bassanio has been wise to the distinction between appearance and essence almost from the beginning. Finally, the ring test forces Bassanio to admit failure—a failure, however, that anyone would suffer since, as Belsey observes, the riddle of the ring makes it "impossible to tell where truth resides" (147).[11]

Bassanio is no longer the unthinking and enthusiastic boy-archer who can ignore consequences, compensate for any loss, or solve any problem, if necessary, on the second try. Although humbled, he is more self-aware and less brash than the child-man of Act 1, and he understands that for those who live in this world, justice and mercy are fully realized only in the presence of the other, just like husband and wife.

LORENZO

Lorenzo, the secondary juvenile lead, is drawn with fewer strokes and less sympathy than Bassanio. Sigurd Burckhardt suggests that Jessica and Lorenzo "stand in the sharpest imaginable contrast to Portia and Bassanio" (223) because the former couple is "lawless," "spendthrift," and "aimless" (224), and the "shame and uselessness" of their lives serve only "by contrast, to make clearer and firmer the outlines of bonded love" (225). On the other hand, Bloom finds Lorenzo so similar to Bassanio that "no one would want the project of distinguishing between" them; they are merely "two Venetian playboys in search of heiresses" (*Shakespeare: The Invention* 179). Although both begin as bright and charming boys, careless of the consequences of their actions to others, as the play progresses, Lorenzo increasingly contrasts with Bassanio.

Lorenzo develops as someone who would never accept the challenge of the casket test, let alone win it. And as clever as he may be, he would not hazard or plan ahead to remedy his insolvency—either foolishly or wisely. Bassanio's acceptance of a loan that jeopardizes the life of his friend remains an admittedly risky plan, but it compares favorably to Lorenzo's thievery of Jessica's identity, at once robbing her of her heritage in exchange for a Christian marriage and of Shylock's familial and frugal house, which brings on his reported despairing cries, "My daughter! O my ducats! O my daughter!" (2.8.15).

But like Bassanio, Lorenzo gains a greater understanding of himself and others by the end of the play. While he remains enamored of Jessica, he gains humility and humor. In Scene 1, he is most of all a foil to the noisy and impulsive Gratiano. Almost an eiron to Gratiano's alazon character,[12] he responds sarcastically when Gratiano describes people who have a false gravity derived from silence. "I must be one of these same dumb wise men," he says dryly, "For Gratiano never lets me speak" (1.1.106–7). Later that afternoon with his friends (2.4), he praises his beloved, Jessica, while explaining how he and she will rob Shylock. What can we feel other than ambivalence toward him? Charm encloses self-absorption. We are not seduced into liking him because we simultaneously hold two opinions; one is approval of his youthful love for Jessica, and the other is dismay over his thoughtless thievery.

When darkness falls and Lorenzo and Jessica meet to run away together, Lorenzo is again generous in his praise for Jessica. He says he is her "love" (2.6.29), and as she gathers more of her father's ducats, he tells his friends that she is "wise, fair, and true" (2.6.57), an accolade similar to Bassanio's praise for Portia as being rich, beautiful, and virtuous. But while he may love Jessica, he steals her and her father's money and offers nothing of his own. Granted, Shylock never would have approved of their marriage, but a stolen dowry remains a felony. Once again, a juvenile lead is attractive but dependent, irresponsible, and unaware of considerations beyond his desires.

Unlike Bassanio, however, Lorenzo shows little energy and activity. It is Jessica who plans and implements the escape, Salerio who brings news of Antonio to Belmont, and Portia who arranges for Lorenzo and Jessica's temporary supervision of Belmont. Although he jokingly claims to be as good a spouse as Portia, his inactivity and dearth of goals differ decidedly from her energy and ambition.

Lorenzo is most impressive in the final scene, as he and Jessica gaze at the stars and catalog memorable but ill-fated mythic lovers whose passions similarly soared "In such a night as this" (5.1.1). These ambiguous sets of lovers, shining in the moonlight for only a moment, were ironically fated to suffer tragedy. Burckhardt calls the interaction between these characters "fly-by-night love: betrayal (Troilus and Cressida), desertion (Pyramus and Thisbe), disaster (Dido and Aeneas), sorcery (Medea) , and theft (Jessica)" (226). All these mythic lovers were gloriously passionate, even though their relationships were limited to the here and now. Finally, the fifth and final set of lovers in Jessica and Lorenzo's catalog is themselves—Jessica who, Lorenzo punningly observes, "did . . . steal from the wealthy Jew," and Lorenzo who, Jessica responds, did steal "her soul with many vows of faith, / and ne'er a true one" (5.1.15, 17–19). They conclude, then, with a joke on themselves.

Lorenzo continues, explaining why even these great lovers are imperfect. Looking at the "floor of heaven," he notes:

> There's not the smallest orb which thou behold'st
> But in his motion like an angel sings,
> Still choiring to the young-eyed cherubins.
> Such harmony is in immortal souls,
> But whilst this muddy vesture of decay
> Doth grossly close it in, we cannot hear it. (5.1.60–65)

He knows that he himself is high on the list of the flawed, undependable beings of earth. Love, limited by the imperfections wrought by flesh and time, is most successfully embraced with laughter because, like life and death, it is beyond human control. Yet the imperfection of the play's earthly lovers and their love make the audience unable to surrender unquestioningly to the play's romance. Audience response to these sometimes selfish lovers is limited by reason; thus the moment, like the entire final act, may seem perfect, but it will neither remain nor bear deep scrutiny.

In the end, Lorenzo is wise enough to accept the grandeur represented by music and the palliative value of laughter, humble enough not to expect a complete remedy to the problems created by his interfaith marriage, and sufficiently aware of his own shortcomings to show gratitude for his inheritance from Shylock: "manna in the way / Of starvd people" (5.1.292–93).[13] In one important sense, Lorenzo reflects Bassanio. He is clever, charming, playful, and self-aware from the beginning. And while he may not develop responsibility nor plan great success, he implicitly recognizes their absence as deriving from himself.

GRATIANO

As a foil to Bassanio and Lorenzo, and a foolhardy alazon who claims to know what is right, Gratiano begins by asking Antonio to let him play the fool, someone who makes others laugh, and by wishing that his liver, the seat of passion, "heat with wine" (1.1.80) rather than that his heart feel pain. In this, ironically, he is aligned with Shylock, who similarly points out his own "affections, passions" (3.1.47).

In contrast to Lancelot Gobbo, Gratiano is, according to Burckhardt, "a true jester, who marries in due form" (224). The fool or jester talks much, acts little, and valuably, serves as a catalyst for the more spontaneous actions of others. He is a financial hanger-on, and in exchange is an entertainer. He also equivocates, using puns to redirect meaning in his own and others' language. This can provoke a sort of happy confusion that regularly encourages love and lust.[14] All this is true of Gratiano, from the opening scene introducing Antonio's melancholy to the final scene promising the pleasure and procreation of sexuality. He is an entertainer and a defender of his comrades, particularly when he fails to consider the consequences of intemperate words. Bassanio chides him, saying that he is "too wild, too rude, and bold of voice" (2.2.152), which are not faults to those who know him but may seem like "wild behaviour" (2.2.154) to strangers. His vociferous loyalty to Antonio never wavers, but it inspires no unusual risk taking.

Although Bloom calls Gratiano "vicious" (*Shakespeare: The Invention* 177), he is unable to cause real harm. In court, his ridicule of Shylock as a dog and a wolf, ugly bigotry as it is, is ineffective; and his later hyperbolic taunts that the Jew should die begin only after Shylock is safely defeated by Portia's citations of the law. He recommends that Shylock hang himself. But since his wealth is "forfeit to the state" and he has not been left "the value of a cord," he sneers that this can only proceed at the state's charge (4.1.360–64); or, he advises, Antonio can be merciful and give Shylock "a halter gratis" (4.1.375). Gratiano also offers, with his usual thoughtless intemperance, his wife's life for Antonio's, not entirely the same as Bassanio's offer of his own life, his wife's, and all he has. From the beginning, he indeed plays the fool. And while his bigotry is offensive, particularly during the trial, he is consistently outspoken and never shrouds his hostility in hypocrisy, which would be uncharacteristic of a fool.

Gratiano's language, particularly colorful and equivocal, also characterizes a fool. As a lover and husband to Nerissa, his deeds and language suggest that he will be faithful, if perhaps not sensitive. His candor, bawdy puns, and innuendoes make him a reasonable choice to speak the play's final lines in which he promises conjugal devotion: "Well, while I live I'll fear no other thing / So sore as keeping safe Nerissa's ring" (5.1.305–6). Like Shylock, he is concerned with his wife's ring, but the turquoise ring that Shylock laments represents a partnership sadly ended by death, whereas Gratiano's lines highlight the fool's equivocation that expands and opens the word to represent the emotional and physical aspects of marriage, appropriate to end this play. Marc Shell identifies the very act of punning, borrowing new meanings for words, as "verbal usury."[15] Herein lies the importance of Gratanio.

Act 5 begins with Lorenzo, as philosopher, recalling the harmony that we, as mortals, will never hear, but that sings in immortal souls. It ends with Gratiano, as fool-catalyst, balancing Lorenzo's observation, loosening verbal and social restrictions so the remaining characters can enjoy the promise of love and regeneration abiding in their flesh.

ANTONIO

The most prestigious Venetian is Antonio, who begins the play and for whom the play is named. In *Il Pecorone,* the Antonio character is Ansaldo, the otherwise childless godfather and benefactor to Giannetto (Bassanio). But Shakespeare alters this godfather figure so that, along with the other source elements, Antonio/Ansaldo deepens into a puzzling paradox who draws considerable literary commentary. Interestingly, much of Antonio's ambiguity develops from his career as a merchant. His mercantile values dominate both his world and him.

This seems not to be the case in the first scene. Antonio describes his unexplained, self-absorbed sadness; the world is a stage, he explains, on which his part is "a sad one" (1.1.78). Many critics, beginning at least with E. M. W. Tillyard in 1966, attribute this melancholy not to the risk of his financial ventures but to his romantic distress over Bassanio's earlier news that he will leave Venice to seek a wife. Others, including Lawrence Danson, disagree, concluding that a homosexual relationship, or even homoerotic passion, raises more problems of interpretation than it solves (40).[16] That we are left with only circumstantial clues and cannot entirely accept a single interpretation of this relationship demonstrates the ambiguity Shakespeare has added to this character.

Whether he is a friend or lover or parent figure to Bassanio,[17] Antonio's love is exceptional even as it is admittedly undefined. But Antonio shows further ambiguity. Even though he is compassionate to Bassanio, he is cruel, disdainful, and arrogant to Shylock. Bloom says that Antonio's anti-Semitism is "even more viciously intense than anyone else's, even Gratiano's" (*Shakespeare: The Invention* 185). In their first encounter in the play when they agree to the bond, Shylock reminds Antonio that he has called him "dog," spat on him, and spurned him; and Antonio agrees, with arrogant self-righteousness, that " I am as like to call thee so again, / To spit on thee again, to spurn thee too" (1.3.122–23). When Antonio agrees to the bond that will help Bassanio, Antonio is again sarcastic to Shylock. At the end of their negotiations, he foreshadows the future: "Hie thee, gentle Jew. / The Hebrew will turn Christian, he grows kind" (1.3.170–171). In short, whenever we begin to develop a positive or negative opinion of Antonio, or of any of the other central characters for that matter, the play dashes it and displays evidence that refutes whatever we had wanted to believe.

We may also wonder about another point: why does Antonio so unquestioningly agree to the bond that puts his life at stake for Bassanio's risky venture, and why, after a brief and fruitless attempt to speak to Shylock in 3.3, does he accept his punishment so fatalistically? Both questions are important because they are both about wealth, the goal of nearly all the activity of Venice.

In the first scene, Bassanio makes clear that his reason for venturing to Belmont is to allay his poverty and repay debt. These are reasons certain to impress Antonio:

> . . . my chief care
> Is to come fairly off from the great debts
> Wherein my time, something too prodigal,
> Hath left me gaged. (1.1.126–29).

If his dear friend Bassanio is experiencing financial difficulty, then Antonio realizes this to be among the worst fates that could befall a soldierly, scholarly Venetian.

Three months later, in his despairing letter to Bassanio in Belmont, Antonio unresistingly submits to the bond, wishing only to see Bassanio before he dies. He does not ask for help. Back in Venice in 3.3, Antonio reveals the reason for his fatalistic, almost meek acquiescence—a key to nearly everything he does. More than a cultural anti-Semitism and more than his attachment to Bassanio, it is at the heart of Antonio's actions. In fact, Antonio's bias against the Jew extends as a corollary from his value system's damning premise. After trying to reason unsuccessfully with Shylock, who angrily exits, Antonio explains to Solanio that the Duke cannot waive a forfeiture and save him. This is not because a contract must be honored, nor because even-handed justice is ethical and moral, but rather for the following reason:

> . . . the commodity that strangers have
> With us in Venice, if it be denied,
> Will much impeach the justice of the state,

Since that the trade and profit of the city
Consisteth of all nations. (3.3.27–31).

Property rights are transcendent, not for the sake of justice but for the goal of commerce, for the smooth and successful acquisition of wealth in Venice. Shylock is naive to think that the goal of Venetian law is justice. Antonio, a part of the power structure that condemns the Jew, accepts his own doom with apparent grace because he respects the social order of Venice, which has as its heart neither justice nor mercy but rather Venetian business and Venetian wealth.

Just as Antonio is entirely respectful of Venetian commerce, he is respectful and courteous to Venetian citizens who participate in that activity. In return, they praise him for his outward show of grace. When another of his ships is lost, Solanio calls him "the good Antonio, the honest Antonio—O that I had a title good enough to keep his name company!" (3.1.10–12). Later, Lorenzo reassures Portia that Antonio is a true gentleman and a dear lover of her husband. In court, Antonio displays his stiff upper-class upper lip, telling the Duke that he is "armed to suffer with a quietness of spirit" (4.1.11–12). He calls himself "the tainted wether of the flock, / Meetest for death" (4.1.114–15), and as he holds Bassanio's hand in readiness for Shylock's knife, he tellingly notes the benefit in dying so soon. He will escape the most frightening fate for a merchant like him, when it is Fortune's cruel use "To let the wretched man outlive his wealth" (4.1.265).

Finally, we must examine how Antonio, a merchant explicitly and implicitly immersed in a world of commerce, is engaged in the religion that runs through the play. The combination of commerce and religion creates an almost Chaucerian irony. Religion is manipulated to serve commerce. Antonio's Christianity serves his livelihood. And almost in a mirror image, Shylock's Judaism serves his livelihood. Like Jacob, who plotted the clever acquisition of his father-in-law's parti-colored sheep (1.3.69–82), Shylock explains that those who seek economic success, "a way to thrive" (1.3.81), will be blessed because "thrift is blessing if men steal it not" (1.3.82). Religion supports energetic financial activities. Granted, Antonio's sentimentality and Shylock's humorous vengeance motivate them in different directions; yet both employ their religion to justify their business. An especially troubling example occurs in Antonio's demand for Shylock's conversion to Christianity. Some readers find this particularly cruel, while others argue that conversion is a gift, the only road Shylock could take to heaven. The play supports the former notion. It is decidedly a punishment because Antonio requires the conversion as a

part of the compensation for the pardon, "this favour" he has just offered.
Antonio insists:

> To quit the fine for one half of his goods,
> I am content, so he will let me have
> The other half in use, to render it
> Upon his death unto the gentleman
> That lately stole his daughter.
> Two things provided more: that for this favour
> He presently become a Christian;
> The other that he do record a gift,
> Here in the court, of all he dies possessed
> Unto his son Lorenzo and his daughter. (5.1.377–86)

In other words, after the court spares Shylock the fine of half his assets,
Antonio demands control of the other half, which will be bequeathed to
Lorenzo and Jessica; Shylock must become Christian and bequeath his remaining wealth to Lorenzo and Jessica. The conversion is neither intended by Antonio as an opportunity for everlasting life in heaven nor as a
cruel denial of the value of Shylock's religion; rather, it sits between two
financial stipulations. It is, in fact, a financial arrangement itself. Shylock
can no longer practice usury, a boon to the Venetians because it theoreti-
cally will result in less expensive credit.

The ending of Act 5 verifies Antonio's morality, oddly but realistically
both mercantile and sentimental, and incidentally, evidenced still today in
thriving oxymoronic corporate charitable foundations. Antonio has regularly given generously and spontaneously to debt-laden Venetians, especially Bassanio. Such charity, with no expectation of return, was highly
regarded in the Renaissance.[18] As a result, although Antonio is not rewarded with a mate as Ansaldo is in *Il Pecorone,* he does merit entry to
Belmont. He fits in easily in this gentle, gentile, and genteel place that values the show of wealth, like that of the splendid suitors, but disdains the
pursuit of wealth, like that of the Venetians. Antonio's sentimental generosity even motivates his offer of his "soul upon the forfeit" (5.1.252) in
the conclusion of the ring plot, when Portia disparages Bassanio's promise
never to break an oath with her. Portia accepts Antonio's "surety" for what
she sarcastically calls Bassanio's "oath of credit" from his duplicitous or
"double self" (5.1.245–46) and soon rewards the merchant with mysterious news that three of his ships, richly laden, have made safe harbor. With
this news, he praises Portia for having "given him life and living"
(5.1.286), the most valuable gift he, a merchant, could receive. The means
by which Antonio gains this good fortune remain unexplained, perhaps

because characters in Belmont are not concerned with the practical means by which wealth is gained. When Lorenzo receives his own eventual financial windfall, his inheritance from Shylock, he properly calls it "manna in the way / Of starved people" (5.1.294–95), a gift from heaven.

Life in Belmont is built on wealth, and Antonio and Portia create the opportunities for many to gain it. But in Belmont, wealth is neither earned nor central, and it is not a goal; rather, it defines the place itself—the servants, the gold, the musicians, the leisure, the dowry. Belmont is where wealth *is,* Bassanio wins it, and Antonio is notified that he has it and Lorenzo that he will have it. On the other hand, in Venice wealth shines as the distant glistening goal of an amoral, continuing quest. The merchant Antonio, both acquisitive and sentimental, participates in both worlds: in one finding melancholia and danger, and in the other celebrating the equivocal and perhaps equivalent blessings, "life and living" (5.1.286).

JESSICA

The sole female of Venice is Jessica, and like the other Venetians, she behaves with increasing virtue as the play progresses. She enters the play in Act 2, at best as a thoughtless child, abandoning her father, escaping the house that she claims has been "hell" because of its "tediousness" (2.3.2–3). Still, it has not imprisoned her sufficiently to keep her from having a romance with Lorenzo. Even when Shylock goes off to Bassanio's banquet, he gives her his keys and can only command her, "Lock up my doors" (2.5.28). She is not locked in, however, and Shylock, like any father, can only hope that she will comply with his wishes. Critics often have little sympathy for Jessica's trials. Bloom calls her "the insufferable Jessica, the Venetian Jewish princess who gets what she deserves in her playboy, Lorenzo" (*Shakespeare: The Invention* 183). Granted, her life with Shylock has not been one of indulgence and pleasure. But her stealing away, taking her father's gold and jewels, and even returning for a few more ducats show greed, a lack of appreciation for either her father or her heritage, and the self-absorption that is the keystone of Venetian behavior. In requesting her to remain indoors away from the partying Venetians, Shylock may have wished to shield his daughter from the pervasive acquisitiveness of the culture, but he has failed. When Tubal brings the information from one of Antonio's creditors that Jessica traded her mother's turquoise ring, which she had stolen from her father, for a monkey, her thoughtlessness seems nearly cruel. Honor for her parents, so strong a part of Jewish and Christian heritage, is missing and leaves a hollowness in her.

But as with other characters, the play gives ambiguous messages about Jessica and hints that she evolves into something better. Like Lorenzo, she is entirely a character whom Shakespeare superimposes on the source story, perhaps inspired by the character of Abigail, the daughter of Barabas in *The Jew of Malta*, by Christopher Marlowe. Just as giving Shylock a daughter creates in him another dimension that allows us to see him as a father in his own house, Jessica herself gains dimension beyond that of an ungrateful daughter. She is a housemate to Lancelot, a lover to Lorenzo, and a newly made Christian to all the rest. Lancelot calls her "most beautiful pagan, most sweet Jew" (2.3.10–11). Lorenzo finds her "wise, fair, and true" (2.6.57), a conventional platitude but still a positive assessment. And after the elopement, she is almost oddly humble, never speaking in 3.4 as Portia asks Lorenzo and Jessica to care for her house in her absence. Later she praises Portia, noting "the joys of heaven here on earth" (3.5.64) that Bassanio may experience in his marriage. Like Portia, she is more clever than her mate because it is she who masterminds her financially profitable escape, sending Lancelot to Lorenzo with messages outlining her plans. Lorenzo is excited to tell Gratiano what Jessica has planned for them—that she will leave with her father's gold and jewels, wear a page's suit, and pretend to be Lorenzo's torchbearer. She is also witty, matching and exceeding Lorenzo's Act 5 catalog of lovers "In such a night as this," with her last line, "I would outnight you, did nobody come" (5.1.23). Her ability to match the ironic repartee of Lorenzo here and in 3.5 with both Lancelot and Lorenzo does not falter.

Jessica has grown up with an unbending, parsimonious father, a fact corroborated by Lancelot. Yet the careless, adventurous young girl in 2.3 behaves as a flexible and witty adult by 5.1—a victor over Venetian self-absorption.

NERISSA

Nerissa enters in 1.2 as a conventional foil to the ingenue, promoting common sense and moderation. She does not characterize Belmont, a place that can, at times, seem like a prototype of a modern tony and affluent suburb. When Portia complains of her world weariness, Nerissa observes that while those with a surfeit of goods are as troubled as "those that starve with nothing" (1.2.5–6), those "seated in the mean" live longer and happier. After Portia admits the wisdom of these words as well as the challenge of their implementation, she begins yet another complaint over the casket test that Nerissa must again rebut. Trustingly, Nerissa praises the inspired virtue of the Lord of Belmont's deathbed decree.

Nerissa is a faithful but unimaginative proponent of the obvious. Always loyal and without the disrespect for the older generation implicit in Jessica, she is not necessarily virtuous and kind; she is satisfied, easily entertained, and uncomplaining, whether to her mistress, her husband, or the Lord who was her master. She is a flatter character than Portia, with far less variety in her responses to events. Accepting the vagaries of fate, she contrasts the restless Portia and serves as straight woman for Portia's sarcastic appraisals of her would-be suitors. She questions almost nothing, most noticeably the unkindness swirling around her, only chiding Portia for her ingratitude for the abundance of her "good fortunes" (1.2.4).

Like Gratiano, she is a convention, a sidekick to the ingenue and a character Shakespeare developed from the briefly mentioned, somewhat disloyal maid in the source story. Her consistency highlights the paradoxes and contradictions of the ingenue. Because neither Nerissa nor Gratiano have a financial stake in any of the proceedings, both seem free to behave as if they have no restrictions, although this is hardly the case since they can marry if and only if Bassanio wins the casket test. She is delighted by Gratiano, who behaves raucously, speaks thoughtlessly, and engages in recreational anti-Semitism. Neither she nor Gratiano gain any money at the end of the play—the only Act 5 characters who do not—but their loyalty to their betters ensures a secure financial future. And somehow, they do have funds enough to wager with Bassanio and Portia over the first son.

Like the other two female characters, Nerissa is more clever and pragmatic than her intended spouse, but she lacks Portia's imagination. "Why, shall we turn to men?" (3.4.78), she asks both naively and suggestively when she first hears of the disguise plan. But she willingly joins in the androgynous plot in the Venetian courtroom and the trickery of the rings, acting the distressed female in Act 5 when she discovers Gratiano's missing wedding ring inscribed with its unheeded warning, "Love me and leave me not" (5.1.150). More than Portia, she inspires sexual double entendres from her mate, both at the time of their betrothal and after the ring plot is resolved. Gratiano's punning promise to spend his life keeping safe Nerissa's ring is more inelegant than any promise Bassanio makes to the "sweet doctor." Thus, in the end, Nerissa awakens and shares Belmont's carefree pleasure in the moonlit here and now.

MOROCCO AND ARRAGON

Before Bassanio's arrival, Morocco and Arragon's appearances in Belmont build dramatic tension with their failures by establishing the risk and wisdom of the casket test. Marc Shell writes that Portia sees the suitors as "not even men" (113). She belittles Morocco behind his back for having the "complexion of a devil" (1.2.107). He is indeed an unattractively boastful warrior, almost a comic Othello; but unlike Desdemona, Portia is not impressed by him. In his casket selection six scenes later, Morocco considers the inscriptions and the caskets themselves. Reading the inscription on the lead casket, he observes that "men that hazard all / Do it in hope of fair advantages" (2.7.18–19). He lacks sufficient self-awareness to admit that hazarding for fair advantage is, in fact, what he is doing; and he forgets that the prize is contained within the casket, not the casket itself. Next he considers the silver casket because he assumes that he deserves the worthy lady—in birth, fortunes, graces, qualities of breeding, and love. But in the end, he settles on the gold casket because he is convinced that "all the world" desires Portia (2.7.38).

The casket test has now been performed, and it works. Morocco does not qualify as a loving husband or even a clever one. The test is also powerful, creating what Shell calls "[in a] legal sense, a castrate" (in Bloom, *William Shakespeare's* The Merchant of Venice 113). When Morocco learns of his failure, he leaves in grief, banished forever to bachelorhood, where he can never have a legal heir—a heavy penalty in this property-revering world.

Arragon is even more foolish in his casket selection, considering only the inscriptions and not the caskets themselves. In his single scene, he dismisses the lead casket because it must "look fairer ere I give or hazard" (2.9.21) and rejects the gold because he does not wish to be counted among the "common spirits ... the barbarous multitudes" (2.9.31–32) who desire Portia. As he considers the silver casket ("Who chooseth me, shall get as much as he deserves"), he is distracted, ruminates on honor given to the undeserving, "the chaff and ruin of the times" (2.9.47), and concludes quickly, "I will assume desert" (2.9.50). Along with a blinking idiot's head, the casket contains a message: "Take what wife you will to bed" (2.9.69). Shell observes that as a white Christian, Arragon is not penalized as harshly as Morocco and is "allowed to try to generate kin in wedlock" (in Bloom, 113).

Clearly both suitors are foils to the third, "a Venetian, a scholar and a soldier," the "best deserving a fair lady" (1.2.92–93, 97).

SOLANIO, SALARINO, AND SALERIO

Solanio, Salarino, and perhaps Salerio have encouraged more scholarly textual study than critical evaluation of their roles. This is because their names change among and within various editions, so editors must determine whether Shakespeare intended two or three characters and what specific names they should possess. John Dover Wilson is the first modern editor to collapse the three characters into two, Salerio and Solanio. When Salerio arrives in Venice in Act 3 with the bad news of Antonio's forfeited bond, Wilson argues that he is really Salarino (or Salerino), who first appears in the opening scene, because of his familiarity with Antonio. The New Arden editor, John Russell Brown, argues convincingly that Salerio and Salarino are one because the name is spelled *Salerino* five times. The New Cambridge editor, J. J. Mahood, argues for three individual characters because Shakespeare often used similar names for different characters and added characters for minor parts played by actors who doubled and even tripled several roles anyway.[19] In the Oxford edition (1993), Jay Halio follows the practice of Mahood.

In any case, this argument is more lively than any discussion of these characters' functions. Even though one perhaps talks more than the other when two appear together, they provide news to other characters and to the audience. The two Venticellis in the twentieth-century play *Amadeus,* by Peter Shaffer, perform a similar function. Their names may be translated as "little winds," and they pass along gossip and information and offer choric commentary that keeps the plot moving. Perhaps in *MV* as well, the similarity in the names of the three Sallies mute their individuality, so their comments provide no more than tonal background for the plot.

SHYLOCK

If *The Merchant of Venice* is Shakespeare's second most frequently performed play, then the presence of Shylock is the main reason. Although he appears in only five scenes and speaks only about 360 lines, he is arguably the most memorable character in all Shakespeare's comedies. This is the case even though Portia is the main character of the play and Antonio the merchant of the title. Indeed, Shylock's very name,[20] evolved into a pejorative noun in the general vocabulary, has grown more famous than the name of the play itself. But troublingly, despite the play's layers of irony, Shylock, the murderous Jew—some commentators would argue murderous *because* he is a Jew—raises questions of whether the play itself is anti-Semitic.

Yet Shylock's villainy alone is not what makes him memorable. What is it then? In a word, ambiguity: both his own energetic ambiguity and the resulting ambiguity we feel toward him. He is a villain, a Jew, hoping to kill a Christian; but we cannot avoid recognizing his motivation. We see him cunningly plot to ensnare Antonio, but we also see Venice's hypocrisy and bigotry, loud and blatant, surrounding and trapping him. The Venetians mock him and then ask his help; they use him for funding their businesses and then disdain his profit. Besides this, Shylock lives in virtual isolation from the Venetians, seemingly by choice.[21] We sense that their scorn has driven him away, and we can sympathize with his sense of separation. Finally, we enjoy the energy and irony of his often cruel words, and we pity his grief for his dead wife and his anguish over his ungrateful daughter. Thus, along with our revulsion for his unbending cruelty, paradoxically we do not entirely lose sympathy or respect for him. This remains unsettling. And on top of all this, we are unsure of how we should respond to the anti-Semitism of the characters—who may include Portia, the heroine of the play, as well as the Venetians who, misguided by mercantilism as they may be, are among those redeemed in Act 5. In any case, Shylock, the Jew, is a would-be murderer and a villain. This fact tantalizingly leads us to ask whether Shylock is presented as a Semitic anomaly or whether his villainy derives from his Jewishness, a condition that would make Shakespeare's play anti-Semitic.

To sort out all this, we first must look at Shylock as the conventional villain who, in the end, must be separated from the group;[22] and second, we must consider him as the suffering malcontent who fails to be contained within his role, almost as if he were self-generating, enlarging beyond the conventions of the two-dimensional villain.[23] Then, we should examine the anti-Semitism that infects not only the characters but the setting of Venice itself.[24] Finally, we need to consider that Shylock's unique villainy, so enmeshed with his Jewishness, is caused by his alien state—his Otherness—which feeds his obsession with revenge. When a society scapegoats and abuses the Other, there will arise dangerous consequences.[25]

Shylock is a comic antagonist, unfestive and ungenerous, who tries unsuccessfully to block the good fortunes of the protagonists and is banished but not killed in the end, since this is comedy and not tragedy.[26] He also derives in part from the prototypic villains, Judas and the Devil, who are characters in early English mystery plays—medieval dramas that depict stories from the Bible.[27] Onstage, these early characters wore distinctive bright red wigs and perhaps beards. In *The Jew of Malta,* Marlowe's Jew, Barabas, wore such a wig and beard as well as a bottlenose in productions first performed just a few years before *MV,* and almost certainly Shylock wore them too. Besides this, Shylock refers to his long coat or "Jewish gaberdine" (1.3.104), which, Irving Ribner observes, may have been a "conventional costume for Jews in Elizabethan theatres" (255).[28] These costume elements encouraged Elizabethan audiences in their association of Shylock and Jews with the devil. Nondramatic medieval mythic stories also portrayed the Jew as devil, an evil being who poisoned wells, crucified Christian children, and drank their blood in secret rituals (Gross 26–27).[29]

Since the Jew was commonly seen as the agent of the devil, and onstage he looked very much like the devil, he could then serve as the evil tempter whose goal is the destruction of Christians. In his first scene, Shylock behaves as such an evil tempter. First, he negotiates with Bassanio over the terms of the bond, using exaggerated, repetitious language that verges on the comic:

SHYLOCK   Three thousand ducats, well.

BASSANIO   Ay, sir, for three months.

SHYLOCK   For three months, well.

BASSANIO   For the which, as I told you, Antonio shall be bound.

SHYLOCK   Antonio shall become bound, well.
  (1.3.1–5)

He continues, perhaps falsely pretending slow, plodding thought, or, as John Gross suggests, "a need to tabulate and enumerate to keep a tight grip on reality and underline what he means" (66). Through repetition, Shylock's spoken thoughts almost become a parody of logical thought. But just before Antonio enters, Shylock strikingly changes his tone, adding a parallelism that brings a powerful and almost frightening conclusion to the interchange: "I will buy with you, sell with you, talk with you, walk with you, and so following; but I will not eat with you, drink with you, nor pray with you" (1.3.28–30). His rhetorical style follows a drumbeat rhythm, and his dictates are unyielding.

In a rare aside, Shylock next discloses his obsessive motives for the hatred he harbors for Antonio. In this, E. E. Stoll says that Shakespeare "is at pains to label the villain . . . at the moment the hero appears on the boards" (265). We can list his complaints against Antonio, which he murmurs in the 11 lines of his first aside (1.3.33–43):

1. "I hate him for he is a Christian;"
2. " . . . in low simplicity / He lends out money gratis, and brings down / The rate of usance here with us in Venice."
3. "If I can catch him once upon the hip / I will feed fat the ancient grudge I bear him,"
4. "He hates our sacred nation,"

5. " . . . he rails" against me, my business, and my wealth in public.
6. "Cursed be my tribe / If I forgive him!"

Interestingly, although Shylock is the antagonist, we hear his motivations before we see his real villainy, a device that encourages audience sympathy. And his motivations both condemn and explain him. His first three complaints betray his own bias, greed, and vengefulness; but his final three complaints describe Antonio's animosity, which is then demonstrated in the following interchange. Antonio self-righteously claims never to take or pay interest, insults Shylock as "a goodly apple rotten at the heart" (1.3.93) and arrogantly admits to spitting at and spurning Shylock in the Rialto.

Yet soon Shylock entraps Antonio as the devil might, duplicitously tricking him into defeat with the appearance of innocence. Disingenuously, he claims that he does not have the 3,000 ducats and must borrow them from Tubal, and then he seems to contradict himself as he departs, saying that he will "go and purse the ducats straight" (1.3.167). Later, Jessica also finds untold numbers of ducats lying around the house as well as one small jewel worth 2,000 ducats, which she steals that night. Shylock seduces Antonio with false humility, claiming, "I would be friends with you, and have your love / Forget the shames that you have stained me with." And he markets his pound of flesh bond as an interest-free "merry sport" saying, " I would . . . supply your present wants, and take no doit / Of usance for my monies" (1.3.131–33). Antonio is ensnared. "I'll seal to such a bond, and say there is much kindness in the Jew" (145–46).

Shylock remains a passionate, irrational villain throughout the play. In 3.1, after he hears of the serendipity of Antonio's losses striking at the same time as his own loss of Jessica and his ducats, Salarino and Solanio question him, doubting his demands for Antonio's flesh. Shylock replies with his "Hath not a Jew eyes?" speech, an argument justifying his revenge, which, he boasts, will be even more destructive than Christian revenge. But in the course of the argument, he unwittingly condemns himself: Jews indeed have eyes, hands, organs, dimensions, senses, affections (sensory inclinations), and passions as Christians do; like Christians, Jews feel hunger, suffer injury, fall ill and become cured, sense warmth and cold, bleed, laugh from tickling, die from poison, and seek revenge. But although this list of similarities between Jews and Christians is lengthy, it fails to include those similarities of the mind and soul from which emanate virtue, compassion, and mercy. It is the qualities of humanness, which Shylock omits from his list, that damn him. In a speech in the courtroom, Shylock similarly explains that he seeks Antonio's flesh rather than the 3,000 ducats because it is his "humour" to do so (4.1.43). He explains an uncontrollable urge, a compulsion governed by the senses. Some people grow mad at the sight of a gaping pig or a cat; others cannot hold their urine at the sound of bagpipes; and he has such a response to Antonio. Again Shylock ignores the higher human responses and ironically, unintentionally, accuses himself of behaving in a beast-like way.

All this straightforward villainy hardly explains, however, why he develops a humanity that grows beyond the confines of the comic antagonist conventions. We are unable to hate him. Sometimes we enjoy him, and we never entirely lose sympathy for him. Scene 1.3 offers a firsthand illustration of the sort of bigotry he has lived with in Venice. The Venetians are arrogant, self-righteous, and regularly cruel. Later, in 3.1, after Jessica has left, the generic Venetians, Solanio and Salarino, meet him and boast that they indeed had known that Jessica was planning to run away. Solanio adds offhandedly, "I for my part knew the tailor that made the wings she flew withal" (3.1.22–23). The two men even mock Shylock's sexuality: "Out upon it, old carrion. Rebels it at these years?" (3.1.29). Shylock continues without acknowledging, or perhaps even noticing, the insult. "I say my daughter is my flesh and blood" (3.1.28–30), he answers. They continue to jeer him ruthlessly, even at this time of obvious grief: "There is more difference between thy flesh and hers than between jet and ivory," Salarino says (3.1.31–32). Sitting in the audience, we may join Shylock in wishing for some revenge.

Later in the scene, we have further reason to sympathize with him. He speaks alone with Tubal, who tells Shylock news of his daughter and of Antonio's losses. As a comic villain, Shylock reacts to the "good" news of Antonio's lost ships and the bad news of Jessica's wasting money with responses that swing widely between joy and despair. At first, the variation and the repetition of language have a comic effect. When Tubal tells Shylock that Antonio's creditors agree that he "cannot choose but break," Shylock is delighted: "I am very glad of it. I'll plague him, I'll torture him. I am glad of it" (3.1.91–92). But finally, Tubal tells him that one of the creditors showed him a turquoise ring he received from Jessica in trade for a monkey. For a moment, all humor is lost; Shylock is horrified: "Out upon her! Thou torturest me, Tubal: it was my turquoise, I had it of Leah when I was a bachelor. I would not have given it for a wilderness of monkeys" (3.1.95–97). He grieves for his wife and for a daughter who thoughtlessly tosses away both him and her mother on giddy impulse.[30] The comic villain then is more than that. He is entirely alone, set apart from his dead wife, his ungrateful child, and a society that despises him. He will revenge all his losses in the final certain destruction of Antonio, who is a symbol, a representative of all that has hurt him. Harold Goddard contends that Shylock "had in him at least a grain of spiritual gold, of genuine Christian spirit," and if Portia and Antonio "had watered this tiny seed," a "miracle" might have taken place (in Bloom, *Shylock* 35)—a position entirely opposed to that of Stoll, who is certain that Shylock was always intended as the villain. That Shylock has reason for his hatred does not lessen his cruelty but forces our horror of him to ebb and flow so we can never settle on condemnation.

This brings us to the anti-Semitism in Shylock's world. No one denies its presence, although Bernard Grebanier is among a minority in his argument that "far too much has been made of Shylock's being Jewish" and that Gratiano "is the only real anti-Semite in the play" (in Bloom, *Shylock* 21). D. M. Cohen notes "seventy-four direct uses of *Jew* and unambiguously related words in the play," a label that separates the character from other humans and dwarfs the 17 direct addresses to the person who is Shylock (54). The inferiority of the Jew is even implied in Doctor Bellario's letter referring to "the Jew and Antonio" (4.1.56). Name calling is rife. In his opening scene, Lancelot says of Shylock that "the Jew is the very devil incarnation" (2.2.20–21), and he is frequently called a "dog," a "cur," and a "wolf." We hear of Antonio mocking him and spitting on him, and we witness the ugly name calling by Solanio and Salerio after Jessica has abandoned him.

The reasons for such bias are of course cultural, nationalistic, religious, and I wish to argue, economic. The Christians of Venice ostensibly hate Jews because, so the polemic goes, Jews killed Christ. James Shapiro contends that in sixteenth-century England, the separation and denigration of Jews served a more nationalistic purpose in helping to draw not a religious boundary around Christians but rather a patriotic boundary around those who were English, "by pointing to those who were assuredly not—e.g., the Irish or the Jews" (5). But in Shakespeare's Venice, as in London, anti-Semitism also serves an economic function. In Venice, success and peace are dependent on the orderly transaction of business. All the major characters in the play agree that this is the goal of government. Antonio says that for the Duke to deny the power of the state and grant him mercy "will much impeach the justice of the state" (3.3.29); Shylock claims in court that the Duke's intervention will "let the danger light / Upon your charter and your city's freedom!" (4.1.38–39); and Portia/Balthazar concludes that "there is no power in Venice / Can alter a decree established" (4.1.214–15). Property rights, not human rights, are transcendent; contract law cannot be whimsically altered, as Shylock himself argues in court:

You have among you many a purchased slave,
Which, like your asses and your dogs and mules,
You use in abject and in slavish parts
Because you bought them. (4.1.90–93)

Just as the law gives property rights to Venetians to purchase, hold, and use slaves, so the law gives Shylock property rights to purchase, hold, and use Antonio's flesh. It is his; it belongs to him to do with as he wishes.

But Shylock does not fully understand the law. Although he thinks it exists to administer justice in support of property rights—the acquisition of wealth and power—in fact, it administers justice (i.e., success) to the conceivers of the law—in this case, the Venetians—and to the mercantile activity that is conducive to their success. That is why aliens may enter into contracts with Venetians. If they could not do this, Venetians would find it far more difficult to accumulate profits from transactions with non-Venetians, including any of Portia's suitors or any Jewish creditors.

Granted, Shylock's bond appears to protect him, the alien creditor, and punish the delinquent Venetian debtor. But if it really did, it would fail to promote Venetian wealth. Therefore, the bond cannot be enforced, even though nearly everyone agrees that somehow the law must be followed for the good of the state. Antonio notes that the court cannot show him mercy by denying Shylock his penalty because that would create skepticism among alien traders in the city. It would hurt business. The laws that Portia cites form the basis on which Venetian justice is served.

The city's ethics, then, are based on the goal of Venetian wealth. Anti-Semitism does not intrude on that goal; in fact, ugly as it is, anti-Semitism benefits the goal. The individual Jew is a member of a minority or weaker group who assists the majority in becoming more wealthy, as do the slaves Shylock ironically mentions or the alien warriors like Othello who fight Venice's battles. When members of weaker groups justifiably feel unfairly treated, they are labeled malcontents or annoying complainers, unable to fit in and succeed with the powerful. But the game has unfair rules that disallow success to minority groups. Thus anti-Semitism is a part of the stacked deck in Venice. Winners are handicapped in their efforts to continue winning even more; the powerless must remain losers who complain, strike back, and suffer condemnation and finally exile.

The final vexing problem remains, however, that Shakespeare's play may seem to condone the anti-Semitism of Venice and therefore itself be anti-Semitic. That would mean that Shylock's badness is unique among the play's characters and that the play anoints him as the representative of all Jews, since Tubal appears only briefly and Jessica converts to Christianity. C. L. Barber writes that Shylock embodies the evil side of the power of money, "its ridiculous and pernicious consequences in anxiety and destructiveness" (167). But this holds true for all the characters in Venice; both Shylock and the Christians are motivated to act on bias and greed, although often ineffectively. Gratiano implies that he understands his own powerlessness to act on his blustering, biased threats; and in his opening scene, Shylock likewise grudgingly accepts that he has little power to act on his bias against Antonio and the Christians. He knows that Antonio's ships regularly reach shore, witness the merchant's understood wealth; as a result, the bond is for Shylock only a fleeting opportunity for control over the merchant, and its pound-of-flesh forfeit no more than a glorious fantasy with only a glimmer of hope of becoming reality.

Similarly, Shylock's greedy desire for money differs little from that of the Venetians, although the Venetians typically accept more risk. To gain wealth, Bassanio risks his progeny; Antonio, "all [his] fortunes" (1.1.176); Lorenzo, a presumed felony arrest; and Jessica, capture by her father. Shylock implies that, at worst, usury can sometimes be a difficult business; it is "well-won thrift" (1.3.42) but promises greater gain after the elimination of Antonio.

At the turning point in 3.1, however, when he seeks aggressive violence, Shylock's evil exceeds that of the Christians. Barber writes that Shylock is "the opposite of what the Venetians are; but at the same time he is an embodied irony, troublingly like them" (168). I would add, however, that he is "opposite" only after the point in the plot when he hopes to destroy Antonio legally with his own hand. Shylock recognizes that he has the chance to successfully gain a murderous revenge some time during 3.1. At first, he tells Solanio and Salarino, "my daughter is my flesh and my blood," and he disdains his "bad match" with Antonio, a "beggar that was used to come so smug upon the mart" (3.1.30, 36–37). Then, putting these facts together, he warns three times, "Let him look to his bond" (3.1.37–41). He promises to "plague [Antonio], torture him, [be] glad of it" (3.1.91–92) and "have the heart of him if he forfeit" (3.1.100–101). He *shall* be violent, because with Antonio's bankruptcy, he *can* be. And this is his singular goal until he is brought down in court. His planned violence sets him apart from the others. Portia supports this in court when she cites the all-inclusive protectionist law that grants revenge to Venetians for threats from aliens who, "by direct or indirect attempts" seek the life of a citizen (4.1.346–47)—a recognition of Shylock's violence.

In his pathetic exit, Shylock is both knave and fool. He does not understand what was all along the precariousness of his position. Venetian justice would not have been served with Shylock's blood or even the transfer of all his wealth to the state. What does serve Venice is the bequest of Shylock's assets to a private individual, namely, Jessica's Christian husband, Lorenzo; Antonio's unforgettably ugly twist of a forced Christian conversion on Shylock, which cruelly denies him a livelihood; and finally, the happy result for all the citizens of Venice—presumably cheaper credit.

Most controversial, however, is whether Shylock behaves with violence because he is a Jew. Rather than labeling his violence as a convention of the generic villain or romantically justifying his actions as the consequence of mean-spirited Venetian bias, Cohen assesses him as "a complete and unredeemed villain whose wickedness is a primary trait. . . . reinforced by the fact of his Jewishness, which to make the wickedness so much the worse, is presented as synonymous with it" (59). If Jewishness were synonymous with wickedness, that would indeed make the play anti-Semitic. The characters' insistence on the label "Jew" and their association of the word with Shylock's various unsavory qualities support Cohen's position. But strictly speaking, this is evidence only of anti-Semitism among the characters themselves and may sully only their virtue and good sense.

More telling is the association in the play between Shylock's viciousness—his desire for the blood—with his unsought role as the Other. He is so alienated, so completely scorned, that, like other living things, he is left with nothing but the instinct to strike back. The inevitability, the naturalness, of striking back, the pleasure in the fantasy of colossal revenge, belongs to neither Jews nor Christians; it belongs to the injured. By the close of the turning-point scene, 3.1, Shylock has been abused, mocked, and overwhelmed with news from Tubal of Jessica's improvidence and Antonio's losses. Almost impulsively, he makes a grand plan: he will have Antonio arrested; he will "have his heart" and be free to "make what merchandise" he will (3.1.100–101). To do this, he tells Tubal to meet him "at our synagogue," repeating "at our synagogue" a second time (3.1.102–103). This is his retreat. Like a powerless child—like any of us—Shylock gains comfort in his own place where he can muster the strength to attack those who abuse him, with a fantasy violence. The passion in this overwhelming response cannot be overestimated, nor has it been unknown in the hearts of the audience.

But it does mean that the powerful must keep to the task of distracting, calming, or containing the powerless. If the powerless are foolish, like Gratiano, they can be duped into believing that they too share the wealth. Gratiano has no wealth, gains no wealth, and has no power, but the hegemony of the wealthy convinces him that he fits in anyway. If the powerless, like Jessica, are attractive, they can become domesticated pets of the powerful who offer their conscience-soothing, token acceptance. Jessica's marriage to Lorenzo and her laudable wifely affection imply that she will live easily among the Christians. But Jessica's marriage also suggests that, in this world, the only good Jew is one who has converted to Christianity. Finally, if the powerless are clever and angry, like Shylock, they must be outsmarted, contained, and banished.

Shylock is a malcontent grown malignant. Because of his wit, he looms far more fearsome than the less dangerous Malvolio in *Twelfth Night*. But like Malvolio, Shylock has neither the easy sociability nor the heritage to fit comfortably within the powerful group. Shylock's passion deludes him into trusting the law. And like Malvolio, Shylock does not understand the law's equivocation and wrongly assumes that the law will treat him with equity, that the playing field is even. Neither Malvolio nor Shylock realizes that his cries of injustice are bootless, that his troubles and complaints are not affective. The pain of the powerless must go unrecognized by those who place acquisition at the top of their moral hierarchy. Ironically, Shylock accepts such a hierarchy as enthusiastically as everyone else does.

NOTES

1. For a discussion of the romantic plot in MV, see Catherine Belsey, "Love in Venice," in *New Casebooks : The Merchant of Venice*, ed. Martin Coyle (New York: St. Martins Press, 1998), 139–160. Belsey calls Portia "the fairytale princess, the sacrificial virgin, the 'unlessoned girl,' the 'lord of her mansion',," and someone who enjoys "sexual multiplicity" (148–49).

2. Leslie Fiedler, not an admirer of the Christians in either Venice or Belmont, claims that Portia "is almost always lying . . . when she is not performing character assassination, talking courtly smut, or indulging in empty platitudes" ["The Jew as Stranger: Or These Be the Christian Husbands," in Harold Bloom's introduction to *William Shakespeare's* The Merchant of Venice (New York: Chelsea House, 1986), 86].

3. See Belsey for a discussion of riddles as devices that exploit "the duplicity of the signifier, the secret alterity that subsists in meaning" ("Love in Venice" 143–50).

4. This music may serve as a metaphor for his victory or loss, as Portia claims; or perhaps, as some readers suggest, the lyrics of the song may offer prearranged clues that she has wittily devised. Clearly, she is capable of such a scheme; and ethically, it fulfills her father's dictates, or at least it does not break his rules. First there is the "bred" / "Head"/ "nourishd" rhyme that may lead Basssanio to the *lead* casket (3.2.63–65); see A. H. Fox-Strangeways, *Times Literary Supplement* (July 12, 1923), 472. Second is the content of the song itself, which instructs that foolish fancy, engendered and fed only through the eye, is superficial and "dies in

the cradle where it lies" (3.2.68–69); see John Weiss, *Wit and Humour in Shakespeare* (1876), 312.

5. For an explanation of the discovery of the song's clues, see M. M. Mahood *The Merchant of Venice,* New Cambridge Shakespeare (Cambridge: Cambridge University Press 1987), 115 n. 66.

6. See Lawrence Danson, *The Harmonies of* The Merchant of Venice (New Haven, Conn.: Yale University Press), 19–55, for a discussion of love and gift giving as described by Seneca.

7. The casket selection is one of the few Shakespearean plots to which Freud refers extensively. In "The Theme of the Three Caskets" (in Bloom 1986), Freud argues that Bassanio, like Lear, faces a choice from among three females, the most desirable being the third. This third woman is mute, a representation of death who is, in fact, a replacement for the "exact opposite" of what she seems.

8. See Leslie Fiedler, "The Jew as Stranger: Or 'These Be the Christian Husbands,'" in *The Stranger in Shakespeare* (New York: Stein and Day, 1972), 85–136 : also in Bloom, *William Shakespeare's* The Merchant of Venice, Modern Critical Interpretations (New York: Chelsea House, 1986), 63–90, for an opposing argument that neither Portia's "morality nor her deepest faith are Christian" (87). Fiedler says that Portia's speech on mercy is an example of "pieties too familiar to be taken quite as truth" and that it is filled with "saccharine banalities. . . . What moves her—and kills Shylock—is hedonism, the pleasure principle" (86–87).

9. See Catherine Belsey, "Love in Venice," for a discussion of the relationship of desire, risk, and riddles.

10. Although for more than 200 years directors have considered Act 5 superfluous and often have chosen to delete it, and critics like Leslie Fiedler have labeled the ring plot "pure farce, though only Portia realizes the fact" ("The Jew as Stranger" in Bloom, 1986, 89), Act 5 is vestigial only if the production becomes a conflict between Shylock and the biased indulgent world of Venice, a limited interpretation of the play.

11. Belsey identifies the riddle of the ring as *amphibology,* a category of equivocation identified by the Renaissance rhetorician George Puttenham in *The Arte of English Poesie* (1589). Puttenham condemns it because it emanates from oracles, pagan prophets, or witches and makes truth impossible to discover.

12. An eiron and an alazon are a conventional comic pair of characters in New Greek comedy. The alazon is loud and foolishly arrogant, while the eiron tempers his partner's brashness with more quiet, practical sense. Contemporary examples of such comic pairs are Oliver Hardy and Stan Laurel, Ralph Kramden and Ed Norton, and Archie and Edith Bunker.

13. *Manna* is honeyed wafer-like food God provided the fleeing Israelites for 40 years in the wilderness after they escaped from Egypt into Israel (Exodus 16). The irony of Lorenzo's Old Testament analogy comparing God's help to the Jews fleeing slavery in Egypt to Shylock's involuntary help to his son-in-law and daughter fleeing his house cannot be ignored.

14. For a discussion of the traits of the natural and artificial clown or fool, see Vicki Janik, introduction to *Fools, Clowns, and Jesters in Literature, Art, and History* (Westport, Conn.: Greenwood Press, 1998), 1–40.

15. See Marc Shell, "The Wether and the Ewe: Verbal Usury," for a discussion of using money and sex to generate wealth and life as well as using words to generate multiple meanings (in Bloom 107–120).

16. Joseph Pequiney takes a middle position in which he identifies characteristics that mark the relationship between Sebastian and Antonio in *Twelfth Night* as being homoerotic and explains that because these characteristics do not occur in the love between Antonio and Bassanio, they share a nonsexual love; see "The Two Antonios and Same-Sex Love in *Twelfth Night* and *The Merchant of Venice*," in *Shakespeare and Gender: A History,* eds. Deboarah Barker and Ivo Kamps (London: Verso, 1995), 178–90.

17. See the section titled "Love and Friendship" in Chapter 5 of this guide.

18. Danson, 50–55, discusses the varieties of giving in the Renaissance, particularly as explained in *De Beneficiis* by Seneca, one of the most highly regarded classical authors of the period.

19. For a more detailed discussion of the three "Sallie's," see Chapter 2 in this guide.

20. Jay Halio includes a useful summary of contending theories of the origin of the name Shylock in the Oxford edition of *MV* (n. 23). Halio concludes that because other names in the play are biblical, the "more likely" derivation is from Sheleph, Shelah, or Shelach, the grandson of Shem, great-grandson of Noah (Gen. 10:26). Tubal is the son of Japheth and grandson of Noah; Leah is the first wife of Jacob; and Jessica derives from Iscah, Abraham's niece. See also Hermann Sinsheimer, *The History of a Character,* 87, and Brown, *MV,* New Arden edition, 3.

21. In fact, the Jews of Venice in the sixteenth century lived in ghettos, two islands known as the Ghetto Nuevo, or New Foundry, and the Ghetto Vecchio, or Old Ghetto; see John Gross, *Shylock: A Legend and Its Legacy* (New York: Simon and Schuster, 1992), 35–40.

22. See C. L. Barber, *Shakespeare's Festive Comedy: A Study of Dramatic Form and Its Relation to Social Custom* (1959; repr. Cleveland and New York: Meridian, 1963) 164–91, for a full explanation of Shylock as the comic "ogre" (169). See Northrop Frye, *A Natural Perspective: The Development of Shakespearean Comedy and Romance* (New York: Harcourt, 1965), for discussion of Shylock as the "supporter of the irrational law" (133).

23. See Stoll, "Shylock," in *Shakespeare Studies: Historical and Comparative in Method* (1925; repr. New York: Frederick Ungar, 1960), 255–336, and Gross 27. For similar arguments, see John Palmer, "Shylock," in *Shakespeare:* The Merchant of Venice: *A Casebook,* ed. John Wilders (1969; repr. Nashville: Aurora, 1970), 114–131; Harold C. Goddard, *"The Merchant of Venice,"* in *The Meaning of Shakespeare* (Chicago: University of Chicago Press, 1951), 81–116.

24. See Gross, 105–352, for a historical perspective on anti-Semitism in Europe and the European and American theater.

25. Strong arguments for anti-Semitism in the play are made by Derek Cohen in "The Jew and Shylock," *Shakespeare Quarterly,* 31 (1980): 53–63, and Bloom, 1–5.

26. See C. L. Barber, 163–191, for a discussion of Shylock as the blocking character—the intruder among the celebrants in the play—who remains its most fascinating character as he was as early as 1598 when the play was alternately called *The Jew of Venice* in the Stationers' Register.

27. See Stoll, 255–336, and Gross, 27.

28. Although Jews were not legally allowed to live in England, in Spain Jews were required to wear full-length cloaks, while other countries required other distinctive dress.

29. See Gross, "Where Does He Come From?" in *Shylock,* 15–30, for a detailed discussion of cultural and literary origins of the Jew as devil.

30. Leo Kirschbaum observed that Shylock's love for his wife "blackens by contrast his inhumanity all the more" (qtd. in Cohen 59).

5

THEMES

The themes in *The Merchant of Venice,* the questions discovered in the play that we might also ask about our own experience, are questions not explicitly stated in the lines but rather suggested by a number of the play's elements. These elements include the events of the plot and the ways they unfold; the nature of the settings; the behavior of the characters; the particular words and sentences spoken; and the play's genre, which serves as the lens through which we view the play's world—the focus set to reveal some combination of comic, tragic, ironic, and romantic visions. For example, the luminescence of a warm and starry night, which is the setting in the final act of *MV,* raises very different questions from the darkness of the cold and mysterious night when the ghost walks in *Hamlet.* Or we may discover questions in language; the variations on "cutthroat dog" used in references to Shylock force us to consider the possible villainy of Shylock juxtaposed against the possible viciousness of the speakers. These dramatic elements—genre, setting, dramatic structure, characters, and language—develop the drama's themes.

Because themes take the form of inquiry, not aphoristic statement, the chapter raises questions about the play as comedy; the values inherent in Venice and Belmont; the nature of the play's anti-Semitism; the qualities of friendship and romantic love; and finally, the play's images of religion, the Bible, justice, and mercy. Many commentators argue that *MV* contains contrasts or oppositions; therefore, the questions about the play often seek an equilibrium or, more challengingly, a blending of or relationship between these supposed opposites—reality and appearance, acquisition and

charity, justice and mercy, Christian hate and Shylock's revenge, or Shylock's hate and Christian revenge.

THE PLAY AS COMEDY

Because *MV* is framed by its tone and genre, we begin by establishing
the play's roots in Tudor romantic comedy. Questions of Bassanio's constancy, Antonio's bias, Portia's mercy, or Shylock's humanity depend on
genre to frame our shifting joyous, ironic, or sometimes troubling responses. Although Aristotle has much to say about tragedy in *Poetics,*
his discussion of comedy is meager. Editors theorize that Aristotle is repeating a fragment from a longer lost analysis when he writes that comedy is "an imitation of lower types though it does not include the full
range of badness" (23). Aristotle continues that comic plots may include
errors and disgraces, deformity and distortion, that lead to laughter but
"not accompanied by pain or injury," and he further notes that comedy
evolved from the Sicilian fable structure, which contained a single unified story and was first used in Athens by Crates (23). Nevill Coghill argues that the "classic definition" of comedy by Vincent de Beauvais in
Speculum Maius (vol. ii, book iii), written in 1250, contains "the true
basis of Shakespearian Comedy: 'Comedy is a kind of poem which
transforms a sad beginning into a happy ending'" (204).[1] The description of comedy as "a tale of trouble that turns to joy" (204) describes, at
least on the surface, Shakespeare's romantic plays, which are different
from the satiric comedy of social commentary written by Ben Jonson.
Shakespeare's comedies partially derive from the Roman New Comedy
of Plautus and Terence but center less on wily trickery than on the ten-
derness of love.[2] The stories often begin in melancholy, as Vincent de
Beauvais's description states; the exposition makes clear that a frustrated young man is seeking his ladylove. Unfortunately, he is plagued
by a society or a family that blocks his desires, usually because of their
biases against his poverty, her youth or low birth, the families' opposition and bigotry to one another, or the demands of another current, unacceptable lover. Contrasting or parallel sets of other would-be lovers are
similarly but less oppressively blocked from marrying. By the end of the
play, love triumphs and festivity begins, promising or celebrating one or
more marriages among the drama's young and fertile couples. Much of
this foundation plot occurs in *MV.* Noting that Ben Jonson calls the end
of a tragedy a catastrophe, a turning down, Northrop Frye calls this
comic ending an "anastrophe, a turning up rather than a turning down"
(72–73).

In the introduction to the New Cambridge edition, M. M. Mahood further classifies *MV* as a Renaissance romantic comedy, a genre that had become highly popular in the two decades before Shakespeare wrote the play. Romantic comedy portrays love and virtue triumphing over evil, a common story line of medieval romances, short stories of the Italian Renaissance, and many English plays like *MV* written after 1570. Romantic comedies follow several conventions that became popular on the public stage: characters like Bassanio experience love as "an ennobling experience" (Mahood 9) rather than as a series of misadventures; wit and silliness are infrequent; language is often sententious; the plot follows a very clear story line and often includes disguise; the heroine is an almost allegorical image of loyalty and love; and settings are often real places. Jay Halio further points out that Shakespeare's handling of romantic comedy "is not without its darker elements," as the assumed death and threat of death in *Much Ado About Nothing* and *A Midsummer Night's Dream* demonstrate (10–11). *The Merchant of Venice* includes or is inspired by all these conventions.

English mystery, morality, and miracle plays influenced the early modern romantic comedy genre of *MV*. Mystery plays dramatize biblical stories that are cast with both heroic Jews from the Old Testament and the red-bearded, red-haired, bottle-nosed Judas, the Christ killer of the New Testament, with whom Lancelot associates Shylock, "the very devil incarnation" (2.2.20–21). Together these characters inspired in the Christian audience a paradoxical image of Jews. In addition, miracle plays, depicting Christian miracles, include Jews, who are the villains inspiring God's miracles. The fifteenth-century drama *The Play of the Sacrament* depicts "the Conversyon of Ser Jonathas the Jewe by Myracle of the Blyssed Sacrament" (242) when his amputated hand is restored and he is christened and promises "to kepe Crystis lawe /And to serue the Father, the Son & the Holy Gost" (275).[3] The morality play, or moral interlude, popular from the late fifteenth century well into the sixteenth century, presents an allegorical Everyman hero tempted by an allegorical spiritual villain, the generic Vice, perhaps the most memorable character convention of English moralities. He assails the hero with enticements and bombast, serving as a treacherous, often farcical villain. David Bevington recalls that the Vice, although never identified as Jewish, is a source for Marlowe's Barabas: "The Vice has been secularized in the person of Barabas" (225);[4] and Halio adds that the Vice further evolves, becoming "multidimensional . . . [and being] made to appear human" in the person of Shylock (9). Mahood suggests an influence from these genres on other elements of the play. She argues that Shakespeare makes changes from his source story, *Il Pecorone,* to add greater seriousness in the morality-miracle tradition, noting that Bassanio's casket selection ostensibly tests his morality far more than his courage or cunning; Portia's father has a god-like quality in his eternal influence over the living; and "benign powers" seem to protect the protagonists from an unsuccessful courtship. Finally, Shakespeare's replacement of *Il Pecorone*'s bawdy bed test with the more moralistic casket test heightens the morality-miracle play influence, even though the inscription on the lead casket secularizes its more religious prototype in *Gesta Romanorum,* the casket plot source.

Intermixed with these serious native plot elements, conventions from Italian comedy highlight the Jessica and Lorenzo subplot. In both extant and lost plays, George Gascoigne, Antony Munday, and undoubtedly other dramatists followed such traditions, which at least in part were popularized in Italian *commedia dell'arte.*[5] Such *commedia* plots conventionally take place in the city, where pairs of young would-be suitors and their clever and courageous ladies triumph over the older people with the sort of trickery, disguise, and confidence. Shakespeare himself had already written an Italian-inspired comedy in *The Taming of the Shrew,* but in *MV,* the Italian comic plot, planned by Jessica and executed by both her lover and her, echoes and varies the main plot, contrapuntally serving as its foil.

Although *MV* contains characteristics of the dramatic genres previously noted, C. L. Barber contends that it is modeled on something larger than drama or theater; it follows an archetypal pattern of human experience itself—saturnalian celebration, which Barber says is the pattern of all comedy.[6] Human societies regularly observe holidays, or carnivals, with wild, rule-breaking antics. These holidays are periodic and necessary prerequisites for reestablishing harmonious order and understanding. They create a pattern in life and art: from disorder to order, from uncontrolled to controlled, or in Barber's words, "through release to clarification" (4). Barber grants that *MV* is developed from traditions that are theatrical, but he finds in the play's archetypal structure many similarities to the forms of festivity in symbolic ritual (166), that is, the tension-release pattern of ritual. Because of celebration's requirement for both tension and release, complementary, opposing types of language and characters are used in the festive form, including "invocation and abuse, poetry and railing, romance and ridicule, and sets of opposing characters: revelers and kill-joys, wits and butts, insiders and intruders" (166). Barber says that the specific positive force represented by the characters in *MV* is "the beneficence of civilized wealth" (167), a gracious and courteous life led by a group of individuals who no longer seek money; and they are counterpoised against the butt, an intruder who covets wealth and gives to money a villainous power to destroy people and set them against one another. In *MV*, the butt is the source of tension, abuse, railing, and ridicule; but by Act 5, the victory of gracious wealth is demonstrated, says Barber, in the "noble magnificence and frolic at Belmont" and yields an ending with "so full an expression of harmony" that Shakespeare does not match it until the late romances. Indeed, he concludes, "no other final scene is so completely without irony about the joys it celebrates" (187).

Over the last 300 years, however, many readers and actors have questioned the unity of the play and its categorization as romantic comedy and have chosen Shylock rather than the lovers as the play's focus. Particularly during the nineteenth and into the twentieth centuries, readers have shown sympathy for Shylock and consequently have found the play dense with irony. In other words, what appears to be true on the surface—the harmony and joy of Belmont—is not real. Belmont is no reflection of the celestial harmony overhead on which Lorenzo and Jessica comment. This means that the play may be seen as ironic comedy that mocks rather than admires its protagonists. Harold Goddard sees in the play Shylock's humanity beset by Christian acts of revenge, the revenge Shylock cites as a model for his own: "If a Christian wrong a Jew, what should his sufferance be by Christian example? Why, revenge" (3.1.54–55). In the Act 4 trial scene, Christians exact a most cruel revenge against Shylock, confiscating Venice's most cherished commodity, money, and denying him the means to acquire more. Then they celebrate audaciously, forgetting Shylock but rejoicing in his wealth that will soon be their own. Goddard writes, "Shylock's conviction that Christianity and revenge are synonyms is confirmed" (111).[7] If the so-called joyous ending in Belmont is built on the misery of another human being, it is hardly a comic celebration of love.

Other modern readers do not find the play comic at all. They argue that the play condones the obvious bigotry of the characters and is therefore anti-Semitic. E. E. Stoll argues that the play condemns both Shylock and his religion;[8] therefore, he is the drama's villain. First, virtually all characters have something bad to say about him; and second, the first impressions we receive about Shylock through the testimony of others are negative. The characters deride and mock some of his behavior, like his cries over his daughter, even before we see it. Finally, in his first appearance as a scheming moneylender, Shylock professes his hatred for Christians. Stoll says that Shakespeare is "at pains to label the villain" (265). He notes that in the courtroom scene, "Shylock's disappointment is tragic to him, but good care is taken that it shall not be to us. Shakespeare is less intent on values than on the conduct and direction of our sympathies through the scene" (317). More than 60 years later, Harold Bloom agrees with Stoll, going so far as to say that the play is "at once a comedy of delightful sophistication and a vicious Christian slander against the Jews" (5).[9] Thus, even though the play derives from romantic comedy, for many readers it is neither comedy nor romance.

VENICE AND BELMONT

Venice and Belmont suggest to many readers the contrast between two opposing value systems: one driven by justice and business and the other by mercy and pleasure. Northrop Frye sees the two settings representationally. The first setting is the anticomic society, which sets up harsh, unbending, seemingly irrational rules for the characters with whom we sympathize. Often sexual activity is limited by these rules, which then challenge the desires of the juvenile leads (heroes) and ingenues (heroines). Venice is such an image of "social reality, the obstacles to our desires that we recognize in the world around us" (73–75).[10] The second setting, Belmont, is a new and festive society that crystallizes at the very end of the play, becoming a place where all participants get along. "It is a world," Frye says, "we want but seldom expect to see" (75). The world of Belmont may also be associated with what Frye calls the natural world, often a green and magical forest. While Belmont is not described as a green forest or woods, it does possess magic, moonlight, and music. Frye proposes that the Venice-Belmont dichotomy presents a "dialectic . . . worked out in an extremely elaborate imagery of worth and value" (143).

Barber also recognizes a central green world of freedom in comedy; in *MV*, it is Belmont, but he sees Belmont and Venice as contrasting images of wealth. Belmont illustrates the "beneficence of civilized wealth, the something-for-nothing which wealth gives to those who use it graciously to live together in a humanly knit group," while Venice represents the "anxieties about money and its power to set men at odds" (167).[11] Such concerns were of interest to 1590s Londoners, who, Barber notes, were experiencing an economic expansion and looked to Venice as a prototype of wealth and commerce (167).

With a more ironic perspective, W. H. Auden questions a dichotomy between a materialistic Venice and a virtuous and loving Belmont, because Venice and Belmont are "so different in character that to produce the play in a manner that will not blur this contrast and yet preserve a unity is very difficult" (221).[12] According to Auden, because Belmont is a "romantic fairy story world" that is incompatible with the "historical reality of money-making Venice," we cannot see the world of Belmont without questioning our natural attraction to it; therefore, Auden sees *MV* as an "unpleasant" play, certainly a problem play (221). He observes that the incompatibility of the two locations is illustrated in the difference in time, as it passes and as it is measured. Venice follows the socially regulated time of clock and calendars, while Belmont exists in the timelessness of the pastoral world.[13] For example, Bassanio leaves for Belmont the evening after Shylock and Antonio agree to the three-month loan. After his ferry ride to Belmont, which takes less than a night on the return trip from Venice, he participates in the casket test without delay; yet on that very day, Salerio brings word of the forfeited bond and Antonio's impending punishment. Thus more than three months have passed in Venice while only a day has gone by in Belmont. Auden explains that in the fairy world of Belmont, time can stand still. He characterizes this world as a place where external appearance represents unambiguously the good or evil of reality. Characters may disguise themselves, but they do not possess contradictory natures; they are either good or bad. This is a place, then, that cannot hold Shylock and Antonio, who come from the mercantile world of Venice, which evolved from the feudal, which evolved from the tribal. They explode the simple fairy-world illusions of right and wrong, because "in the real world, no hatred is totally without justification, no love totally innocent" (235). More important, in the real world, money and machinery force us into an interdependency that succeeds only if no one is an "other" and all are "brothers." Belmont's simple values are betrayed as foolish and cruel when they are superimposed on what Auden calls the real world of Venice.

Contemporary critics offer a more historical interpretation that compares three places with fictional Belmont: the Venice of the play, Londoners' mythic Venice, and historic Venice. Of the play's Venice, John Gross says, "there is a contrast in the play between Belmont and Venice, [but] a much sharper contrast within Venice itself between two versions of capitalism" (53):[14] that of Shylock and that of Antonio and Bassanio. Focusing on the play's Venice, Gross says that both Antonio and Shylock operate on the premise that Venice is dependent on the wealth of foreigners and that this cosmopolitan economy requires that foreigners enjoy comparable legal rights with the Venetians. In the play, "the business of business is business" (58), and even the despised Shylock can enjoy financial benefits from this pragmatic objective. Shakespeare's Venice, Gross writes, is "a coarser place than Belmont" (99), but not so coarse that it produces irredeemable boors unfit for the gentle world of Belmont.

Shakespeare's Venetian court is more mythically golden than the reality and is based on Londoners' exaggerated notions of the justice of Venetian law. The play presents what may be generously called a flexible court that tolerates an unknown visiting young doctor who cites two implicit restrictions in the bond and then, with a third restriction, transforms the civil proceeding to a criminal trial that yields a verdict and sentence based on a Venetian law against threatened violence from aliens. The presiding Duke offers little more than biased support for the Venetians, who taunt Shylock at every opportunity. Although Shakespeare follows a few practices of the real courts of Venice, such as the figurehead Doge cum Duke, critics argue that this mythical legal system serves as commentary on the existing legal system of Elizabethan England. Mahood suggests that its fictional procedures pleased law-focused Londoners who saw in it the upholding of the spirit of the law and the vanquishing of evil, an ideal though uncommon model. Shakespeare's placing such an equitable outcome in faraway, romantic Venice rather than in London, Mahood says, supported Londoners' respect for the law as well as some elements of their popular myths of the lavish and just world of Venice.

The Venice of the play is more mellow than the generic "myth" of Venice in Tudor legend, a paradoxical place Londoners of the second half of the sixteenth century believed was fraught with darkness and social license as well as enlightened by independence, wealth, art, political stability, respect for law, and tolerance for foreigners. Katharine Eisaman Maus speculates that the mythic Venice offered Shakespeare "an alternative social prototype . . . unusually tolerant of diversity" in the sixteenth century (1081). The romance of Venice inspired Elizabethan and, later, Stuart dramatists to set many dramas in the city, drawing on its traditions of aesthetic and sensory pleasures, wealth, political sophistication, legal equity, and successful worldwide trade, which, in reality, was declining at the end of the sixteenth century.

This near-mythically sophisticated Venice far transcends the historic reality, a more prosaic place that many scholars conclude Shakespeare knew. They speculate that he could have traveled to the city during the plague years between 1592 and 1594, that he likely was acquainted with a small community of theatrical and musical Italians living in London who could have told him about the city, and that he certainly read the many guidebooks and travel books written by visitors to Venice,[15] which provided the local color of the region included in the play—the gondolas, ducats, Duke, doctors of law at Padua, and synagogue. His royal Venetian merchant, Antonio, however, is inaccurately presented, because Venetians no longer had the opportunity to trade all over the world in the 1590s, and no Christian like Lancelot Gobbo could have been a live-in servant to a Jew. Venice was, however, accurately known for the legal rights it granted to foreigners. They could openly practice their religion, engage in contracts and bonds with Venetians, and seek justice for injury in the courts. Consequently, Jews, as foreigners, enjoyed some freedoms.

In any case, Gross contends that Shakespeare understood the many differences between the Venice of his play and the real city. The reality was not as golden as the myth Londoners read about or the myth created in the play. Jews were moneylenders and pawnbrokers by default, since they were restricted from most other means of earning a living and paid much higher taxes. Jews indeed could charge interest on loans, but the loans were primarily granted to the poor so that the state would not need to respond to their annoyingly inconvenient distress; furthermore, by the end of the century, interest was limited to 5 percent. Restricted to living in the Jewish ghetto after 1516, Jews in Venice were easily identified since they were forced to wear high-pointed red hats or turbans and yellow badges.[16]

But most Londoners were ignorant of all this, and intoxicated by the myth of Venice, they likely paid more attention to the opulence of Shakespeare's Venice than to its differences from Belmont. Although the two places may seem a simple contrast between aggressive acquisition and gentle charity, they share an important quality—wealth. Both are saturated with money, one with its acquisition and the other with its pleasures. If Belmont existed in the measured time of Venice, we might even imagine Belmont as a result of Venice—the cleaned-up, bourgeois consequence of the city's prosperity. After an earlier generation had successfully engaged in business, they could offer the following generation the serenity of the suburbs, a place where only gentle people lived. Money earned in one place could be enjoyed in another. But the play does not align the two in time, even though we, like Bassanio, visit Belmont as a fortunate consequence of successful Venetian capitalism.

Rather, Belmont seems to float beyond society's clocks and calendars as an imaginary pastoral world to which young women and men migrate to experience love's pleasures. But when Auden suggests that Belmont is a state of being, a pastoral world, there are two jarring anomalies. First, a pastoral world makes no racial distinctions. The more noble and, in a sense, appropriate of Portia's two unsuccessful suitors is Morocco; but his skin is dark, a fact he suspiciously believes will diminish his chances of winning Portia. Although a harsh and racist "justice" in Venice conspires against Shylock, leisurely and lenient Belmont, a place that is generous but also exclusive and elite, does not admit Shylock at all.

Second, a pastoral world has no money, no thoughts of it, no need for it, no curiosity about it. Belmont already possesses wealth and therefore has no need for the greed and ambition that motivate Venice. Antonio and

Lorenzo do not earn or "deserve" the sudden, unearned wealth Portia gives them in Belmont because, in Belmont, wealth is not longed for or labored for but simply *is*. Material possession in Belmont is not a glistening temptation to acquire more, as it is in Venice. If the wealthy characters truly have no need for further acquisition, it is only because with a most unpastoral materialism, Belmont bestows wealth on the indolent with no restrictions—an externally delightful if internally questionable fantasy.

ANTI-SEMITISM

Because anti-Semitism infected early modern London (see Chapter 2), we must examine whether and how it fits into the play. There are three general positions we may take. First, and least convincing, is the notion that the play does not contain anti-Semitism at all. Shylock is selfish and greedy, traits incidental to his Jewishness, but the sole reasons other characters shun him. John Russell Brown, the editor of the New Arden edition (1959), claims that only two anti-Semitic remarks occur in the text, one by the clown Lancelot who says, "my master's a very Jew" (2.2.100), and one by the condemned Antonio in court, who blames Shylock's "Jewish heart" (4.1.80). With somewhat forced logic, Brown argues that Shylock is a villain not because of his Jewishness but because of "the hate he bears Antonio, the Christian" (xxxix).

The other two positions allow that Shylock's Jewishness, as well as his villainy, sets him apart from the other characters. Walter Cohen reports that the play contains 74 direct uses of the word *Jew* ("Jew," "Jewess," "Jews," "Jew's," "Jewish," and "Hebrew"). The term is in no sense neutral, considering its juxtaposition with such words as *dog, cur,* and *Devil.* With the perspective of a resident in Israel, Harold Fisch even argues that Shylock is intended to seem "Jewish." He possesses those qualities our culture randomly associates with Jews of the Diaspora (outside Israel): "his dark and gloomy resentments, his feverish care of his possessions, his sense of family (prizing the jewel left him by his dead wife), his loyalty to his fellow Jews, his love for his daughter, his gestures, his faith in the absolute validity of the written bond . . . [and] his appeal to law as against sentiment" (qtd. in Gross 45). Gross agrees that "much of this seems to be true" (45). Shylock is intended to be the Other: wearing a Jewish gaberdine; making money in a stereotypical Jewish fashion (although it is necessary to repeat that in England, Jews were not prominent moneylenders at all); citing biblical stories from the Old Testament; attending a synagogue; and, along with his wife, daughter, and friend, having an Old Testament name.[17] He is a stereotype even when very few English citizens knew Jews directly and rarely saw Jews portrayed on the stage. Lawrence Danson reminds us that of the extant plays written between 1584 and 1627, only nine, including *MV,* contain a recognizable Jew, and only *The Jew of Malta* portrays a Jew who is a central character; three other lost plays may have had a Jewish character (58–59). But as Berek argues, the stereotype entered drama with a vengeance with Marlowe's Barabas. We may conclude, then, that Shylock's greedy and biased actions are not merely those of a mean-spirited man; they are intended to be associated with being Jewish.

Yet granting that Shylock's Jewishness sets him apart, most of his unattractive traits do not. Shylock may be wicked, but the Christian characters share his avarice, false seeming, possessiveness, lack of spirituality, and materialism. Furthermore, Shylock is forced into unattractive behavior to survive—a likely consequence of the play's materialistic value system, its mercantilism.

Shylock's avarice is highlighted in his first entrance when, in 22 lines, he repeats his first words three times, voicing his always-financial concerns: "Three thousand ducats . . . For three months" (1.3.1, 3). Then his first aside presents his motives: "I hate him for he is a Christian . . . and [he] brings down the rate of usance here with us in Venice" (2.3.34, 36–37). For him, Antonio is the very devil, who keeps him from realizing greater economic success. But if this inspires us to a generic disdain for Jews, that disdain must also extend to members of the Venetian economic community, because the Venetians too want more wealth: Bassanio seeks marriage to Portia for money; Lorenzo willingly participates in robbery for money; Antonio's existence is based on the acquisition of money; and even after death, Portia's father insists on controlling which man will possess his estate as well as his daughter. Ironically Shylock, supposedly the greediest of all, does not directly seek money in the bond or in the court of Venice.

Shylock's words are also filled with false seeming from his opening scene. In his negotiations with Bassanio, he uses a standard "It's going to be very difficult for me to raise so much cash" refrain:

> I am debating of my present store,
> And by the near guess of my memory
> I cannot instantly raise up
> Of full three thousand ducats (1.3.45–49)

Granted, some critics accept the ingenuousness of this statement,[18] but later lines seem to refute the possibility of his good-faith negotiations. After his aside to the audience verifying his hatred for Antonio, he claims to seek the friendship of Antonio: "I would be friends with you, and have your love, / Forget the shames you have stained me with" (1.3.131–32), a comment apparently accepted by the idealistic Antonio but hardly believed by members of the audience, who have heard the aside. Shylock continues, cheerfully calling the transaction a "merry bond" and concluding with the wish to Antonio that "for my love, I pray you wrong me not" (1.3.163). Is such false seeming sufficient reason for the audience to agree with the Venetians' bias against Jews? It might be, but only if we ignore similar false seeming in the Christians—like Bassanio's facade of wealth, Portia's arrogant artifice with Morocco and Arragon, and the false obedience of Jessica, a Christian convert, to her father. If the play illustrates that "a gracious voice obscures the show of evil" (3.2.76–77), then our condemnation of Shylock should extend to a generalized contempt for all Venetians.

Third, even though Shylock is portrayed as a possessive father who limits the freedom of his daughter, an arguably even more possessive father is the Lord of Belmont. Shylock warns his daughter:

> . . . Hear you me, Jessica,
> Lock up my doors, and when you hear the drum
> And the vile squealing of the wry-necked fife,
> Clamber not you up to the casements then
> Nor thrust your head into the public street . . . (2.5.27–31)

But Portia complains about the restrictions on her life set by her strict and willful father. "I may neither choose who I would, nor refuse who I dislike, so is the will of a living daughter curbed by the will of a dead father" (1.2.19–21). If tight control of one's family is a Jewish paternal trait to be mocked, then the Lord of Belmont's audacious control over Portia illustrates that paternal control is not exclusive to Jews.

Finally, Gross agrees with Fisch in observing that Shylock lacks "the whole region of Jewish spirituality" (qtd. in Gross 46). Gross attributes that spiritual vacuum to Shakespeare's limited knowledge of Jews and the society's built-in assumptions about Jews. He says that "Shylock's stage-Judaism is a pseudo-religion, a fabrication: there is no piety in it" (46). But we can see equally clearly that the Christianity of the play is also a pseudo-religion, a fabrication, and that there is indeed no piety in it either.

Shylock and those around him in Venice, however, do show adulation for a very different idol, although it is both non-Jewish and non-Christian. For everyone, Jew and Christian, material property transcends all in Venice. Because of it, they have reverence, enjoy fellowship, build an ethical system, and tolerate others. Its omnipotence gives Shylock faith that its laws supersede all sentiment, while Antonio is willing to serve as its holy martyr.

> The Duke cannot deny the course of law;
> For the commodity that strangers have
> With us in Venice, if it be denied,
> Will much impeach the justice of the state. (3.3.27–29).

When we meet Shylock during the exposition and the first half of the conflict, almost through 3.1, the third of his five scenes, he is despised by the Venetians as a greedy, deceptive, possessive, and materialistic Jew. But Shakespeare suggests an irony in this Venetian anti-Semitism, because the Venetians hate Shylock for qualities they themselves possess. Thus, in the first half of the play at least, we cannot help but offer Shylock our sympathy for the trials of his far-too-challenging life as an alien in Venice. The final position some hold concerning *MV* is that the play itself promotes anti- Semitism. This means that its main characters, like Antonio and Portia, are sensible and correct to hate Jews in general and Shylock in particular because he is a Jew. D. M. Cohen claims that Jewish audiences and readers are justified in feeling "fear and shame" throughout the play and that "such an intuitive response is more proper and accurate than the critical sophistries whose purpose is to exonerate Shakespeare from the charge of anti-Semitism" (53). In the first sentence of his 1998 essay on the play, Bloom agrees: "*The Merchant of Venice* is . . . a profoundly anti-Semitic work" (171).[19]

I suggest that until the end of 3.1, Shylock's villainy could be explained by the biased treatment he receives and that his course of action, a response to the greedy materialism that permeates the mercantile world of Venice, is the only one available to a powerless individual who hopes to survive and thrive. It is, in fact, modeled on the greed of the Venetians.

However, the dominant image of Shylock as victim fades at the end of 3.1, when passionately, after grieving for his daughter, his ducats, and his lost turquoise ring from Leah, he threatens to take advantage of Antonio's unexpected penury. He arranges with Tubal to go to the synagogue to plan the death of Antonio, an event that will free him to charge higher interest rates. It would be difficult to argue that such a speech does not feed anti-Semitic sentiments in the audience. Venice has hated Shylock all along because he is a Jew, and now the audience is encouraged to agree because Shylock's greed has been wed to plans of violence.

Indeed, society's hatred is the inevitable fate of Others—when they fail to submit to victimization and fight back. Then they are not falsely accused of villainy, because they in fact begin to perpetrate it. Thus Shylock's Jewishness is inextricably enmeshed with both his continuing greed and his increasingly murderous violence. This identifies a cause and effect between Jewishness, or Otherness, and greedy violence. Unavoidably, society's victims are more likely to become society's bad people, a condition that is perhaps one of the most damning traps with which the red-haired devil has ensnared humankind. It makes villains of us all.

Shylock, the Jew, stands alone at the apex of the play's villainy. We see the evidence of his expanded evil in the contrast between his brief second and fourth scenes, 2.5 and 3.3. In 2.5, he is still a victim, leaving his home and daughter for Bassanio's feast with a warning that he senses "some ill-abrewing towards my rest" (2.5.17). But by 3.3, he Shylock has created the brew for the doomed Antonio. He seems to have expanded horribly, looming large over his Christian victim. Shylock, the abused outsider, has been overcome by the venom of his passion. We must assume that this intensification of revenge is unprecedented; even the anti-Semitic Venetians do not hold such feelings. Thus, in the first half of the play, the bias the Venetians hold against Shylock is not shared by the audience. We feel some sympathy for Shylock as a spat-upon loner who serves only as a convenient cash machine to Venetians needing extra money, and as a still-grieving widower and a worried parent of an obviously wayward daughter. But the ending of 3.1 and the two subsequent Shylock scenes reroute our sympathy.

D.M. Cohen observes that at the end of the trial scene, the audience regains some of their sympathy for him as he suffers under the fiercely protectionist law of the Venetians (61). No alien can threaten the life of a Venetian. Shylock, who had trusted the law entirely, is traumatized into near speechlessness. He must submit to any punishment or die. Yet he remains the Jew-villain until his final exit.

Why is this so? Cohen concludes his essay with the idea that "it is as though *The Merchant of Venice* is an anti-Semitic play written by an author who is not an anti-Semite—but an author who has been willing to use the cruel stereotypes of that ideology for mercenary and artistic purposes" (63). Shapiro suggests that Shakespeare's anti-Semitism contributes to the establishment of an exclusionary English national identity. We cannot know whether either of these claims is accurate. Perhaps Shakespeare felt the dramatic energy heightening unstoppably with the growing monstrousness of Shylock. Perhaps the Marlovian Barabas presented so great a rival that Shakespeare felt he had to match him. Perhaps the political mood in London was still deeply colored by the hanging of Ruy Lopez. Or perhaps Shakespeare wished to dramatize unstoppable human frenzy, hatred ignited into rage by the brazen theft of goods and child.

In any case, although a large part of the play is sufficiently ironic to show similarities between Shylock and the Venetians, the final lines of 3.1 and the following two scenes with Shylock (3.3 and 4.1) force us to agree that Shylock's Jewishness, his Otherness, contributes to what becomes his irrefutably brutal violence.

LOVE AND FRIENDSHIP

That *MV* centers on love (or, as various commentators label it, giving, bonds, and mercy) is both a function of its genre, as discussed in the previous section, and the time in history of its creation. Writers of the early modern period—the Renaissance—were especially interested in the nature of love as defined by Plato and contemporary interpreters, particularly the Italian Count Baldasarre Castiglione (1478–1529), who wrote *Il Cortegiano* (*The Courtier*) in 1528. Soon translated into the other European languages, this work was available in an English translation, *The Courtyer,* by Sir Thomas Hoby (1530–1566) in 1561.[20] In a dialog divided into four books, several historical persons who actually lived at the court of the Duke of Urbino from 1504–1508 spend the evening (and night) describing the ideal courtier—implicitly, the ideal man. The speakers contend that the courtier is distinguished by *sprezzatura,* an easy and natural grace, or, as M. Bernard Bibiena, one of the speakers, says, "the grace that oughte of nature to make hym so amyable" (51). He should be "well-borne and of a good stocke" (368), "of a meane stature, . . . and well made to his proportion. . . . amiable in countenance unto whoso beehouldeth him" (368), have a "principal and true profession of . . . arms" (48), and ought also to be "a good scolar" (58)—all qualities, incidentally, first recollected by Nerissa about Bassanio: "a Venetian, a scholar, and a soldier that came hither in company of the Marquis of Montferrat," who "of all the men that ever my foolish eyes looked upon was the best deserving a fair lady" (92–94, 96–97).[21]

M. Peter Bembo, another key participant in the dialog, later offers his description of the sort of love such an ideal courtier might enjoy, which, following Plato, is "a certein covetinge to enjoy beawtie" (342), while beauty itself is a heavenly light shining into the lover. He says that a man may long for his beloved in three ways, each manner becoming closer to the angels: first, beastly appetite flows through sense; next, human choice emanates from reason; and finally, angelic will arises through the understanding. This platonic progression, then, implies that a younger courtier is less fortunate in love because his soul hungers for beauty with the greater agonies and frustrations of appetite; in contrast, the older courtier (or a godly younger one) is guided by reason and understanding and, consequently, enters into a spiritual or holy love that transcends the destruction wrought by time, because such beauty is bodiless. Such a lover may kiss his beloved "to joigne hys mouth with the womans beloved with a kysse: not to stirr him to anye unhonest desire, but bicause he feeleth that, that bonde is the openynge of an entry to the soules" (355). At the conclusion of his discourse, "Lady Emilia, pluckinge hym a litle, warns, 'take heede [M. Peter], that these thoughtes make not your soule also to forsake the bodye.'" And M. Bembo replies wittily, "it shoulde not be the first miracle that love hath wrought in me" (363).

This influential dialog informs themes of love and friendship in *MV*, including the ambiguous kiss between Portia and Bassanio after the casket selection, the play's increasing focus on the physical considerations of love in Act 5, and the nature of the love between both sets of major lovers, Antonio and Bassanio and Portia and Bassanio.

Antonio and Bassanio's relationship presents two questions: Is it homoerotic? How does it relate to the romance between Bassanio and Portia? Proponents of the homoerotic theory argue that Antonio's sadness in the opening scene is too great to have been begotten by other than romantic love:

> I hold the world but as the world, Gratiano:
> A stage where every man must play a part,
> And mine a sad one. (1.1.76–78)

The older and richer of the two men is more smitten and generous, while Bassanio has been a self-admitted irresponsible spendthrift who, in the first scene, continues his past practice of taking advantage of Antonio's love. Even to the play's conclusion, when Portia feigns anger over the supposedly lost ring, Antonio remains devoted, confessing that he is "th'unhappy subject of these quarrels"; and he justifies Bassanio's loss of the ring, saying, "I once did lend my body for his wealth, / Which but for him that had your husband's ring / Had quite miscarried" (5.1.249–51).

Danson warns, however, that commentators often support the notion of a homoerotic love between the two men using a circular logic: Antonio's homoerotic feelings cause his sadness and his sadness results from his homoerotic love (35). E. M. W. Tillyard, for example, concludes that Antonio is indeed isolated, lonely, and forlorn, but he is not a "'study in homosexuality'" Danson observes, which, implies that homosexuals are normally lonely. Leslie Fiedler says that Antonio loves Bassanio with "an austere, Uranian love, for whose sake the older lover educates to manliness the boy he adores" (Bloom 1986, 87). The older man agrees to die for the boy, even though his love cannot be fulfilled and he must accept the role of rival to Portia. Nevill Coghill concludes that to justify Antonio's willingness to secure the loan with his life, "nothing less than a high homosexual affection, worthy of the *Symposium,* would poetically suffice" (212). Bloom similarly concludes that Antonio "lives for Bassanio and indeed is willing to die for him" (*Shakespeare: The Invention* 179), that the relationship they share is sexual, although Bassanio is bisexual; and the bond Antonio agrees to is sadomasochistic. On the other hand, Joseph Pequiney finds the love between Bassanio and Antonio nonsexual because it lacks many of the features of the homoerotic love between Sebastian and Antonio in *Twelfth Night* (185–195). Finally, noting the ubiquity of the homoerotic theory in the second half of the twentieth century, Catherine Belsey grants that it is "not one that I wish to discredit" ("Love in Venice" in Coyle 150), but she concentrates instead on the difficulty in determining the precise meaning of words, wisely asking, "Possibly our difficulty resides in the plurality of the word *love?*" (155).[22]

Danson argues that theories of Antonio's frustrated homoerotic love are "quite wrong" because they are "not coherent with the play's overall shape and tone" (35–36) and place Antonio in an unwinnable competition with Portia. He concludes that the play resolves in harmony, and even though "the love of Antonio and Bassanio . . . is a textual fact . . . a sexual competition between Antonio and Portia is not, and to invent one raises more problems of interpretation than it solves" (40). Barber similarly notes that the relationship is a deep friendship "between young people of the same sex which Shakespeare frequently presents, with its positive emphasis, as exhibiting the loving and lovable qualities later expressed in love for the other sex" (245).

Indeed, educated people in the Renaissance viewed friendship between men as the most ideal human relationship, described by Plato in "Phaedrus," a dialog between Socrates and Phaedrus,[23] and idealized in the loving relationship between David and Jonathan, King Saul's son, in the first Book of Samuel in the Old Testament. Jonathan selflessly and regularly saves David from his father's wrath and even brings it down on himself. "The soul of Jonathan was knit with the soul of David, and Jonathan loved him as his own soul" (I Sam. 18:1). Even though Jonathan is Saul's son, he accepts that he will be second to David, who will be king (I Sam. 31:5). In the Renaissance, such a relationship was thought to involve neither sexual attraction nor resolution; to coexist with love for a woman; and to serve as a higher, more spiritual bond than the latter. Yet there are qualifications: the love of one friend, Jonathan, is greater than that of the other, David; and Jonathan suffers martyrdom. Mahood further compares Antonio and Bassanio's love to the uneven relationship narrated in Shakespeare's first 17 sonnets between the persona and the fair-haired youth. The older lover bestows on the younger a greater love, which indulges the younger and places within him an imagined, perhaps longed for, requited love. M. Bembo praises such a love by a "Courtier not yonge" (355), because while it may lack equity, it attains a satisfying spiritual level of human love.

Antonio and Bassanio might be seen as sharing such a spiritual love, a far more significant motivation for their behavior than any romance based on "appetite," for which the play gives no evidence. Each offers to die for the other. In fact, Bassanio's courtroom offer in 4.1 of his life and all he possesses is a far more immediate sacrifice than Antonio's in 1.3, when the likelihood of actual payment of the flesh forfeit to Shylock seems absurd. Bassanio's offer elevates him and, incidentally, confirms his ability to love someone with reason and understanding as well as sense. Thus, although the play concludes with Antonio as unattached as he was in 1.1, he gains new evidence of Bassanio's (and Portia's) love for him, and he remains a successful merchant.

What is the nature, then, of the love between Bassanio and Portia? She gives Bassanio her wealth and self with the ring, and he vows constancy, promising that the arrangement is off if he removes the ring from his finger. If that happens, he announces, he may be pronounced dead. So important is the ring, Sigurd Burckhardt says, that it is "the bond transformed" (234).[24] But by the end of the next act, Bassanio does indeed part the ring from his finger, without parting from life, and sets aside his extravagant pledge of constancy. But for several reasons, he is a faithful lover and, by play's end, worthy to be Portia's husband. First, he has the makings of a courtier—grace, according to at least two meanings of the term: personal *sprezzatura* (modesty, ease, and humility to admit wrong and seek mercy) and the "undeserved" mercy of God's grace. In 3.2, immediately after reading the alarming letter from Antonio, Bassanio confesses to Portia, "I was a braggart. When I told you / My state was nothing" (3.2.257–58); and in the final scene, he admits to the missing ring and asks forgiveness with a promise, "Pardon this fault, and by my soul I swear / I nevermore will break an oath with thee" (5.1.247–48). His loyal love and willingness to risk all for Antonio compares favorably to Gratiano's courtroom offer, which fails to include his own life but only that of his wife:

> I have a wife who I protest I love;
> I would she were in heaven, so she could
> Entreat some power to change this currish Jew (4.1.286–88)

Bassanio has also proven himself far more than an adventurous and charming soldier and scholar. He is perceptive, constant, and clever in his mistrust of Shylock's words, in his willingness and wisdom to select a casket, and in his loyalty to Antonio and ultimately Portia. Finally, the predicament of the lost ring is contrived, a conflict that is almost a play within a play, with Balthazar as an imaginary blocking figure who is responsible for the problem. The conflict is unwinnable. Had Bassanio chosen to keep the ring, he would have been guilty of ingratitude. As a result, he must be forgiven and allowed to remain in what Danson calls the circle of love arranged by the bond, represented by the ring, and maintained throughout the story.[25]

Portia's love for him is similarly worthy. Even before Bassanio's correct choice, she declares a love of the understanding:

> [Your eyes] have o'er looked me and divided me:
> One half of me is yours, the other half yours—
> Mine own, I would say: but if mine then yours,
> And so all yours. (3.2.15–17)

While this image is admittedly a commonplace, her offer of help to Antonio is based on this yoking of souls:

> . . . . Antonio
> Being the bosom lover of my lord,
> Must needs be like my lord. If it be so,
> How little is the cost I have bestowed
> In purchasing the semblance of my soul
> From out the state of hellish cruelty! (3.4.16–21)

Like Antonio, she does not need evidence of devotion from Bassanio to demonstrate her own.

In examining love in *MV*, we gain insight from Renaissance ideas such as those expressed in *The Courtier*. But even what Castiglione fails to say illuminates the play. At the end of the book, the Duchess asks M. Bembo to explain "whether women be not as meete for heavenlie love as men" (364). But the group has been talking all night and dawn has arisen, so she suggests that he respond on the following night. The book ends, and the

Duchess never receives an answer. But *MV* suggests one. In Acts 3, 4, and 5, Portia shows that she is capable of heavenly love expressed through appetite, reason, and understanding.

Like Antonio and Bassanio, Portia is a gift giver. Danson reminds us of the "peculiarly Elizabethan preoccupation" (51) with giving, as described by Seneca in *De Beneficiis:* "'the chief bond of human society'" is the passing of gifts from hand to hand and includes three "equally necessary branches—giving, receiving, and returning willingly without thought of payment"(51). The spontaneity with which Antonio extends his credit to Bassanio in the first scene and offers his soul as surety in the last follows this pattern. With her ring, Portia bestows herself and her possessions on Bassanio, which Bassanio then offers along with his own life in exchange for Antonio's life. Act 5 concludes with Portia's gift of wealth to Lorenzo and Antonio and, with the return of the ring, wealth encircled by generous love to her husband.

Portia also personifies the understanding explained in the Act 5 choric commentary of Jessica and Lorenzo, which offers insight into the couple themselves but also into the other lovers who will soon return to Belmont. Humans are imperfect, grossly enclosed by the flesh, and doomed to err and misstep; but when music, the symbol of love's harmony, begins, Lorenzo remembers the joy that a human may know when "music for the time doth change his nature" (5.1.82). Muddy as we may be, Lorenzo suggests, we may still find harmony and respond to the music of the moment. Finally, implying the reason for Shylock's absence from Belmont, he adds:

> The man that hath no music in himself,
> Nor is not moved with concord of sweet sound,
> Is fit for treasons, stratagems, and spoils . . . (5.1.83–85)

Portia understands that perfection—beauty—exists, but mortals must graciously settle for the transient, and therefore imperfect, joys of earth. Portia, Antonio, Bassanio, and all the rest are destined to remain flawed. Evidence litters the final scene—Antonio is still excruciatingly earnest, even in Belmont, having pledged to Portia that he will offer his own soul to serve as the surety for a renewed bond between Bassanio and her because of the missing ring. With this promise, of course, he plays into a parody of the earlier bond with Shylock:

> I dare be bound again,
> My soul upon the forfeit, that your lord
> Will nevermore break faith advisedly. (5.1.251–53)

Bassanio is still well intentioned but impulsive. He apologizes disarm-
ingly for losing the ring, but in the loss, he fulfills his promise to give and
hazard all he has; unfortunately, that can have questionable results. With
humility and good humor, he admits his defeat with his highly equivocal
final lines: "Sweet doctor, you shall be my bedfellow; / When I am absent
then lie with my wife" (5.1.284–85). Portia understands, perhaps like Bassanio himself, that he could err again; but she knows too that, for now, he
responds to the harmonies of the heavens through the music of Belmont.

In Belmont, the paradox of continually forgiving others and one's own
flawed self, while simultaneously aiming at perfection, is very much at the
heart of the so-called Christian ideal of the play. Yet the play transcends
religion. The strongest characters admit their weaknesses but do not
thereby lose their responsiveness to the harmony of the night's music, a
redeeming human gift.

The audience too must be self-aware. Norman Rabkin wisely comments on the play: "It is time to recall that all intellection is reductive, and
that the closer an intellectual system comes to full internal consistency
and universality and application—as with Newtonian mechanics—the
more obvious become the exclusiveness of its preoccupations and the limitations of its value" (116). Therefore, when we reach our own "enlighten-
ing" conclusions about *MV*—about the love or the music or the
giving—we cannot surrender our suspicions that such reasoned neatness
ignores contradictions still hidden in the play's enigmatic lines.

THE BIBLE, JUSTICE, AND MERCY

Another theme in *MV*, in what Coghill calls the "Christian tradition of a
former age" (216), is the unity of justice and mercy, which commentators
associate with the Old and New Testaments, with the Old and New Laws,
and even with men and women. Coghill goes so far as to explain the
forced conversion of Shylock in these terms, since "in the name of mercy,
Antonio offers him the chance of eternal life, his own best jewel" (220).
Coghill concludes that Act 5 in Belmont completes the intertwining of justice and mercy. It portrays "Lorenzo and Jessica in each other's arms.
Christian and Jew, New Law and Old, are visibly united in love" (220).

The many biblical references in the play would seem to support
Coghill's analysis. Among Shakespeare's plays, *MV* has an unusual number of biblical allusions, echoes, and references from both the Old and the
New Testaments. In *Shakespeare's Biblical Knowledge,* Richmond Noble
cites well over 50 references.[26] In Shakespeare's time, familiarity with the

Bible was common among even the poorly educated, simply because citizens were required to attend lengthy services where they heard or antiphonally responded to at least four passages from the Bishops' Bible at each Sunday morning service and two more at evening prayer. Additionally, as children, more-educated citizens like Shakespeare would have studied the Old and New Testaments and the Apocrypha in petty and grammar schools. T. W. Baldwin outlines the readings Shakespeare would have memorized as a small child and then later translated from English into Latin in grammar school. Finally, like other educated adults in Anglican London and Stratford, Shakespeare would have owned and read the Geneva Bible.[27] Noble's study distinguishes Biblical echoes in *MV* from both the Geneva and the Bishops' Bible at a one to four ratio, but Mahood points out that Shakespeare likely was reading the Geneva version "when *The Merchant of Venice* was in the making" because of the echoes from the marginal glosses in the Geneva text" (Mahood 185). It is probable that he owned and referred to both.[28]

The unusual number of biblical allusions in the play suggest to some commentators that the play is more than thematically based on the Old and New Testaments; rather, it is an elaborate religious allegory of justice represented by Shylock and of mercy represented by Portia. The old and supposedly unforgiving, vengeful law of the Old Testament is contrasted to the new and unquestioningly compassionate law of the New Testament—an eye for an eye versus turning the other meek cheek. And because this play emanates from a Christian society, commentators suggest that the far more attractively presented New Law wins. In "Biblical Allusion and Allegory in *The Merchant of Venice*" (1962), Barbara Lewalski argues that the play is religious allegory following the comic form of Dante, which has "a beginning in troubles and a resolution in joy, reflecting the fundamental pattern of human existence in this world" (236). She submits that this "may organize the total work" (236), although the dimensions of the allegory are not consistent throughout the play. She says that the play explores Christian love and its various antitheses "using Antonio as a representation of "the very embodiment of Christian love" (238) and Shylock as its most obvious antithesis. Antonio hazards but Shylock hoards, and when each has the opportunity to choose between revenge or charity, Shylock selects revenge, while in the courtroom, Antonio picks charity. His demand for Shylock's forced conversion to Christianity is not vengeful, Lewalski continues, but is a part of "a perfect embodiment of Christian love" (240). Generally, Lewalski sets up dichotomies that signify the New Law in opposition to the Old Law, mercy countering justice, a Christ figure contrasting a devil figure.[29] Movement throughout the play is away from the old and toward the new: in Lancelot's decision to run from "the Jew," in Jessica's stealing away at night with Lorenzo, and finally in Shylock's conversion. Meanwhile, Antonio plays a Christ-like role of sacrificing martyr for humanity through divine justice, and Shylock, the devil, holds humankind "in bondage through sin." The trial scene most clearly presents these allegorical roles; however, at its conclusion, Lewalski says, Shylock's conversion is "not anti-Semitic revenge: it simply compels Shylock to avow what his own experience in the trial scene has fully 'demonstrated'—that the Law leads only to death and destruction, that faith in Christ must supplant human righteousness" (247).

Mahood, however, cautions against a conclusion that the consistent presence of biblical allusion supports a biblical allegory. Biblical echoes pervade the Tudor culture, so Shakespeare's use of phrases from the Bible may simply reflect current usage. The question of the play's religious allegorical structure requires careful examination.

Because the play has an unusual number of references to the Bible and its central conflict is between the self-righteous Christians and the ultimately violent, greedy Jew, at the very least, biblical allusions inform the play, even though these allusions may not prove the play to be a religious allegory. Shakespeare could have known few accurate facts about Jews or Orthodox Judaism, and in London, any New Christians he may have known would have been practicing Christians; therefore, Mahood proposes that for this play, Shakespeare used the Bible, particularly the lives of the three Jewish patriarchs in Genesis, as a resource for the creation of Shylock (185).[30]

Mahood notes four important references in the play to well-known stories in Genesis. First, in 2.5, as Shylock readies himself to leave for dinner with the "Christian fools," he mutters to Jessica, "By Jacob's staff I swear / I have no mind of feasting forth tonight" (2.5.35–36). Mahood explains that the staff by which he swears is the staff Jacob takes with him as a young man when he leaves his father and mother, Isaac and Rebekah. Jacob must leave because he has just won his father's blessing through trickery, in collusion with his mother. Isaac had intended the blessing for Jacob's older twin brother Esau. With only the staff, Jacob then travels across the River Jordan to Pandanaram to stay with his mother's brother, Laban. On the journey, Jacob lies down to sleep and dreams of a ladder with angels reaching up to heaven and God standing above it promising to give Jacob and his children the land where he lies (Gen. 28:13). The staff, then, has come to be the symbolic, material starting point on which Jacob builds both the land of Israel and his own personal fortune (Gen. 28–32:10). While Jacob's staff is not commonly used in oaths, Shylock, the wealth seeker, would surely find the staff worthy of oath taking.

In the next lines, Shylock turns to Lancelot the clown and asks him to precede him to the banquet to announce his arrival. As Lancelot leaves, he whispers to Jessica, "There will come a Christian by" (2.5.40). Shylock cannot make out what the clown has mumbled so he asks in irritation, "What says that fool of Hagar's offspring?" (2.5.42). This is a reference to Hagar, the Egyptian handmaid of Sarah, Abraham's wife. She bore Abraham a son named Ishmael some years before Sarah bore Isaac. The angel of the Lord predicts that Ishmael will become a wild man living in the presence of all his brethren. Years later, Ishmael mocks his younger half-brother Isaac when he is weaned. Sarah becomes angry, so Abraham sets both Hagar and her son out into the wilderness with only bread, water, and God's promise to save them (Gen. 16:21), which He indeed does. Ishmael, then, is remembered as a less-than-civilized, mocking fool, appropriate in Shylock's epithet to Lancelot. Thus, in condemning a figure representing Ishmael, Shylock can again be identified with the three Jewish patriarchs, Abraham, Isaac, and Jacob, the latter two of whom triumph when their brothers are cast aside.

In his opening scene with Antonio and Bassanio (1.3), when he justifies his collection of interest on loans, Shylock cites a third reference, another story about the third Jewish patriarch, Jacob. The Genesis tale describes Jacob's arrival at his Uncle Laban's lands. Jacob falls in love with Laban's daughter, his cousin Rachel; and Laban orders him to work for seven years to gain her hand. But when the marriage takes place, Laban tricks Jacob into marrying Rachel's older sister, Leah, instead. Her name, the same as that of Shylock's dead wife, is a fourth echo from Genesis in the play and is ironic because she is the lesser-loved wife of Jacob. Laban explains that an older sister must marry first, so Jacob agrees to work another seven years for the hand of Rachel, whom he finally marries. In all these years, Jacob causes Laban's flocks to thrive. Finally, Jacob tells Laban that he wants to return to his father's land of Canaan with his family and asks in payment for his years of work all the speckled and spotted goats and sheep. In yet a third bit of trickery, Laban secretly removes those animals to a faraway place. Jacob, however, is more clever. He cuts tree branches, carves white streaks in them, and sets them in front of the strongest animals, thus causing them to conceive parti-colored lambs. He then informs his wives of their planned departure, and they agree that "all the riches which God hath taken from our father, that is ours, and our children's: now then, whatsoever God hath said unto thee, do." Additionally,

Rachel steals images that are her father's (Gen. 31). Danson writes that Shylock cites this story to show that Jacob's seemingly artificial breeding of the sheep allows him to be "blest" by God; therefore, by extension, Shylock's apparently artificial breeding of money is also right and good. When Antonio asks whether gold and silver are like ewes and rams, Shylock jokingly dismisses the question: "I cannot tell, I make it breed as fast" (1.3.88). Danson notes that "it is unlikely that Shylock's sly argument would have converted many of the audience from the deep-seated prejudice against the moneylender's trade" (149–50). Also implicit in Jacob's success with his father-in-law is the notion that he should be applauded for his wit in gaining just payment for his many years of unjust labor. God rewards the shrewd. With this precedent, Shylock concludes that interest on money he has lent at some risk to the citizens of Venice is just. Ironically, if Shylock were to continue the story of Jacob's departure, he would reach the point where Laban's daughters, Rachel and Leah, leave their father, taking much of his wealth and even his most-valued images. Thus the outcome for the story's villain, Laban, foreshadows Shylock's own grievous fate.

Another Old Testament reference in the play to the three patriarchs (but by no means the only one remaining) occurs in the scene introducing the play's clown, Lancelot Gobbo (2.2). It parodies the scene in Genesis 21 in which Jacob tricks his blind father, Isaac, into giving him the blessing that Isaac intended for Jacob's twin brother, Esau. Hearing the voice of Jacob, Isaac feels his son's hands, made falsely hairy with coverings of goatskin provided by his mother, and smells his clothes, filled with the scent of the field, and is fooled into thinking that Jacob is Esau. In parody, Lancelot kneels before his father, old Gobbo, and asks, "Give me your blessing" (2.2.64–65). But Gobbo does not recognize his son's voice at all and thinks that he has in fact too much hair on his chin, "more than Dobbin my fill-horse has on his tail" (2.2.77–78). He is convinced in the end that it is really his son because Lancelot knows his own mother's name—Margery, a conventional name for a comic lower-class woman in Tudor literature. In a sense, this scene mocks the Genesis patriarch that Shylock so venerates, thereby lessening the reverence the audience may hold for both the Jewish patriarch and his acquisitive admirer in Venice.

The New Testament also inspires verbal echoes and allusions in the play, four of which will be noted here. In Shylock's opening scene, he recalls to Bassanio the story of pork becoming "the habitation which your prophet the Nazarite conjured the devil into" (1.3.27–28). Jesus met two men who were possessed of devils and taunted him, daring him to send the devils into a herd of pigs. Jesus accepted the challenge, accomplished the transfer, and sent the pigs running into the sea where they drowned (Matt. 8:28). Shylock ignores Jesus's elimination of the possessed pigs altogether and selectively recalls only the portion of the tale that serves his purpose.

Second, when Antonio enters, Shylock murmurs in an aside, "How like a fawning publican he looks!" (1.3.33). A publican was a Roman tax collector in Jerusalem who had a reputation for flattering the rulers of the land and treating the Jews harshly. However, in one of Jesus' parables, a publican is an unexpectedly humble hero in contrast with a self-pronounced, self-righteous Jewish pharisee. Based in the premise that one's external appearance does not predict one's inner heart—an idea stressed in *MV*—the parable illustrates that he who exalts himself shall be abased, while he who humbles himself shall be exalted. Shylock's reference to Antonio, then, backfires; he has mistakenly praised Antonio when he intended to mock him.

The third New Testament reference occurs later, after Jessica has left with Shylock's valuables. He cries, "The curse never fell upon our nation till now, I never felt it till now" (3.1.67–68). This curse is one that Jesus placed on Jerusalem: "Behold your house is left unto you desolate" (Matt. 23:38). It is noteworthy that in his grief, the Jew Shylock gives such credence to these words of "the Nazarite."

Finally, in the courtroom scene, Shylock refers to the life of Jesus when he wishes that his daughter might have married "any of the stock of Barabbas" rather than a Christian (4.1.282). Barabbas was the thief who nearly was crucified alongside Jesus but whom the Jewish crowd chose to save on Passover instead of Jesus. The lowest Jew is better than a Christian, Shylock implies, which is also a reflection of the crowd's opinion at the crucifixion (based, of course, on the anachronistic premise that Jesus is a Christian).

These selected allusions and most others are spoken by Shylock who, we have seen, takes them out of context and regularly misses the ironic meaning they may hold in the play. Act 5, in which Shylock does not appear, contains multiple references to the classical world but a dearth of allusions to scripture. If this is due to Shylock's absence, then Antonio's aphorism predicted correctly that it is the devil (Shylock) who "can cite Scripture for his purpose" (1.3.90). Shylock, the source for most of the play's biblical allusions, intentionally or unintentionally misuses them to support his arguments. Therefore, the play's most detailed biblical allusions are not necessarily to be trusted. Lewalski argues that the structure of the plot follows the medieval comic form of religious allegory used by Dante. But if we are to base our assumption that the play is religious allegory on its abundant biblical allusions, at least in part, then we are ignoring Shylock's regular misuse of those allusions. Therefore, unless we filter his words through Antonio's warning about the devil, our conclusion that they directly support a religious allegory is specious.

NOTES

1. Coghill, "The Basis of Shakespearian Comedy," *Essays and Studies* 3 (1950), 1–28. Coghill's essay includes definitions of comedy presented by a number of commentators, beginning with the Latin grammarians of the fourth century—Evanthius, Diomedes, Donatus—and Isidore of Seville (560–636), Matthieu de Vendome (c. 1150), and several who are contemporary with Shakespeare. Coghill explains how they differentiate between what evolved into the harsher social commentary of Ben Jonson's satiric comedy and the love-focused romantic comedy of Shakespeare.

2. The two most well-known dramatists of Roman New Comedy are Plautus (250–184 B.C.E.), who wrote comedies for a diverse audience, and Terence (195–159 B.C.E.), who wrote for a more elite audience of scholars and members of the court. Plautine comedy, far more influential in Tudor and Stuart England than Terentian, takes place in Greece and contains bawdy, wordplay, slapstick, and unlikely plots with foolish slaves and young people tricking older and more prestigious characters. About 20 extant plays remain from a probable canon of 130 works. Among many excellent studies of Roman New Comedy is Gilbert Highet's *The Classical Tradition: Greek and Roman Influences on Western Literature* (Oxford: Oxford University Press, 1967).

3. This play is printed in John Matthews Manly, ed., *Specimens of the Pre-Shakespearean Drama* (New York: Dover, 1967), 239–76.

4. For a useful discussion of the relation of Marlowe's play to earlier drama, see David Bevington, *"The Jew of Malta,"* in *From Mankind to Marlowe: Growth of Structure in the Popular Drama of Tudor England* (Cambridge: Harvard University Press, 1962), 218–33.

5. *Commedia dell'arte* performances were most popular in Italy from 1550 through 1750 and have only a plot outline on which the actors improvise. The genre has very defined conventions: the setting is a busy street corner in front of the lovers' families' houses; and standard character types, called masks, usually appear in pairs: two opposing older men, two servants, two young women—such as the clever, pure, and genteel daughter of one of the older men and her servant girl. The plot and subplots ultimately resolve with the defeat of the father and the victorious marriage of the various sets of lovers, similar to the Italian comedy. We must view this form as an influence on *MV* with caution, however, because Shakespeare may never have seen *commedia dell'arte,* and there are no actual scripts; thus he may have known only those elements of *commedia* that are shared by other Italian comedy. A useful study of *commedia dell'arte* is in Allardyce Nicoll, *The World of Harlequin* (Cambridge: Cam-

bridge University Press, 1963).

6. C. L. Barber's important work comparing comic structure to the forms of ritual and containing a full chapter on *The Merchant of Venice* is *Shakespeare's Festive Comedy: A Study of Dramatic Form and Its Relation to Social Custom* (1959; repr. Cleveland and New York: Meridian, 1963).

7. See Harold C. Goddard, "*The Merchant of Venice,*" in *The Meaning of Shakespeare* (Chicago: University of Chicago Press, 1951), 1: 81–116, for a generally sympathetic reading of Shylock.

8. See E. E. Stoll, "Shylock," in *Shakespeare Studies: Historical and Comparative in Method* (1927; repr. New York: Frederick Ungar, 1960), 255–336.

9. Harold Bloom's three useful volumes include a set of essays on *MV*, another on Shylock [*Shylock: Major Literary Characters* (New York: Chelsea House, 1991)], and a lengthy study of Shakespeare's entire canon [*Shakespeare: The Invention of the Human* (New York: Riverhead Books, 1998)]. The cited lines are taken from *William Shakespeare's* The Merchant of Venice, *Modern Critical Interpretations* (New York: Chelsea House, 1986).

10. Northrop Frye is an important structuralist critic who seeks an archetypal, systematic framework within literary works that helps to organize its plot and its ideas, particularly those of comedy and romance. His important works include *An Anatomy of Criticism* (Princeton: Princeton University Press, 1957) and *A Natural Perspective: The Development of Shakespearean Comedy and Romance* (New York: Harcourt, 1965).

11. In *Shakespeare's Festive Comedy*, 3–35, Barber compares the temporary misrule and return to order of such social forms as local holiday celebrations to the form of dramatic comedies.

12. The essay "Brothers and Others" is included in *The Dyer's Hand and Other Essays,* a collection first published in 1948 (repr. New York: Vintage, 1968) that contains Auden's essays on a number of literary works.

13. The accurate measurement of time with clocks and calendars, in the face of a seemingly inharmonious pattern of the phases of the moon with the rise and fall of the sun, was important in the early modern era. Such measurement had to align the church year, with its celebration of Easter, to natural seasonal change. See David Ewing Duncan, *The Story of the Calendar* (1998; repr. London: Fourth Estate, 1999). On the other hand, sixteenth-century writers responded to contemporary social problems by describing an imagined perfect pastoral world. Inhabited by shepherds and shepherdesses who know neither war nor commerce and feel no ambition, the pastoral world exists in a timeless dimension.

14. Gross's book *Shylock: A Legend and Its Legacy* (New York: Simon and Schuster, 1992) focuses on the history of performance but includes one chapter on the history of Jews in drama and another on Jews in London. See also James S. Shapiro, *Shakespeare and the Jews* (New York: Columbia University Press, 1996); Walter Cohen, "*The Merchant of Venice* and the Possibilities of Historical Criticism," *Journal of English Literary History* 49 (1982), 765–89; and Peter Berek, "The Jew as Renaissance Man," *Renaissance Quarterly* 51 (1998), 128–62.

15. Books praising Venice written by Italian authors or English travelers begin with William Thomas, *History of Italy* (1549) and extend through Sir Lewis Lewkenor in an introduction to Gasparo Contarini, *La repubblica e i magistrati di Venezia* (1543, trans.1599) as cited by John Gross in *Shylock: A Legend and Its Legacy.*

16. See David C. McPherson, *Shakespeare, Jonson, and the Myth of Venice* (Newark: University of Delaware Press, 1990), for discussions of historical and mythic Venice described by writers of Tudor England.

17. See Barbara Lewalski, "Biblical Allusion and Allegory in *The Mechant of Venice,*" in ed. Harold Bloom *Shylock: Major Literary Characters* (New York: Chelsea House, 1991), 236–251. In a note (17) to her article, Lewalski suggests her theories for the derivation of the names of the Jews in the play: Leah is of course the first wife of Jacob; Jessica derives from Jesca, a form of Iscah, who was the sister of Milcah, Abraham's sister-in-law, who bore Lot (Gen. 11:29); Tubal is named after the grandson of Noah (Gen. 10:2); and Shylock likely derives from Shalach, which translates as "cormorant" (Levit. 11:17; Deut. 14:17). These derivations are similar to but not the same as the name derivations given in the Chapter 4 (see n. 20).

18. Marc Shell writes that Shylock "does not have sufficient funds for Bassanio" ("Wether and the Ewe," in Bloom, 1986, 109). But later that night, Jessica manages to carry away more than enough wealth for Shylock to have funded the bond.

19. This appears in Bloom's *Shakespeare: The Invention of the Human* (1998).

20. Strongly influenced by Plato and influential in many Renaissance works, *The Courtier* is available in Hoby's original translation with an introduction by Walter Raleigh. See Thomas Hoby, *The Book of the Courtier. The Tudor Translations,* ed. W. E. Henley (New York: AMS, 1967).

21. Interestingly, the summary list of attributes required of a courtier, which concludes the text (368–73), identifies many qualities shown by Bassanio and Antonio, neatly informs the flaws Portia describes in her earlier suitors, provides commentary on Gratiano's behavior (the courtier must "not mocke . . . persons given to mischeef, which deserve punishment"), and even points out the weaknesses of Lancelot (the courtier must "not be sensual or fleshlie" and must "not . . . waite upon or serve a wycked and naughtye person").

22. Belsey's reference to the now-popular notion of a homoerotic love relationship between Antonio and Bassanio was proposed at least as early as 1966 by E. M. W. Tillyard [in *Shakespeare's Early Comedies* (New York: Barnes & Noble, 1965), 182–208]. See Lawrence Danson's refutation in *The Harmonies of The Merchant of Venice* (New Haven: Yale University Press, 1978), 34–40.

23. Plato's Dialogs strongly influence writers of the Renaissance throughout Europe, including Castiglione, whose book *The Courtier,* in turn, informs *MV.*

24. See Sigurd Burckhardt, "The Merchant of Venice: The Gentle Bond," in Shakespearean Meanings (Princeton: Princeton University Press, 1968), 206–36, for his well-regarded analysis of the circularity of the plot, themes, and creation of MV.

25. For Danson's full discussion of love and friendship, see "'The Semblance of My Soul': Love and Friendship in *The Merchant of Venice*" in *The Harmonies of* The Merchant of Venice, 19–55; and for a discussion of the topic of gift giving in marriage, see Karen Newman, "Portia's Ring: Unruly Women and Structures of Exchange in *The Merchant of Venice*," *Shakespearean Quarterly* 38 (1987): 19–33, which is also discussed in the section titled "Portia" in Chapter 4 of this guide).

26. Useful studies of Shakespeare's education in and knowledge of the Bible are in T. W. Baldwin, *William Shakespeare's Small Latine and Less Greeke*, 2 vols. (Urbana IL: University of Illinois Press, 1944), vol. I; and M. M. Mahood, ed., *The Merchant of Venice*, New Cambridge Shakespeare (Cambridge: Cambridge University Press), 184–88.

27. The Geneva Bible was compiled by Marian exiles and first published in 1560; the New Testament was revised in 1595. Private individuals usually purchased this Bible because it was cheaper, smaller, and printed in clear Roman type. Shakespeare was also familiar with the Bishops' Bible; in *MV* he refers to sections of it that were not used in public worship. He probably used the 1584 quarto edition when he was writing *MV,* because the play contains echoes of it. The King James Version, which is familiar to modern readers, was not be published until 1611.

28. In the New Cambridge edition of the play, Mahood provides useful glosses for at least 50 Biblical echoes and allusions. See also the index in Jay Halio, ed., *The Merchant of Venice*, Oxford Shakespeare (Oxford: Clarendon Press, 1993).

29. Explanations of comic structure as an archetypal victory of virtue over evil or, in *MV,* of New Law over Old Law, may be found in Frye, *A Natural Perspective* 1–33; Barber, *Shakespeare's Festive Comedy* 3–15; and Coghill, "The Basis of Shakespearean Comedy," 1–28.

30. At the end of the New Cambridge edition of *MV,* Mahood includes her essay titled "Shakespeare's Use of the Bible in *The Merchant of Venice*," 184–88.

6

CRITICAL APPROACHES

Like celebrities, critical theories ascend, eclipse others, and descend in popularity; they replace old ones and are replaced by new ones, reflecting the values of the contemporary culture. Literary critics use existing theory to explain a work of art like *The Merchant of Venice,* or they postulate methods and goals of new critical trends. In previous chapters, I have excerpted comments from critical essays, but in the present chapter, I examine selected twentieth-century essays that serve both as representatives of particular critical theories and, more valuably, as individual interpretations of the play. As a jumping-off point, however, I look briefly at nineteenth-century criticism because, as Heather Dubrow writes, a literary movement "can best be understood by identifying what it reacts against" (35).[1]

I begin with three important cautions. First, literary theory is not tidy; theories overlap, and each is variously defined, even by a single commentator over several years. Second, *MV* is not clarified by all major literary theories; proponents may not have found some theories useful in examining the play or may not yet have gotten around to writing about the play. On the other hand, some theories may be highly relevant to the play, but this chapter can examine only a few representative studies. Finally, and very important, we must avoid reading literary criticism as if its primary function were to explain how a work like *MV* embodies a particular critical theory. Criticism may explain, inform, respond to, unify, illuminate, or categorize art; or, as some critics suggest, it may fill in the blanks left by the artist. But although a work of art may be said to represent its author, her or his culture, the text itself, or even the present audience and its culture, it transcends the conventions of any theoretical critical trend.

NINETEENTH-CENTURY CRITICISM

Expressionism and Expressive Realism

Nineteenth-century critical theory moved beyond the mimetic criticism of the Renaissance and eighteenth century, which assessed art in its achievement of a pleasing, unified imitation of nature and of valuable moral instruction.[2] Romantic nineteenth-century commentators valued self-expression in art. In 1800, William Wordsworth (1770–1850) famously wrote in the "Preface to the Second Edition of *The Lyrical Ballads*" that poetry expresses the artist's "spontaneous overflow of powerful feelings" (678), but by mid-century, critics argued that art should achieve expressive realism. John Ruskin (1819–1900) describes such a fusion of Wordsworth's expressive and earlier mimetic values in a discussion of painting:

> [Painting] must always have two great and distinct ends: the first, to induce in the spectator's mind the faithful conception of any natural objects whatsoever; the second, to guide the spectator's mind to those objects most worthy of its contemplation, and to inform him of the thoughts and feelings with which these were regarded by the artist himself. In attaining the first end . . . he sets himself before the landscape and leaves him. . . . [T]he artist is his conveyance, not his companion, his horse, not his friend. . . . [B]ut in attaining the second, the artist not only *places* the spectator, but *talks* to him, makes him a sharer in his own strong feelings and quick thoughts. . . . [The spectator is] ennobled and instructed, under the sense of having not only beheld a new scene, but of having held communion with a new mind, and having been endowed for a time with the keen perception and the impetuous emotions of a noble and more penetrating intelligence.
> (vol. 3, 133–34)

Art, and more specifically, literature, must express truth by simultaneously representing objects in the world and representing thoughts within the artist. This may be called an empiricist-idealist aesthetic because it holds that art should present the real but should also filter out the meaningless and focus on the ideal that remains.

William Hazlitt and Heinrich Heine present expressionist responses to *MV,* while Ruskin himself illustrates an expressive-realist approach to *MV.* Hazlitt (1778–1830), an English essayist, comments on *MV* in *The Round Table: Characters of Shakespear's Plays* (1906, 1964), at least partially inspired by a performance he had seen by Edmund Kean as Shylock, who refashioned, from Charles Macklin's portrayal of a villain, a human being wronged. Hazlitt reacts with emotion to the character's humanity and is the first to identify Shylock as a "*good hater;* a man no less sinned against than sinning" (320). Respecting and even sympathizing with Shylock, Hazlitt recognizes that Shylock has become "a half-favourite with the philosophical part of the audience, who are disposed to think that Jewish revenge is at least as good as Christian injuries" (320); and he argues that Shylock has "strong grounds" for his hatred of Antonio and the other Christians, which he "explains with equal force of eloquence and reason. . . . We can hardly help sympathising with the proud spirit, hid beneath his 'Jewish gaberdine,' stung to madness by repeated undeserved provocations" (320). And in the end "we pity him, and think him hardly dealt with by his judges." Shylock's adversaries, on the other hand, are "So far from allowing of any measure of equal dealing, of common justice or humanity" and show only "the rankest hypocrisy, or the blindest prejudice" (321). He expresses similar subjective perceptions of Portia: "[she is] not a great favourite with us; neither are we in love with her maid Nerissa [because of] her affectation and pedantry"; moreover, her mercy speech is "very well, but there are a thousand finer ones in Shakespeare" (322).

Heinrich Heine (1797–1856), a German poet and critic, responds similarly in 1839 to Kean's performance:

> When first I saw the play presented in Drury Lane there stood back of me in the box a pale British beauty who wept violently at the end of the fourth act and frequently cried out, "The poor man is wronged!" Hers was the face of the noblest Grecian cut, and her eyes were large and black. I could never forget them, those great black eyes, that wept for Shylock! But when I think of those tears, I am forced to include *The Merchant of Venice* among the tragedies.
> (672)

He assesses the characters with like subjectivity:

> [Shakespeare's] drama in reality exhibits neither Jews nor Christians, but oppressors and oppressed, and the madly agonized jubilation of the latter when they can repay their arrogant tormentors with interest for insults inflicted on them. . . . Truly, except for Portia, Shylock is the most respectable character in the play. . . . Lorenzo is the accomplice of a most heinous theft and under the Prussian code would be sentenced to fifteen years at hard labor, branded and pilloried. . . . Bankrupt Antonio is a nerveless creature without energy, without strength to hate, and hence without strength to love, a gloomy insect-

> heart. . . . .Bassanio is a 'genuine fortune hunter'; he borrows money
> to make sumptuous display so as to bag a rich wife and a fat dowry.
> (673–74)

While these Romantics record their emotional reactions to the play, Ruskin's evaluations are foregrounded by his reasoned eye. Writing in 1880, he rejects Henry Irving's sympathetic interpretation of Shylock: "I entirely dissent (and indignantly as well as entirely) from his general reading and treatment of the play" (34: 545). Elsewhere he explains that "in the tale of *The Merchant of Venice;* in which the true and incorrupt merchant, kind and free, beyond every other Shakespearean conception of men, is opposed to the corrupted merchant, or usurer; the lesson being deepened by the expression of the strange hatred which the corrupted merchant bears to the pure one, mixed with intense scorn" (17: 223), and Ruskin regrets that the "the public . . . consistently and naturally enough, but ominously considers Shylock a victim to the support of the principles of legitimate trade, and Antonio a 'speculator and sentimentalist'" (24: 418). Ruskin is led to this position by his distaste for usury, "the mercantile form of pillage. . . . The idea that money could beget money, though more absurd than alchemy . . . [leads to] the wealth of villains and the success of fools" (23: 161). He regrets that Shakespeare made his famous usurer a Jew, since that has diverted Christian hatred from the practice of usury to "religious hatred of the race of Christ. . . . Shakespeare himself . . . suffered himself to miss his mark by making his usurer a Jew" (23: 161).

In their observations, Hazlitt and Heine flood the reader with their passion; Ruskin bestows on readers an evaluation he implies they would be foolish to ignore.

TWENTIETH-CENTURY CRITICISM

In the twentieth century, literary commentators developed a variety of theories that diverged from expressive realism. These theories did not neatly evolve one from the other; and those that became popular in the final 30 years of the century, notably changed from earlier approaches, were often derived from other disciplines—history, linguistics, economics, sociology, psychology, philosophy. These theories exploded almost simultaneously in the latter part of the twentieth century. This section examines criticism of *MV* from the entire century in a makeshift chronology that separates the first 70 years from the final 30. I avoid the misleading notion that literary criticism *evolves*—a word that often implies progress or improvement—because changes in theories have not inevitably led to greater insight. Valuable commentary was written throughout the century, its benefit depending not merely on showing how a literary work expresses current literary theory but rather illuminating the work itself and using the work to find a new awareness of the world.

1900–1970

A number of useful perspectives on Shakespeare's works developed in response to expressive realism, although commentators often chose to apply them to the tragedies rather than the comedies and other genres. Furthermore, most valuable commentary defies categorization into any single critical perspective, so the labels that follow apply loosely.

Historical Criticism

Historical criticism of the early part of the twentieth century is based on the premise that the works of an author are best understood in the context of the time in which he or she lived. In varying degrees and versions, the major historicists, who were influential well into the 1940s, saw *MV* as an expression of the Elizabethan world, its philosophies, politics, and mores.[3] Certainly, historical criticism is a response, in part, to the Romantics and Victorians, who engaged in subjective interpretations that often turned out to be anachronistic. For example, while nineteenth-century Romantics might conclude that in *MV* the Venetians' hatred for Shylock implicitly expresses Shakespeare's presumed disdain for anti-Semitism, early twentieth-century historicists might argue that Venetian bigotry is a direct reflection of pervasive anti-Semitism in Elizabethan England.

E. E. Stoll (1874–1959), a historical critic who taught at the University of Minnesota, discusses the play as a product of the time in which it was written.[4] Stoll begins by comparing it to Marlowe's *The Jew of Malta,* noting the conventions shared by the two characters who are Jews: probable red wig and beard, false nose, obsession with wealth, and desire for violence. Stoll excuses Shakespeare for this biased representation: "Now a popular dramatist, even more than other artists, cannot play a lone hand, but must regard the established traditions of his art, the rooted sentiments and prejudices of his public" (272). Stoll then describes several other conventional stage Jews of the period and before in England and Germany and "the opinions, or antipathies, of the time—a sorry tale to tell" (275). He concludes that Shakespeare portrays Shylock as a hated enemy who returns that hatred with hypocrisy and trickery yet desires the same sorts of power over the Christians that they seek over him:

> Had [Shakespeare] cared to make a serious and sympathetic figure of
> Shylock, he would not have made him after the similitude of those
> created by the prejudices and misconceptions awake or slumbering in
> his day—not one avaricious and miserly, crafty and treacherous,
> hard-hearted and pitiless, . . . thirsty for the Christians' blood and
> hungering—pork excepted—for his goods—not made him a cur and
> devil, in short to be spurned and spit upon, despoiled and forcibly
> converted.
> (288)

Thus, in the mode of the historicist, Stoll describes in a broad sweep the
society's prevailing attitude toward Jews and its artistic representations,
which, he argues, explains the malignant character in Shakespeare's play.

Other commentators follow related critical approaches. A popular and
fruitful perspective in the first part of the century, Arthur Quiller-Couch
(1863–1944) emphasizes the relationship among the play, a supposed
older, nonextant version, and the two fantasy source stories. This mongrel
background, he believes, explains much of the weakness of the work,
which finally is supplanted by the beauty in Act 5.

John Middleton Murry further develops this perspective but does not
consequently judge the play as weak. In the chapter titled "Shakespeare's
Method: *The Merchant of Venice*" in his book *Shakespeare* (1936), Murry
contends that of all the plays of this period, *MV* is Shakespeare's most typical, clearly expressing what Coleridge calls his "omni-humanity";
nonetheless, Murry agrees that *MV* is "more than any other of Shakespeare's plays, a matter-of-fact fairy tale: a true folk story, made drama"
(189). It contains "tragedy, comedy high and low, love lyricism; and notably, it not does [sic] contain any Shakespearian character" (190). He suggests that the popularity of the play, matched only by that of *Hamlet*, may
be explained by its folktale origins and its historical prototypes in Renaissance drama and literature. Because of these folk origins, some characters
only minimally "derive from the situation . . . [and] the remainder of the
characterization floats as it were free of the situation" (209). Murry continues that this concept is often too simple to grasp, and as a result, critics of
MV explain away the cloudy or absent character motivations as arising
from Shakespeare's unwise excisions or lack of excisions from the now
missing presumed earlier version of the play. For example, Murry notes
that the New Shakespeare editors find Jessica an especially ungrateful,
thoughtless daughter whose testimony in Belmont against her father should
have been deleted. But Murry maintains that since the play is a folktale,
Jessica is not a lifelike daughter but rather "a princess held captive by an
ogre" (194). Similarly, although some critics argue that Antonio's melan-

choly is unexplained because Shakespeare unfortunately deleted its cause, Murry finds the melancholy appropriately "motiveless" in the context of a fairy tale. Finally, Murry notes that although some argue that Shylock hates Antonio because of Antonio's disdain for usury or, more pathetically, because of his daughter's desertion, his hatred for Antonio actually is "a fairy-tale hatred of the bad for the good" (195). Thus Shylock is *both* a fantasy character with an irrational hatred and a "credible human being. . . . He is neither of these things to the exclusion of the other. If we ask how can that be? the only answer is that it is so" (199).

Stressing the history of ideas, Charles Read Baskerville recognizes the Renaissance philosophical ideas within the play. He establishes platonic influences on images of love in the play. Platonic ideas and ideals permeated Renaissance thought. For example, as noted earlier, in Booke IV of *The Courtier*,[5] Baldassare Castiglione (1478–1529) outlines platonic ideals in the three ascending faculties of the soul—sense, reason, and understanding—which influence Bassanio in the casket scene as he considers each casket and finally selects the most spiritual. Bassanio understands that love requires self-sacrifice for the sake of the beloved. Later, in Act 5, Lorenzo more obviously reflects on ideal Platonic love.

The analysis of stagecraft in the early twentieth century produced other rewarding insights.[6] The director, playwright, and actor Harley Granville-Barker (1877–1946), who Dubrow calls "probably the most influential student of Shakespeare's stagecraft" ("Twentieth-Century Shakespeare Criticism" 30), compiled the highly regarded six-volume *Prefaces to Shakespeare* (1927–1974). Of the *MV*, he begins with his famous assessment:

> *The Merchant of Venice* is a fairy tale. There is no more reality in Shylock's bond and the Lord of Belmont's will than in Jack and the Beanstalk.
> (89)

Like other commentators of the first half of the twentieth century, Granville-Barker directs attention to character, which is of particular interest to him since he approaches the play as stage performance.[7] Having successfully directed John Gielgud in a production of *MV* in 1938, Granville-Barker argues that the play's improbable plots come alive with the humanity of the characters. The plots, in fact, move in two streams of time; "they do not naturally march together" (89).[8] The casket plot seems to have occupied far less time than the three months of the bond's term; yet Shakespeare alternates between scenes from both plots because the less acutely dramatic casket plot must stand up to the life-threatening bond plot in Venice. As a director, Granville-Barker observes that the most effective way to act the part of Portia is as an "unlessoned schoolgirl" whose "little body is aweary of this world" and who later becomes the "Portia of resource and command" (102), planning the courtroom victory in Venice and winning the life of Antonio and the negotiated wealth of Lorenzo and Jessica.

Commenting on the all-male casts of the sixteenth century, Granville-Barker notes that the original boy-actors of the part had certain advantages, particularly in fulfilling the need to appear young and fresh, both in the earlier scenes and later in the courtroom scene where Balthazar must be "alert, athletic, modest, confident" (103). Granville-Barker views Portia as "the slave of the caskets" (101) until she is freed by Bassanio and can become a fully drawn character. It is then that Shakespeare "lets us feel its whole happy virtue in the melody of her speech . . . she is a great lady in her perfect simplicity, in her ready tact . . . and in her quite unconscious self-sufficiency" (101). He warns that playing the part of the androgynous Balthazar must not "lapse into feminine softness," for this "damns the scene and herself and the speech, all three" (103). The dichotomy in the part of Portia, the schoolgirl turned courtroom victor, must still yield "one Portia, a wise and gallant spirit so virginally enshrined" (102). Indeed, actresses playing many of the heroines in Shakespeare's comedies must have "a twofold artistry" in which their characters must have a "delicacy and humour" but must also present a "contrast between womanly passion or wisdom and its very virginal enshrining, . . . which the limited resources of the boy [actor] left vivid, which the ampler endowment of the woman too often obscures" (101).

Shylock plays against this heroine and loses. But Granville-Barker does not find him weak: "He is not a puppet, neither is he a stalking horse; he is no more a mere means to exemplifying the Semitic problem than is Othello for the raising of the colour question." Both merely set up the circumstances for the conflict; "but at the heart of it are men"; and Granville-Barker speculates "that from a maturer Shakespeare we should have had, as with *Othello,* much more of the man, and so rather less of the alien and his griefs" (106). Although he has "a savage certainty of revenge, . . . a satanic heroism," his concluding lines show him as being banal: "I am not well." He exits with "an all but ridiculous appeal to our pity, such as an ailing child might make that had been naughty; and we should put the naughtiness aside" (116). Giving Shylock an extravagant exit negates the simple elimination of the villain and confuses the tone of the final act.

New Critical Theory

New Critical theory developed in response to historicism, placing a re-newed emphasis on the play itself rather than on its historical background. It challenges the notion that literature takes meaning from the world of the author, or even from the author's own intent; rather, readers must look only to the words of the text for "meaning." In her analysis of American New Critics of the 1940s and 1950s, including William K. Wimsatt and Cleanth Brooks, Catherine Belsey explains that such critics view the text "as belonging to the public because language is public" (*Critical Practice* 16). They advocate close and detailed readings of the text to find its unity, subtlety, and design. This means that the text itself offers an experience; it is not mimetic—a representation of a "real" experience—nor the author's expression of her or his own world or personal response to experience. A piece of literature has an independent unity, has an internal coordination, and results in an impact of words on the imagination and the emotions. New Critics also warn that the writer's intent and the reader's present mindset do not affect the "meaning" inherent on the page, because that meaning is solitary and unchanging. By disallowing outside influences, New Critics argue that textual criticism must analyze apart from outside readings or other disciplines. As in other areas of life, isolationism has its limitations; yet many excellent readings result from the New Critical theory. Although several commentators discussed in the following sections are categorized as writing from other critical perspectives, most follow Wimsatt and Brooks's tenet of close reading and attention to unity and design.

Analysis of Image and Theme

Some of the most insightful commentary of the mid-century analyzes the play as if it were a dramatic poem, paying close attention to symbolism, imagery, word choice, metrical and syntactic structure, and the patterning and variation of themes or ideas within the play.

In his essay "The Three Caskets," in *The Meaning of Shakespeare* (1951), Harold C. Goddard illustrates such careful reading and, at times, cites Freudian references. Goddard proposes that this play is best informed by the casket theme, which is based in the fact that the outward appearance of the gold, silver, and lead caskets is very different from what is contained within them. The golden world of pleasure in Belmont is supported by the trade and commerce of the silvered money in Venice, and under the surface of both is an ugly and hypocritical exclusivity. In this setting, most of the main characters are sad, weary, living in hell, even as their outward lives seem idyllic. Like the caskets, Goddard says, nearly every character in the play is a poseur, offering to the world an exterior personality that covers a very different interior being. In his casket-selection scene, Bassanio wears the elaborate new clothes he bought with Shylock's money but righteously says that he will not choose "gaudy gold." He is actually the gold casket, Goddard argues, because in the end he gets what he desires, "a wealthy wife" (86). Antonio's outward show of anti-Semitism is rather self-hatred; unconsciously, he sees too much of himself in Shylock, the worship of money and commerce, venture and profit. "Anger at himself, not a conventional anti-Semitism" is what makes Antonio the personification of silver casket. In the end, "he got as much as he deserved," Goddard concludes, "material success and a suicidal melancholy" (92). Shylock is the lead casket in his offer of an interest-free loan to Antonio. The offer is a genuine act that shows Shylock to be, deep down, "humane, kindly, and patient" (111), because he has no reason to believe that the wealthy Antonio will become bankrupt in the next three months. "Shakespeare is at pains to make plain the noble potentialities of Shylock" (95). However dark he is on the outside, Shylock is the lead casket with the gold within (101); he is "spiritual gold" (111). Finally Portia is "the darling of a sophisticated society" who, like the others, is not what she appears. Most of all, Goddard claims, Portia is an actress who assumes that she deserves the attention and devotion of all those around her. Her carefully scripted courtroom performance gains her accolades, but in the end she is unable to act with the mercy she has urged. This is in keeping with her prescient speech to Nerissa in her first scene: "I can easier teach twenty what were good to be done, than be one the twenty to follow mine own teaching" (1.2.13–15). Like Bassanio, Goddard says, Portia is the golden casket getting what she desires, "admiration and praise" (112).

Derek Traversi's essay *"The Merchant of Venice"* focuses on themes and symbols as well as considerations of genre.[9] He admires *MV* in comparison with earlier plays as a "transition to a more elaborate conception of comedy . . . an approach to some of the permanent features of his mature comic creation," although the play's "incompletely worked out contrasts between romantic love in Belmont and quests for wealth in Venice," its "dark and twisted" reality of Shylock, and its overly heavy allegory carried by the delicate casket plot result in a play that is "tentative, imperfectly assimilated to a single dominating conception" (39–40). Traversi also finds the play's "relation of reality and make-believe" a base from which Shakespeare presents themes "more triumphantly and coherently" than in later comedies (470).

The two heroes of the play demonstrate the risk and self-dedication of love—Portia's self-surrender to Bassanio after the casket test and Antonio's acceptance of "the rule of friendship" (Traversi 40). But reflecting his vision of the play as a dramatic poem, Traversi warns that "to read" Shylock with sentimentality is a mistake. While Shakespeare conceived him as "the melodramatic villain, the heartless usurer, and the enemy of Christianity" (40), his "human solidity threatens at times to break through the elaborate poetic fabric of [Shakespeare's] romance" (43). Antonio's disdain for him and Jessica's abandonment of him bring "verisimilitude and depth to his passion." (43). His flawed nature brings on his climactic doom in the courtroom, initiated with Portia's "quality of mercy" speech, the "deepest, the most permanent 'meaning'" of the play, in Traversi's estimation (46). Shylock casts away his opportunity to temper justice with mercy, to act out the lesson of the caskets—namely, that the universal human condition requires us to "give as well as to exact" (46). In 5.1, Traversi finds "the absorbing beauty of life," which becomes "the pervasive background of Shakespeare's comic devices" (47) and, finally, a comic coda in the rings, which the women had seized in the name of Venetian justice and now return with loving mercy.

Traversi's examination of the play's dramatic form and substance is valuable even though it rests on the premise that Shakespeare created his canon in a relatively smooth evolutionary process, and *MV* lies at the end of the "necessary preliminaries" and just before "mature achievement" (48).

In his essay titled *"The Merchant of Venice:* The Gentle Bond," in *Shakespeare's Meanings* (1968), Sigurd Burckhardt uses the structure of the entire plot to explain the play. The plot is the controlling metaphor of the play, not, as Murry writes, merely the union of stories lifted from *Il Pecorone* and the *Gesta Romanorum.* The plot is circular; Portia is able to save Antonio from the deadly bond in Venice only because Bassanio chose the lead casket and married Portia, only because he was able to fund his quest to Belmont, only because Antonio borrowed the money from Shylock with the deadly bond. "So seen," Burckhardt continues, "one of Shakespeare's apparently most fanciful plots proved to be one of the most exactingly structured" (210). The play, then, is "about circularity and circulation" and the method by which the "bond's law can be transformed into the ring of love," which, Burckhardt says, is "through a literal and unreserved submission to the bond as absolutely binding" (210). The two worlds must interact. Each responds to the needs of the other, and each uses the other to gain success. To win Portia, Bassanio needs the wealth of Venice; to save Antonio, Bassanio needs the lady of Belmont. Unlike Antonio, Shylock already understands the use of barren metal and the inter-action between money and flesh. He also uses action-filled "better lines" that are "so fully part of the dramatic situation, so organically flesh of the play's verbal body, that they resist excision. . . . It is because Shylock speaks this language that he is able to transform barren metal into living substance; the very mode of his speaking here becomes the mode of his doing" (215).

Burckhardt says that Venice and Belmont are the realm of law and the realm of love, but both demand submission to laws—laws that are fol-lowed to the letter in Venice but in substance and more intrinsically in Belmont. When Bassanio selects the lead casket, he ignores the letter—the enigmatic inscriptions the caskets bear—and listens only to the sub-stance—the caskets themselves. In court, Portia learns from Shylock how to transform the written word into flesh, and as a result, she is able to use the letter of the law to save Antonio. In contrast, Jessica and Lorenzo transform the metal and the symbolic value of the ring into something far inferior. They invert and diminish action and use; their love is financed by theft, experienced in nomadic wandering, and uncommitted by a ring. In thoughtlessly trading away the ring for a monkey, they create a foolish parity of metal and life. The play's ethos is based on use, which the main characters fulfill but Jessica and Lorenzo do not. In Act 5, "the scapegrace lovers have an unearned, nocturnal grace which transcends all that is earned and useful, and as their actions prove, they were not to be trusted" (227). Later in the act, Burckhardt concludes, "the ring is the bond trans-formed, the gentle bond" (234), so transformed by Portia, who speaks with a double voice of woman and man, of Belmont and Venice. The ring becomes the gentle bond that closes the circle of the plot.

Lawrence Danson presents an invaluable amalgamation of several crit-ical perspectives in *The Harmonies of* The Merchant of Venice (1978). Oddly, *MV* has inspired very few book-length studies, unlike its famous villain, about whom several excellent volumes have been written. Dan-son's work would be unusual, then, merely as a lengthy study of the play itself. But it also stands as an excellent analysis of the play's major themes. Danson devotes entire chapters to love and friendship, religion, the dilemmas of divine law, law and language, the problem of Shylock, and fulfillment and reconciliation. Also valuable is Danson's examination of the play within the genre of comedy, its detailed observations of char-acter, and its historical commentary as it builds on Burckhardt's emphasis on the image of the ring.

Danson begins with an observation with which I agree: "Shakespeare may after all have been master of only a single dramatic genre" (1). Each comedy or tragedy or history is so infused with elements conventionally assigned to other so-called genres that such expectations may in fact limit our understanding of a play. As a corollary, any Shakespearean play, if considered carefully, becomes a problem play. In *MV*, the wise and worldly heroine is right, but then, so is the savage and suffering Shylock. The play contains both comic heroine and tragic hero. "It makes the conflict," Danson observes, "eternally interesting" (17). It also challenges literary critics to search for a compromise, a particular ratio of comic to tragic.

Danson points out the importance of music in the final reconciliation scene, from which Shylock is excluded. He "will hear no music, and he will 'have no speaking' (3.3.17)" (181), a fate he desires and one that results from his "spiritual tone-deafness" (183) and from his goal to "silence the humanizing voice" (191). He is not witness to the night in Belmont in the final scene because he cannot admit "touches of sweet harmony." The lesson on harmony, describing music's role in human and cosmic nature, is presented by his son-in-law Lorenzo, through both description and demonstration. His is not the sole voice of harmony at the end of the play, however, because Portia develops meanings of love and charity in the emblem of the ring. But Danson warns, "It would be labor lost to sum up a play as rich as *MV* with a single rhetorical figure or flourish. It will always 'exceed account'" (194).

Psychoanalytic Criticism

An early multidisciplinary perspective on Shakespeare's works, psychoanalytic theory, developed during these decades, led by the influential Ernest Jones, a student of Sigmund Freud.[10] Norman Holland, perhaps the most significant psychoanalytic Shakespearean critic, wrote in *Psychoanalysis and Shakespeare* (1964) that Sigmund Freud's "inconspicuous discovery of the unconscious mind at the end of the nineteenth century bids fair to be the defining event in the intellectual life of the twentieth century" (3). Freud's work has provided insight and inspiration to nearly a century of literary critics, but Freud did not write an extended study of art; rather, he commented on it throughout his work. Freud says that "art is intended to allay ungratified wishes" of the unconscious and preconscious in the artist and the audience. To explore so beneficial a use for art, critics must consider the artist, the work, and the audience.

Interestingly, in 1913 Freud wrote one of his few essays on a specific work, "The Theme of the Three Caskets,"[11] in which he identifies *MV* as a symbolic folktale of a man choosing from among three females. Freud compares Bassanio's casket selection to three other tales: Lear's selection among his three daughters, the myth of Psyche and Cupid, and the tale of Cinderella. Freud continues that Bassanio's choice of the lead casket, and Lear's choice-that-should-have-been of his youngest daughter, Cordelia, are archetypically the selection of the youngest, the fairest, the most silent, the most faithful. Such a choice of quiet perfection, Freud claims, actually represents the black choice of death, or a replacement by the opposite, which is a common occurrence in dreams and myths that identify fertility with death and choice with necessity.

But interestingly, as a Jew himself, Freud elected not to develop other dominant themes from the play, which seem odd in their omission from his psychoanalytic inquiry—namely, the anti-Semitism surrounding Shylock and the role of the powerful female, Portia. Many years later, in "Shakespeare's Ghost Writers" (1987), Marjorie Garber suggests a reason for Freud's disregard for these themes. She says that Freudian analysis easily recognizes that the caskets are substitutions for females and that the lead or black casket is a substitution for Portia herself. But she continues that Freud's personal concern for this theme is itself a substitution within his own mind for his feelings for his third daughter, 18-year-old Anna. Hence the quick segue from Bassanio and the caskets to Lear and his daughters, and hence Freud's probable stronger identification with Lear than with Shylock.

Later, so-called psychoanalytic critics have not similarly ignored Shylock. Among major psychoanalytic critics writing about *MV* in the later half of the century were Holland, Leslie A. Fiedler, and Leonard Tennenhouse. Holland reviews earlier studies of the play by psychoanalysts (numerous, he suggests, because "many psychoanalysts were Jewish")—Ludwig Jekels, Otto Rank, Theodore Reik, E. E. Krapf, and Robert Fliess—and uses a symbolic focus to identify the two worlds in the play. Holland identifies Venice as the hard and masculine world, presided over by Shylock "as a kind of malignant deity" and defined by hoarding and stealing, and Belmont as the world of females, romance, and generosity, where solving the riddle of the woman leads to song and feasting. These worlds are, respectively, anal and oral; Venice is the anal world of withheld wealth, and Belmont is the oral "beautiful mountain" or bountiful breast. Finally, Holland sees a third phallic or oedipal level contrasting the bountiful mother, Portia, and the castrating father, Shylock (236). The play grants the wish to "have," which includes the wish to breed, both in the bountiful Belmont manner and in the aggressive Venice manner. But the wish to have, Holland warns, includes accepting risk.

Psychoanalysis may also be applied, but less easily, to the characters as if they were real people. This focuses most of all on Shylock and Antonio. Shylock is in a transition stage between an anal-erotic personality, which is explosive, irritable, and eager to possess money as power, and an oral personality, which is starving for vengeance. Antonio is a homosexual lover, probably unconscious rather than conscious, almost certainly continent, and possibly unconsciously fixated on Shylock. Thus Antonio's love supports the image of a masculine Venice; it is a place of passive homosexual submission from which heterosexual lovers like Jessica and Lorenzo flee.

Holland also discusses in detail Fliess's analysis of Shylock's speech in court, in which he explains his hatred for Antonio (240–42). He refuses to justify that hatred and instead concludes, "So can I have no reason, nor I will not, / More than a lodg'd hate and a certain loathing / I bear Antonio" (4.1.60–61). In other words, he defiantly describes himself as childishly irrational. He also twice cites other men's irrational impulses as being similar to his—their revulsion for a rat, a gaping pig, a cat, and a bagpipe. This is much as a child would argue that she or he must have permission to do something because other children have permission. Furthermore, all the irrationally loathsome animals, Fliess notes, have mouths and exhibit oral behavior except the phallic "woollen bagpipe," which causes "unrestrained wetting," an image of Shylock's "moral incontinency" (242). Fliess concludes that since Shylock states this response two times, his speech pattern edges toward childishness, and the logic of his explanation is generally childish; Shylock's language represents his slide toward an irrational childishness in the plot itself. Holland comments that these ideas of Fliess's may all seem "farfetched"; but even though a psychoanalytic reading of a single image may seem "strained, even fantastic, it is not so when placed in the context of hundreds of similar and related images" (242). Holland argues that just as traditional critics find a controlling idea "at work in each specific speech," the psychoanalytic critic finds "the nuclear fantasy of the whole play shaping the images, symbols, diction, and style of each speech" (242).

In "The Jew as Stranger: Or 'These Be the Christian Husbands,'"[12] Leslie A. Fiedler acknowledges that "the play in some sense celebrates, certainly releases ritually, the full horror of anti-Semitism" (98). Like Joan in *Henry VI Part I,* Shylock as stranger is a figure to whom we wish to give new meaning. The old image of villainous Jew offends our modern sensibilities, particularly since Adolf Hitler's hideous real-life response to the irrational fear of Jews held by far too many Christians. When we see the play, we try to alter the meaning of the Jew as stranger and give him some contrived, pathetic humanity. We see that he loves his dead wife, is betrayed by his daughter, is bullied by the Christian mob, and is composed of the same human qualities as everyone else.

But we should see Shylock as one of many images or symbolic characters, objects, and acts in the play. Fiedler contends that Portia represents hedonism—the pleasure principle—in contrast with Shylock's "puritan austerity" (131–37). To the anti-Shylock interpreters, she is the heroine, but she has no loving heart. She mocks, lies, and mouths platitudes, beginning with her catalog of xenophobic biases against all her suitors, including the foolish Spaniard Arragon and the black-skinned Morocco. In court, she begins with banal truisms and then "acts out a ritual of Jew-baiting" (101) that speaks for the anti-Semitism of all the other characters. Fiedler proposes that she maintains the images of Shylock as devil, dog, and wolf or, he sums up, Shylock as "ogre" (109). As in myth, Shylock, an image of the stranger, is "the ogre father [who] seeks to swallow down his son, keeping his natural daughter for himself," . . . twin threats of cannibalism and incest"(109). Finally, Portia introduces the ring plot, which contains another "father" image, Antonio, who hopes to use the ring against her. He seeks to hold on to his "son," Bassanio, by attempting "to preempt the ring," a symbol of marriage that becomes a shackle to both him and presumably Bassanio. Even though he has convinced Bassanio to give up the ring in 4.1, it is "only a delusive victory." In Act 5, Portia insists that Antonio himself place the ring on Bassanio's finger. Along with the ring, Fiedler identifies several other symbols in the play: Shylock's bond stands for his efforts to destroy Antonio with his knife, certainly a symbol of castration; the caskets signify "the mortmain [property left after death] of Portia's father" (132); and Gratiano reveals in his final bawdy couplet that female genitalia are yet another meaning for the ring.

Leonard Tennenhouse writes in "The Counterfeit Order of *The Merchant of Venice*" (1980)[13] that although psychoanalytic criticism focuses on "the disturbing or incoherent features of a text" (54), it takes into account the context of the rules, codes, and languages of the author's culture. An unusual number of such rules usually develop around issues that generate stresses and contradictions within the society. Similarly, in art, dramatic or poetic conflicts arise where historical facts contradict cultural codes and ideals. The author's personal manipulation of these contradictions is fertile territory for psychoanalytic work (55). In the Elizabethan period, for example, the historical suspicion of women conflicts with the literary ideal of courtship and virgin female virtue, and intense male rivalry in the newly exploding mercantile society conflicts with the ideal of selfless male friendship. In *MV*, Shakespeare attempts to resolve the tensions of oppositions—female and male, the quests for wealth and love—and create an ordered world (55).

Perfect order is thwarted, however, because many characters are subject to betrayal, as in real life. Women betray, making them indeed worthy of suspicion, but men do also. Jessica betrays her father when she abandons him, Bassanio betrays Portia in the courtroom, and Portia betrays her wifely role in the courtroom when she becomes an androgynous figure and when she completes the ring plot, "threatening to cuckold her husband hermaphroditically" (Tennenhouse 66). Tennenhouse says, she "is sexually self-enclosed and threatening" (66) when she teases her husband: "Pardon me, Bassanio, / For by this ring the doctor lay with me" (5.1.259–60). Paradoxically, her androgyny is responsible for her successful rescue of Antonio in Venice. Act 5 concludes with less-than-perfect order, a counterfeit order, because Antonio is left alone, suggesting that the ideal of male friendship cannot be maintained in a world of heterosexual marriage. Affecting all these relationships is the acquisition of wealth and wealth's role in initiating and maintaining love. Tennenhouse concludes, "the play ends in Belmont, where marriage substitutes for patronage, and love is wealth" (66).

Myth and Archetypal Criticism

Northrop Frye is perhaps the most well-known critic who rebuts New Critical theory's isolationist requirement (73–78). Instead of reading a work without considering external influences, he offers a system for classifying literature that identifies similarities among works. In *A Natural Perspective* (1965), Frye describes a poetics, or a systematic framework for literature. After we read a piece of literature, "we see it as a simultaneous unity" (8–9). The key word, he says, is *structure,* a particularly useful term in understanding comedy and romance, in which "we must surrender ourselves to the structure and accept its conventions" (9–10). He claims that tragedy contains actions that seem to be a logical result of behavior and character, while comedy stylizes characters and "may force them to do quite unreasonable things"; thus Shakespeare's "Moor of Venice [Othello] belongs to humanity and his Jew of Venice to folklore" (14). Frye outlines the generic three-part comic plot, which first presents "an anti-comic society" that blocks and opposes "the comic drive"; second, the comic plot narrates a "period of confusion and sexual license" with temporarily lost identity or "the stock device of impenetrable disguise"; and third, the plot concludes with "the discovery of identity, which may be a new social group, a new individual identity, or newly revealed sets of lovers" (73–78). Showing how critical theories, such as structuralism and Freudianism, overlap, Frye observes that "the action of comedy is intensely Freudian in shape; the erotic pleasure principle explodes underneath the social anxieties sitting on top of it and blows them sky-high" (78). "The mythical or primitive basis of comedy is a movement toward the rebirth and renewal of the powers of nature . . . from death to rebirth, decadence to renewal, winter to spring, darkness to dawn" (121).

Finding archetypal myths in comedy, Frye examines *MV* as it fits into a mythic comic plot configuration. He sees in Portia an Andromeda figure who is placed in an "exposed condition" by her dead father "who arranged the scheme of the caskets" (90). She laments her fate: "so is the will of a living daughter curbed by the will of a dead father" (1.2.20–21). In the archetypal myth plot, the rebirth of the new society occurs because of the actions of an Eros figure, who encompasses both sexes, or an ingenue like Portia, who plays a bisexual role and uses a male disguise to gain "the birth of the new society and the reconciliation of the older one with it" (83). The harsh and irrational law or social contract that begins the plot in *MV* therefore is not ignored; rather, it is reconciled, "internalized, transformed to an inner source of coherence" (127). Frye also sees the law in *MV* as undergoing such a transformation, similar to the transformation of the law in the Christian myth: mankind loses the peaceable kingdom of the Garden of Eden, suffers through human history struggling under a tyrannical law, and "eventually regains . . . [God's] original vision . . . not by breaking the law, but by internalizing it: [the law] becomes an inner condition of behavior" (133).

Shylock, however, can only insist irrationally on the tyrannical law. Frye compares him to the Jews at the trial of Christ when he claims that he would prefer his daughter marry "any of the stock of Barabbas . . . rather than a Christian" (4.1.292–93). Frye suggests, "The redeeming power which baffles [Shylock] is the blood that he cannot have. When he finally renounces mercy entirely, then his bond is denied" (134). *The Merchant of Venice* is almost flawed because of the exclusion of Shylock from the final triumph. But Frye qualifies this exclusion as being aimed not at Shylock the father but at an abstraction, "the spirit of legalism," which disallows mercy, and he adds that it "nearly destroys the comic mood of the play" (91). He labels Shylock, like other Shakespearean antagonists who can only be spectators to the final resolution, *idiotes,* which he defines as technical villains or the "focus of the anticomic mood." But Shylock is quantitatively different for he "is also misanthropic and opposed to festivity on principle" (97). As a result of his exclusion from the Act 5 festivity, we feel "there is always a part of us that remains a spectator, detached and observant, aware of other nuances and values" (103). Consequently, by the end of the play, Shylock is not a part of the new society, but "we never quite forget him" (103).

Predating Frye's overview of structuralism as an interpretation of the comedies is C. L. Barber's "The Merchant and the Jew of Venice: Wealth's Communion and an Intruder," a chapter in his now famous text, *Shakespeare's Festive Comedy* (1958). In this structuralist study, Barber hypothesizes that Shakespeare's festive or idyllic comedies (those before *Hamlet* in 1601) and clowns of misrule mirror the annual Elizabethan holidays of sport and feast, in which brief designated periods of misrule and merrymaking lead to extended periods of renewed order and traditional rule. Barber says that "festive" comedy here refers to the structure or the saturnalian pattern by which comedy organizes experience. This may be "summarized in the formula, through release to clarification by means of humorous understanding" (4). In his chapter on *MV,* Barber observes that while the play is "not a theatrical adaptation of a social ritual," it contains symbolized social rituals and occasions throughout. Misrule evolving into grace, disorder into order, is embodied in the conventions of character: killjoy and reveler, butt and wit, intruder and insider. Language itself evolves from abuse to invocation, railing to poetry, ridicule to romance.

Shylock, of course, is the negative character, using negative language, devising negative events, and serving as the negative symbol. He is "the evil side of the power of money" placed up against the "beneficence of wealth" (167). But the community has set Shylock outside the "easy bonds of community" for good reason; he has threatened the grace of accord, even if only in the false and unreal form of a legal bond, insubstantial verbal machinery. Furthermore, the key concept of the play—mercy—has always been beyond Shylock to give (or receive) so, as Barber euphemistically puts it, in Act 4 Shylock "is plainly told that he is a snudge" (187) and kept from participation in Act 5 where the celebration of community, grace, and the proper use of wealth conclude the play. Shylock, Barber says, has "appallingly inhuman" attitudes which rest "on a lack of community of grace." On the other hand, Barber comments on the persistent virtue of the Portia-Bassanio group. They are "so very very far above money . . . it would be interesting to see Portia say no, for once" (190). Yet Shylock fits perfectly into the design of the play, even if his strong humanity, which is not "ipso-facto good," is enough to form the basis of another entire play (191).

Barber concludes that the more one remembers the high design of the play, which promotes grace in the community expressed through Shylock, "the less one wants to lose the play Shakespeare wrote for the sake of one he merely suggested" (191). Thus structure is the key to understanding, even if its broad strokes make Shylock and the Portia-Bassanio group into a black-and-white design, progressing from the darkness of misrule to the brightness of grace and order.

1970 to the Present

Dividing twentieth-century literary criticism at the beginning of the eighth decade is in some ways arbitrary, since the later commentary depends on methods of analysis developed earlier, and the observations themselves from earlier decades remain persuasive. Yet in or around 1970, commentators change direction. Inspired by other disciplines—philosophy, linguistics, psychology, or perhaps political science—they often base their observations on continental theory, political and gender-based hegemony, and skepticism about the independence of authorship. Many reject the notion that language holds consistent meaning; rather, the concepts that language represents shift according to the demands of social hegemony.

This broadening of the meaning of *meaning* in the later part of the twentieth century further strengthens the relationship of literature to other disciplines by adding interpolated subtexts. This leads to contemporary rereadings of important earlier scholars, including Freud; Carl Jung (1875–1961), a Swiss psychologist and Freud's sometime colleague; Karl Marx (1818–1883), a German political philosopher; Martin Heidegger (1889–1976) and Friedrich Nietzsche (1844–1900), both German philosophers; and Ferdinand de Saussure (1857–1913), a Swiss linguist. Later scholars who initiated these rereadings and formulated new concepts of literature include Louis Althusser (1918–1990), who examined literature through political philosophy; Jacques Lacan (1901–1981), a psychoanalyst; Jacques Derrida (1930–) and Mikhail Bahktin (1897–1975), both philosophers; Claude Levi-Strauss (1908–), a cultural anthropologist; and Michel Foucault(1926–1984) and Roland Barthes (1915–1981), who studied literature from the perspective of linguistics and discourse studies.

Post-Saussurean theory is named for Saussure, who in 1916 published *Course in General Linguistics,* the basis for semiology or semiotics, the science of signs. His theory of linguistics describes the relationship between *signifiers,* sounds or written images, and *signifieds,* the concepts or things the signifiers supposedly represent. Saussure argues that although signifiers appear to be transparent signs clearly representing signifieds, they are actually separate and distinct from the signifieds they are called on to stand for. Signifiers, or signs, carry their own inherent weight of meaning. Societies must have signifying systems and agree through common practice to attach certain meanings to signifiers. As isolated sounds or markings, signifiers would be arbitrary, but in social use they gain broad and evolving meanings from the changing society. The meanings of signifiers come not from the signifieds on which we imagine them pasted but from one another; signifieds differentiate from one another in their own construct of a language system.

Just as signifying systems in language are preset and constantly reset by the society, change in signifying systems occurs in areas other than language, such as dress, gesture, and behavior, thus becoming an important consideration in drama and theater studies. A production reworks the ambiguities of a play, edits, highlights, and reorders it to reflect prevailing relationships among signifiers in order to present a favored interpretation and shroud others. For example, in Bill Alexander's 1987 production, Salanio and Salarino shoved and kicked Shylock to the ground in 3.1 as they taunted him, thus highlighting his victimization by the Christian mob. In many nineteenth-century productions, when Portia delivered her courtroom speech, she looked as if a supernatural force had surprisingly compelled philosophical thoughts to proceed from her pretty mouth, which implied passivity in the ingenue. Post-Saussurean theory makes of expressive realism a tautology; just as Ruskin wrote that the writer's discourse reflects the world and her or his responses to it, post-Saussurean critics say the world and the writer's responses to it reflect the writer's discourse. Most important, no final "meaning" of a work of literature exists, because literature is constructed of language—by definition a commodity filled with infinite meaning and forever in flux. This premise of the fluidity of language inspires most contemporary commentary, including New Historicist, Marxist or Cultural Materialist, feminist, and queer readings.

A Note on Deconstruction

Since ideas from deconstruction theory have become ubiquitous in the criticism of the last third of the twentieth century, I will briefly review their background. In *Mythologies* (1957), Roland Barthes began the process of examining a work of art, a discourse, not as a reflection of the world but rather as a construction—material arranged to fit within a form but inevitably to break out from that form with contradictions the reader may recognize and then interpret. With the consequent variety of interpretations, a text is said to be plural, and the process of examining the text's construction is said to be *deconstruction,* a term coined after Barthes had begun this investigative process. Deconstructing may also be described as decentering, probably first coined in the study of literature by Pierre Macherey, who saw that the silences in the text, what it does not say, give meanings to what it does say. This parallels the work of Freud, who labeled the unspoken in the individual the "unconscious" and proposed that it gives meaning to the conscious. Catherine Belsey summarizes that "it is the task of criticism, then, to establish the unspoken in the text, to decenter it in order to produce a real knowledge of history" (136). A theatrical production or a critical essay shares this function.

While Freud decentered the individual, Marx decentered history, and Saussure decentered language itself, we must finally recognize perhaps the most famous "decenterer," Jacques Derrida, whose philosophical-linguistic study, *Of Grammatology,* published in French in 1967 and in English in 1976, along with his other works, reveals a complex analysis of language he exemplifies in his own writing. Among the many principles he advances is that language does not originate in the speaker or subject; rather, the subject is created from or inscribed in the language, which is a system of differences. In fact, there could never be subjectivity at all without language, because subjectivity is founded in the separation of I from the rest of the world. If I am conscious of myself, then I must recognize the differentiation between the world and me.[14]

While I cannot delve into the complexities of Derrida's work, we can agree that he too would not seek a single meaning from the play. Granted, *MV* contains a closed set of words (assuming that we can agree on a single text of the play); but those words gain meaning only as they differ from one another in a linguistic calculus of relationships, which are fluid, flowing through time and space, dissolving and reshaping the subjectivity of each reader. This suggests that even though Shakespeare's sixteenth-century audience, virtually all Christians, would have disapproved of Shylock and his scorn for Christianity, other audiences can see him as the tragic hero with the lovely blond-haired Portia and the Venetians cheering her on as his hard-hearted persecutors.

New Historicism

New Historicism, like the more traditional historicism of the earlier decades of the twentieth century, deals with clarifying our understanding of the world in which the play was written to better understand the play itself. First developed by Stephen Greenblatt,[15] new historicism, however, deals less with well-known historic events, royal or noble figures, and broad philosophic ideas than with the details of the lives of common people, which are thought to more accurately inform our understanding of the entire period. As James Shapiro writes, New Historicism deals "with the history of the Other in the Renaissance" (86), and that might include witches, hermaphrodites, Moors, Turks, prophets—those who existed among the mainstream but were overlooked in general historical or literary studies. Greenblatt explains that his purpose for such study is his "desire to speak with the dead" through fictions that are "simulations . . . undertaken in full awareness of the absence of life they contrive to represent" (*Shakespearean Negotiations* 2). He investigates "the margins" of texts for traces of "energia," the "compelling force" or social energy of the culture, lying "however transformed and refashioned . . . [yet] initially encoded in those works" (6).

Greenblatt observes that theater, with its "circulation of energy by and through the stage," provides representations of that culture through gesture and language as well as through props and the "symbolic acquisition of social practices" (*Shakespearean Negotiations* 6). For example, Greenblatt cites the convention in comedy of transvestite freedom (the implicit hermaphroditism of boys dressed as girls dressed as boys), which excites sexual energy in the audience (20). He calls this "erotic chafing" (88) because it creates real-life sexual excitement. In *MV*, the practice of usury and the biblical precepts against it create what we might also call "chafing" because the newly developing mercantilism of England fascinated the Elizabethan audience. As a result, New Historicists might examine the business dealings among theater owners, acting companies, banks, and moneylenders in Elizabethan England to inform a study of *MV.*

During the Renaissance, drama was a form of literature easily accessible to the common people; therefore, applying New Historicist inquiry to Renaissance drama and theater studies can be fruitful because drama influenced and reflected common society. Yet some critics argue that drama's relationship to the common people is difficult to identify. First, plays were highly regulated by both church and state; therefore, they may offer to us only official and therefore false notions and not present an "accurate" image of society. Second, a play might have been written in the first place as pure propaganda, offering beneficial instruction and serving as an effective government voice that could help convince the audience that cooperation and compliance with the rules of the state are golden. Finally, a playwright may have included in his work clever hidden irony that would escape the censor's notice. Even as it seemed to be promoting order and obedience to the state, between the lines, the play may have mocked that order and criticized the state. Thus it might contain two simultaneous

messages, one straightforward and the other ironic. We question its effectiveness, however, in dispensing a more seditious, hidden message to a
public that was generally far less sophisticated than the Master of the Revels.

But granting these considerations, a New Historicist study of drama, in
particular of *MV*, remains especially fertile. The play is about economic
and social-religious issues that affected and interested common people
then as they do now: money, usury, marriage, and ethnicity. Outwardly,
the play posits that wealth and marriage accompany virtue, and that Jews
and usury lead to evil. But we must ask whether the play actually supports
these positions. At the end of the sixteenth century, a gentle life required
wealth, but many methods for its acquisition were officially condemned.
Jews were scorned as violent murderers; yet they had suffered a long and
ugly history in England and Europe and regularly served as convenient
scapegoats. Marriage remained a means to acquire riches, but it also could
be motivated by love. Finally, usury was a necessity to capitalism, yet it
was condemned as a sin. These ambiguities support the value of New Historicist and Marxist inquiries into the text.

In *William Shakespeare:* The Merchant of Venice (1993),[16] Graham
Holderness evaluates the play as a document that both reflects and influences the past and continues to speak differently to changing audiences.
First, Holderness considers its inclusion among the comedies. He proposes that the sixteenth century had "a broader and more elastic" conception of comedy (8), so that a romantic comedy like *MV* could still include
the threat of "physical mutilation . . . [that] would not be out of place in a
Senecan melodrama like *Titus Andronicus* or in a Jacobean tragedy" (9).
Furthermore, the Venetian setting is a real place, so "the teasing interplay
of the real and the imaginary" produces a particularly difficult crux for the
modern reader. Even more difficult, however, is Shylock—on the one
hand, a conventional, miserly senex from Italian drama and folktale who
blocks the marriage of the young lovers, but on the other, a Jewish moneylender, a role that today we find "unacceptably racist" (11). Our responses to him as senex are "destabilized by our acute awareness of the
complicating factor of race," and we do not approve of the dominant
Venetian culture "conspiring to rob and humiliate the representative of a
minority ethnic group" (11).

Holderness next looks at the play and history. He suggests that we may
look at the problem of casting a Jew as the revenge villain in two ways.
We assume the play to be "essentially historical" (13), belonging to the
belief systems and the prejudices of the age in which it was produced. As
a consequence, modern audiences may read the play "as if [they] were

Elizabethans" or acknowledge "the deep divergences between the ideologies of the past and the culture of the present" (13–14), which implies that it is not the text that contains "inherent complexities" but rather "the subsequent evolution of cultural differences" (14). Contradiction and complexity arise because of historical change, according to this traditional historicist approach. Conversely, New Historicists might argue that "we should recognize the past as an enemy" and therefore "expose the crudity and prejudice of the play and create a "critical account that foregrounds the past and [the] continuing dominance of repressive and exploitive ideologies" (14). New Historicists might alternatively add "that all the complexities discovered by modern criticism were embodied within the Elizabethan text from the outset," but Holderness observes that the notion of a single authoritative voice in drama is less likely because "drama is 'dialogic'—composed by the juxtaposition of different and divergent voices" (15).

Finally, Holderness comments on the text and performance, concluding that performance history further suggests "a poststructuralist model of interpretation" (15). He notes that the racial problems as well as the representation of a Christian culture "dedicated to the uninhibited pursuit of wealth" suggest that complexity is embedded in the text. In his overview of performance history, Holderness notes the changes in the presentation of Shylock from stock villain to tragic hero, to noble victim, back again to anachronistic stock villain, to generic outsider. He warns against describing Elizabethan ideas with confidence and assuming that Shakespeare presents orthodox ideas in his plays. He suggests that we read the plays dialectically with historical imagination and an awareness that "subsequent historical developments and modern beliefs may have changed the play's possibilities of interpretation" (17). Whether the play is inscribed with these inconsistencies or whether history has imposed them remains a question.

Kiernan Ryan also presents a New Historicist and Marxist view of the play in his essay "Re-reading *The Merchant of Venice*" (1995), arguing that the contradiction between a racist capitalism and humanity is "what the play exposes to the gaze of a fully historical reading" because "conditions of literary production in Shakespeare's time made it possible for his drama to undermine rather than underwrite the governing assumptions of his society" (37). The play holds "conflicting impulses" that Shakespeare sets on one another so that in Shylock, the play subverts the values of the Venetians that it appears to uphold.

A key line, according to Ryan as well as other commentators, is in the conclusion of the "Hath not a Jew eyes?" speech: "The villainy you teach me I will execute" (3.1.56). In other words, Shylock's evil is "the deliberate mirror-image of [the Venetians'] concealed nature. The revenge is a bitter parody of the Christians' actual values" (38), and gaining Antonio's heart is the mirror image of the Christians' heartlessness. Shylock is the creation of the greedy, wealth-centered culture of the Venetians. Their hatred of Shylock's "wolfish, bloody, starv'd and ravenous" behavior is transferred self-hatred for the same sorts of actions (4.1.138).

Ryan warns that this does not imply sympathy for Shylock; rather, it indicts "an apparently civilised society . . . as premised on barbarity, on the ruthless priority of money values over human values, of the rights of property over the elementary rights of men and women" (40). The play serves as a commentary on the entire society of the Venetians as well as on the actions of the alien.

Ryan points out the corollaries to such a perspective on the play. The casket plot underscores the "the disparity between the visible and the veiled nature of people and things, between supposed worth and actual value," (40) sharpening our scrutiny of the opposite hidden beneath the observed. Lancelot Gobbo's dilemma over remaining with Shylock reflects the audience's confusion over whom to offer allegiance—charitable Christians or victimized Shylock. Finally, the unknown source of Antonio's sadness, the mystery of his affections, and his final yet wealth-filled isolation may be seen as "the void at the heart of Venice," an expression of "Shakespeare's anguished rejection of the values invading Elizabethan England" (41–42). The flawed values of Venice extend to the play's "preoccupation with women as the alienated objects of men's vision, choice and possession" (42). This is especially evident in the final scene in Belmont with its "alleged romantic harmony [that is] fraught with sinister insinuations" (41), including Jessica's and Lorenzo's catalog of tragic lovers, Portia's and Nerissa's "nagging reproaches" (Ryan's unfortunate adjective) and their threats of future unfaithfulness, and Antonio's offer to pledge his soul to Portia for Bassanio's faithfulness—an offer uncomfortably echoing his pledge in 1.3 to Shylock, the other repressed figure in the play. Ryan argues for "a determinate range of verifiable readings genetically secreted by the play" (42), not readings that arise from later, changed cultures.

In "Historical Difference and Venetian Patriarchy" (1998), John Drakakis examines the play as a comedy in the theater and, like Ryan, argues that the text questions the religion and ideology of its own culture. He argues that *MV* contains "discordant effects" that block "generic conformity" (185) and are uncomfortably woven into a formal comic resolution. He explains that the Elizabethan theater as an institution of leisure stood in "tense opposition" to the "values and norms of Elizabethan culture," which valued work; hence the theater held a more distant and therefore broader vantage point from which to comment on that culture. This produced a voice not entirely ironic but rather discordant, expressing "a variety of positions, all of which could be contained within a single text" (185). "The theatre itself," Ryan writes, "charged with imitating ideology, also exposes its workings, and can thus be said to function as the 'mirror' of Elizabethan culture insofar as its function is mimetic, but also as the means whereby the ideological underpinnings of that culture are displayed" (204).

Shylock is less a realistic character and more a primary *means* by which *MV* challenges the values of Venice. He is "both a subject position *and* a rhetorical means of prizing open a dominant Christian ideology no longer able to smooth over its own internal contradictions. He is also a challenge and a threat—in theatrical terms, as a stage Jew or villainous vice, and in sociological terms, as a puritanical voice opposing pleasure." Drakakis writes that in the figure of Shylock, Shakespeare "represents a convergence of a multiplicity of identities . . . against which Venetian identity defines itself" (188).

Drakakis also observes that the play "appears to confront economic questions directly" (189), and in such questions, once again, Shylock, as the usurer, is the "other," different from the dominant order, without "independent existence or self-definition" (189). He draws a parallel between Portia and Shylock as "foci of resistance" because "both are possessed of material wealth which Venice needs" (198), but while Shylock acquired his wealth only through the unnatural practice of usury, Portia's wealth is available to the Venetians through the accepted means of marriage. But Portia focuses resistance by representing the pleasures of excess that challenge the patriarchal need for constraint that governs the actions of her father (and Shylock). Finally, the role of Portia, as well of Nerissa and Jessica, even raises questions of gender fixity since the roles were played by young boys. Drakakis warns against submitting to the experience of the play without pointing out its troubling cruxes. "To abrogate this critical responsibility is to propose a complicity with texts such as *MV* which lays the critic open to the charge of disseminating its prejudices" (209).

In *Shylock: A Legend and Its Legacy* (1992), John Gross offers valuable scholarly research to explain the changing role of Shylock since his inception. Gross divides his study in three parts: first he traces literary, mythic, and historic influences on the character of Shylock and discusses him as usurer, Jew, father, husband, and demon in relation to the other characters in the drama—Antonio, Portia, Jessica, and the other Christians. Second, Gross provides a history of English-speaking performance and criticism, often as it reflects the prevailing attitudes toward Jews; and finally, he looks at Shylock since 1939 as "A Citizen of the World." Particularly in this section, Gross notes the way Shylock has been borrowed by popular culture, by psychology, and by government to further a variety of ideologies. As a miserly usurer he represents the worst of capitalism; as a possessive father he manifests an anal retentive neurosis; as a demon, he has served as a justification for anti-Semitism; and as a victim of discrimination, he has become a pathetic or even a tragic symbol of the racist world in the twentieth century.

The ethics in *MV,* Gross concludes, remain murky, particularly on the key question of whether the play presents Christians ironically and thus gives sympathy to Shylock. Gross doubts it. "The Christian characters have admirable ideals, and on the whole—in their dealings among themselves, as opposed to their dealings with Shylock—they live up to them." It cannot be proved of course, that they are not to be viewed ironically, but "great stretches of the play do not feel ironic" and "the fantasy, though it is sometimes shaken, is never shattered." This isolates Shylock as the villain who is hated all around for "the moneybags and the knife." Were he not Jewish, Gross hypothesizes, we would not mind his punishment. But he is Jewish, and to some readers, the play rests on the assumption that Jewishness means vileness. The other characters, who "represent, at their best, some of the leading values of their civilization," implicitly believe that Jewishness is "an offense in itself." This does not mean, Gross explains, that "there is a direct line of descent from Antonio to Hitler," but he admits, "the ground for the Holocaust was well-prepared" (350–52).

In *Shakespeare and the Jews* (1996), a study of Elizabethan culture, James Shapiro, like Gross, supports a critical position with extensive scholarship. He works within a narrower but complex focus, examining "what Shakespeare and his contemporaries thought about Jews" (1). He proposes that as the English struggled for a national identity at the end of the medieval and into the early modern period, they used so-called aliens, Jews and Irish, to identify, perhaps silhouette, what the English were not. Thus Jews served to outline the characteristics of English nationalism rather than the characteristics of English Christianity. Jews' inferiority rested in their alien status, not in what was then considered their paganism. By the eighteenth century, the English had begun to identify Shakespeare with what it meant to be English; he represented English culture as a whole. Thus, Shapiro argues, Shakespeare's portrayal of Shylock as a morally inferior Jew fit conveniently with the notion of English ethnic superiority.

In the first section of his text, Shapiro defines and describes the small groups of Jews who were in England during the Renaissance. Next he presents Elizabethan notions of Jews as criminals, originally the killers of Christ, who, some thought, were killers of Christian children, poisoners of water, and circumcisers (read castrators) of Christians. Shapiro also suggests that questions of the Jewish Diaspora were unconsciously coded questions for the English about their own ethnic unity. Shapiro then examines Jewish conversion to Christianity—whether it was possible and whether it was accepted. Finally, he investigates the post-Reformation period beginning in 1660 through the period of the Jewish Naturalization Act ("the Jew Bill") controversy in 1753, when the inclusion of practicing Jews as English citizens was a turbulent issue.

Jews in England during the Renaissance have received little attention because so few Jews had lived there presumably since 1290, when Edward I expelled them. Even Stephen Greenblatt comments that the particular study of Jews as the New Historicist's Other in Renaissance England could be of little use because there were "scarcely any Jews in England." But Shapiro questions this, based on what he calls the sixteenth- and seventeenth-century English "obsession" with the Jews. They appear in a broad range of discourses, in both Tudor and Stuart drama, historical chronicles, travel narratives, sermons, and works on trade, usury, magic, race, gender, nationalism, and alien status. Their meager numbers in England belie their cultural impact (90). Shapiro further argues that Shakespeare was familiar with Jews. Such familiarity could explain the sympathy he shows for Jews, which, Shapiro claims, is indicated in his works.

The sympathy or scorn Shakespeare had for Jews, then, is an ongoing political as well as literary matter. Shapiro scrupulously details in his book the importance of Jews to English culture during Shakespeare's time and beyond—even in current historical and literary inquiries. He concludes that "the story that has never been far from the center of this [Shapiro's] book has been Shakespeare's *The Merchant of Venice;* . . . its vitality can be attributed to the ways in which it scrapes against the bedrock of beliefs about the racial, national, sexual, and religious difference of others" (228). Just as post-Saussurean critics suggest, history affects the discourse called *MV,* and the discourse affects history.

An article further illuminating elements of Shapiro's book is Peter Berek's "The Jew as Renaissance Man" (1998). Focusing on the theater in the 1590s, Berek expands Shapiro's notion that "discussion of Jews in late medieval and early modern England was less about Jewishness than about what it meant to be English," which was assuredly superior to being non-

English. Berek argues that Christopher Marlowe's *The Jew of Malta* is "the crucial initiatory text" (130), because during the 1590s, the theater was "obsessed" with questions of nature versus nurture—whether one could achieve social success through accomplishment in spite of birth.

New Christians or Marranos exemplified such social fluidity and thus encouraged an ambiguous attitude in non-Jewish English people about such mobility. Berek writes that Barabas is a wealthy Jew but is vicious and murderous and always outside the circle of Christian power. This does not remain only Marlowe's mimetic representation of Jews. Following the post-Saussurean premise, Berek argues that the character of Barabas becomes the model for society and art. Along with his Christian enemies, he is "the ground for mimesis" (130), since theater "both mirrors and creates" society in a "transactional relationship" (130). Shylock follows in that lineage. Jewish characters after Marlowe "are far more indebted to theater than to history" (131).

Berek traces the history of Jews in England from the time of William the Conqueror into the seventeenth century. Because they were forced to appear as Christians, the few Jews who lived in England had to live lives that were "a succession of useful fictions," what Berek suggests was their "most important quality in Elizabethan England" (134). As outsiders, either New Christians or "New Jews," Marranos were forced to wander on the periphery of the society, without the identity of a place they could call home. In Marlowe's play, Barabas lives such a fiction, seeing religion and morality "as childish toys," because "the strong and successful man invents his own rules as he invents his own personality" (137). One element of Barabas's Jewish evil, in Marlowe's eyes, is being duplicitous. Marlowe's "peculiar vision" of Jews is hostile and expresses his own, but not necessarily the society's, anxiety over the social change represented in the Jew, a template for later representations.

Berek explains Renaissance images of Jews, first the biblical portrayal of the Jews who chose to save Barabbas over Jesus at the Crucifixion, and then the contemporary English portrayal of Jews who lived abroad. Such sketches are sometimes sympathetic, often harsh, but on the whole no worse than the descriptions of other foreigners. Berek explains that to the English, Jews abroad were harmless since they did not threaten English nationalism and social change.

Two subsequent sections tell of usury and the Jews in England and the affair of Roderigo Lopez in 1593–1594. He notes that in contemporary documents telling of Lopez, little is made of his Jewishness, perhaps, Berek suggests, because he was a convicted spy, an unambiguous criminal. Berek concludes his article with a section titled "Jewishness and

Genre," in which he identifies the stage conventions of character derived from Marlowe and Shakespeare in later Jewish characters. The convention continues to create "social energy" that encircles the character of the Jew, for better or worse.

Marxist Criticism and Cultural Materialism

Related to New Historicism, Marxist criticism and Cultural Materialism are premised in economic determinism—that one's class predetermines one's economic fortunes and overall fate. Marxists vary widely, but most examine the hegemony—the process by which powerful people manipulate the weak by brainwashing them into believing that the powerful and the weak share common goals, which obviously are the goals of the powerful. Thus, unbeknownst to them, the weak do not hold beliefs of their own, nor do they espouse ideas that are at all self-serving. Marxists further state that individuals lack autonomy and identity.

Since 1970, Marxism has become a notable basis of Cultural Materialism. Like New Historicists, Cultural Materialists question the relationship between literature and the prevailing culture but with at least three differences: in the study of Shakespeare, Cultural Materialists examine the relationship of Shakespeare studies to the current culture, perhaps more than to Shakespeare's culture; they seek to initiate social change and influence current culture; and as implied above, they are often strongly Marxist. Although Cultural Materialism and Marxism use terminology loosely and historical evidence selectively, both encourage vitality in literary interpretation and rebellion from tradition.

Walter Cohen warns of the limitations of historicism in "*The Merchant of Venice* and the Possibilities of Historical Criticism" (1982). Cohen presents an approach to *MV* that combines history with structure, connecting "the historical moment" with "the interpretive categories" (765). He argues that an interpretation of *MV* often serves to limit the play's meaning rather than deepen it, noting, "Perhaps no other Shakespearean comedy at all has excited comparable controversy." He explains why some commentators "view the play as a symptom of a problem in the life of late sixteenth-century England" (767), providing an overview of the period and place, the society's fear of the rise of capitalism, and the attendant ubiquitous practice of usury, which people scorned but needed. All levels of society required credit, debt, and banking. Cohen notes that in the following century, when the nobility had successfully adapted to a capitalist and therefore credit-bearing society, even though the lower classes remained endangered by credit practices, art, as a reflection of this hegemonic upper-class society, no longer represented usury as an evil. At the time of *MV,* however, usurers were considered opposite from merchants; usurers were represented as victimizers of the poor; they offered no benefit to the borrower and risked nothing—unlike brave, risk-taking merchants.

But the play is art, not a coded statement about English life. Cohen says that Shylock is neither a tight-fisted Mediterranean Puritan, nor is Antonio an apparent retro-anticapitalist. In fact Shylock serves as a powerful antagonist, ironically, because he does not practice usury with Antonio. Instead, he imposes a horrible kind of interest, defined as payment after the bond is forfeit. With an irrational resolve, Shylock refuses to forgive the bond, even for a great deal more money than he had lent in the first place, ostensibly because he believes that Antonio's demise will pave the way for Shylock himself to gain greater profits. Cohen suggests that, like the terms of the bond itself, Shylock's behavior is in the realm of folktale.

Cohen proposes that the Venetian setting for the story allays fears of capitalism because Venice and Italy were understood to have successfully adopted capitalism. Thus, Cohen says, "in *MV* English history evokes fears of capitalism, and Italian history allays those fears. One is the problem, the other the solution, the act of incorporation, of transcendence, toward which the play strives" (772). But even with a harmony of economic themes achieved with the superimposition of Venice on the concerns of England, Cohen notes that still "many critics have been unable to read a final coherence to *MV*" (773). In the play, there remains a bifurcation between the English and the Italian and between the need to bring closure to a literary work and to betray problems of economic and social injustice. This leads to the fallacious distraction, Cohen continues, that there is "a congruence between economic and moral conduct, between outer and inner wealth" (776), between the pastoral and the urban. The play also tries to unite feudal and more modern values of love and marriage. In the beginning, a woman is dominated by a dead father, property rights, and sexual hierarchy; but in the end, a virtuous wife is her husband's equal, both socially and legally. The "play reconciles the ideologically unreconcilable" (777).

Cohen also explains how the lower-class dramatic characters, namely, Lancelot Gobbo and Shylock, subvert the Christian social hierarchy. Typical of the clown, Lancelot offers puns that demonstrate chaos in language, which in turn implies an anarchy within all order. Lancelot also says that he listens to both the devil and to his conscience and foolishly equates the mortal Shylock with the superhuman Devil. Similarly, as a disruptive character derived from the conventional medieval Vice figure,

Shylock serves the devil, is the enemy of Christianity, and, Cohen adds, is "an incisive critic of Christian society" (780–81).

Cohen further sees in *MV* a questioning of the romantic comedy genre. This genre celebrates married love, resolves improbable problems through "playing and pretense," and subordinates social mimesis to focus on a joyous celebration of "comic, anarchic freedom". But in *MV,* the presence of "potentially antagonistic classes" highlights the limits of the form (782), because their presence questions the romantic order of the conclusion.

Finally, Cohen draws a comparison between the romantic comedy genre and Marxist theory because both suffer from a gap between theory and practice. In theory, the romantic comedy genre is far more narrow than it is in the diversity of its practice. Similarly, Marxist theory remains isolated from and more narrow than the reality that is now "a scarcely existent, larger, contemporary movement for social and political transformation." Yet, Cohen concludes, "Marxist theory provides Shakespearean drama with its most resonant context at least since the early seventeenth century" (784–85).

In *Rereading Literature: William Shakespeare* (1986), Terry Eagleton "rereads" the major plays "as an exercise in political semiotics," locating "the relevant history in the very letter of the text" (ix), particularly the "pious self-deception of a society based on routine oppression and incessant warfare" (1–2). He writes about *MV* in terms of the law. Just as language is paradoxically both a regular grammatical structure using lexical terms as well as a particular moment's event, "always this or that utterance in this or that situation" (35), so is the law. The law exists as an impartial set of decrees that must be enforced for all groups lest one group be granted "private" and more privileged law than another. It also must become a series of events of the moment, applications or interpretations that uphold its spirit and are "not narrowly technical or pedantic" (36). Eagleton asserts that it is Shylock, not Portia, who argues for the spirit of the law. Portia uses "ingenious quibbling" that would be "ruled out of order in a modern court" and "is aberrant because too faithful" (37).

Eagleton sees the possibility that Shylock did not plan to be victorious because he is "a solitary, despised outsider confronting a powerful, clubbish ruling class" (37). Eagleton speculates that it is almost as if he expects the Christians to lay a trap but cannot imagine what it might be. And his refusal to offer a reason for his vengeance is a challenge. But whatever the courtroom outcome over the bond, says Eagleton, Shylock wins; he either kills Antonio or mocks the justice of the court. To save one of its own from "the odious Jew," the court risks "deconstructing itself, deploying exactly the kind of subjective paltering it exists to spurn"(38).

Eagleton then compares spoken and written words and concludes that those written are more permanent but stifling, while speech is passing, unfixed, and deceptive. Portia's mercy speech is a case in point. She is deceptive in her false identity, false objectivity, and use of a hidden, hair-splitting trifle to win the proceeding. Shylock's written bond confirms that order in Venice is maintained with a written code, not transient human speech. As a powerless outcast in Venice, Shylock needs the support of a written or fixed contract to protect him. Granting mercy, as Portia requests, would be a foolhardy casting off of his minimal legal safeguard. If the law is allowed an *ad hoc* interpretation like that which Portia argues, then, Eagleton says, the difference between anarchy and authoritarianism is erased, since both give free rein to individual judgment.

Shylock's irrational insistence on Antonio's flesh "must be read in the light of his sufferings at the hands of anti-Semites; not just as revenge for them—though this is no doubt one of his motives—but as a scandalous exposure of that which Antonio owes him—his body, an acknowledgment of common humanity with Shylock—and arrogantly denies." It is perversely a "bitter inversion of the true comradeship Shylock desires, the only form of it now available to him" (43). In granting the bond in the first place, Shylock "demonstrates favouritism and partiality, risking a bad exchange" (44). But when he demands the forfeit of the bond, he demonstrates his capriciousness, an integral element of human nature, and thus the evidence of "the absolutely binding nature of a common humanity" between him and the equally whimsical, subjective Portia and Venetians (45).

Concerning the casket scenes, Eagleton says that although they imply "the acceptably idealist face of mercantile society, with their naive contrasts of appearance and reality"(46)—that the worthless is precious—Bassanio does indeed gain money from the marriage. Eagleton observes that this is typical; "the bourgeoisie have always pretended that sex transcends utility, at the very moment they debase it to a commodity" (45). Because both love and money share "measurelessness, transmutability, inexplicable mystery," Eagleton concludes, "money is less the opposite of erotic desire than its very image" (46). Bassanio's bottom line is that winning Portia is winning wealth. Eagleton proposes that Shakespeare rejects any simple counterpointing of appearance and reality and, like Lenin, believed in "the reality of appearances" (46).

Finally, Eagleton writes of the need to sustain impartiality in the law to yield justice and charity. The law and its implementation in Venice are not impartial. They are intended to promote trade and business by offering the appearance of fairness to all. But, Eagleton says, if the law is entirely impartial and indifferent, there is "something deconstructive" about it because it steamrolls over individuals for the sake of equality and uniformity (48). Law, he concludes, is "metaphorical, seeking a balance of similarities and differences" that is always in danger of splitting apart and "reducing unique situations to singular identity or fostering—what is strictly unthinkable—a cult of pure difference" (48).

Feminist Criticism

Evidence of the impact of feminist criticism on Shakespearean criticism is the breadth of its diversity.[17] The more popular Anglo-American feminism focuses on the experience of being female, while French feminism, as might be expected, explores the effect of language as a tool that forms gender in the first place. In her essay "Broken Nuptials in Shakespeare's Comedies" (1981), Carol Thomas Neely identified three broad groupings or modes of feminist criticism that have remained useful: the compensatory mode highlights female characters and their inherent strengths; the justificatory mode explains the patriarchal tone in the plays as a consequence of the patriarchal worlds of both the sixteenth and the twentieth centuries; and the transformational mode examines feminism as one of many gender issues that relate to Marxism. Some readers question this approach because it subsumes feminist issues into gender issues so that, once again, there is "the erasure of women" (Dubrow 44).

Feminist criticism also shows a broad range of influences. Neo-Freudian psychoanalysis, or cultural analysis, generally points out a more or less patriarchal, misogynistic, or suppressive attitude in Shakespeare's society and plays. Associated with French feminists, post-structuralists dismiss interpretation of the plays because it is mere language, an always-changing construction of the prevalent culture. Materialist feminism, arising from Marxism, questions the ways gender, class, race, and social marginality in a society affect depictions of the power of women characters in drama. Gender studies, more difficult to delineate, argue issues of gender and its construction from any number of positions, but most hold that plot conflicts may be explained not through fate or differences among characters but rather as conflicts programmed into a patriarchy, which silences the female voice.

In "Giving and Taking in *The Merchant of Venice*" (1984), Marianne Novy argues for the strength of the female character, saying that the play distinguishes between Antonio's self-sacrificial and ultimately depressing giving and Portia's more assertive, realistic, and sexual giving and taking. At the beginning, both Shylock, the Jew, and Portia, the woman, represent the Other in Venetian society. Each is identified with a form of giving strictly codified by society: giving money as a loan must be done with no thought of personal financial gain, and giving the flesh in sexual union must be done with no thought of pleasure. Novy says "both money-lending and sex were supposed to be for the benefit of others more than for oneself" (64). But as the Elizabethan world moved toward greater individuality and mercantile competition, these existing religious norms were threatened, as *MV* reflects. "Women and Jews could be seen as symbolic of absolute otherness—alien, mysterious, uncivilized, unredeemed." Thus they were associated with the flesh—sexuality and acquisitiveness (66).

Portia is the strongest character in the play because, Novy says, her form of giving involves "mutuality." Antonio speaks and behaves asexually, supporting Bassanio in his quest for Portia, and he "denies the acquisitiveness inherent in being a merchant and instead attacks Shylock" (66). Bassanio behaves irresponsibly with a "naive love of fine gestures," and he holds a childlike notion that he can later regain what he has lost— an arrow, money, or even a wife. Finally, Shylock seeks to serve himself as an isolated and separate individual; and he accumulates wealth without regard to a larger society. Portia's mutuality, the give and take of mutual exchange, is more successful than the extreme asceticism of Antonio, the individual acquisitiveness of Shylock, or the irresponsibility of Bassanio (70). She behaves with none of Antonio's self-sacrificial courtroom love, "which gives without asking for any return"; rather, in Act 5, she shows eros, "which desires also to receive" (77). Each character in Venice either gives or takes; and because each is an extreme, both merchant and lender fail. Portia brings to this world a mean in which Shylock is forced to give and Antonio responds by taking. In Act 5, Portia reaps a benefit from her heroic androgyny in Venice—self-assertion. Novy writes that Portia's "self-assertion . . . is also a celebration of the way that people manage to love one another with all their differences" (82). Portia proves to Bassanio that she will never be possessed. Love requires two separate, independent individuals who can experience the "mutuality in love with which the play ends" (80).

Another successful female in *MV* is Jessica, discussed by Camille Slights in "In Defense of Jessica: The Runaway Daughter in *The Merchant of Venice*" (1980). Slights admits that Jessica elicits both praise and blame from readers. Some see her escape from her father as a victory of the New Law over the Old, an analogy between her behavior and that of Jacob to Laban in Genesis or that of the Jews following God's command to Moses in Exodus that they despoil the Egyptians before leaving the land of bondage. It is a move from "the devil to Salvation" and a foreshadowing of the triumph of love in the casket-selection and flesh-bond plots. Other readers cannot ignore Jessica's deception, disobedience, theft, and abandonment of her father. Slights says "that in Jessica Shakespeare has created a character who elicits the audience's good will and yet disturbs it with moral doubts." The goal is "to explain the significant relation of the joy and love to the pain and loss embodied in her dramatic role" (360).

Slights says that Jessica is consistent throughout the play, unlike other characters. She is not greedy but seeks financial support for her flight with an impoverished lover. She is fun, courageous, ingenious, and far more thoughtful than many of Shakespeare's other heroines who escape tyrannical fathers. Although she cannot escape the charge of disloyalty, Jessica abandons her father and her religion for what Slights calls "a conscious, positive choice, involving danger and sacrifice" so that she might enter "the familial, social, and divine harmonies that bind people together in Christian society" (364). Unfortunately, she causes pain to others, an inevitable part of change. This includes her father and even Antonio, whose victimization is likely entrenched by Shylock's anger and grief over her departure. We therefore have ambivalent feelings over her move from old to new, from law to love. Slights claims that, even in the conclusion when Jessica's wealth is assured, readers know that it is "fortuitous" and not ensured by the law as is Portia's good fortune; it is, according to Lorenzo, miraculous.

Slights concludes that Jessica's greatest strength is her "receptivity to beneficent influences" (366), like marriage and Christianity, that require "humility and flexibility" (367). This receptivity is especially apparent "in her commitment of her gentle spirit to Lorenzo's guidance" and her immediate melancholy response to music, so different from Shylock's hatred:

> She listens attentively and so can discern true worth and give people their right praise. By attaining knowledge through hearing rather than through sight, she indicates her spiritual understanding that 'faith cometh by hearing' (Romans x.17). Jessica's gentle, attentive spirits do not always make for merriment, but they testify that by risking pain people may change their natures and grow toward true perfection. (368)

In "Broken Nuptials," Neely discusses marriage as the "subject and object" of Shakespearean comedies. She sees the plays as comments on the patriarchal world and explains how they contain the insistent motif of "parodic, unusual, or interrupted ceremonies and premature, postponed, or irregular consummations which occur in nearly every comedy" (61). These contrapuntal motifs expose the most serious impediments to "comic fulfillment" as being those within the lovers themselves. Neely notes that in both *MV* and *As You Like It*, the threat of male friendship to the union of lovers and its confrontation by the women in the form of "parodic ceremonies" mock the "extravagant commitments of the men and hint of the counterthreat of infidelity." This threat also gives substance to the previously unacknowledged sexuality of women. In the final scene in *MV*, Bassanio is forced to admit the seriousness of the injury he inflicts on his marriage, which is implicit in the missing ring, and to reaffirm the vows of his marriage, with Antonio "in effect giving Bassanio away" as he hands the ring from Portia back to Bassanio (65).

Janet Adelman further examines the patriarchal world as it is based in male relationships like that between Antonio and Bassanio in "Male Bonding in Shakespeare's Comedies" (1985). She sees women as "a disturbance to the bond" between men and to their "identity so constituted" (73). Although the classic dramatic obstacle to marriage, which generates a new family unit, is the will of the father, the male lover in *MV* and in other plays harbors an internal impediment, namely, a double loyalty to wife and male friend. While the earlier plays offer a magical resolution to the friend-versus-wife conflict, *MV* shows that "a fantasy solution is impossible" (79). Portia wins only insofar as Antonio loses the contest for Bassanio, and "the return of Antonio's three ships provides only poor compensation" (80). It is an "uncomfortable ending" that cannot be eased or ignored.

Coppélia Kahn continues the explication of the ring plot in "The Cuckoo's Note: Male Friendship and Cuckoldry in *The Merchant of Venice*" (1985). As a patriarchal romantic comedy, the play at once establishes marriage as the symbol of "the ideal accommodation of eros with society and as the continuation of both lineage and personal identity into posterity" (104); yet it "undercuts" the genre by questioning the success of marriage in accomplishing these goals. Such undercutting occurs in the ring plot, which begins in 3.2, continues in 4.1 and 4.2, and concludes in 5.1. The plot parallels and contrasts the rivalry between Portia and Antonio in the main plot and highlights the "conflict between male friendship and marriage which runs throughout [Shakespeare's] works (104). And just as such male friendship threatens the period before marriage, cuckoldry threatens during marriage. Kahn proposes that an interdependence binds these two motifs. Renunciation of such friendship and fear of eventual cuckoldry are the twin anxieties borne by Shakespeare's men as they seek exclusive possession of their women. Ironically, this is emphasized by the double standard that tolerates men's infidelity but condemns it in women.

As rivals for Bassanio's affection, Antonio and Portia enter the play in similar states of ennui, and both show remarkable generosity to Bassanio, so remarkable, in fact, that each could be accused of making Bassanio feel indebted. Yet it is Portia who triumphs, thanks to Antonio's ironic urging that Bassanio give up the ring. Kahn notes that "it takes a strong, shrewd woman like Portia to combat" the men's attachment for one another (107), but she succeeds at first because of her wealth and later because of her will and her wit. Her disguise, Kahn observes, makes "her something of a man as well . . . as though images of her as male and as female are super-imposed" (108). Her androgynous condition in 4.1. gives way to a more specifically "female power as wife to establish her priority over Antonio" in the ring plot (108). Using the ring both as a symbol of the marriage bond and as a symbol of female sexual parts, she responds to Bassanio's courtroom expression of loyalty to Antonio, which includes sacrificing his life and wife, by retaliating "with the only weapon at a wife's command: the threat of infidelity" (109). Kahn concludes:

> One facet of Shakespeare's genius is his perception that men don't see women as they are, but project onto them certain needs and fears instilled by our culture. He and a few other writers stand apart in being critically aware that these distorted but deeply felt conceptions of women can be distinguished from women themselves—their be-havior, their feelings, their desires. From Portia's point of view, women aren't inherently fickle, as misogyny holds them to be; rather, they practice betrayal defensively, in retaliation for comparable in-juries. (109–10)

Thus the ring plot presents a "tug of war," Kahn observes, between women and men for the affections of men. And, we may add, this "war" is won by the participant who arranged and controlled it from the beginning.

In "Portia's Ring: Unruly Women and Structures of Exchange in *The Merchant of Venice*" (1987), Karen Newman sees in the play both the strength of women and the power of the patriarchy, purposely leaving Shylock out of her reading. She comments on the male structures of ex-change that serve as powerful acts and cement relationships among men. Men offer and receive gifts—land, women, money, goods—to gain status, gain a credit bank for reciprocal gifts, and gain and maintain bonds with one another. Newman notes that this has been conventional practice among most peoples of the world from the nobility of Renaissance England to the "Big Man" in New Guinea, who gains unusual status by giving gifts that are too valuable to be returned in kind. *The Merchant of Venice* at first appears to maintain this tradition. In the first three acts, Portia appears to be the possession of her father, waiting to be won by the most worthy suitor. Although she is frustrated by this plan, she seems to accept it joyously when she is won by the dashing Bassanio in Act 3. She promises him that "This house, these servants, and this same myself / Are yours, my lord's! I give them with this ring" (3.2.170–71).

But even in these lines, the play does not follow the convention of man as exchanger of gifts and woman as gift because it is Portia who gives herself with the ring. This foreshadows her subversive role as Big Man, powerful enough to solve everyone's problems in Acts 4 and 5. Some readers argue that power in the female, particularly verbal power, is like that of the clown, who temporarily speaks rebellious subversive ideas, using wordplay that alters meaning. The woman's and the clown's contrary language serves as a safety valve that ultimately supports and verifies the status quo because their ideas lack permanence, and the status quo is always restored. But Newman contends that this is not the case with Portia's increasing power in the final two acts of the play. The ring that she gives to Bassanio as a symbol of his possession of her becomes a symbol of her power to reclaim herself as she reclaims the ring. As the ring then passes from Portia to Bassanio to Balthazar to Portia to Antonio and back again to Bassanio, it gains broader and deeper meanings. No longer does it merely represent love pledges and a man's possession of a woman. Bassanio's act of giving the ring to "an unruly woman" broadens its meaning so that it represents "forces of disorder, bisexuality, equality between the sexes, and linguistic equivalence in opposition to the decorous world of Renaissance marriage" (Newman 28). Therefore, this empowerment of a woman is no brief interlude after which the Renaissance norm of male exchanges returns. In Act 5, Portia's "mastery speech and gift-giving" (32) is not subversive, not a transient aberration of the norm of gender opposition and hierarchy that will be predictably overthrown. Rather, it is a simulation of male behavior that "perverts authorized systems of gender and power" and suggests that gender-coded norms of behavior are not natural (33). Women are not destined to one thing and men another. The permanence of Portia's inversion of the norm proves that behavior is a continuum of differences.

In her essay "Love in Venice" (in Coyle 1998), Catherine Belsey contributes to the discussion of sexual politics and the cultural history of gender. Belsey argues that in *MV*, love undergoes "a radical transformation"

(140). She explains that in the late sixteenth century, perceptions of love as "anarchic, destructive, and dangerous" were being replaced with an understanding of love as "marriage, concord, consent, and partnership" (141). Traces of the earlier and more dangerous love exist in the text; it is "desire . . . only imperfectly domesticated" (141). Belsey cites Lacan, who explains that the danger of desire lies in lack—"what you don't have." It is "the residue of demand, the unutterable within and beyond it" and the difference remaining when the signified is subtracted from the signifier (142). Because desire is hazardous, it is "immoderate, disproportionate, unstable, thrilling" (142), a condition Bassanio understands and explains after he correctly selects the lead casket.

Riddles are similarly dangerous since they "exploit the duplicity of the signifier, the secret alterity that subsists in meaning" (143). Riddles equivocate, showing that "language itself seduces and betrays those who believe themselves to be in command of it" and "are posed by the wise to isolate the foolish" (144). They may be likened to desire itself because both share uncertainty, enigma, and danger. Both "cease to fascinate," evaporating when "the *otherness* of the other is mastered" (145). An equivocation or riddle governs the marriage of Portia, the bond trapping and finally releasing Antonio, and the ring that represents a "new kind of marriage, where a wife is a partner and a companion" (146). Belsey notes George Puttenham's distinction (in *The Arte of English Poesie,* 1589) between a riddle, which has closure in its solution, and the more troubling amphibology, which has no solution because it lies, misleads, and seduces and has as its source oracles, pagan prophets, and witches who intend confusion, like the witches who beguile Macbeth. Portia's riddle posed to Bassanio in 5.1 can be solved only with the acknowledgment that "Portia has more than one identity." She "has always been other than she is. . . . fairytale princess, sacrificial virgin, 'an unlesson'd girl,' 'the lord /Of this fair mansion, master of my servants, Queen o'er myself' (3.2.159, 167–69)" (148). Belsey argues that the ring episode asks, what "does it mean to be a wife?" (149). Because of her success as "Bassanio's fellow-warrior, partner and friend," and because of her solution to the riddle of the rings, she presents "a utopian vision of the new possibilities of marriage" (149), a vision that also disrupts the patriarchal social order. This revolutionary basis for marriage proceeds not only from the "otherness" requisite to desire but also from the equality requisite to comradeship.

Finally, Belsey compares the play's representations of marriage and friendship, observing the differences between sixteenth-century values and those of today. She notes the supreme priority given to friendship but also the confusion of the newly evolving practice of identifying friendship in marriage, and she questions the notion that homosocial relationships lie in a natural progression of development. In determining whether homoeroticism was the basis of these relationships, Belsey cites Eve Kosofsky Sedgwick in her observation that "the sexual context of that period is too far irrecoverable for us to be able to disentangle" the meanings in the language.[18] Additionally, Belsey concludes that understanding marriage and friendship in *MV* may well reside "in the plurality of the word 'love'" (155), since the same word describes homosocial love and heterosexual passion. Meaning remains hidden in the language of the sixteenth century, and perhaps in our language as well.

Queer Theory, Gay and Lesbian Studies

Queer theory of the 1990s, arising from gender studies, breaks down gender divisions, since the label "queer" clouds the confining terminology—*homosexual* and *lesbian*—that separates gay men and gay women and mirrors the separation between male and female heterosexuals. It also neutralizes the pejorative implied meaning of the word "queer," a result of the post-structuralist premise that a stable linguistic identity in anything is fantasy. Queer theorists further point out that before the beginning of the eighteenth century, specific sexual labels did not exist, and individuals simply did or did not engage in certain sexual acts. After that time, linguistically regulated sexual identities developed. Some queer theorists propose that varieties of female-female and male-male relationships exist on a continuum of emotional and physical relationships without any defined borders marking off so-called homosexuality.

In *Homosexual Desire in Shakespeare's England: A Cultural Poetics* (1991), Bruce R. Smith raises a number of issues relating to homoeroticism and relates three to *MV*. First, he refers to several classical sources that speak of homoeroticism. One is Plutarch's debate over the superiority of the gender of one's lover in "Of Love" (*Moralia*). Two characters, Protogenes and Daphnaeus, discuss the relative merit of men loving boys versus men loving women. Protogenes argues that love for women is unsatisfying and debilitating while love for boys "inspires virtuous action." Daphnaeus responds that love toward boys "is against kinde" while that toward women is "according to nature" and significantly notes to Protogenes that "the passion of Love" toward either boy or woman is "all one & the same" (qtd. in Smith 38). Smith hypothesizes that Renaissance readers of Plutarch would agree with Daphnaeus. He continues that most critics agree that Shakespeare's plays reflect that position and give greater merit to "the ideal of husbands loving wives" (69). We remember that this ideal seems victorious in *MV* at the end. But if Act 5 does nothing else, it establishes the mutability of the present moment and the need to take from it the fullest advantage. The past has been less lovely, containing Bassanio's courtroom pledge to give his life and wife for Antonio's survival, followed by Portia's deception and mockery of her husband with the ring. Similarly, the future contains an exiled Shylock and the ambiguous fate of Antonio, who remains a loving and virtuous friend to Bassanio. That leaves only the moonlit moment holding with certainty "the ideal of husbands loving wives."

Second, Smith discusses the insistent theme in Shakespeare's plays of the conflicts between two male friends that are brought on by a woman, calling Antonio "the most pathetic" of all the severed friends (67). He notes the inability of Antonio and Bassanio in the first scene to speak of emotions and love in male-dominated Venice when they are finally left alone. Bassanio chatters on, in prose, about the loquacious Gratiano; and then, after a pause, Antonio awkwardly but with gravity broaches the topic of the mysterious lady, in blank verse. The self-conscious clumsiness of their conversation compares interestingly with Portia's and Nerissa's easy exchange in the subsequent scene in which they also discuss love. By the end of the play, Smith writes, "Portia and Nerissa teach Bassanio and Gratiano truths about men loving women and women loving men that the two male friends clearly do not know in Act I, scene 1" (68).

Finally, Smith speaks of the convention of cross-dressing in Renaissance drama, an important plot element in the play. Sixteenth- and seventeenth-century testimony of playgoers suggests that boys in women's clothes were simply an accepted convention. But some contemporaries did not approve. The Puritans saw cross-dressing as a major reason for closing the theaters. To that end, John Rainolds wrote in his 1599 polemic against the theater that cross-dressing "may kindle . . . uncleane affections" (147). The practice is officially condemned in Deuteronomy 22:5 in the Geneva Bible as that which "were to alter the ordre of nature, & to despite God." Smith notes three assumptions about theatrical cross-dressing, presented in 1989 by Stephen Orgel, that give credence to Rainolds's concerns. First, the "basic form of response to the theater is erotic"; second, "the theater is uncontrollably exciting"; and finally, "an essential form of erotic excitement for men is homosexual" (147). Many feminists agree, saying that in plays written by men, performed by men, and viewed by men, "homosexual titillation was *always* a factor," which furthers the modern notion that homosexuality is "all about men wanting to be like women" (148). He observes, for example, the bawdy language accompanying the cross-dressing of Portia and Nerissa.

But cross-dressing also is "the magic that turns tragedy into comedy" with its "retreat to a liminal landscape where social identities, and sexual identities, dissolve in the half-light" (152–53). Smith outlines various reasons that this is true. Perhaps Shakespeare was an "incipient feminist," at least temporarily allowing women to "enjoy a man's latitude of action" (153). Or more philosophically, cross-dressing may demonstrate that women, however briefly, may be perfectible to the level of men. Or following a Freudian interpretation, cross-dressing may mimic males' rite of passage from loving mirror images of themselves to loving women, from the homosexuality of adolescence to the heterosexuality of manhood.

Smith argues, however, that cross-dressing is more than this. Similar to Barber and Frye, he argues that it loosens the boundaries between society and nature, one person and another, and one's own internal and external self, particularly relating to one's sexual identity. Thus the play safely "indulges" the audience's homosexual desire with a boy playing a girl masquerading as a boy. As the play concludes, so does the play's implicit sodomy, which conveniently remains *within* the play. Yet this loosening of limitations is beneficial. If "we may take with us as we leave the theater some of the liminal freedom we allowed ourselves during the play" to go beyond the boundaries of our external gender roles, perhaps we can be like the play's characters, "better lovers, brothers, and rulers" (155). Certainly *MV*'s suggested exit to bed states where this might occur, much to the despair of contemporary Puritan attackers of the stage. But one can scarcely avoid noting that Smith fails to acknowledge female audience members. If a play's cross-dressing gives "a relaxation of the social rules that hold man's animal passions in check" (153) by allowing male characters to be sexually attracted to young boys, then Smith might expand his argument to include the effect and value of such actions for women in the audience.

In "The Two Antonios and Same-Sex Love in *Twelfth Night* and *The Merchant of Venice*" (1995), Joseph Pequiney examines the relationship between Antonio and Bassanio and offers a method to identify same-sex passion among Shakespeare's characters. He dismisses critics who either ignore homoerotic passion in the plays, deny its presence, or admit that homoerotic impulses are suppressed, unrequited, or punished in the world of the play (178). His essay focuses on Shakespeare's two comic Antonios, the merchant and the sea captain in *Twelfth Night,* a lesser character created about five years after *MV*'s Antonio. Each loves a male friend more than anyone else, risks his life and fortune for that friend, and watches as the friend chooses to marry a woman. Pequiney establishes norms to identify same-sex passion, which he finds inscribed in the homoerotic friendship between Antonio and Sebastian in *Twelfth Night,* and he uses these norms to discuss Antonio's and Bassanio's bond in *MV.* Pequiney's norms are based in diction, particularly the relative amorousness of the two Antonios' language; the conduct, personality, and history of the characters; the specific scenes between the two sets of companions; and the structure of the main plots. Although Pequiney offers ample evidence establishing a homoerotic liaison between Antonio and Sebastian in *Twelfth Night,* he concludes that in *MV* "there is almost nothing to suggest a sexual dimension" (187). The merchant's "love for his friend is philia instead of eros" (187). Neither Antonio nor Bassanio speaks in amorous terms or refers to physical beauty; they do not live together or keep to themselves, and one willingly seeks a wife while the other assists, although sadly. They share "same-sex" love, a more inclusive term than homosexual love. In an analysis of the ring episode, Pequiney further contends that Bassanio has little choice but to surrender the ring and that Antonio is not "relegated to the outer cold," as the other Antonio is at the end of *Twelfth Night* (188).

He also argues that "a Christian-Jewish opposition is fundamental to *MV*" (189); religion, however, is described not in theological or scriptural terms but is merely implied as right conduct by Portia's father in the casket test. Consequently, the risks, charity, and venture capital of Antonio, Bassanio, and Portia are victorious over the legal bonds, hoarding, and credit of Shylock in the comic world that also showers worldly bounty in the here and now on the heroes. "The graspers and hoarders lose; the givers gamble and win," and the "moral law peculiar to this comedy coincides with the law common to all Shakespearean comedies" that abundance and joy reward the virtuous (190). Antonio gains such a reward. When Portia requests that he place the wedding ring on Bassanio's finger a second time, Pequiney contends, she illustrates his "incorporation into the marriage. . . . He is permanently and more closely than ever bound to his friend," as well as to Portia. Pequiney further suggests that the "nearly universal" and incorrect assumption that at the end of the play Antonio remains unhappy is evidence of "the bourgeois attitude that confirmed bachelors deserve to suffer loneliness and lovelessness for failing to marry and have children" (191); yet he agrees that homosexuality is introduced in 5.1 with the wordplay of the two couples over the rings.

In "How to Read *The Merchant of Venice* Without Being Heterosexist" (1996) Alan Sinfield comments on the play "as a gay man," a reader "not situated squarely in the mainstream of Western culture today" (162). He intends that his commentary should not be limited to explanations of *MV*'s exclusion of his own group but instead should clarify the sixteenth century's benign acceptance of limited same-sex passion within friendship and around the periphery of marriage.

First, unlike Pequiney, Sinfield accepts W. H. Auden's premise that Antonio is in love with Bassanio. In 1.1, the other Venetians recognize that they should allow the two men a private conversation, Bassanio's mercenary marital goals are intended to reassure Antonio, and Antonio is the more intense lover, seeming "to welcome the chance to sacrifice himself," which contributes to an "air of homoerotic excess, especially in the idea of being bound and inviting physical violation" (163–64). Most convincing, Portia behaves with a rival's need to compete with Antonio. That Portia triumphs over Antonio in 5.1, with the ring remaining the symbol of cross-sex marriage rather than same-sex partnership, is "a slap in the face of a very familiar kind" to the gay man (166). It is not commentators who look on this victory as natural in the evolution of homosocial bonds into heterosexual ones; it is the play itself.

Sinfield offers "two routes through *MV* for out-groups: first, one that shows how the circulation of Shakespearean texts privileges some groups and marginalizes others, and second, one that explores "the ideological structures in the playtexts—of class, race, ethnicity, gender, and sexuality—that facilitate these exclusions": the "enticements, obligations and interdictions" that compel us to maintain our somewhat negotiable social roles as children, servants, wives, citizens, suitors, friends, but privilege the rich, the male, the Christian (167). Although today same-sex passion "polices" our roles, limiting our sexuality and thus our potential for disrupting society, sixteenth-century England may not have given the fear of same-sex relations as great a power to control society. Indeed, even though sodomy was condemned, during the 68-year period of Elizabeth's and James's reigns in England, records show only six men indicted on charges of sodomy and only one convicted (169). In fact, art regularly celebrated same-sex passion,[19] likely in imitation of classical Greek and Roman standards. Social orderers consciously ignored same-sex passion, not because it was harmless but because it was less harmful than cross-sex passion. Relations with boys could provide diversion; but relations with girls invited the chaos of unwanted pregnancies that could interfere with lineage, property, and alliance. In the sixteenth century, when art portrayed a disrupted society, it was women, not boys, who resisted marriage, committed adultery, failed to produce male heirs, ran away, and, in widowhood, held on to power (170). Boys, like Lancelot, Jessica as the page, Nerissa as a boy, and Gratiano, are only servants who lack the danger implied in young females.

Sinfield also discusses friendship, explaining that in practice, homoerotic relationships and same-sex friendship overlapped. He proposes that the absence in the text of explicit reference to erotic passion between Antonio and Bassanio "may well mean that it didn't require particular presentation as a significant category" (172). Portia hints at the possibility that Bassanio has slept with the young (presumably male) doctor:

> I will become as liberal as you,
> I'll not deny him anything I have,
> No, not my body, not my husband's bed. (5.1.226–28)

Since same-sex passion did not yet hold the privilege it has today, Sinfield says that play texts explored "an ideological terrain, opening out unresolved faultlines, inviting spectators to explore imaginatively the different possibilities"—the "uncertain, unresolved, contested value of same-sex and cross-sex passion" (174). He notes that the drama could accept a pattern of limited acceptance of same-sex passion, but it had to be replaced, "set aside," because it represented what Valerie Traub calls " non-reproductive sexuality" (176). Ultimately, children were needed in the family. Finally, Sinfield hypothesizes that Antonio's most virulent hatred of Shylock may lie in his sexual orientation, since "gay people today are not more immune to racism than other people, and transferring our stigma onto others is one of the modes of self-oppression that tempts any subordinated group" (177).

NOTES

1. For a valuable overview of twentieth-century critical theories most frequently applied to Shakespeare's plays, see Heather Dubrow, "Twentieth-Century Shakespeare Criticism," in *Riverside Shakespeare,* 2nd ed., ed. G. Blakemore Evans (Boston: Houghton Mifflin, 1997), 27–48.

2. In *The Works of Mr. William Shakespear* (1709), Nicholas Rowe (1674–1718) comments on the purity of imitation in Shakespeare's art and specifically in *MV:*

> . . . . some of his Comedies, are really Tragedies, with a run or mixture of Comedy amongst 'em. That way of Tragi-Comedy, was the common Mistake of that Age. . . . though the severer Critiques among us cannot bear it, yet the generality of our Audiences seem to be better pleas'd with it than with an exact Tragedy.. . . .
> The Tale indeed, in that Part relating to the caskets, and the extravagant and unusual kind of bond given by Antonio, is a little too remov'd from the Rules of Probability: But taking the Fact for granted, we must allow it to be very beautifully written. ("Some Account of the Life Etc" 1: xix)

After the actor-manager Charles Macklin revived Shakespeare's original play in 1741, playing Shylock as a villain, Francis Gentleman commented in 1770 on a much different production that still maintained a mimetic aesthetic ("The Dramatic Censor," in Wilders 25–26). He outlines the plot, calling Portia's courtroom argument "a very natural and most agreeable turn" and Gratiano's comments as "admirably pleasant" against "the bloodthirsty hopes" of the Jew, who is "a most disgraceful picture of human nature" with "not a gleam of light" (30). The play itself, he continues, does not have "a general moral, yet from many passages, useful, instructive inferences may be drawn" as well as the particular lesson "that persevering cruelty is very capable of drawing ruin on itself" (qtd. in Wilders 25–26).

3. E. M. W. Tillyard's *The Elizabethan World Picture* (London: Chatto, 1943) is the traditional example of a study based in historical criticism. More-recent commentators warn of the simplistic ideas presented in this well-known volume, although among some, Tillyard bashing is waning. More nuanced is Hardin Craig, *The Enchanted Glass: The Elizabethan Mind in Literature* (New York: Oxford Univesity Press, 1931).

4. See "Shylock," in *Shakespeare Studies: Historical and Comparative in Method* (1927; repr. New York: Frederick Ungar, 1960), in which Stoll emphasizes character. Stoll also can be grouped with commentators of the study of character, typified in A. C. Bradley, who, however, examined characters with less regard to the historical time and place of their creation.

5. *The Book of The Courtier* was translated from the Italian of Count Baldassare Castiglione by Sir Thomas Hoby in London in 1561. See *The Book of The Courtier. The Tudor Translations,* ed. W. E. Henley (New York: AMS, 1967).

6. A valuable study of the staging of *MV* emphasizing the historical record of production, information not detailed by Harley Granville-Barker's more general observations, is Toby Lelyveld's *Shylock on the Stage* (Cleveland: Press of Western Reserve University, 1960).

7. See J. C. Trewin, *Going to Shakespeare* (London: George C. Allen, 1978), 107–12, for a similar, production-oriented commentary on the play written almost 50 years later, and a like conclusion: "In essence, the play is what Granville-Barker said" (111).

8. H. H. Furness discusses this topic in "Duration of Action," in *The Variorum Edition of* The Merchant of Venice (1888), 332–45. He compares "two different computations of time" in the play to the movement of time in Aeschylus's *The Agamemnon.*

9. This essay is the sixth and final among a useful but small 60-page volume of essays titled *Shakespeare: The Early Comedies* (1960; repr. London: Longmans Green, 1964), by Derek Traversi.

10. To examine Ernest Jones's significant work in applying Freudian analysis to the plays of Shakespeare, see, for example, Ernest Jones, *Hamlet and Oedipus* (New York: Norton, Anchor edn., 1954).

11. This essay is excerpted in *William Shakespeare's* The Merchant of Venice, ed. Harold Bloom (New York: Chelsea House, 1986), and is published in vol. 12

of *The Standard Edition of the Complete Psychological Works of Sigmund Freud,* eds. James Strachey and Anna Freud (1911–1913).

12. See *The Stranger in Shakespeare* (New York: Stein and Day, 1972), 85–136. The volume of essays, all by Fiedler, offer a psychoanalytic perspective on Shakespeare's works.

13. This essay appears in an anthology titled *Representing Shakespeare: New Psychoanalytic Essays*, eds. Murray M. Schwartz and Coppélia Kahn (Baltimore: Johns Hopkins University Press, 1980), which includes essays that represent "an emerging consensus on the recurrent, defining features of Shakespeare's art as it is reflected through contemporary psychoanalytic concepts" (xi).

14. See Catherine Belsey, *Critical Practice* (London and New York: Routledge, 1980), for a useful overview of modern critical viewpoints.

15. See Stephen Greenblatt, *Renaissance Refashioning: From More to Shakespeare* (Berkeley, CA: University of California Press, 1980), for a beginning of New Historicist examinations of Renaissance literature, and *Shakespearean Negotiations: The Circulation of Social Energy in Renaissance England* (Berkeley, CA: University of California Press, 1988), a study focused more directly on Shakespeare.

16. In this volume in the Penguin Critical Studies series, Holderness devotes chapters to a variety of subjects that shed light on the play, including Venice and Belmont, economics and sexuality, Jews and Christians, law and power, the Elizabethan stage, and "endgames" (the final act).

17. A useful overview of feminist criticism of Shakespeare is found in *Shakespeare and Gender: A History,* eds. Deborah Barker and Ivo Kamps (London: Verso, 1995), and Dubrow's overview of twentieth-century criticism cited in note 1 in this chapter.

18. See Eve Kosofsky Sedgwick, *Between Men: English Literature and Male Homosocial Desire* (1985).

19. Sinfield cites Bruce Smith for a discussion of the six "cultural-scenarios" of same-sex passion (13–14, 74–76).

7

THE PLAY IN PERFORMANCE

After *Hamlet, The Merchant of Venice* is Shakespeare's most frequently performed play. Furthermore, the elusive unity of its script has generated more changes, alterations, and adaptations than any other Shakespearean play (Bulman 27). As a result, its performance history, spanning more than 400 years, offers a particularly broad range of topics for study. First among them, of course, are the changes in the conventions of its production: from the bare-thrust stage style of Shakespeare's time; to the unused stage of the interregnum of 1649–1660, when theater performances were forbidden; through the increasingly elaborate stages within the proscenium arch of the eighteenth and nineteenth centuries; and finally to the varied, less realistic, "upholstered" twentieth-century stages of the theater, cinema, and television—stages which, for example, may be impressionistic, fantastic, realistic, bare, on location, thrust, in the round, or framed by curtains.

But with *MV,* other issues of performance arise. Because the play is based on at least two ancient fables, elements of fantasy invariably lurk somewhere in the productions, perhaps in the costumes of Arragon and Morocco, the composition of the caskets, the music played in Belmont, or the androgyny of Portia. And these fairy tales intertwine with the always-contemporary themes of wealth, materialism, family relationships, romance, sex, prejudice, and gender roles—topics responsible for much of the public's fascination with the play. Thus evolving social norms are reflected in productions over the centuries, and audience responses to the characters—Antonio, Portia, and the rest—evolve similarly. Finally, and perhaps most strikingly, the play remains perplexingly current because it reflects what remains an ongoing and overpoweringly stormy problem in western and Middle Eastern society—anti-Semitism. Directors' and actors' interpretations of the play through its 400-year history have both represented and helped create whatever form of anti-Semitism was percolating through the culture at the time. An early eighteenth-century production, for example, with Shylock raging through the courtroom scene in a red beard and a false nose and waving a knife, could reaffirm the English image of the Jew as being kin to the devil and of the stage Jew as being a comic Vice who will be eradicated conveniently by the play's conclusion. Such a production may also have included a gentle Duke, a compassionate Portia, and a noble Antonio, who together would reaffirm the audience's conception of Christians as personifications of love and mercy. On the other hand, a Romantic nineteenth-century production could have included a rowdy and drunken group of biased Venetian revelers the night before they leave Venice and a lonesome, isolated Shylock returning home, futilely knocking on his door and waiting for a daughter who will never appear to open it. The audience would have disdained the Venetians and pitied the Jew. Most memorable in the play, of course, is that Jew, Shylock, the outcast alien who is both brutally destroyed and almost brutally destroying. In nearly all productions, he arises as the most memorable character, particularly because the actor playing the role, until this century, has also served as the actor-manager or director of the production.

The usual way to learn about a play's long performance history is through theater artifacts (playbills, inventory lists, and the like) and written descriptions and commentary by critics, audience members, and performers, whose views are, in turn, influenced by the aesthetic, social, and political conventions of the period in which they lived.[1] This chapter on performance history examines such materials as well as historical studies of theater conventions and primary records from the twentieth century, that is, films and tapes of stage performances.

SIXTEENTH AND SEVENTEENTH CENTURIES

Shakespeare wrote *MV* in 1596 or 1597, but no extant records prove the frequency of the play's performances before 1600 except an implied reference to several performances in the first edition of the play. When he printed Quarto 1 of *MV* for Thomas Heyes in 1600, James Roberts set on the title page, "As it hath beene diuers times acted by the Lord Chamberlaine his Seruants." This suggests frequent performances at the end of the sixteenth century. Also implying the play's popularity are the two performances—the only ones recorded in either the sixteenth or seventeenth century—given at the command of the King: one on Shrove Sunday, February 10, 1605, by the King's Men,[2] and the second on the following Tuesday, a sign of favor, since undoubtedly the King had believed the play merited a second performance. The royal Chamber and Revels accounts of court performances record these two productions before King James himself:

> 10 Feb . . . John Heminges one of his M*ates* plaiers . . . [received] . . . £40 [for the performance of this play and three others] . . . By his M*atis* plaiers. [performed] . . . On Shrousunday A play of the Marthant of Venis [by] Shaxberd.
> . . . .
>
> 12 Feb . . . by his M*atis* players.[performed] . . . On Shroutusday A play cauled the Martchant of Venis againe comanded By the Kings M*atie* [by] Shaxberd.
> (Chambers 4: 172)[3]

After these, no performances are recorded for 136 years, until 1741.

We can, however, make some assumptions about the earliest performances, those before 1605. In 1598, Francis Meres listed *MV* among "the excellent" comedies by Shakespeare in *Pallidis Tamia: Wit's Treasury;*[4] consequently, several performances had almost certainly been given by 1598. The play required a full company for performance because it includes 20 speaking roles and 8 or 9 nonspeaking roles, called mutes or supers. Because acting companies conventionally doubled roles, the performing cast comprised approximately 12 men and 4 boys playing all speaking and nonspeaking roles, the usual number of actors in the Lord Chamberlain's Men. The role of Shylock was probably played by Richard Burbage and less likely by William Kempe, the company's popular actor who performed in clown roles and who probably played Lancelot Gobbo. Although the English character convention from which Shylock derives is comic, the character himself is not, so we may conclude that Burbage, the lead actor in the company, played him. Furthermore, a villainous stage Jew would have been popular, since Christopher Marlowe had introduced the infamous Barabas in *The Jew of Malta* (c. 1590).[5] Evidence that the stage Jew wore the red hair and beard used by the actor playing Judas Iscariot in the mystery plays and associated with the recently hanged Dr. Roderigo Lopez exists only in a forged poem, an elegy on the death of James Burbage, written by John Payne Collier.[6] The poem states that Burbage wore a red wig. Even though the document is fantasy, Collier's forgery is based on the strong odds that Burbage did indeed wear the conventional dress of the stage Jew (Lelyveld 13). Additionally, like Barabas,

Shylock probably wore a large false nose. We might imagine that Shylock resembled the Pantalone character who is the stock avaricious Venetian tradesman in *commedia dell'arte*. A 1601 illustration shows Pantalone with false nose, beard, hat, cloak, and knife in his belt.

The play was performed in about two hours with no pauses. As a result, the alternating scenes of Venice and Belmont followed fast on one another, with one group of actors exiting through the door on one side of the stage while another entered from the other. In contrast to later productions, in which Venice and Belmont were often separated by the several minutes needed to change an elaborate stage setting, such a close juxtaposition between scenes does not support the mid-twentieth century notion of a sharp thematic dichotomy between mercy, or the New Law of Belmont, and justice, or the Old Law of Venice; rather, it heightens the plot similarities in the two locales.

EIGHTEENTH CENTURY

Between 1605 and 1741, the play disappears from written record. Since the theaters were closed from 1641 to 1660, the question of public performance is moot. The Restoration, beginning in 1660 with the reinstitution of the monarchy in England in the person of Charles II, brought theater back to London and, along with 15 other plays of Shakespeare, *MV* was assigned to Thomas Killigrew and the King's Company in 1669, although no performance is recorded. During the Restoration, writers such as Colley Cibber, William Davenant, George Granville, and Nahum Tate refashioned many of Shakespeare's plays for "improvement," with music, spectacle, and emended scripts with narrower plots that more clearly defined and appropriately rewarded good and evil.

George Granville, later Lord Lansdowne, adapted *MV* in *The Jew of Venice,* which was introduced in May 1701 at Little-Lincoln's-Inn-Fields and published in six separate editions by 1736.[7] Granville's play begins with a prologue, a lengthy poetic statement spoken by the ghosts of Shakespeare and John Dryden who are "crowned in laurel." They describe Shylock, the play's obviously comic villain who appears in only four scenes (against the five in Shakespeare's play):

> Today we punish a Stock-jobbing Jew.
> A Piece of Justice, terrible and strange;
> Which, if pursued, would make a thin Exchange . . .

Interestingly, these lines hold anti-Semitic references that contemporary business people understood easily. In 1697, 12 Jews were legally permitted to join the group of 100 who traded on the London stock exchange, a law far too liberal for the traders and businesspeople in London. They argued that Jews engaged in "stock-jobbing," that is, cheating in the buying and selling of shares of stock. This contemporary reference to London's world of finance, then, begins the play, gives it contemporary interest, and suggests a somewhat elite audience—those who were aware of the issues surrounding the London financial exchange.

Unfortunately, Granville mutilates Shakespeare's play with a variety of alterations in language, plot, and character. He recasts Shylock's prose into a strange and stumbling blank verse, so bad that William Winter labels the script a "perversion" and a "jumble" (134–35). He also slows the action with a lengthy and "dreary" masque titled "Peleus and Thetis" in the Venetian banquet scene before Jessica's departure and places Shylock in attendance, sitting alone and, supposedly comically, offering a toast: "Money is my Mistress! Here's to Interest upon Interest!" (Winter 134). The well-known master comic actor Thomas Doggett played Shylock, while Thomas Betterton, whom Winter calls "the greatest actor of his time," played Bassanio. Betterton had been so much a favorite of King Charles II that the King had given Betterton his coronation robes. Consequently, Granville, wishing to spotlight the famous actor, excised Salanio, Salerino, Lancelot Gobbo, old Gobbo, Tubal, Morocco, and Arragon, and reduced Shylock's scenes by one. Bassanio stood as the central romantic lead, and Shylock became a character of low comedy. George Odell observes that the Shylock of the play is "a comic creation" (1:79), but his lines are no funnier than Shakespeare's, so the humor must have lain in Shylock's action and appearance.[8] With the Gobbos eliminated from the script—ostensibly because of the laws of unity, which were important in the eighteenth century[9]—Shylock served as a clown figure. Odell concludes that the play is "a vulgarization of the great original . . . almost like a rouged corpse—a thing too ghastly to conceive of" (1:79). Similarly calling the play a "marked vulgarity," Toby Lelyveld proposes that "the actors who were involved in this parody . . . probably worked uninhibitedly at the task of devastating whatever charm and nobility was left in Shakespeare's play" (18). Still, Shakespeare's play remained ignored for production, even though it was included in excellent editions of the complete works being offered by scholars and writers such as Alexander Pope (1725) and Lewis Theobald (1733). In fact, after 1733, a revival of Granville's *Jew* was performed with great success at the new Covent Garden Theatre in London, a large house with more than 1,000 seats.

In 1741, the actor-manager[10] Charles Macklin produced and starred in Shakespeare's play at the Drury Lane Theatre after announcing that he would not play the part in the comic tradition of Granville's modified Shylock popularized by Doggett's performance. By most accounts, Macklin's was a tragic version, what Lelyveld calls "relentless, savage, ominous, venomous" (22), and Odell notes that "despite the chill goddess of Elizabethan Unity," the cast listed in the playbill discloses that Macklin followed Shakespeare's script closely with two Gobbos, two suitors, and Tubal. Macklin portrayed so vicious a Shylock that audiences believed Macklin himself to be as malicious and vengeful as the character he played. He did, in fact, deserve a reputation for violence. Six years earlier, he had stood trial for murder after killing a fellow actor in a dispute backstage over a wig. He was acquitted because the jury agreed that he had been strongly provoked (Lelyveld 23); furthermore, other actors, not a savory lot in those times, had killed their fellows too. The theater was a rough and tumble world. Exacerbating his reputation for violence was Macklin's own face, a caricature-like image of Shylock, with a large chin, a small upper lip, a large nose, and dark, deeply set eyes—a template for a villain. In 1775, a German scientist and aphorist, Georg Christoph Lichtenberg, described Macklin in detail: "[He had] a nose which is by no means lacking in any one of the three dimensions, a long double chin or dewlap; and in making his mouth, nature's knife seems to have slipped and gone all the way to his ears" (*Furness* 374). He had a red, pointy, wispy beard and wore a long black cloak (perhaps the "Jewish gaberdine" Shylock mentions in the play), long and broad pantaloons, and a red three-cornered hat. Although his performance was precedent setting with its serious and frightening reading of Shylock, some critics of the time claimed Macklin was less than successful. Charles Churchill writes that he was "hard, affected and constrained"; and John Bernard complains that he had "a barking or grunting delivery more peculiar than pleasing" (qtd. in Gross 114). On the other hand, Thomas Davies, the biographer of the English actor David Garrick, records that Macklin was "the only actor he had ever seen 'that made acting a science'" (qtd. in Winter 143). Lichtenberg adds, complimenting the character Macklin created, "Shylock is not one of your petty cheats, who can spend an hour talking about the excellence of a cheap watch-chain. He is slow, calm in his impenetrable cunning, and when he has the law on his side, unflinching, to the very limit of malice. . . . It is not to be denied that the sight of this Jew suffices to awaken at once in the best regulated mind, all the prejudices of childhood against this people" (*Furness* 374–75). Francis Gentleman recalls that "his voice is most happily suited to the sententious gloominess of expression the author intended" (*Furness* 373). Winter concludes that from extant records, Macklin "has never been excelled in ideal or in terrific power" (143); indeed, George II was said to have been kept awake all night after attending a performance, and in 1781, a young man in the audience supposedly fainted from the horror of Macklin's portrayal.

In contrast, Macklin cast Kitty Clive as an energetic, lively, mocking Portia. Odell points out that the selection of so "sprightly" an actress as Clive was odd, unless it was "a last concession to the spirit that had for so long regarded Granville's *Jew of Venice* as a funny, not to say, farcical, entertainment" (1: 262). In the courtroom scene, Clive parodied a famous lawyer of the time, Lord Mansfield; while in Belmont, she sang songs, always countering Macklin's tragic and somber, devil-like Shylock. Gentleman praises her performance: "in petticoats she showed the woman of solid sense and real fashion; when in breeches, the man of education, judgement, and gentility" (*Furness* 384).

Through 1789, at the age of nearly 90, Macklin continued playing Shylock. Then suddenly, during a performance in that year, he could not remember his lines; he apologized, and, according to Gentleman, "the audience accepted his apology with mingled applause of indulgence and commiseration" (*Furness* 374). He retired shortly after and lived until 1797, when he died in poverty. His interpretation of the role, however, remained the standard. It reflected the anti-Jewish sentiment of England, where a legal attempt to naturalize Jews in 1753 was rescinded by popular demand and Jews still were denied citizenship.[11]

NINETEENTH CENTURY

Edmund Kean

By the end of the eighteenth century, after Jews had gained citizenship in France in 1791, the portrayal of Jews in other English dramas began to vary. The character conventions of male Jewish characters evolved from vicious devils and stock clowns to roles with greater humanity. At the Drury Lane Theatre on January 26,1814, Edmund Kean, another actor-manager, portrayed an innovative Shylock with a breadth of humanity that contrasted with Macklin's relentlessly evil character kept alive by his imitators. Kean played to only a partially filled house of fewer than 50 on the first night of performance, but the meager audience enthusiastically supported his performance. The English Romanticist William Hazlitt attended the opening performance and praised it in his review in the *London Morning Chronicle*. He later wrote that Kean's more sympathetic portrayal of Shylock was closer to Shakespeare's intentions: "Shylock is *a good hater*. . . . When we first went to see Mr. Kean in Shylock, we expected to see, what we had been used to see, a decrepit old man, bent with age and ugly with deformity . . . that [Shylock] has but one idea is not true; he has more ideas than any person in the piece" (269, 276).[12] Hazlitt decried the critics' less than enthusiastic response for Kean: "a man of genius comes once in an age to clear away the rubbish, to make it fruitful and wholesome. They cry 'Tis a bad school: it may be like nature, it may be like Shakespear, but it is not like us.' Admirable critics!" (277).

A small man only 27 years old, Kean was poor and relatively unknown and nearly lost his chance to play Shylock. After he had signed a contract, the directors of the Drury Lane asked him to recite, to play a minor role, and finally, to play Richard III. He insisted on the part of Shylock. After three other actors failed in the part, it was finally granted to him, but he had only one rehearsal. When he appeared backstage wearing a black rather than a red wig, the house manager scorned him; yet his performance was remarkable. Winter writes that "at the fall of the curtain after the Street Scene, one of the most signal victories had been gained that ever have been achieved in the history of the Stage" (149). Wearing a black gaberdine, crimson vest, and black hat and carrying a knife, he made what had been a one-dimensional Vice into an injured human, using a demonstrative and passionate style of acting (later called "romantic") that was imitated throughout the century (Lelyveld 40). Shylock's anger over mistreatment motivated his single-minded revenge, and the audience was able to understand. The high point of his performance was his scene with Tubal (3.1), in which Shylock vacillates between horror over his ungrateful daughter and vengeful glee over news of Antonio's losses at sea. Many directors agree that this scene, requiring a quick alternation between two contrasting moods, all spiraling downward, shows greater dimension in Shylock than the single-minded revenge of the 4.1 trial scene. Yet in his Act 4 final scene, Kean completely collapsed in agony, and his final lines, "I am content," and, "I pray you give me leave to go from hence, / I am not well," along with his defeated and downcast exit, were said to carry the sympathy of the nineteenth-century audience (Winter 147–50). Shylock no longer terrified those who saw him, as Macklin's grotesque monster had done; rather, he subdued others as an inflexible and austere representative of the Old Law, before his own horrifying destruction.

Kean played the role through 1832. Interestingly, his portrayal of Barabas in *The Jew of Malta* was judged ineffective, perhaps because Marlowe's character lacks the depth and humanity that became prized by nineteenth-century audiences, who favored emotional and romanticized visions of suffering, troubled villains. Barabas is a flatter, one-dimensional villain exaggerated into what many consider a parody. In Kean's Shylock, the audience saw humanity in a stage Jew, created by Kean's emotionally romantic modeling of a heretofore predictable, exaggerated, and comic character.

William Charles Macready

The nineteenth century brought greater tolerance of Jews in England, which was reflected in other characterizations of Shylock. By 1800, 20,000 Jews lived in England, a far cry from the hundred or so in London during Shakespeare's lifetime. A liberalization of laws in England brought new rights to Jews. They could be admitted to the bar in 1820 and to other municipal offices in 1843; many of their legal rights were established in 1846; and in 1847, Baron de Rothschild, a practicing Jew, was elected to Parliament, although he did not take the seat until 11 years later when he was freed of the requirement to profess that he was a Christian.

This England, increasingly friendly toward Jews, appreciated the passionate, wronged, vengeful, but finally dignified portrayal of Shylock by subsequent nineteenth-century actors who took their lead from Edmund Kean. William Charles Macready debuted in the role in 1823 at Covent Garden, wishing to outdo Kean even though he claimed that he was not pleased with his own performance. "I acted Shylock very nervously" he said in 1841 (Lelyveld 49). He followed the text carefully, used sixteenth-century dress, and made Shylock a neat and richly dressed but harsh and cruel man. Winter notes that Macready believed that the character is "composed of harshness" and that even his lament over the loss of Leah's ring "is only the suffering of wounded cupidity" (152). He stressed a murderous violence as the defining trait of Shylock, exemplified in his delivery of one sentence, "'*Nearest his heart*'—those are the very words, which was horrible in its expression of hatred and exultant cruelty" (152). Reviews of Macready's entire production were positive and sometimes effusive. The critic in the *Times* wrote that "the scenery is in the best possible taste . . . the moonlit garden in the fifth act is particularly beautiful, sparkling with soft light, and melting away into a poetic indistinctness" (qtd. in Odell, *Shakespeare* 1:227).

Charles Kean

Another actor in the wake of Edmund Kean was his son, Charles, an actor who lacked great beauty, voice, or technique, and, in fact, Winter notes, enunciated poorly, substituting "d" for "th" and thus creating a

Macklin as Shylock. Drawing by J. Borfone (n.d.). By permission of the
Folger Shakespeare Library.

"pudding voice" (152–53). He presented a grandly tragic image of Shylock, which, Winter maintains, was often "noble and winning" and therefore "incongruous" with Shakespeare's character (152). His most
important contribution was a new and significant emphasis on staging to
impress the audience. By the 1850s, as actor-manager, he had created an
extravagant production of pageantry and splendor with as many as 100 ex-

tras in the courtroom scene, including a little flower girl who later became the greatest Portia, Ellen Terry. He demanded historically accurate costumes, based on illustrations researched at the British Museum, and elaborate sets, including a bridge over which characters entered and under which gondolas passed. Charles Kean edited the text heavily, although he claimed the opposite, explaining that he maintained all the casket scenes "for the purpose of more strictly adhering to the author's text, and of heightening the interest attached to the episode of the caskets" (qtd. in Odell, *Shakespeare* 1:296). He cut Morocco's casket selection speech from 48 to 16 lines and Arragon's from 34 to 25. Even in Bassanio's casket selection, Kean cut two 35-line speeches to 19 and 15 and Portia's two speeches from 24 lines to 6.5 and 23 lines to 6.5. Although his production techniques overshadowed both his rigor in following Shakespeare and his own acting, Charles Kean's contribution to the play was a historical authenticity that influenced many later productions. He produced what Odell calls "a good acting play without undue favour to lines that happen to be poetical" (*Shakespeare* 1:296).

Junius Brutus Booth and Edwin Thomas Booth

In America, the Booths, made infamous by one son, John Wilkes, played Shylock memorably on the American stage. The father, Junius Brutus Booth, played Shylock with a sympathy many attributed to his own ecumenical if somewhat superficial response to a variety of religions, including Judaism, Catholicism, and Islam. Thomas R. Gould, chronicler of Booth, found in his performance "the representative Hebrew: the type of a race as old as the world. He drew the character in lines of simple grandeur, and filled it with fiery energy. In his hands it was marked by pride of intellect; by intense pride of race; by a reserved force, as if there centred in him the might of a people whom neither time, nor scorn, nor political oppression could subdue" (qtd. in Winter 151). Not everyone agreed, however; in 1885, Walt Whitman wrote in the *Boston Herald* that his performance was "inflated, stagey, and antiquated" (qtd. in Lelyveld 65).

Junius Brutus Booth's son Edwin, on the other hand, from his first performance as an American actor in London in 1861, emphasized the economic conflict between Shylock and the Christians and almost ignored their religious differences. Booth's friend, Horace Howard Furness, the editor of the *Variorum Edition of Shakespeare's Works,* quoted Booth's notion that Shylock was, most of all, mean and corrupt (384). Like Macready, Booth argued that Shylock's anguish over his wife's ring was dismay over financial loss (Winter 152). Further, his treatment of his daughter was unloving (*Furness* 384), and from his opening scene, his single goal was economic victory over Antonio and the other Christians. His was a far more subtle performance than that of his father; he was crafty and often sarcastic as he used the deadly bond to ensnare Antonio, the nemesis to his increasing fortune.

Booth's promptbook and acting edition give details of his delivery and show that he continued the usual nineteenth-century practice of ending the play after Shylock's courtroom exit in Act 4 with Gratiano's line, "To bring thee to the gallows, not the font." He also cut scenes to establish Shylock as the preeminent character and transposed lines to emphasize his fearsomeness. For example, at the end of the bond scene (1.3), as Antonio and Bassanio walk away, Shylock watches them with loathing, threatening them under his breath with lines borrowed from 3.3: "Thou call'st me dog, before thou hadst a cause; / But since I am a dog beware my fangs!" Working closely with Booth, Winter edited the 16 plays in Booth's acting repertoire and so had intimate knowledge of Booth's ideas about the performance of *MV*. He came to agree with the actor that Shylock should not be a generic representative of the ancient Hebrews but rather a man of "subtle craft . . . grim humour, . . . and Oriental dignity"—a figure enhanced by "the glow of [Booth's] spirit and the music of his tones" (156).

Edwin Booth's staging of the play was strongly influenced by Charles Kean's intricate productions. It was considered the finest production of any play in America when it opened at the Winter Garden Theater in New York on January 28,1867, and then at the Booth Theater on April 12, 1869. The scenery was painted by Henry Hilliard and Charles Witham and impressively portrayed famous Venetian locales—the Rialto, the Church of San Giovanni, the Place of St. Mark, and the Hall of the Senate. Most scenes were populated with large numbers of supers who recreated the bustle of Venetian society. Booth's own costume was distinctively Hebraic—dark green gown, red leather pointed shoes, multicolored scarf tied at his waist, leather purse, cap with a two-inch rim, earrings, and many rings. He carried a long staff, reminiscent of the Old Testament, and his beard was grizzled while his wig was balding and black and, in later performances, gray (Winter 158). Although he performed the play over three decades, the tragedies of Booth's life left him with little energy—the death of his first wife, the assassination of the president by his brother, the fire in the Winter Garden Theater in New York that destroyed all his theatrical equipment, and the death of his second wife (Lelyveld 72). He continued playing the role, but weakly: "mechanically correct but artistically false" according to one London critic in 1881.

In the late 1870s, Edwin Booth made a significant change in his production inspired by the script of Henry Irving; he restored the end of Act 4 and all of Act 5, excepting, Winter writes in 1913, "those few lines in it of indelicate speech, which good taste does not tolerate and always must exclude" (155). This addition showcased the talented Polish actress Helena Modjeska as Portia. Having seen her performance, Winter recalls it as "a delicious impersonation of Portia, upon which memory delights to linger. She specially revealed and exulted in, the tender, ardent, intrinsic womanhood of that golden girl of Italy, and I remember that the love-light in her eyes when Portia looked at Bassanio, while he was making choice among the caskets, was one of the most expressive, artistic, fascinating beauties of her beautiful performance" (212–13).

Henry Irving

The finest Shylock of the century, and some believe of all time, was Henry Irving, whose interpretation of the role reflected both his genius and the less anti-Semitic period in English history during which he lived.[13] Jews no longer were denied civil liberty; the Rothschilds were powerful European bankers, and Benjamin Disraeli was a respected British prime minister. No longer did the actor need to imagine what it would feel like to be despised as a Jew, as Edmund Kean had done, since Jews, according to the law, were far less despised. Now the actor of Shylock could express passion and power and wrath without the screaming rage of a victim. Shylock's dignity could remain through all his scenes. Irving created a villain who did not rant but rather maintained a gentlemanly mystery begotten in persecution and expressed in frightening but dignified cynicism.

His peers agreed that Irving himself was "a man with an inner devil," who, unlike Shylock, was careful to control his nature. Born Henry Brodribb in 1838, he changed his name to save the family from the notoriety of his stage career. He took over the Royal Lyceum Theatre in London in 1878 and produced and starred in *Hamlet* in the first year. After a performance as Hamlet, and after playing the roles of Bassanio and Salerio in *MV*, Irving, as actor-manager, made his debut as Shylock with remarkable success. For the next 25 years, Irving played Shylock and served as actor-manager more than a thousand times, which included eight tours in the United States. The part became identified with him and was the final role he played at the Lyceum in 1902, and the one he had intended to play the day after he suddenly collapsed and died in 1905 (Gross 147).

His first production opened at the Royal Lyceum Theatre with the beautiful actress Ellen Terry as Portia on November 1, 1879, the beginning of a run of 250 consecutive performances over the following seven months (Brown xxxiv); the production opened in New York at the Star Theater on November 6, 1883. Irving was a shrewd producer who boasted that his production costs were limited to 1,200 pounds in 1879 and 2,061 by July 1880 (Odell 2: 421). In New York, he created a new production and still kept costs low, spending only $60,000 on exquisite sets, many with supers creating local color and pageantry; he had detailed paintings of St. Mark's, gondolas on the canal, an opulent home in Belmont, pageantry in Venice, and a moonlit garden in Belmont (Winter 176). Reviewing Irving's production on November 7, 1883, the *Herald* critic praised its overall artistic effect: "It is not so much the opulence of the costumes, the picturesqueness of the groupings, or the beauty of the scenery which makes of this production a triumph of stage art, as the taste, the discretion, the poetic tact with which they are applied" (qtd. in Lelyveld 81). Indeed, his was a sumptuous effort, complete with a bridge like that in Kean's 1858 production. James C. Bulman speculates that elaborate realizations of specific locales, so alien to the neutral space of the Elizabethan theatre, may have been an inevitable cultural byproduct of British imperialism, "resonant of the material wealth which conquest brought" (30). Irving's sets were generally painted, however, perhaps because of the constraints of time but, according to his acting edition, "to avoid hampering the natural action of the piece with any unnecessary embellishment" (qtd. in Bulman 30). They were brilliantly colored by painter Hawks Craven, like the rich costumes inspired by the clothes in the paintings of Veronese, Moroni, and Titian. All fit together in pleasing proportion.

Irving claimed that his interpretation of Shylock was inspired by a North African (Levantine) Jew, whom he had met in Tunis on a Mediterranean cruise hosted by the Baroness Burdett-Coutes, and "whose romantic appearance and patriarchal dignity against the background of his native landscape was so much at variance with the popular conception of his race which was held by Western Europeans" (Irving qtd. in Bulman 29). At the beginning of his lengthy run as Shylock, Irving further explained, "The tendency of the play is undoubtedly to show that the worst passions of human nature are nurtured by undeserved persecution and obloquy" (qtd. in Bulman 29). Hence, his performance stressed both the cause and the effect. The coming century would develop that perspective in a number of ways; for example, in the axiomatic twentieth-century notion that people who are raised in violence become violent adults. This does not forgive or lessen the wrongness of their violence, it merely explains it. But as Irving proved, acknowledging the reasons for Shylock's attempted brutal act inevitably softens it.

On the stage, Irving compensated for his naturally weak speaking voice by developing a stronger, nasal tone, and although he was 5 feet 9½ inches tall, he adopted a presence that made him seem overpowering, "a towering stage presence—an ungainly carriage and a stride that caricaturists loved" (Bulman 29). It was almost as if he did not become Shylock, Shylock became Irving, a mysteriously multidimensional character. He played Shylock as an older man, stooped, tired, and thin, dressed in robes of the Orient to increase his mystery. He wore a dark brown, fur-trimmed robe edged in black, a matching tunic, gold earrings, a striped sash, and a black cap marked with the age-old ugly yellow bar separating Jews as different and thus never equal. His wispy gray beard and his walking stick were not oddly alien, but the walking stick sounded his entrance before he appeared onstage (Bulman 34).

More than any other actor, Irving sought authenticity both in the portrayal of the period and in Shakespeare's script, cutting far fewer sections than previous actor-managers had—only the Prince of Arragon scene and the Jessica, Lorenzo, and Lancelot scene after Portia's departure (Odell, *Shakespeare* 1:422).[14] Unlike earlier actor-managers, Irving maintained the jailer scene, the remaining casket scenes in full, and the entire fifth act (which Booth had been eliminating thus far and Charles Kean had badly bowdlerized). Unfortunately, the elaborateness of Irving's sets led to the transposition and binding of several scenes since set changes were very time-consuming. This led to the alternation of "big" scenes with "front" scenes (played before a painted cloth), and merged scenes, such as some Act 2 scenes in Venice, which strung together scenes in Venice and then in Belmont. Bulman observes that "the quick alternation of scenes which Elizabethan staging had facilitated, with the attendant juxtaposition of ideas and values, was replaced by a simpler and structurally damaging isolation of the Venetian (here, tragic) scenes from the Belmont (comic) scenes" (Bulman 37). This upset the balance that Shakespeare had striven to create and led, eventually, to Granville-Barker's observation that "the play's two distinct plots may be irreconcilable" (39). Additionally, Irving made cuts that emphasized Shylock's tragedy. He cut lines critical of Shylock, including those by Salanio and Salarino in 3.1, minimized Lancelot Gobbo by cutting his conversations with Jessica in 2.3 and 3.5, eliminated the scene with Arragon so that the audience could not know that the least dazzling lead casket was the correct choice, and diminished "the women's sphere" of Belmont by shortening speeches. As a result, Irving's acting script has, in fact, fewer lines than that of Charles Kean's production or the elaborate London production by the Bancrofts in 1875 (Bulman 39). Lines also were cut to serve the sensibilities of Victorian London. Irving transformed Portia into a proper and dull young lady from her opening scene, when she does not comment on the parsimonious Scotsman, the poorly educated Englishman, the Neapolitan prince who gives evidence of being an illegitimate son of a smith, or the drunken German. Later she has no words of resentment over her father's casket test, pleasure in the potential of her man's disguise, or wit in teasing Bassanio about going to bed with the doctor. Bulman says that Irving "was robbing her of a wit and earthiness that had once made her a credible antagonist for Shylock" or perhaps was "blatantly" suppressing "the romance of the casket plot in favour of the bond plot" (40), which was further constrained in the elimination of Bassanio's passionate expressions of love in 3.2. The result of this unobstructed flow of highly edited Belmont scenes left a dichotomy between Belmont and Venice and made of the romance an earnest and unconsummated marriage that justified Portia's presence in Venice.

In *Annals of the New York Stage,* Odell praises the production, noting most of all "the very human Shylock" Irving created on the stage (431). Irving himself writes of the sympathy he feels for the character: "I look on Shylock as the type of a persecuted race; almost the only gentleman in the play and the most ill-used . . . Shylock was well-to-do, a Bible-read man . . . and there is nothing in his language, at any time, that indicates the snuffling usurer" (264). Irving's sympathy for the character reflected that of the society, although Jew-baiting still continued in America. For example, the *Saturday Review* saw in Irving's Shylock "an air of a man feeling the bitterness of oppression, and conscious of his own superiority in all but circumstance to the oppressor"; *The Theatre* similarly noted that "in point of all intelligence and culture he is far above the Christians with whom he comes in contact . . . this fact . . . is gall and wormwood to his proud and sensitive spirit"; and Robert Hichins noted that he had "something of the eternal man, subject to the striving and suffering which is the common lot of all human beings, pierced through the crust of his greedy Jewishness. . . . One almost forgave him" (qtd. in Lelyveld 83). Irving's Shylock became a tragic hero embedded in a romantic comedy. This did not make him any less vengeful. In fact, Irving's Shylock began the plan for revenge in his opening scene when he clearly tricked Antonio into agreeing to sign the bond in front of a notary. Irving notes in his script that this line must be spoken hurriedly so that Antonio will not notice the potential danger of the signing.

Overall, Irving evoked pity and fear, the conventional audience response to a tragic hero who shows more passion than irrational devilishness. Perhaps audience sympathy was further assured because Irving gave to Shylock not one but two momentous defeats. First, Irving embellished 2.6, the departure of Jessica and Lorenzo, and then added an extra scene, which contained no dialogue. Both additions were highly praised by critics. As Jessica readied herself to go, she was serenaded by singers in a passing gondola and then left with Lorenzo amidst carnival revelers. The tone was joyous and self-indulgent. Then the stage emptied as an extra scene began. The sound of Shylock's walking stick was heard as he slowly walked home over the bridge. In the dim light, he approached his door, knocked once, and then twice again. As he patiently waited at the doorstep, he knocked three times again, looked in the upper windows, and began to realize the horror of what his daughter had done; then the curtain slowly fell. Throughout, he remained silent and only looked ahead. Bulman writes that no one criticized the scene as non-Shakespearean in its melodrama because it appealed to the Victorian value of respect for parents, and no one commented on its derivation from a similar scene in *Rigoletto*. The scene generated the most sympathy for Shylock, and Ellen Terry writes that in all of her experience in theater, "nothing . . . could compare with it" (Odell, Annals 423).

The second scene of loss is Shylock's in the courtroom, which Irving also admirably underplayed—waiting for the duke's affirmation of the bond, losing everything as the bond is found to be illegal and criminal, and finally accepting Antonio's pronouncement that he "presently must become a Christian" (Lelyveld 90). His final lines and exit from the stage elicited the audience's pity, just as Gratiano's taunting created audience disdain and revulsion. As in Charles Kean's production, Irving crowded many extras into the courtroom scene. Besides Christians, Irving effectively included a group of Jews who responded without dialog to Shylock's answers to Portia's pleading and arguments. Their position was a seemingly rational one, that Shylock should accept Bassanio's offers of extra money and leave. But in the end, after he had been ground down by Antonio's demands to sacrifice and break from his Jewish roots, Shylock dully stared at his oppressor, inaudibly murmured, sighed, and arose to leave. Winter describes his exit "as if he had been stricken by a fatal weakness and were opposing it by inveterate will. At the door he nearly fell, but at once recovered himself, and with a long, heavy sigh he disappeared. The spectacle was intensely pathetic, awakening that pity which naturally attends upon despoiled greatness of character and broken, ruined power, whether that character and that power be malignant or benign" (195–96). Both Jews and then Christians followed after him, and then suddenly from without, their loud screams arose as they sought revenge from the solitary Jew, whom both Christians and Jews disdained (Gross 149, Lelyveld 90, Mahood 45).

THE THEATRE, NO. 1, THIRD SERIES·   WOODBURYTYPE·

"How like a fawning
publican he looks"!

Shylock

Henry Irving: 1879:

PHOTOGRAPHED BY LOCK & WHITFIELD, LONDON.

Henry Irving as Shylock. Photograph with Irving's
handwritten lines from Act 1, Scene 3, and signature
(1879). By permission of the Folger Shakespeare
Library.

Some critics found inconsistency in Irving's performance because he stressed both the humanity of the abused tragic hero and his vindictive, sly revenge. How could the audience feel pity for so mean-spirited and cruel a character? This paradox is an inconsistency in the play itself. The play forces the audience to ask and never quite answer whether evil can be more easily accepted when it is given justification. Irving's production highlights that question.

Fortuitously, Irving's production also included the greatest Portia to date, Ellen Terry. Earlier, she had debuted as Portia opposite Charles Coghlan's unmemorable Shylock in the elaborately staged production by Squire Bancroft and his wife, Marie Wilton, in 1875 at the small Prince of Wales Theatre. They had commissioned their scene painters to go to Venice to recreate accurate and beautifully constructed settings, but Coghlan's less-than-lackluster performance closed the show in three weeks. Terry was as beautiful as the elegant production itself, wearing a blue-and-white brocade dress and a red rose at her breast. In Act 3, she openly showed passion and devotion to Bassanio, and began the plea for mercy to Shylock in Act 4 as if she had faith that she could achieve success, although she seemed only an innocent medium for some external force of wisdom. Winter's commentary on Terry's performance reveals as much about Victorian sensibilities as her performance itself. Unlike previous Portias, who, Winter said:

> [were] heavy formidable females, unlively, unromantic, hard, cold, practical, matter-of-fact, some of them provided with the stalwart legs of a piano and the booming voice of a trombone . . . Ellen Terry occasionally disfigured her performance of Portia by irrelevant and farcical interjections, but the most spontaneously feminine, completely symmetrical and absolutely enchanting embodiment of that part was the one given by her, as she presented it in the earlier days of her professional association with Henry Irving. [She was] essentially feminine, possessing a deep heart and a passionate temperament, and, at the same time, possessed of that arch, buoyant, glittering piquancy and playfulness which are fluent from health, innocence, and kindness toward all the world.
> (218–19)

Four years later, playing opposite Irving, she remained an affecting Portia. F. J. Furnivall, a noted Shakespearean scholar and philologist of the nineteenth century, wrote that her romantic, loving, and open Portia epitomized the character Shakespeare had written: "one longs that he could be here to see you. A lady gracious and graceful, handsome, witty, loving and wise, you are his Portia to the life" (qtd. in Gross 153). Yet her innocent virtue, so dominant in the courtroom and casket scenes, seemed to contradict Irving's victimized Shylock. Audience sympathy could not logically attach itself to either one; how could so generous a spirit treat Shylock with so little of her highly acclaimed gentle mercy? Ellen Terry wrote in her autobiography that Irving "had made not merely a tragic hero but an heroic saint" (163). The other characters became superfluous, save Portia, thanks to the strength of Terry's performance.

As the years passed, Irving's 1879 interpretation lapsed into one with less subtlety and more superficial, villainous excitement, possibly as a result of waxing anti-Semitism in Europe and America and a resulting decline in sympathy for Shylock. Since an almost chauvinistic nationalism was spreading in Europe, and Jews were not a part of any homogeneous national group, their alien identity seemed more apparent, and the image of Shylock as the alien to be removed began to surface. In any case, playbills from the Lyceum in 1880 show that Irving again began ending the play with the courtroom scene of Act 4 that excised Shylock from gentle society. Thus the play became more the property of the actor-manager, more a political tool using anti-Semitism to bolster nationalistic pride, than a production of Shakespeare's authentic script.

TWENTIETH CENTURY

The Edwardian Period and the War Years

The twentieth century began with the Edwardian Period (1901–1910) and initiated an important transformation in aesthetics, including those of theater production. In *Shakespeare Refashioned: Elizabethan Plays on Edwardian Stages,* Cary Mazer argues that the changes in "theatre art and organization," the methods by which productions were staged, were more significant in this transformation than the work of any single director or actor. Further, Mazer says that the older style from the previous two centuries overlapped with the changing production values of the new century until after the First World War, when modernism became the dominant style.

Most of Shakespeare's plays continued to be produced with a traditional actor-manager. The star served as the manager who made artistic decisions consistent with Victorian aesthetics. The traditional style included "romantic costumes" (Mazer 3) and lavish spectacle, sometimes called "upholstered" (Mahood 48). The goal was detailed "pictorial representationalism" (Mazer 7). Mazer notes that traditional staging aimed for unity within the world on the stage and for a separation with the proscenium arch from the passive audience. This created an internal consistency and a conventionally "'real' space" (8). The traditional power of the actor-manager extended also to the script. He not only directed and played the starring role, he also had the liberty to alter significantly the playwright's script by deleting whole scenes and other lengthy sections, adding sections, and reordering the sequence of scenes and events. But by the end of the Great War, modern values had become increasingly popular. Such values called for unedited scripts, nonrealistic settings, modern dress costumes, and the replacement of the actor-manager with the Director's Theatre, all of which continue today.

William Poel

Early exceptions to the traditional style before the turn of the century were the productions of William Poel (1852–1934) and the Elizabethan Stage Society, which first presented *MV* in 1898. The Society, founded by Poel in 1894, sought to create productions of Shakespearean plays that were "authentic," in other words, like those Shakespeare himself might have presented. Poel was critical of current productions, saying that directors did not understand "the way Shakespeare conducts his story and brings his characters on and off the stage, a matter of the highest moment. . . . Elizabethan dramatists had to round off a scene to a conclusion, for there was no kindly curtain to cover retreat from a deadlock" (119, 122).[15] Poel argued that directors changed too much: "When you have collected, at vast expense, labour and research, this interesting information about a country of which Shakespeare was possibly entirely ignorant, thrust all this extraneous knowledge into your representatives, whether it fit the content or not, let it justify the rearrangement of your play, the crowding of your stage with supernumeraries, the addition of incidental songs and glees, to say nothing of inappropriateness of costume and misconception of character [the play barely survives]" (121). As a result, Poel eliminated bowdlerism, additional music, slower line delivery, elaborate sets seen through a proscenium arch, and "stars" in leading parts. The generally amateur group performed in Elizabethan costumes, in bare auditoriums, and with Elizabethan music. *The Merchant of Venice* was the first Shakespearean play Poel had ever seen, so he was inspired to participate actively in the productions of November and December 1898. He hired a professional actress, Eleanor Calhoun, to play Portia, and he was Shylock. He played the part as a clownish villain whom the audience had neither the desire nor need to pity. In his final exit, he left the stage in great indignation with everyone laughing that he had finally become the dupe. Following what was likely Renaissance tradition, he wore a red beard and large false nose while the more than usually somber and earnest Portia dressed like Queen Elizabeth, which scholars at the time believed to be historically accurate.

The production was not popular, nor was its 1907 revival. Poel argued that the play is romantic, and Shylock is a conventional character from the Roman comedy of Plautus. He serves as the miserly, surly older senex or blocking figure to the young lovers and is eventually dismissed from the social order. Poel ignored that Shylock is also a miserly, usurious Jew. While he may have found Irving's earlier interpretation of Shylock a simplistic exaggeration of the victimized outsider and Terry's Portia a china-doll ingenue, his production was equally stylized, giving Portia almost godlike wisdom and Shylock little more than a well-staged pratfall. Poel was historically correct in his notion of the clown; Aristotle indeed writes that the clown is first of all ridiculous and consequently, unthreatening. But Shakespeare's Shylock is neither.

Herbert Beerbohm Tree

More commonly, Edwardian productions were traditional, unlike those of Poel and the Elizabethan Stage Society. One of the best remembered was that of Herbert Beerbohm Tree in 1908. It was nearly baroque in its lavishness. Many elements outdid even those of the Bancrofts and Henry Irving at the end of the previous century. To create local color, Tree recreated the Doge's procession at the beginning of the play; he gave to both Morocco and Arragon elaborate exits in dumbshows, and, in an attempt to be historically accurate, he used a set that included a non- Shakespearean ghetto, complete with synagogue and clotheslines. His Shylock was an exaggeration of Irving's. For example, he retained Irving's tiny but dramatic additional scene of Shylock's return home after Jessica's departure. But Tree did not create dramatic tension with Shylock's terrible mute shock. Rather, Shylock cried Jessica's name, entered the house, ran from room to room (visible through windows), and was sobbing as the curtain fell. Later, he sat on the ground, rent his clothes in grief, and put ashes on his head (Trewin, *Shakespeare on the English Stage* 41).[16] Equally emotionally, he fainted into Tubal's arms at the conclusion of the courtroom scene. The effectiveness of all this was debatable, even to Edwardian tastes. While Winter categorizes Tree as one of a number of "comedians" who played Shylock, like Edward Hugh Sothern (200), Tree intended serious drama. His entire portrayal was so melodramatic, so sympathetic with Shylock, so faithful to traditional Jewish customs, and so typical of the many roles of other Jews he had played, that the public believed Tree himself was Jewish; but he was not. His half brother, the theater critic Max Beerbohm, wrote favorably of the production even though he was not partial to the play, especially the non-Shylock elements, saying it was "a study of racial strength against contempt and persecution" (Gross 167). J. C. Trewin dismisses much of the production, however, as "hysterically theatrical" (*English Stage* 41).

Franck Benson

The actor-manager Franck Benson made his debut as Shylock in another Edwardian production in 1901. He was educated at Oxford, had begun his career working with Irving, and had performed Shakespearean plays for two decades in England outside of London. Generally, his productions were done in a high oratorical style, perhaps a reflection of his education. Beerbohm Tree was not one of his strongest admirers, but for *MV,* he made an exception, writing that Benson showed "much more of imagination, and much less of angularity, than is his wont" (qtd. in Gross 168). Still, the play was in the upholstered style and much bowdlerized, with the scenes in Belmont strung together, those in Venice joined together, and Act 4 serving as the final scene on the exit of Benson himself as Shylock. As a last gasp, the Old Bensonians offered a final matinee of this production honoring Benson, who had been knighted in 1916. He played Shylock at Stratford-Upon-Avon on a Whit Monday matinee, May 16, 1932, well after styles had changed and Benson's conventions had been dropped. He had retired as manager of the Shakespeare Festival in 1919 (Bulman 53) but his work, highly influenced by Irving, was well-respected and of enormous influence. As a result, when Benson's performance concluded and the audience continued to cheer loudly, the director, W. Bridges-Adams, stepped forward and placed a laurel chaplet at his feet (Trewin, *English Stage* 137).

Edward Hugh Sothern

In the United States, the most popular production of this most popular play starred the famous Edward Hugh Sothern and Julia Marlowe, claimed by Winter in 1911 to be "the best Shakespearean actress of the present period on the American stage" (209). They opened in the production in New York on February 16, 1907, at the Lyric Theater, after two years of touring throughout the country, and they continued performing Shakespeare together through the 1920s. Sothern's interpretation of Shylock was melodrama, according to Lelyveld; in other words, his actions exaggerated the original language (104–5). In the courtroom, as Portia began, apparently in support of the bond, Shylock knelt and kissed the hem of her robe, calling her "a Daniel come to judgement!" But when Antonio required that Shylock convert to Christianity, in what Gross calls a "stunt" (170), Sothern's Shylock tried to run and was held down by guards. Winter's assessment of Sothern's performance is harsh. Calling himself "the wearied beholder," Winter writes that Sothern's performance was "an abortive effort to blend greed with benevolence, the crafty usurer with the majestic Hebrew patriarch, the bloodthirsty schemer for revenge with the noble, loving father, the would-be murderer with the austere, righteous minister of Justice, and once more the union of those antagonistic components was seen to be impossible" (209). Winter continued that Sothern's pronunciation was nasal and "pudding" and his face expressionless and overly made up, and he concluded that Sothern's stage business of sitting down during the street scene was sufficient evidence of "how completely unworthy his performance of Shylock was" (Winter 209).

1918–1932

Between the two world wars, production styles became more like those popular in Elizabethan England (1558–1603), which were far slimmer and simpler. The proscenium arch was often replaced by theater-in-the-round or a thrust stage jutting out into the audience. Scenery ceased to be elaborate and realistically detailed and was exchanged for symbolic sets that often were abstract in shape. Finally, productions no longer focused on the actor-manager. An ensemble presentation created a unity among all the actors and the disparate elements in the play.

Maurice Moskovitch

By the 1920s, when styles had changed, *MV* continued to be the second most frequently produced Shakespearean play. Between 1918 and 1939, 29 separate productions were offered in Stratford-Upon-Avon and at London's Old Vic and West End theaters. Two important productions, one in London and the other in New York, offered contrasting views of Shylock, both with Jewish actors. In London, Maurice Moskovitch (1871–1940) played Shylock as a character entirely motivated by hate who could elicit only a similar response from those around him. The 1919 production, staged by J. B. Fagan, ran nine months on the strength of Moskovitch's performance; critics agreed that the rest of the production was mediocre

(Trewin, *English Stage* 92–93; Lelyveld 106–8). A tall man who had acted in many productions in Yiddish, Moskovitch played Shylock with the body movements of a conniving devil—self-deprecating shrugs, seemingly uncontrolled shaking, genial effusiveness, and melodramatic tears, all in the service of hate for the Christians. Sympathy was an impossible audience response. His replacement, Louis Bouwmeester, was even more fiend like and maniacal.

David Warfield

In direct contrast, a 1922–1923 New York production starred David Warfield who, Gross writes, "went further than any previous interpretation in portraying the moneylender as a sad-eyed victim" (Gross 186). Its grand and ornate excess seemed to "dwarf the anxious little Shylock" (Lelyveld 108–9).[17] In this production, he was stooped and small, more so because of the extravagance of the set, a Rialto dominated by a synagogue in the center. Staged by David Belasco, the production was a financial success but failed to give Warfield the prestige he desired after a career as a vaudeville comic playing Jewish stereotype roles in comic sketches. The script is highly bowdlerized, with additional lines clearly intended to simplify the story, and filled with details of setting, costume, and stage action. Warfield's Shylock began as a simple lender who indeed sought the friendship of Antonio, and only as his fate darkened irrecoverably did his motivation evolve into revenge. He never showed the power necessary to be a convincing adversary to Antonio. He was mocked by the Christians in his final exit, as a man dwarfed by the enormity of his pathetic fate. A leading critic of the period, Stark Young, wrote that the character Warfield created had humanity and "infinite pathos," but that was, of course, inappropriately tame for Shylock and left a "distressing" imbalance in the play (188). Still, the script must be held responsible for much of the production's artistic mediocrity.

George Arliss

A second and far different American and Jewish Shylock was George Arliss in a 1928 production. He was sober and dignified, lacking in so-called Jewish stage mannerisms. Lelyveld suggests that he was attempting to neutralize the evil and conventionalized Jew that Moskovitch had popularized (109–10). Arliss urged that the play be made into a film, inevitably "an expensive production," he admitted, and one to which Jews would object; but such an objection, he argued, was foolish, because Shylock was far superior to the Venetians, of whom he said, "a greater collection of dishonorable cads than Antonio and his set it would be difficult to find" (qtd. in Gross 190). The play did give an important boost to his career, since it was at one of the performances in Los Angeles that Jack Warner and Darryl F. Zanuck saw him and offered him a role in a sound film that marked the beginning of his film career.

Lewis Casson

Following the newer conventions that evolved between the wars, Lewis Casson starred as Shylock at the Lyric, Hammersmith, in a noteworthy version in 1927. He played a "mean and warped" villainous Shylock (Mahood 48) with what Gross calls "pawnbrokerishness" (191). Acknowledging the strong presence of other actors in the ensemble, a headline of the *Evening News* praised Casson as the "Best Shylock Since Irving" (Gross 191). He played Shylock as an ordinary sort of lower-class cheat who spoke in dialect to underscore his ghetto background, pronouncing w's as v's in the contemporary Yiddish accent of London Jews ("I vill not eat vit you . . . "). When St. John Ervine wrote in a review that he lacked "magnificence . . . and courageous abandon," Casson answered that he could read none in the text.

Theodore Komisarjevsky

In 1932, two months after Franck Benson's overwrought farewell performance of *MV,* Theodore Komisarjevsky was invited to be the first guest director at the new Shakespeare Memorial Theatre at Stratford-Upon-Avon. A daring choice, he had served as director (he preferred the title *regisseur*) at the Imperial and the State Theatres in Moscow and at other more avant-garde theaters throughout Europe, particularly as a director of Chekhov (Bulman 54).[18] His production of the play manifested ideologies of the time, both aesthetic and political. His was a "fantastic comedy playfully and wildly eclectic, its elements unified only by the 'creative work of [his] irrational self,'" inspired if not based in the cubism and expressionism of the earlier part of the century (Bulman 56). But more important, Komisarjevsky's satiric production responded to what he perceived as the greed of bourgeois decadence in the theater and in all of society, which "could lead to racial prejudice" (72). To bring to life this ideological aesthetic, he wrote, a *regisseur* seeks to be "a spiritual leader, a kind of magician, psychologist and technical master . . . who respects the creative individualities of his actors and knows that no more can be achieved by

Herbert Beerbohm Tree as Shylock. Photograph (1916). By permission of the Folger Shakespeare Library.

the methods of the drill sergeant than by committee meetings" (qtd. in Bulman 67–68). But he also believed that *regisseurs* guided social reform and had their political counterparts in leaders who recognized the failures of European democracies, like Lenin, Stalin, Hitler, and Mussolini (Bulman 72). He abhorred what he considered the dictatorial actor-manager, whose "megalomania" made of *MV* a study in character development, a means to bloat the vanity of the actor playing Shylock, and who did not preserve the ensemble production of the Elizabethan theater.

Komisarjevsky's production began and ended in the fantasy of *commedia dell'arte,* with Bruno Barnebe, an actor who had trained in mime and had studied the clowns of the *commedia dell'arte,* playing Harlequin.[19] Barnebe entered, dressed in the traditional black and white patches and high peaked hat, leading a group of pierrots in an acrobatic dance. Behind them the Venetians magically appeared and began the first scene. Barnebe then changed costume and became Lancelot Gobbo for the remainder of the play. He and Old Gobbo were depicted as the *commedia* figures, Scapino and Pantalone, and wore conventional clown costumes. After the added prologue, action continued, seeming like an implicit dream of Harlequin, a play within a play, much as *The Taming of the Shrew* is the dream of Christopher Sly. This dream also served as a convenient explanation for the fantasy of the bond, the caskets, and the cross-dressing within the plot. Furthering the tone of fantasy were the continuing revelry and slapstick of the Gobbos, who appeared together when only Lancelot is named in the script. Characters entered and exited oddly from without and within the proscenium and from beneath and above the playing space, thereby yielding a disorienting, surreal, and dreamlike atmosphere. At the end of Act 5, all the players departed except Lancelot, who again summoned the pierrots who danced and finally left as Lancelot stretched and yawned.

Scenery and costumes were similarly expressionistic. Dress at first seemed sumptuous and historically appropriate to the beginning of the Stuart reign but then revealed itself as fantasy—"fancy-dress" (57). Portia entered as the pastoral and pure *commedia* figure, Columbine; Gratiano had the parted and pasted-back hair of Rudolph Valentino; Morocco looked like Al Jolson in a sombrero; Arragon was "a foppish grotesque" with a little fat attendant; and Antonio wore flame-colored tights and an exaggerated ruff as he kept admiring himself in a small mirror hanging around his neck. The set, alternately lit in pea-green or crimson light, represented a brilliantly colored, cubist Venice. The perspective of angles and lines were opposed to those of the natural world but supported the timeless moments of a dream, where no sweep of time and space ordered reality and single images were juxtaposed and spotlighted without ever fitting together. Towers leaned dangerously, tops of buildings were too large and heavy to be supported by their bases, bridges spiraled rather than lay flat. Such places were ideal for characters who secured loans with flesh, won wives in lotteries, and cross-dressed to argue the law in court.

The novel and comically carnivalesque production hinted at humor, comedy, and satire that was not to be muddied with somber meditation. But Komisarjevsky's script, with only 14 lines cut from Shakespeare's script, was not monotonic or monothematic; and Komisarjevsky's conclusion that Shylock is "little more than a caricature of malice . . . [and] can receive no sympathy because his goal is revenge" could not have been possible without cutting and moving lines with the abandon of Henry Irving or Charles Kean. Again, Shylock rested in the center of the thematic paradox. Wearing brightly colored clothes and behaving like a trickster or even a music hall performer or Italian Pantalone who deserved whatever punishment he received, Shylock was intended to generate none of what Komisarjevsky called the "false pathos" of the nineteenth century. But Randle Ayrton played a Shylock of greater dimension, if for no reason other than it is in the script, which, Trewin concludes, was out of place in this fantasy production (*English Stage* 137).

Komisarjevsky's production was not frivolous, because he believed that as *regisseur* he played an important role in the destruction of decadence and greed, like the socialist dictators of Europe. This noble goal, he claimed, justified the suffering of Russians or Jews that is "however regrettable, an understandable and even necessary consequence of 'any mass progressive movement' . . . for there has never been progress 'without bloodshed and injustice being inflicted on certain groups of people, and however sentimental we may be, our feelings must not be allowed to blind us to the positive and progressive side of the Fascist, Communist and Nazi movements'" (qtd. in Bulman 73).

He sought to dehumanize the bourgeois tragic hero that Shylock had become in the nineteenth century and reshape him into "a twisting comic devil"; yet paradoxically, he acknowledged that in *MV*, Shylock is "victimised by 'the crash of justice in the face of prejudice'" (Bulman 73). Bulman observes that expressing such apparent contradictions is hypocritical, but I would argue that it also illustrates the sometimes careless logic of the ideologue. Any performance of *MV* in the twentieth century is difficult because of the play's alleged anti-Semitism, but *MV* becomes dangerously risky when a production is intended to support a preexisting ideology that blames capitalism, as represented by the Venetians, for worldwide poverty resulting from sharp class distinctions. Capitalistic greed, Komisarjevsky implies, encourages anti-Semitic bias; but on the other hand, the two-dimensional villainous Jew deserves loathing. This popular production was revived in 1933 in part because such a flawed logic and finger-pointing ideology resonated at the nadir of the Great Depression and gave intellectual and artistic support to the military invasions that began World War II.

Ernest Milton

A highly praised production of the play, also in 1932, was presented at the St. James Theatre in London. Ernest Milton (1890–1974) both managed and played the part of Shylock in a performance that Trewin called "proud and inflammably racial" (*English Stage* 133). The then elderly critic Graham Robertson exclaimed that this production was superior to that of Irving, another he had reviewed, and was very different from it. "The blessed memory of Irving's crucified saint remains with me quite undisturbed, but it wasn't Shylock," he wrote. Milton's production had a well-designed set, an excellent supporting cast, and an interpretation of Shylock that, Robertson said, "performed no tricks" and followed Shakespeare's lines "straight and with wonderful effect" (qtd. in Gross 194). No one at the time labeled it racially incendiary. After a very recent failure with a production of *Othello,* Milton hoped for a long run of his highly acclaimed production, but because of weak box office sales, it closed in three weeks. The Depression, the increasingly acute problem of anti-Semitism, and the production's lack of excitement all contributed to its demise.

Depression and Wartime Performances

At the end of the decade, well after Nazi Germany had begun its surreal devolution of humankind in 1933, the English stage continued obliviously presenting lovely Venices, pretty Portias, and vile although less spotlighted Shylocks. Whether this was politically or historically significant is questionable, but it does imply that the theater was not guided by the liberal inspirations it often claims. One of the finest English actors, John Gielgud, played the role of Shylock in 1938 at the Queen's Theatre, six years after having directed it. The production was romantic and lovely, as Gielgud's 1932 production had been. Venice brimmed with wealth, Belmont was almost magical, the Venetians were handsome and courtly. All served as the pastel canvas upon which Shylock was an ugly stain. He did not fit; he needed to be removed. One reviewer implied that Gielgud's Shylock was a Dracula-like, bloodsucking, and fervent revenger: "a Transylvanian usurer" with the "ardor of an Old Testament prophet" (qtd. in

Gross 200). Trewin, on the other hand, describes Gielgud as "a drab, un-sentimentalised, young-looking Shylock, though almost bald, with ear-locks, a straggling beard, and gummy, blinking eyes. . . . .who refused to let the man dominate" (*English Stage* 176). Whether this production, or any production at all, was prudent at a time when news articles reported that mass numbers of Jews were being brutalized is perhaps not an artistic consideration. But artistic considerations are not always most important.

During the period between the wars, the English and Americans largely ignored the play's relationship to the horror that was developing in Europe: the escalating scapegoating of the Jews and the eventual attacks, torments, and ultimate genocide by the Nazis as well as by the Soviets. Productions in England and America maintained a villainous Shylock but lessened his importance. Directors also made the play more a springlike fantasy than a moralistic statement about Jews and money. Yet this play is undeniably political. The Nazis took advantage of it, and the rest of the world played innocent.

Nazi Performances

Because of the potential for the play's becoming useful political persuasion for anti-Semitism, as discussed earlier, Nazi Germany encouraged important propagandistic, if aesthetically and morally repellent, performances, which served the obvious function. Even with the Nazis' pervasive censorship of the arts, performances of many of Shakespeare's plays continued because the Nazis considered Shakespeare ideologically Germanic. *The Merchant of Venice* was, of course, especially popular, being presented in 20 productions in 1933 and 30 between 1934 and 1939. The government even provided commentary to convince the audience of the frightening evil in the Jew. For example, if anyone might have misinterpreted the Nazi assessment of Shylock—perhaps dangerously admitting that he is, at least, hardworking and industrious, while the Venetians appear slothful, a Koenigsberg newspaper essay in 1935 provided government-approved notes to a local production. It argued that despite his appearance of hard work, Shylock is "malicious and cowardly," and despite their apparent indolence, Antonio and his friends are "selfless." The play itself, the essay continues, presents two opposing worlds that "are the expression of racial opposites . . . a problem that is of the highest relevance to us today" (Gross 319).

As expected, the Nazis also enjoyed Marlowe's *The Jew of Malta*, presenting it on Easter Sunday in 1939 in Weimar. A contemporary monograph said that the director, Otto zur Nedden, had created in Barabas a "racially determined portrait of a real Jew . . . a pitiless, vengeful, Christian-hating Jew" (Gross 320) even though most critics see in Barabas an almost comic, exaggerated parody of the image of the Jew in the Christian Renaissance.

Shylock, however, offered more interiority, and potentially had a far more damning influence. But to assure the audience of Shylock's utter villainy, in 1942 Paul Rose planted extras in the audience to curse and scream at Shylock in the courtroom scene. Possibly the most slanted and hateful production occurred in Vienna in May 1943 at the order of the Baldur von Schirach, Gauleiter for Vienna. He used the performance of the play to celebrate the deportation of Vienna's tens of thousands of Jews to certain death in concentration camps. He proudly said of this horror, "I see it as a positive contribution to European culture." Werner Krauss was Shylock, having played the roles of a variety of unattractive Jews in the 1940 film *Jew Suss,* a production ordered by Joseph Goebbels. Krauss's Shylock, three years later, was a repugnant character, with bright red hair and beard, cunning eyes, greasy caftan, shuffling walk, clawlike hand movements, and explosive rages. Gross notes that after the war, Krauss was tried and convicted as a minor offender, paid a $125 fine, and continued on in the 1950s to receive prestigious awards from the German theater and government (322).

Postwar Productions

While two English productions during World War II, starring Donald Wolfit and Frederick Valk, are considered noteworthy, those after 1945, haunted by the Holocaust, were finally compelled to respond to its horror. At first, however, few war-inspired productions took place, almost as if the theater were shocked into paralysis. Even eight years later, in 1953, Shylock remained a conventional villain as portrayed by Michael Redgrave. More interesting was Peggy Ashcroft's Portia, which she had performed successfully in 1938. Ashcroft personified a lawyer who had studied the case and who argued from wisdom, skill, and research, not lucky revelation (Mahood 51). That convention, typified in Ellen Terry's courtroom presentation, had been to portray a beautiful but mysteriously inspired Portia. This implied that the only means by which a woman could ever successfully argue a case in court were through strange and exotic inspiration. In the 1950s, another notable production in England starred Emlyn Williams (1956) as Shylock, and a second, in America, starred Morris Carnovsky. The latter played Shylock as an American no-nonsense bad guy; but even as such, he gained sympathy as a noble victim. In 3.1,

Carnovsky startlingly stepped forward into a spotlight to declaim the Act 3 "Hath not a Jew eyes?" speech. This transformed the speech into an oration, elevating it through the diminution of the taunting Venetians, Solanio and Salarino, who became mere unworthy listeners. In the United States, Joseph Papp directed a memorable postwar version in 1962. Cleverly cast, Shylock was George C. Scott, who, 10 years later, played a similarly mean, rough, and gruff film character as the general in *Patton*. His Shylock was clever and fearless, even in the face of Venetians dressed for the masque in white sheets with holes cut for their eyes.

Michael Langham, Director

The most important production of the time, however, occurred in 1960 at Stratford-Upon Avon, where Michael Langham directed Peter O'Toole as Shylock. Expressing the inescapable response to the Holocaust, Langham made petty, superficial materialists of the male Venetians, and adolescent, silly girls of the three females, with Portia dressed as a bellhop. All the Christians lacked depth in the courtroom when they ganged up on the handsome, gentlemanly O'Toole. Again, Peggy Ashcroft portrayed Portia as a lawyer who knew the case and argued with wisdom, not an inexplicable revelation (Mahood 51). While the postwar audience found this production laudable, one critic, Nigel Dennis, looked at it more skeptically. He suggested that this ironic version of the play drew upon the self-righteousness of the audience. He continued that it mistakenly implied that Shakespeare had been on Shylock's side all along against the Christian bullies. Lelyveld notes, however, that the reviewer for *Punch* (April 27, 1960) found O'Toole's Shylock "refreshing" and the production "simple, intelligent, and unostentatious" (132). In any case, Langham's World War II–inspired English version of the play had required the passage of 15 years to gestate. Apparently, only then could the theater grasp the immensity of the Nazi horror and develop an artistic response.

Jonathan Miller, Director

In 1970, at the National Theatre in London, Jonathan Miller created a production perhaps most characteristic of the period because, as Gross points out, "it was the one which established the principle that a director is free to do whatever he likes with the play" (329).[20] It starred Laurence Olivier as Shylock and was set in late-nineteenth-century Venice, where the overriding value of the emerging modern world was the acquisition of money and power. Miller said this setting was more compatible with certain speeches in the play than a sixteenth-century setting (Bate and Jackson 222), since many of the play's themes are relevant to the flourishing capitalism of that era. The play implies that acquisition is the motivation driving modern capitalism and its inevitable persecution of minorities, who can be depended on to enhance profits with low labor costs in the execution of unattractive tasks. Olivier's Shylock, however, was a member of a minority group who had become affluent—as dignified looking as the other Venetians but distinctively wearing a skullcap yamulka under his top hat. Within himself, however, he held dense emotion. He experienced despair when Jessica left, he mourned the loss of his wife's gift of a turquoise ring, and at this most painful time, recognized around him the racial hatred lying only marginally below the surface of the Venetians. It was in this scene (3.1) that "it occur[red] to him *for the first time* that the bond [might] serve as a vehicle for retribution: an Antonio for a Jessica" (Bulman 89).

Several additions and cuts in the play degraded the Venetians into tormentors and elevated Shylock into a persecuted, grieving father. Shylock's 1.3 aside in which he describes his hate for Antonio as a Christian who lowered the rate of usance in Venice was entirely deleted. Bassanio's casket selection had the unmistakable look of having been fixed. Two singers sang lyrics asking where fancy is bred, as they stared directly at the lead casket. Lorenzo and Jessica ignored any meaning in their Act 5 conversation, as Lorenzo paused in his philosophical musings to smoke his pipe so often that Jessica finally fell asleep. Arragon acted the fool, a characterization that has become a near convention; and Portia bordered on rudeness when she met Jessica in 3.2. The production excised all of Shylock's lines that might have betrayed his hatred for Christians or his usurious greed. Therefore, he became a character motivated solely by fatherly grief for a runaway child, a development beginning at the end of Act 2.

Admittedly, Shylock was as affluent as the Venetians, but his attempt to blend in with the Christians remained slightly out of focus. His accent was clipped and theatrical; his mannerisms were broad, stylized, and oddly awkward. He danced a strange little jig at good news and gestured with his cane to emphasize his words and moods. The trial scene, the climactic moment in the play, took place in a judge's chambers but still centered around a table, as it had since the eighteenth century. Portia (Joan Plowright) dominated and seemed to talk down to an unsuspecting Shylock. She began with her cool and theoretical "quality of mercy" speech and moved in for the kill, attacking Shylock with ultimately lethal punches across the table. After her onslaught, Shylock could no longer walk alone from the room. His role in the play ended with an unscripted coda of horror. After his final exit, the audience as well as the remaining Venetians heard from offstage his final hideous and shattering wail. Jessica suffered too. Lorenzo revealed himself as a less-than-ideal husband who would never appreciate his financial good fortune or his lovely wife. And in the final scene, Jessica seemed to grieve over her father's fate and undoubtedly her own, walking out slowly to a Kaddish, or Jewish dirge, a musical addition to the play that has been adopted by other contemporary productions.

Gross suggests that "the whole theme of assimilation and rejection was something which the production tried to graft on to the play from outside, and the result was a high degree of incoherence" since Olivier's Shylock "did not grow out of Jewish history or Shakespeare's text" (329). Bulman, however, reminds us that Miller "refuses us the comfortable closure" we expect from Act 5, because in 1970, it was inevitable that such hatred was seen as "the core of the play" (99); thus the production reflects its time in history.

Besides this, some critics argue that with its cuts and obvious bias, the production encourages "an overall view of the play which is bound to seem restricting after the experience of multeity afforded by repeated readings" (Mahood 50). Gross admits that this production is "the key production of its period" because of its unusual directorial freedom, and he adds that such freedom governs productions of nearly all Shakespeare's plays over the past 30 years, although more so with *MV*, given the subject matter of this play and the history of the past 60 years. Mahood cites Miller's comment that limited or sharply focused vision is appropriate in a theatrical production because "a successful production can reveal only so much of the structure of a play" (50).

Indeed, a production presents a unity within a play that emphasizes certain elements and ignores others. The production is the creation of the director, who begins with the drama and creates from it something unique. This something inevitably does not include all the paradoxes and unanswerable questions present in the play. Additionally, a director coordinates the unity so that actors do not work at cross-purposes, which results in tonal confusion. For example, in the courtroom scene, an inspired, virginal Portia and a tragic, victimized Shylock could dissipate the tension necessary for a resolution because no one plays the villain. Thus the drama lacks energy. Past productions have in fact been flawed with this sort of disjointed effect. As actor-manager, Charles Macklin kept his interpretation of Shylock a secret until opening night, when he and Kitty Clive played their roles for tragedy and gaiety, respectively—an odd combination, particularly when they finally met in the courtroom. Similarly, Henry Irving, a suffering and victimized antagonist, and Ellen Terry, a virtuous and sincere ingenue, created what many thought to be a muddled tone (Mahood 50). Miller's production reflects the cynicism of 1970, the unity of action Miller wished to emphasize, and the ensemble created by the actors. By definition, memorable productions, like Miller's, lead audiences to new and valuable understanding of the text.

Ellis Rabb, Director

Productions that followed further debased the Christians, making them animal-like wastrels. In a 1973 New York production in the Vivian Beaumont Theater in Lincoln Center, directed by Ellis Rabb, Venice consisted of decadent beaches and bars, and Belmont was a yacht anchored in a lagoon filled with the wealthy and bored. The relationship between Bassanio (Christopher Walken) and Antonio (Joseph Sommer) was stereotypically homosexual, threatening the marriage of an older Portia and a younger Bassanio. The Christians even slipped into violence: a drunken Lorenzo slapped Jessica in Act 5; Portia (Rosemary Harris) slapped a foppish Bassanio in Act 5 as the ring plot unfolded; and in an orgy, Jessica was surrounded and stripped of her blouse by the Venetians in Act 2. In contrast to such unstable behavior, almost any Shylock (Sidney Walker) would have seemed dignified, but Rabb further ennobled him with sophisticated dark clothes and no stereotypic Jewish character conventions except his speaking Yiddish to Tubal (Bulman 146–47). The production indicted a decadent, superficial society that could not accept an alien who scorned its dissolute life. Again, like Miller's production, Rabb's interpretation comments on its time in history. That the play can contain so contemporary a voice adds to its merit.

John Barton, Director

Even more laudable were two different but related productions directed by John Barton, the first in 1978 at the Other Place in Stratford-Upon Avon and later at the Warehouse in 1979 by the Royal Shakespeare Company, and the second in 1981 at the main theater in Stratford-Upon-Avon and then in London at the Aldwych Theatre in the same year. Like Jonathan Miller's production, these were set in the late nineteenth century, and Mahood writes that the 1978 production is what "many consider the finest production in recent years" (52). Together, the two productions demonstrate the flexibility of the play, since Barton directed the outwardly similar productions (although the second was larger than the first). But because the cast changed, the two presentations were tonally very different. In 1978, Patrick Stewart played Shylock and Marjorie Bland (in Stratford) and Lisa Harrow (in London) played Portia; while in 1980, David Suchet was Shylock and Sinead Cusack was Portia.

In a videotaped conversation, Barton, Stewart, and Suchet discuss the two productions;[21] and in a separate essay, Cusack offers observations on her experiences with the play in 1981.[22] Together these commentaries offer unusual insight into the acting of *MV*. Barton begins his edited publication of the discussion noting that neither Stewart nor Suchet saw the other play the role but both, along with Barton, agree that Shylock is a "bad Jew and a bad human being, but this in itself does not make the play anti-Semitic. If it were we would not have done it" (169). Shylock alone among the three Jews in the play is an entirely unmerciful, would-be murderer (169). Yet noting that some actors and directors use the prejudice of the Venetians to justify his hateful behavior, Barton concludes that "the deliberate ambiguities and inconsistencies . . . *are* the character: flawed, contradictory, human" (170). Suchet, a Jew himself, argues against any anti-Semitism in the play by warning that it cannot be seen in relation to the twentieth-century Holocaust and suggests rather that the play is much less "heavy going" than *The Jew of Malta* and is unique because of Shylock's opportunity to save his soul at the end of the play. Stewart finds the anti-Semitism a "distraction" and played Shylock as an outsider rather than a Jew. Suchet disagrees, saying that "as Shylock, I'm not an outsider who happens to be a Jew but because I'm a Jew" (171). Stewart adds that the character is "a very modern creation" that should therefore not be dressed with the conventional gaberdine, long hair, and hooked nose. Most important, Shylock's motivating force is "money, possessions and finance" over race, religion, even family. His clothes must be shabby because he would not choose to spend his wealth on his attire; yet his speech must be unaccented so he seems to fit into the society of Venice. He cannot eliminate his foreignness, however, since his language patterns are unique—"truly strange and exotic" (172).

Suchet agrees that money is Shylock's main consideration, but he did use a generic foreign accent, not only to demonstrate his foreignness, but also to "exploit it." Both actors deleted Irving's extra sixth scene of Shylock's Act 2 return but agree that the remaining scenes give broad dimension to the character. Suchet and Stewart agree that the ambiguities must be played so that Shylock is the multidimensional character Shakespeare created, not a "baddie or a goodie." Both stress the humor in Shylock's lines, but Stewart played an "ingratiating and cringing" moneylender in

1.3 while Suchet was dignified (175). Both actors found the next scene with Jessica alone in his house far more difficult and revealing. Shylock's only intimate scene, the interchange with Jessica should reveal "a man from whose life love had been removed," a scene that Stewart describes as "a harsh, bitter unhappy scene, and it lay at the very heart of the part for me" (175). In the scene, he strikes Jessica and then tries to reconcile with her, but it must fail because "it is impossible for him to show the undoubted love that lies there underneath" (176). Suchet, on the other hand, believes that he "didn't solve" the scene at all. His goal was to make Jessica claustrophobic from his over-possessiveness so she would have a reason to run from him, but the brevity of the scene and the lines themselves do not lend themselves to this interpretation.

Shylock's next scene (3.1), containing the "Hath not a Jew eyes?" speech, developed very similarly for both actors. They began believing that it was the traditional call for understanding and racial tolerance that it seems to be at its inception, but both actors then realized that it is, ironically, a justification for revenge. They both played a weary and defeated Shylock who is motivated to speak at all only because of Solanio's and Salarino's taunting. More unusually, they both waited until the end of the scene, when Shylock is speaking with Tubal, to decide to take revenge on Antonio. Slowly, Shylock ponders his words: "Go, Tubal, fee me an officer." Barton adds, however, that Tubal's attitude is critical in representing the Jewish community as being at best dispassionate, at worst, disapproving. In speaking of the end of the trial scene, Stewart observes that Shylock's exit is "the great question for any actor" (179) and explains that he humiliated himself and crawled because a Shylock whose main concern is money would do anything to safeguard what he still possessed. Barton observes that Suchet's exit was very different, which supports his thesis that "the end result will always belong rightly to the actors . . . And that is how it should be" (180).

Sinead Cusack played opposite Suchet, whom she calls "a consummate actor" although she notes the unusual rehearsal plan of John Barton, who does not meet with the cast to discuss the play and often rehearses actors alone in isolation from the rest of the cast. Cusack praises many of Barton's interpretations; for example, the relationship between Portia and Nerissa is that of a very young and mercurial Portia and an older and more sophisticated Nerissa dressed in hot pink. Belmont was dark and autumnal, reflecting the misery of Portia, who mourned her father. Portia wore her father's old raincoat and highlighted her imprisonment in the casket test by dragging the caskets around with her wherever she went, like a victim, and even having a rope placed over her lap during the casket selections. She had no notion of trying to be attractive, living as she did in an entirely female Belmont where even Balthazar was transformed into Betty Balthazar. Cusack played the part as if she had already fallen in love with Bassanio at their earlier meeting to which both refer in Act 1, but she seemed much more smitten than Bassanio (Jonathan Hyde), who in 3.2 concentrated on selecting the correct casket. Cusack regrets that in many of her lines in this scene, she emphasized Portia's distress rather than her humor and that the declarations of love she offered Bassanio as he tried to choose correctly were often muddled. Portia was alone under a spotlight as she sang the song about fancy. Cusack argues that Portia's discipline during the scene foreshadows "her courage and endurance . . . that she later takes into the courtroom in Venice" (347). After Bassanio's selection, she picked up each casket and threw it clear across the room. Cusack believes that like Bassanio, Portia matures through the play, "particularly in the casket trial," since it is during the test that Portia must remain silent and Bassanio "has to rise to the occasion to pass the test" (347).

The trial in Venice was another story, because during the exchange between Portia and Shylock, downstage right, Antonio began to disrobe slowly with Bassanio sufficiently close by to exchange several kisses, obviously a distraction from the famous lines. Cusack explains, however, that Portia has a carefully planned strategy not to save Antonio with the speech but "to save Shylock, to redeem him—she is passionate to do that" (349). She regrets the somber setting maintained in Belmont even in 5.1, yet she concludes that she too lost the lighthearted ending in Belmont— "and that is why, she says, "I failed when I played Portia" (350).

Although Gross finds the interpretation "small-scale because its significance had been reduced" (330), Mahood applauds Barton as having successfully diminished the focus on Shylock and the bond and emphasizing the plot's several quests: Bassanio's courtship of Portia, Portia's attempt to gain the husband of her choice, Jessica and Lorenzo's elopement, and Shylock's long-sought revenge. The overall romantic plot is tempered by the mourning in Belmont for the dead Lord, the Edwardian middle-class costumes, and the self-serving values of Venice represented in the wild and thoughtless behavior of the young Venetians at the turn of the century. The emphasis on ensemble performance adds to the strength of these two productions.

Bill Alexander, Director

A particularly daring production was Bill Alexander's *MV* for the Royal Shakespeare Company in 1987, revived in London in 1988, starring Anthony Sher as Shylock.[23] Portrayed as an especially foreign Levantine Jew with clothes and accent far different from those of the rest of the cast, Shylock was, according to Bulman who saw the production three times, "grotesque—at once comic, repulsive, and vengeful" (117). Alexander emphasized those elements of the script that had traditionally generated the greatest controversy—the bias and self-indulgence among the Venetians and the repulsive villainy in Shylock—for the audience not merely to observe prejudice among the characters onstage but to experience it and examine it within themselves. He deliberately sought to create audience disdain but, in the process, received attacks that he was promoting anti-Semitism. Alexander fashioned Shylock into the equivalent of a Middle Eastern terrorist demon, like those "associated in the western mind with frightening and unpredictable extremes of behaviour, with Islamic fundamentalism, death threats, and acts of political terrorism" (Bulman 121). For example, in 4.1 when Portia admitted that Shylock has a right to his pound of flesh, Antonio was bound to a pole in a Christ-like pose while Shylock removed his gaberdine, replaced it with a Tallith or shawl, poured blood onto a white cloth, set it at the feet of Antonio, violently ripped off Antonio's shirt, waved his arms rhythmically, cupped Antonio's chin in one hand, and raised his dagger above his head, all while chanting an apparently Hebrew prayer (Bulman 118). Bulman notes that Sher, a South African Jew, was disappointed when, at this climactic moment, the audience applauded as Portia called out "Tarry a little!" (4.1.301). But this points out the risk in a production that arouses prejudice, even if only to prove its ugliness: audiences may be taken in by Shylock's violence and, rightly, condemn him. This response, however, does not lead to the conclusion that the audience hates Jews. According to Sher, audiences were "to suspect that they were being coaxed into the very racial intolerance which . . . the production took pains to expose" (qtd. in Bulman 119). Shylock in no way represented Jews, since westernized Jews no longer elicit fear in middle-class England.

The Venetians were awful in equal measure, intended to be the Dr. Frankenstein whose brutal violence created the Shylock monster. Spitting dominated the production, with almost everyone following Antonio's self-admitted mode of insult, thereby showing "the reciprocity and the violence of prejudice" (Bulman 124). The Venetians spit at Shylock (as he did at Antonio in his bankrupt state), threw stones at him, taunted him, mocked him, kicked him, shoved him, prodded him with a stick, and nearly rolled him into a canal. Their lavish clothes and self-absorption made their biased attacks even more arrogant. Provocatively, Alexander further tested audience bias by making Antonio a "depressed homosexual" hopelessly in love with the manipulative, selfish bisexual, Bassanio. Salerio and Solanio, similarly, were "reduced to type" in their own January-May erogenous relationship. The audience was provided no safe harbor for its sympathies, since it was the arrogant, flawed Venetians who produced their near-crazed scapegoat. While Tubal and Shylock had large yellow Stars of David sewn onto the backs of their coats, likely a historic reality, the Venetians sported large crucifixes around their necks and regularly crossed themselves; the Duke even wore a religious robe and silver crucifix. These symbols were, of course, ironic, and, as Shylock was forced out of the courtroom, a crucifix was dangled in his face, "the mocking gesture," Bulman observes, "of a closed society for whom Christianity signifies power and exclusion, not mercy and acceptance" (133).

The near-bare stage emphasized the similarity between Venice and Belmont. Both had as a backdrop the cracking plaster of the brick back wall of the theater itself, although Belmont was given a soft carpet, a Bible on a stand, and warmer lighting. The effect drew parallels between the two locales rather than differences, so that Belmont was a roseate reflection of the city's smug Christianity.

Alexander intended to emphasize the racism of both Shylock and the Venetians by identifying him with not only Jews but also Third World minorities. The brutality of the scene is praised by Bulman (118) and criticized by Gross (331); certainly the excesses of the production show the variety of interpretation by twentieth-century directors, if not their attention to the subtleties of the text.

Peter Hall, Director

Peter Hall staged the play in 1989 in the West End in London with his private company and Dustin Hoffman as Shylock, Leigh Lawson as Antonio, and Geraldine James as Portia. He later videotaped it for television. Between 1973 and 1987, Hall had been the director of the National Theatre in London, replacing Lawrence Olivier and being replaced by Trevor Nunn. When he left the National, he created his own company, but he continued to follow the practices he had used in the six large-scale and three studio productions of Shakespeare's plays he had directed at the National. Labeling his style "militant classicism," Hall followed an uncut text, rearranged no scenes, reassigned no lines, and did not impose unusual scene and costume design that might have expressed the director's taste more than Shakespeare's play. His productions at the National received mixed reviews after the first, *Hamlet,* in 1976, often because of the inappropriate casting of the star. Albert Finney played Macbeth (1978), Paul Scofield played Othello (1980), and Ian McKellen played Coriolanus (1984). But according to Samuel Crowl, the post–National Theatre production of *MV* with Hoffman was "most notably" successful. Stanley Wells notes Hoffman's ironic emphasis, less common than a passionate or even a comic interpretation of Shylock (*Shakespeare* 160). Gross agrees on its success, saying that Hall's production "was a sound conventional staging of the play" with a "small-scale" Shylock, but also with an unfortunate and unoriginal bit of stage business, a "regrettable outbreak of spitting" (332).

Trevor Nunn, Director

A recent production staged in 1999 at the National Theatre in London was Trevor Nunn's *MV,* placed in a 1920s continental Gatsby-era Venice. A hedonistic café with piano playing and singing often was the setting for the scenes in Venice, while Belmont was, most of all, luminous light. Antonio (David Bamber) was a troubled older romantic lover of a carefree and younger Bassanio. Shylock (Henry Goodman) was controlled by a tension that banished joy, locking it out from his daughter, a child he loved but rigidly protects from attacks by disdainful Christians. Jessica departed from her father with glee, almost like a naughty child. Even though he slapped her, Shylock's pain over his missing daughter was numbing and made more awful by Nunn's inclusion of Irving's added homecoming scene. Yet audience sympathy fell to him only by default. While he showed an internal gravity that the Venetians did not, he remained inflexibly harsh. In the end, Jessica, too, suffered for her disrespectful behavior. When the lovers exited arm in arm in the moonlight of Belmont, Jessica, and not Antonio, was the single character remaining on the stage. She slowly exited alone to a Jewish Kaddish, much as in Jonathan Miller's 1970 production. Cutting herself off from her heritage did not open a world of joy for her. The *New York Times* praises "the care and balance of Mr. Nunn's direction"; and sees in Goodman's Shylock a character who has a "rare capacity for feeling . . . [and] vastly more moral and spiritual weight than the flighty, frivolous Christians." The review judges Goodman's "perhaps the finest performance currently in London," and he won the Olivier Award for its excellence.

Film and Video

The unusual popularity of *MV* made it an early candidate for film: 10 silent films entitled *The Merchant of Venice* were produced, 2 others proposed, and several more produced roughly or closely as adaptations with other titles. In France, *Shylock, ou le More de Venise,* directed by Henri Desfontaines, was released by Eclipse in February 1913, starring the Jewish actor Harry Baur as Shylock. He became an excellent film actor, and when the film was shown in the United States, his performance was reviewed by George Kleine in the *Moving Picture World.* Kleine wrote that his "interpretation of the role is somewhat different from those we have seen in America, inasmuch as he portrayed a less dignified Jew, yet it is done with a remarkable skill, and shows what a finished actor he is" (qtd in Ball 178). Baur died in 1943, tortured by the Nazis.

Der Kaufman von Venedig (1923), a German version of the play written and directed by Peter Paul Felner, was released in the United States in 1926 with the title *The Jew of Mestri.* Shylock, named Mordecai, and his family's experiences are the focus of the story, and the casket plot is deleted. The only surviving copy is an English version, two reels shorter than the original German. Felner adds major characters who are not present in either the play or Shakespeare's source stories, among them a wife for Mordecai and mother for Rachela (Jessica), and a son, Elias, for Tubal.[24] Filmed in Venice, the film stars Werner Krauss as Shylock, who, Robert Hamilton Ball writes, "makes a striking Mordecai . . . his creation is made impressive and convincing" (296). But Gross reminds us that he is the actor whose stage version of Shylock was so pleasing during World War II to Nazi audiences.

One British production (1916) was simply Matheson Lang's stage production at the St. James Theatre transported to a glass-roofed studio in Walthamstow and filmed during daylight hours. Ball finds the film "an artistic failure" because "the titles take more time to read than what is presented in pantomime . . . [and] it is far too respectful of Shakespeare's text" (252).

After sound films became the convention in the 1930s, filming *MV* was less likely than it had been during the silent film era. Gross notes, "the subject matter was too sensitive for Hollywood to handle" (190). George Arliss, the English actor whose stern and dignified Shylock had been so successful on the stage in America (1928), writes in his memoirs that he attempted to film the play with sound, believing that "it would make a magnificent movie. . . . [But] unfortunately the Jews don't like it, and as they are great supporters of the cinema and the theater in the United States, the American producer doesn't care to hurt their feelings—or his own" (qtd. in Gross 189–90). It was Arliss's contention that the play was as critical of the Christians as it was of the Jews, and in fact, "Shylock was palpably their superior" (190). Few filmmakers shared his opinion.

Orson Welles, Director

Although Orson Welles never released a film of *MV*, he began a production in the late 1960s that remains incomplete. Michael Anderegg notes a few intriguing extracts of this project in a faded work copy shown in a documentary titled *Orson Welles: The One Man Band*, directed by Vassili Silovic (1995).[25] Along with his other productions, including *Hamlet, Julius Caesar, Othello, King Lear,* and *Macbeth,* this demonstrates Wells's attraction to the standard Shakespeare repertoire (Anderegg 18–19). He completed a cut version of *MV* for Mercury Text Recordings, playing both Shylock and Morocco. This was a part of a larger project in which he recorded four of the plays during 1937–1938, reading from editions that he had created. Anderegg notes that in the recording, he uncharacteristically underplays Shylock, seeming nearly distracted in his opening scene. In the "Hath not a Jew eyes?" speech, he begins with tight and quiet control, moderately builds volume, and then at the call for revenge, nearly whispers his frightening intention. Welles plays the courtroom scene, however, with "the bombast and declamatory style" we associate with this scene, this character, and this actor. Anderegg concludes that "the production as a whole is quite good" (52).

Jonathan Miller, Director

The most well-known television production of *MV* is the ABC Theatre Special presentation, filmed in 1973 and telecast in 1974, of Jonathan Miller's 1970 National Theatre Company's stage production starring Laurence Olivier and Joan Plowright. Robert Hapgood judges this televised version "the best of Jonathan Miller's efforts" (qtd. in Wells, *Cambridge Companion* 284). But, as expected, some Jewish groups argued that it should not be shown because of its arguably anti-Semitic ideology. The *New York Times* published an article by Fred M. Hechinger (March 31, 1974) defending the airing because Shylock (as played by Olivier), "though vengeful, had much to be vengeful about" (qtd. in Danson 4). As in the stage production discussed above, Olivier's affluent and well-dressed Shylock does indeed elicit both audience sympathy and scorn because he is given obvious justification for revenge against the materialistic and biased Venetians. Hechinger points out the irony in the actions of both the Duke and Portia in the courtroom as they praise the virtues of mercy only moments before they approve the destruction of Shylock (Danson 4). With the camera serving to focus the attention of the audience, Miller highlights Shylock's suffering in conspicuously affluent late nineteenth-century Venice surrounded by vice-ridden Christians. One of the moments most sympathetic to Shylock takes place near the end of 3.1 in his well-appointed home. In tight close-up, the audience watches the intense emotion in Olivier's face as Tubal alternately informs him of Antonio's bad fortune and then of Jessica's thoughtless dissipation of wealth. Finally, Tubal tells him that Jessica has traded a turquoise ring for the foolery of a pet monkey. The camera focuses on the grieving face of Shylock: "I had it of Leah when I was a bachelor," he utters slowly. "I would not have given it for a wilderness of monkeys." With this, he embraces a large elaborately framed picture of Leah and falls to his knees crying. The television camera heightens the image of the suffering Jew, which had already been emphasized in the stage production.

Jack Gold, Director (Video Recording, BBC Production)

Another major television production was produced by the British Broadcasting Corporation (BBC) in association with Time-Life Television in their series of the 37 plays of Shakespeare taped between 1978 and 1985 and shown in Britain on the BBC and in America on the Public Broadcasting System (PBS).[26] The BBC had presented an earlier production of *MV* in 1955 and a 30-minute film of the trial scene alone entitled *Shylock versus "The Merchant of Venice"* in 1969. The 1980 production was a part of the enormous feat of producing approximately six plays per year for more than six years. The project was sometimes called "the First Folio of television." The BBC production of *MV,* taped May 15–21, 1980, and telecast on December 17, 1980, in Britain and on February 23, 1981, in America, was produced by Jonathan Miller and directed by Jack Gold.

The American telecast of *MV* met expected resistance from groups such as the Anti-Defamation League. They argued that while censorship is wrong, the production of this play would be "awash in bad taste" (qtd. in Willis 37). Morris Schappes, the editor of *Jewish Currents,* observes in a letter to the editor in the *New York Times* that Orson Welles had cancelled a production of the play in 1960 because it might enflame continuing anti-Semitism" (Willis 38). The president of PBS, Lawrence K. Grossman, responded that both producer and director were Jewish, as well as Warren Mitchell who played Shylock, and that PBS would not censor Shakespeare anymore than they would ban *Huckleberry Finn* on the grounds of racism (Willis 39).

The production itself is impressionistic. Gold uses what he explains are "totally real and very beautiful" costumes but only minimal, stylized settings—"a backcloth with a 'semi-artificial column or piece of wall'" because, he says, the play is "not about sitting down and about props. It's about people speaking to each other, relating to each other. It's also a very dynamic piece: I could see it with a lot of movement" (qtd in Willis 209). A 360-degree scrim, a blue, airy, gauze backdrop, surrounds the stage area. Belmont, rolled in on casters, is a gazebo, wide stairs, some columns, and some obelisks; and Venice is archways, walls, and columns. With so wide a stage, camera work was complex and in fact won a prize for Geoff Feld as Best Cameraman from the British Association of Film and Television Artists (BAFTA). The production emphasizes the cruelty of the Christians, including Bassanio (John Nettles). In press materials, Gold says that Shy-

Dustin Hoffman as Shylock. Photograph. Phoenix Theatre, Royal National Theatre (1989). "Taking the Stage: An Exhibition of Photography." By permission of John Hayes.

lock's Jewishness in the play "becomes a metaphor for the fact that he, more than any other character in Venice, is an alien," and Miller adds that "it's not about Jews versus Christians in the racial sense; it's the world of legislation versus the world of mercy" (Willis 38). Mitchell played the part as "not a murderous, money-grasping villain, but a sympathetic and much sinned against man" (Willis 38). For example, after Jessica has run away and Shylock cries to Salarino and Salerio that his own flesh and blood has rebelled, Solanio cruelly mocks him and grabs Shylock's crotch, saying, "Out upon it old carrion! Rebels it at these years?" (3.1.32). The courtroom scene, with three rows of onlookers, includes far more close-ups than pre-

Henry Goodman as Shylock. Photograph. Cottesloe Theatre, Royal National Theatre (1999). By permission of John Haynes.

vious scenes, perhaps to intensify the climactic events taking place. The Venetians' cruelty is again highlighted with close-ups of Shylock and his knife, Portia (Gemma Jones) and her mercy argument, and finally Salerio forcing a tortured Shylock to kiss a cross at his newly created conversion. He exits alone from 4.1, which Willis suggests parallels Antonio's (John Frankyn-Robbins) isolation at the end of 5.1. While Gold has a logical justification for the minimalist production, it can, at times, seem dull for television, which conventionally provides an audience a great deal more to look at than listen to. Still, the controversial presentation brought a response from viewers unlike that of any other play in the series.

Trevor Nunn, Director

A Performance Company's presentation of the National Theatre's 1999 stage production of MV was taped for television and presented in October 2001 on PBS's *Masterpiece Theater.* Like the original theater version, this telecast stars Henry Goodman as Shylock and Derbhle Crotty as Portia. Caryn James in the *New York Times* gives the production excellent reviews, saying that it "makes Shakespeare's questions seem eye-openingly fresh." She finds Goodman's performance especially noteworthy and writes that his "mesmerizing performance as Shylock reveals why he is so haunting a character. . . . [T]his Shylock is vengeful, imperfect, unlikeable, but also persecuted, emotionally wounded and deserving of sympathy." Although the production "remains unapologetically stage-bound," it is "so vibrant and rich, . . . that it makes you wish you had seen it onstage."

NOTES

1. The reader may find detailed analyses of performances over the past 400 years in Toby Lelyveld, *Shylock on the Stage* (Cleveland: Press of Western Reserve University, 1960); Bill Overton, The Merchant of Venice: *Text and Performance* (Atlantic Highlands, New Jersey: Humanities Press International, 1987); James C. Bulman, *Shakespeare in Performance:* The Merchant of Venice (Manchester: Manchester University Press, 1991); "Part 3: The Play in the Theater," in The Merchant of Venice: *Critical Essays*, ed. Thomas Wheeler (New York: Garland, 1991), 315–74; John Gross, *Shylock: A Legend and Its Legacy* (New York: Simon and Schuster, 1992); and in three modern individual editions of *MV*: John Russell Brown, New Arden Shakespeare (1955; repr. Cambridge: Harvard University Press, 1959); M. M. Mahood, New Cambridge Shakespeare (Cambridge:

Cambridge University Press, 1987); and Jay Halio, Oxford Shakespeare (Oxford: Clarendon Press, 1993), 58–83. Additionally, commentary on performances before 1888 is available in H. H. Furness, *The Variorum Edition of Shakespeare's Works* (1888).

2. The King's Men is the name given to Shakespeare's acting company after 1603, when King James became its patron. It had formerly been known as the Lord Chamberlain's Men (and the Lord Hunsdon's Men in 1596–1597), when first Henry Carey, the Lord Chamberlain, and then his son, George, the two Lords Hunsdon, served as protectors and patrons of the company. George married Elizabeth Spencer of Althorp, ancestor of the present Prince William of Wales, in 1582. See E. K., Chambers, *The Elizabethan Stage* (1923; repr. Oxford: Clarendon, 1961), 2: 192–95, for a full discussion.

3. See Chambers, *Elizabethan Stage,* 4: 172, for information on the two recorded performances of the play during Shakespeare's lifetime; 2: 192–220, for background on the acting company with which Shakespeare was affiliated; and 3: 484, for information on the play's publication and aspects of the title.

4. In *Palladis Tamia, Wit's Treasury* (1598), Francis Meres (1565–1647) identifies Shakespeare as an English dramatist comparable to Plautus and Seneca. As they are "the best for Comedy and Tragedy among the Latines: so Shakespeare among the English is the most excellent in both the kinds for the stage"; he then lists six comedies, including *MV,* as evidence of Shakespeare's excellence in this genre.

5. Jewish characters were not yet common on the stage, and the few examples include Abraham, the poisoner in *Selimus,* by Robert Greene, and Gerontus, the sole virtuous stage Jew, in *The Three Ladies of London.*

6. John Payne Collier forged other documents intended to prove the veracity of other popular suppositions. The influence of his fraudulent hoax is seen in William Winter's 1913 identification of Collier's elegy on the death of Burbage as evidence of Burbage's use of a red wig and long false nose to play Shylock; see Winter, *Shakespeare on the Stage: First Series* (1911; repr. New York: Benjamin Blom, 1969). Winter does add that "a reasonable doubt" exists over "at least a part of" the poem (133).

7. The text of Lansdowne's play is included in the Furness variorum edition of *MV,* 346–69.

8. See George Odell, *Shakespeare From Betterton to Irving,* 2 vols. (1920; repr. New York: Benjamin Blom, 1963), for detailed descriptions of early performances.

9. A proper plot in the eighteenth century was expected to adhere to the principles of the three unities: unity of place, time, and plot. A play had to take place in one locale and on one day and contain only one plot line.

10. The position of actor-manager continued well into the nineteenth century and was held by popular actors of the day who played favorite roles and who were responsible for other elements of a stage production, including its direction.

11. For a complete discussion of the Jewish Naturalization Act of 1753 ("the Jew Bill") in England, see James Shapiro, *Shakespeare and the Jews* (New York: Columbia University Press, 1996), 195–224.

12. See William Hazlitt, *The Round Table: Characters in Shakespear's Plays* (1906; repr. London: Everyman's Library, 1964) for detailed observations that exemplify nineteenth-century Romantic aesthetics.

13. For an excellent modern discussion of Henry Irving's production, see James C. Bulman, "Henry Irving and the Great Tradition," in *Shakespeare in Performance,* 28–52; and for a detailed description by one of Irving's contemporaries, see Winter, 129–231.

14. See Winter, 174–97, for a detailed description of Irving's production and dramatic interpretation of Shylock.

15. See William Poel, *Shakespeare in the Theatre* (London: Sedgwick and Jackson, Ltd., 1913), 119–33, for Poel's full discussion of the play and his observations on its production.

16. J. C. Trewin's two texts describing Shakespeare's plays are easy-to-read observations about, first, the plays themselves in *Going to Shakespeare* (London: George C. Allen, 1978), and second, somewhat more detailed descriptions of performances in the twentieth century in *Shakespeare on the English Stage 1900–1964: A Survey of Productions* (London: Barrie and Rockliff, 1964).

17. See also David Belasco's production script, *A Comedy by William Shakespeare As Arranged for the Contemporary Stage by David Belasco* (New York: Privately printed, 1922), which is highly edited and minutely detailed with stage directions.

18. See Richard E. Mennen, "Theodore Komisarjevsky's Production of *The Merchant of Venice,*" 386–97, for a full detailed description of this landmark production; also Sally Beauman, *The Royal Shakespeare Company: A History of Ten Decades* (1982).

19. See also Trewin, *Shakespeare on the English Stage,* 137, for analysis of the production.

20. See James C. Bulman, "Aesthetes in a Rugger Club: Jonathan Miller and Laurence Olivier," in *Shakespeare in Performance,* 75–100, for a detailed history and analysis of the performance, and Patrick J. Sullivan, "Strumpet Wind—The National Theatre's *Merchant of Venice,*" in Wheeler, 315–37.

21. See "Exploring a Character," in John Barton's *Playing Shakespeare* (London: Methuen, 1984), a 12-chapter, edited version of a taped series of conversations on acting Shakespeare by a variety of well-known Shakespearean actors. Barton conducted the set of nine workshop programs that were taped in 1982 and presented on London Weekend Television on Channel Four in 1984.

22. See "Portia in *The Merchant of Venice*" in Wheeler, 339–50, for Cusack's full explanation of why she "failed when [she] played Portia."

23. Bulman includes a highly detailed description of Alexander's work, praising many aspects of the production (117–42).

24. The text of the entire six-reel English version is included in Robert Hamilton Ball's *Shakespeare on Silent Film: A Strange Eventful History* (New York: Theater Arts, 1968), 288–95, along with details and illustrations of other films.

25. See Michael Anderegg, *Orson Welles, Shakespeare, and Popular Culture* (New York: Columbia University Press, 1999), for a history of Welles's work with Shakespeare's plays.

26. See Susan Willis, *The BBC Shakespeare Plays: Making the Televised Canon* (Chapel Hill and London: University of North Carolina Press, 1991) for a thorough study of the history and production of this BBC series.

SELECTED ANNOTATED BIBLIOGRAPHY

The following list identifies major sources and editions used in this book as well as other articles and texts that may be useful in understanding *The Merchant of Venice*. The editions included here are easily available and are texts of the single play only (save the First Folio facsimile edition), not texts included in current editions of Shakespeare's complete works, which are listed in Chapter 1. This bibliography is in no way comprehensive. The reader who seeks an exhaustive listing of works on *MV* may use the bibliographies included below as well as the bibliographies included at the end of virtually all of the sources. This list may assist readers interested in further study of the play who wish to read a complete study which is only summarized or noted in this book, investigate a single aspect of the play more deeply, or broaden their understanding of Shakespeare's entire canon.

SINGLE EDITIONS OF THE PLAY

Shakespeare, William. *Shakespeare's Comedy of* The Merchant of Venice. Ed. William J. Rolfe. 1870. New York: American Book Co., 1911.

> This is an excellent example of a bowdlerized text common a century ago.

————. *A New Variorum Edition of Shakespeare, Vol VII*. The Merchant of Venice. Ed. Horace Howard Furness. Philadelphia: J.B. Lippincott Company. 1888.

————. *Mr. William Shakespeare's Comedies, Histories, & Tragedies. A Facsimile Edition Prepared by Helge Kökeritz*. New Haven: Yale UP, 1954.

> This is a reduced facsimile edition of the First Folio owned by the Elizabethan Club of Yale University preceded by a 29-page introduction by Charles Tyler Prouty.

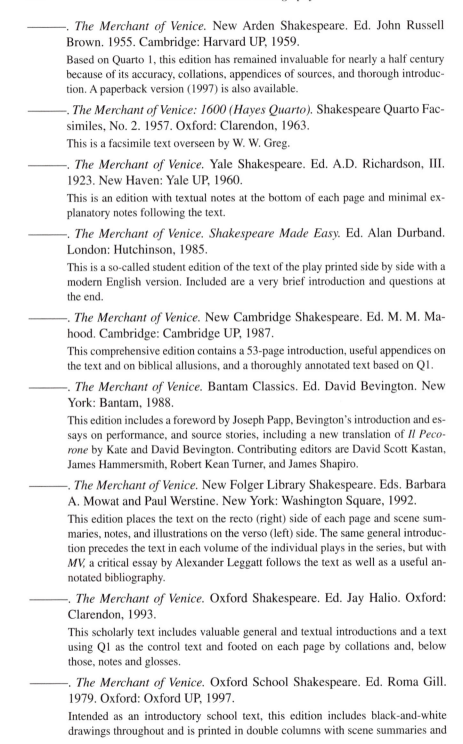

———. *The Merchant of Venice*. New Arden Shakespeare. Ed. John Russell Brown. 1955. Cambridge: Harvard UP, 1959.

Based on Quarto 1, this edition has remained invaluable for nearly a half century because of its accuracy, collations, appendices of sources, and thorough introduction. A paperback version (1997) is also available.

———. *The Merchant of Venice: 1600 (Hayes Quarto)*. Shakespeare Quarto Facsimiles, No. 2. 1957. Oxford: Clarendon, 1963.

This is a facsimile text overseen by W. W. Greg.

———. *The Merchant of Venice*. Yale Shakespeare. Ed. A.D. Richardson, III. 1923. New Haven: Yale UP, 1960.

This is an edition with textual notes at the bottom of each page and minimal explanatory notes following the text.

———. *The Merchant of Venice*. *Shakespeare Made Easy*. Ed. Alan Durband. London: Hutchinson, 1985.

This is a so-called student edition of the text of the play printed side by side with a modern English version. Included are a very brief introduction and questions at the end.

———. *The Merchant of Venice*. New Cambridge Shakespeare. Ed. M. M. Mahood. Cambridge: Cambridge UP, 1987.

This comprehensive edition contains a 53-page introduction, useful appendices on the text and on biblical allusions, and a thoroughly annotated text based on Q1.

———. *The Merchant of Venice*. Bantam Classics. Ed. David Bevington. New York: Bantam, 1988.

This edition includes a foreword by Joseph Papp, Bevington's introduction and essays on performance, and source stories, including a new translation of *Il Pecorone* by Kate and David Bevington. Contributing editors are David Scott Kastan, James Hammersmith, Robert Kean Turner, and James Shapiro.

———. *The Merchant of Venice*. New Folger Library Shakespeare. Eds. Barbara A. Mowat and Paul Werstine. New York: Washington Square, 1992.

This edition places the text on the recto (right) side of each page and scene summaries, notes, and illustrations on the verso (left) side. The same general introduction precedes the text in each volume of the individual plays in the series, but with *MV*, a critical essay by Alexander Leggatt follows the text as well as a useful annotated bibliography.

———. *The Merchant of Venice*. Oxford Shakespeare. Ed. Jay Halio. Oxford: Clarendon, 1993.

This scholarly text includes valuable general and textual introductions and a text using Q1 as the control text and footed on each page by collations and, below those, notes and glosses.

———. *The Merchant of Venice*. Oxford School Shakespeare. Ed. Roma Gill. 1979. Oxford: Oxford UP, 1997.

Intended as an introductory school text, this edition includes black-and-white drawings throughout and is printed in double columns with scene summaries and detailed notes on the left and text on the right. Commentary, background material, questions, class work, and exams are placed at the end of the volume.

————. *The Merchant of Venice.* Signet Classic Shakespeare. Ed. Kenneth Myrick. 1965. New York: Penguin, 1998.

This edition, based on Q1, offers only brief notes but includes notably thorough explanations with 81 pages of introductory material and 64 pages of excerpts from essays by critics from 1709 through the present.

BIBLIOGRAPHIES

Bevington, David, comp. *Shakespeare.* Goldentree Bibliographies in Language and Literature. Arlington Heights: AHM, 1978. 175–78.

Bevington lists selected studies of the play on these pages as well as more general studies in other sections.

Kolen, Philip C., comp. *Shakespeare and Feminist Criticism: An Annotated Bibliography and Commentary.* New York and London: Garland, 1991.

Kolen's annotated list includes works written between 1975 and 1990, a 48-page introduction, and 53 listings on *MV.*

Wheeler, Thomas, comp. *The Merchant of Venice: An Annotated Bibliography.* New York: Garland, 1985.

Wheeler offers a useful annotated list of works about *MV,* most of which were written between 1940 and 1980 and concern criticism, sources, textual studies, bibliographies, editions and translations, stage history, films, music, recordings, adaptations, and synopses.

Woodbridge, Linda, comp. *Shakespeare: A Selective Bibliography of Modern Criticism.* West Cornwall: Locust Hill, 1988. 144–49.

Woodbridge focuses on criticism from the last half of the twentieth century.

SCHOLARSHIP AND CRITICISM

Adelman, Janet. "Male Bonding in Shakespeare's Comedies." *Shakespeare's "Rough Magic": Renaissance Essays in Honor of C. L. Barber.* Eds. Peter Erickson and Copplia Kahn. Newark: U of Delaware P, 1985. 73–97.

Adelman focuses on male friendship and love, not the will of the father, as the greatest obstacle to marriage, and she concludes that a successful resolution to the conflict between friend and wife is impossible.

Auden, W. H. "Brothers & Others." *The Dyer's Hand and Other Essays.* 1948. New York: Vintage, 1968. 218–37.

Calling *MV* "one of Shakespeare's Unpleasant Plays (221)," Auden argues that it intertwines the incompatible mercantile world of Venice with the fairy life in Belmont.

Bacon, Francis. "On Usury." *Essays, Civil and Moral in 'The New Atlantis' by Francis Bacon; 'Areopagitica' and 'Tractate on Education' by John Mil-*

ton; 'Religio Medici' by Sir Thomas Browne. Ed. Charles W. Eliot. New York: P. F. Collier, 1909.

Bacon's essay presents the newly developing and pragmatic seventeenth-century approach to usury, which marked an important change from the religion-based notions of the sixteenth century.

Barber, C. L. *Shakespeare's Festive Comedy: A Study of Dramatic Form and Its Relation to Social Custom*. 1959. Cleveland and New York: Meridian, 1963.

Barber's respected text explains Shakespeare's comedies as dramatic rituals representing the movement from chaos to order.

Barker, Deborah, and Ivo Kamps. *Shakespeare and Gender: A History*. London: Verso, 1995.

This volume contains a useful overview of the topic followed by several valuable essays, including two on *MV.*

Belsey, Catherine. *Critical Practice*. 1980. London and New York: Routledge, 1987.

Belsey offers a chronological survey of twentieth century critical theory with detailed literary illustrations and focusing on post-structuralist theories and theorists.

———. "Love in Venice." *New Casebooks: The Merchant of Venice*. Ed. Martin Coyle. New York: St. Martin's Press, 1998. 139–60.

Belsey compares the relationship between Bassanio and Antonio with that between Bassanio and Portia and concludes that the language of both relationships is similar.

Berek, Peter. "The Jew as Renaissance Man." *Renaissance Quarterly* 51 (1998): 128–62.

Berek examines the English theater in the 1590s, contending that Christopher Marlowe's *The Jew of Malta* is "the crucial initiatory text identifying Jew as Other in the nationalistic effort in England to create a unique English identity. (130)."

Bevington, David. *"The Jew of Malta." From Mankind to Marlowe: Growth of Structure in the Popular Drama of Tudor England*. Cambridge: Harvard UP, 1962. 218–33.

Chapter 15 of this valuable text examines *The Jew of Malta* and its relationship to other English medieval and Tudor plays.

Bloom, Harold. *Shakespeare: The Invention of the Human*. New York: Riverhead Books, 1998.

Bloom's 745-page volume of critical essays on all of Shakespeare's plays provides the general reader with insightful explanations.

———, ed. *Shylock: Major Literary Characters*. New York: Chelsea House, 1991.

This anthology includes 12 complete critical essays and 23 excerpts by American, English, and other European critics primarily of the twentieth century, introduced with an essay by Bloom.

————. *William Shakespeare's* The Merchant of Venice. Modern critical interpretations. New York: Chelsea House, 1986.

> Introduced with an essay by Bloom, this anthology contains eight interpretative
> essays by various twentieth-century critics.

Brown, John Russell. Introduction and appendices. *The Merchant of Venice.* By
William Shakespeare. Arden Shakespeare. 1955. Cambridge: Harvard UP,
1959. xi—lviii, 140–74.

> Brown's introduction and appendices of sources are invaluable—accurate, in-
> sightful, and convenient to use.

Bullough, Geoffrey, ed. *Narrative and Dramatic Sources of Shakespeare.* Vol. 1.
London: Routledge, 1957. 443–514.

> After an 18-page introduction to *MV*'s sources, Bullough includes texts of eight
> probable sources and analogues for the play.

Burckhardt, Sigurd. *Shakespearean Meanings.* Princeton: Princeton UP, 1968.

> Burckhardt's interpretation of a number of the plays depends on reading with at-
> tention to detail to determine discoverable messages in the text.

Chambers, E. K. *The Elizabethan Stage.* 4 vols. 1923. Oxford: Clarendon, 1961.

> This four-volume series remains an invaluable source for scholarly study of En-
> glish theater during the Elizabethan period.

Christensen, Jerome. "The Mind at Ocean." *William Shakespeare's* The Merchant
of Venice. Ed. Harold Bloom. New York: Chelsea House, 1986. 121–28.

> This is a post-structuralist analysis of language in *MV*, concentrating on Samuel
> Taylor Coleridge's analysis of 2.6.14–19 in chapter 1 of *Biographia Literaria.*

Coghill, Neville. "The Basis of Shakespearean Comedy." 1950. *Shakespearean
Criticism: 1935–1960.* Ed. Anne Ridler. London: Oxford UP, 1970.
201–27.

> Coghill examines Shakespeare's use of the comic genre from the more Plautine
> early comedies such as *A Comedy of Errors* to *The Tempest.* See *ES* III (1950), for
> the full text of this essay.

Cohen, D. M. "The Jew and Shylock." *Shakespeare Quarterly* 31 (1980): 53–63.

> Cohen argues that the play is anti-Semitic and that even though Shakespeare
> clearly understood the humanity of Jews, he was willing to use a sensational ste-
> reotype—a "profoundly troubling" conclusion about Shakespeare.

Cohen, Walter. "*The Merchant of Venice* and the Possibilities of Historical Criticism." *Journal of English Literacy History* 49 (1982): 765–89.

> Moving beyond a single literary theory, Cohen interweaves background material
> from history, economic and social theory (particularly Marxist), and early modern
> literary conventions to gain useful insights into *MV.*

Danson, Lawrence. *The Harmonies of* The Merchant of Venice. New Haven: Yale
UP, 1978.

This is an excellent and oddly rare study of the entire play (rather than of the character of Shylock) that argues that the play's structural and thematic unity is based on order, harmony, and circular imagery.

Donawerth, Jane. *Shakespeare and the Sixteenth Century Study of Language.* Urbana: U of Illinois P, 1984.

Following a general study of the nature of language during the Elizabethan period, Donawerth includes studies of various plays, including a chapter on language as a determinant of character in *MV.*

Drakakis, John. "Historical Difference and Venetian Patriarchy." The Merchant of Venice: *William Shakespeare.* New Casebooks. New York: St. Martin's, 1998. 181–213.

Drakakis argues that *MV* contains unresolvable discord in the text, a position appropriate to Elizabethan theater, which itself held the role of Other—that which was inherently different—in the sixteenth century.

Dubrow, Heather. Twentieth Century Shakespearean Criticism. *Riverside Shakespeare.* 2nd ed. Ed. G. Blakemore Evans. 1974. Boston: Houghton Mifflin, 1997.

Dubrow's introduction is a clear, chronological description of literary critical trends that affect all Shakespeare's plays and are applicable to individual plays.

Duncan, David Ewing. *The Story of the Calendar.* 1998. London: Fourth Estate, 1999.

Duncan presents a history of the world's attempts to precisely record time with calendars and clocks.

Eagleton, Terry. *Rereading Literature: William Shakespeare.* Oxford and New York: Basil Blackwell, 1986.

This is a study of 17 of Shakespeare's plays that interrelates language, desire, law, money, and the body; it is "an exercise in political semiotics" that seeks the relevant history in the text. 27–48.

Erickson, Peter, and Copplia Kahn, eds. *Shakespeare's "Rough Magic": Renaissance Essays in Honor of C. L. Barber.* Newark: U of Delaware P, 1985.

This series of essays, addresses, and lectures about a variety of Shakespeare's plays includes several directly about *MV.*

Fiedler, Leslie A. "The Jew as Stranger: Or 'These Be the Christian Husbands.'" *The Stranger in Shakespeare.* New York: Stein and Day, 1972. 85–136.

Fiedler says the play, with its austere Jew and pleasure-seeking Venetians, highlights the anti-Semitism of the past as well as the anti-Semitism still smoldering in contemporary society.

Freud, Sigmund. "The Theme of the Three Caskets." *William Shakespeare's* The Merchant of Venice. Ed. Harold Bloom. New York: Chelsea House, 1986. 7–14.

Although only a brief section of this essay concerns *MV,* it is one of Freud's few discussions concentrating on a specific work of Shakespeare.

Frye, Northrop. *A Natural Perspective: The Development of Shakespearean Comedy and Romance.* New York: Harcourt, 1965.

> This is an important structuralist explanation of comedy as archetypally mythic in structure.

Garber, Marjorie. *Coming of Age in Shakespeare.* New York and London: Routledge, 1981.

> Garber uses anthropological and psychological perspectives to analyze the plays and includes some insightful references to *MV.*

Girard, René. "To Entrap the Wisest: Sacrificial Ambivalence in *The Merchant of Venice.*" *A Theater of Envy: William Shakespeare.* New York: Oxford UP, 1991. 243–55.

> Girard argues an ironic reading of the text based on the explicit venality of Shylock, which is challenged by the implicit and expanding venality of the Christians.

Goddard, Harold C. "*The Merchant of Venice.*" *The Meaning of Shakespeare.* Vol. 1. Chicago: U of Chicago P, 1951. 81–116.

> Goddard views Portia and Bassanio as the golden casket, Antonio as the silver, and Shylock, generously, as the lead casket, acknowledging anti-Semitism in the Venetians that does not permeate the play itself.

Granville-Barker, Harley. "*The Merchant of Venice.*" *Prefaces to Shakespeare.* Vol. 4. 1946. Princeton: Princeton UP, 1965. 88–119.

> As an actor and director as well as a scholar, Granville-Barker discusses the performance and critical interpretation of *MV.*

Grebanier, Bernard. *The Truth About Shylock.* New York: Random House, 1962.

> In great detail, Grebanier analyzes a character, less a Jew than a larger-than-life man, who is possessed by greed and abides in a fantasy world of fellowship that excludes him.

Greenblatt, Stephen. *Renaissance Refashioning: From More to Shakespeare.* Berkeley, CA: U of California P, 1980.

> This work contains Greenblatt's early presentation of the New Historicist perspectives on Renaissance literature.

———. *Shakespearean Negotiations: The Circulation of Social Energy in Renaissance England.* Berkeley: U of California P, 1988.

> Unlike his earlier *Renaissance Refashioning,* this work of Greenblatt focuses more specifically on the plays of Shakespeare in the application of New Historicist perspectives.

Greg, W. W. *The Editorial Problem in Shakespeare: A Survey of the Foundation of the Text.* Oxford: Clarendon, 1951.

> This study covers a variety of topics and explains problems in editions of *MV*; namely, its original registration, its 1619 edition, and Q1 typesetting.

———. *The Shakespeare First Folio.* Oxford: Clarendon, 1955.

> Greg's text remains an outstanding source on the text of the First Folio of 1623, with a thorough bibliography.

————. *Some Aspects and Problems of London Publishing Between 1550 and 1650.* Oxford: Clarendon, 1956.

Greg discusses various topics in six chapters, but the most relevant to *MV* is the concluding chapter, which explains blocking entries.

Gross, John. *Shylock: A Legend and Its Legacy.* New York: Simon and Schuster, 1992.

Gross surveys the history of the play's performance but also includes extensive background material on the history of Jewish characters in drama and the history of Jews in London.

Halio, Jay. Introduction. *The Merchant of Venice.* The Oxford Shakespeare. Oxford: Clarendon, 1993. 1–93.

Halio's thorough research is matched by his clear style. This is a praiseworthy study that sets a standard for others.

Hardin, Craig. *The Enchanted Glasss: The Elizabethan Mind in Literature.* New York: Oxford University Press. 1931

Hazlitt, William. *The Round Table: Characters of Shakespear's Plays.* 1906. London: Everyman's Library, 1964.

Hazlitt writes insightful and emotional impressions of the characters in the plays.

————. *Shakespeare's Library: A Collection of the Plays, Romances, Novels, Poems, and Histories Employed by Shakespeare in the Composition of His Works.* Vol. 1. 1875. New York: AMS Press, 1965.

Hazlitt offers five sources for the play in original spelling and, interestingly, *Il Pecorone,* which Hazlitt calls "The Adventures of Giannetto," in the original Italian.

Heine, Heinrich. "Shylock." *The Poetry and Prose of Heinrich Heine.* Ed. Frederick Ewen. New York: Citadel, 1948. 674–81.

Heine's descriptions and responses to the plays demonstrate the romantic responses of the time.

Highet, Gilbert. *The Classical Tradition: Greek and Roman Influences on Western Literature.* Oxford: Oxford UP, 1967.

This is an excellent standard study of the topic.

Hoby, Thomas. *The Book of The Courtier. The Tudor Translations.* Ed. W. E. Henley. New York: AMS, 1967.

This edition of a highly influential text in the Renaissance uses original spelling and includes an introduction by Walter Raleigh.

Holderness, Graham. *New Casebooks: The Merchant of Venice.* Ed. Martin Coyle. New York: St. Martin's Press, 1998. 23–35.

Holderness's introduction to the play has a New Historicist perspective.

Holland, Norman, N. *Psychoanalysis and Shakespeare.* New York, Toronto, and London: McGraw-Hill, 1964.

Holland's study is an important early text relating Freudian and other psychoanalytic perspectives to the plays.

Joseph, Sr. Miriam. *Shakespeare's Use of the Arts of Language*. New York: Columbia UP, 1947.

> An exhaustive study of classical rhetoric as Shakespeare learned and used it, which one may use to study the language of Shakespeare and other writers of the period.

Kahn, Copplia. "The Cuckoo's Note: Male Friendship and Cuckoldry in *The Merchant of Venice*." *Shakespeare's "Rough Magic": Renaissance Essays in Honor of C. L. Barber*. Newark: U of Delaware P, 1985. 104–12.

> Kahn sees the ring plot as highlighting male anxieties over cuckoldry after marriage and the male need to renounce close male relationships before marriage.

Lewalski, Barbara. "Biblical Allusion and Allegory in *The Merchant of Venice*." *Major Literary Characters: Shylock*. Ed. Harold Bloom. New York: Chelsea House, 1991.

> Lewalski argues that the play is a religious allegory in the comic form established by Dante that begins in troubles and resolves in joy.

Long, William B. "Stage-Directions: A Misinterpreted Factor in Determining Textual Provenance. *TEXT* 2 (1985): 121–37.

> Long argues against the established premises of the New Bibliographers that neatness and form necessarily indicate the provenance of a printed text.

Lyon, John. *The Merchant of Venice*. Twayne's New Critical Introductions to Shakespeare. Boston: Twayne, 1988.

> Lyon gives a thoughtful act-by-act analysis of the play.

Mahood, M. M. Introduction. *The Merchant of Venice*. By William Shakespeare. The New Cambridge Shakespeare. Ed. M. M. Mahood. Cambridge: Cambridge UP, 1987.

> The 53-page introduction, text history, and biblical analysis cover a variety of scholarly subjects with particularly useful examinations of performance history with accompanying illustrations and text.

Manly, John Matthews, ed. *The Play of the Sacrament. Specimens of the Pre-Shakespearean Drama*. Vol. I. New York: Dover, 1967. 239–76.

> This is an edition of the play in original spelling.

Marlowe, Christopher. *The Jew of Malta. Complete Plays and Poems*. Ed. E. D. Pendry. 1976. London: J. M. Dent, 1997.

> This is the Everyman Library version of the play originally published in 1906.

Maus, Katherine Eisaman. Introduction to *The Merchant of Venice*. The Norton Shakespeare. Ed. Stephen Greenblatt. New York: W.W. Norton, 1997. 1081—88.

McPherson, David C. *Shakespeare, Jonson, and the Myth of Venice*. Newark : U of Delaware P, 1990.

> McPherson presents an extensive discussion of historical Venice and mythic Venice described by writers of Tudor England.

Muir, Kenneth. *Shakespeare's Sources*. Vol. 1. 1957. London: Metheun, 1961. 47–51.

Muir provides a brief summary of the sources for each play.

Murry, John Middleton. *Shakespeare.* 1936. London: Jonathan Cape, 1961. 188–211.

In his essay on *MV,* Murry discusses the play as deriving from a folk tale, which explains its lack of realism.

Neely, Carol Thomas. "Broken Nuptials in Shakespeare's Comedies." *Shakespeare's "Rough Magic": Renaissance Essays in Honor of C. L. Barber.* Ed. Peter Erickson and Copplia Kahn. Newark: U of Delaware P, 1985. 61–71.

Neely examines the threats to marriage in the patriarchal world and, more specifically, male friendship.

Newman, Karen. "Portia's Ring: Unruly Women and Structures of Exchange in *The Merchant of Venice. Shakespeare Quarterly* 38 (1987): 19–33.

Newman explains that although in many cultures men have used women as possessions for exchange, in *MV,* Portia inverts this norm. She gives herself to Bassanio and maintains the power to reclaim herself when she wishes, thus demonstrating that women are not permanently destined to subordinate roles.

Nicoll, Allardyce. *The World of Harlequin.* Cambridge: Cambridge UP, 1963.

This is a detailed study of an influential genre in western drama.

Novy, Marianne. "Giving and Taking in *The Merchant of Venice." Love's Argument: Gender Relations in Shakespeare.* Chapel Hill: U of North Carolina P, 1984. 63–82.

With a feminist perspective, Novy concludes that Portia is the wisest and most powerful character in *MV* because she loves most effectively—with the mutuality of giving and taking.

Oz, Avraham. *The Yoke of Love: Prophetic Riddles in* The Merchant of Venice. Newark: U of Delaware P, 1995.

This study examines the rhythm of riddle and prophecy in the play from a deconstructionist perspective.

Pequiney, Joseph. "The Two Antonios and Same-Sex Love in *Twelfth Night* and *The Merchant of Venice." Shakespeare and Gender: A History.* Eds. Deborah Barker and Ivo Kamps. London: Verso, 1995. 178–95.

Pequiney compares the language and action in the love relationships of Antonio in *Twelfth Night* and Antonio in *MV* and concludes that although the former relationship is homoerotic, the latter is not.

Plato. *The Dialogues of Plato.* Vol. 1. Trans. B. Jowett. 1892. New York: Random House, 1937. 233–85.

This is an excellent translation of a work whose influence during the Renaissance cannot be overestimated.

Rabkin, Norman. "Meaning and Shakespeare." The Merchant of Venice: *Critical Essays.* Ed. Thomas Wheeler. New York: Garland, 1991. 103–25.

Rabkin uses *MV* to discuss the process of finding meaning in a Shakespearean play. The original essay may be found in Norman Rabkin, *Shakespeare and the Problem of Meaning,* (Chicago: U of Chicago P, 1981).

Ruskin, John. *The Complete Works of John Ruskin.* London: George Allen, 1903.

Ruskin's *Works* may nearly serve as an unalphabetized encyclopedia, and his observations in various volumes on *MV,* usury, and Shylock are well phrased, direct, and economically written.

Ryan, Kiernan. "Re-reading *The Merchant of Venice 1995.*" In the Merchant of Venice: *William Shakespeare.* New Casebooks. New York: St. Martin's, 1998. 36–43.

Ryan's New Historicist premise includes the notion that *MV*'s "true achievement consists in its subversion of its own conventional commitments. (37)"

Schwartz, Murray M., and Copplia Kahn, eds. *Representing Shakespeare: New Psychoanalytic Essays.* Baltimore: Johns Hopkins UP, 1980.

This anthology includes essays (one of which is on *MV)* that represent "an emerging consensus on the recurrent, defining features of Shakespeare's art as it is reflected through contemporary psychoanalytic concepts" (xi).

Sedgwick, Eve Kosofsky. *Between Men: English Literature and Male Homosexual Desire.* New York: Columbia University Press. 1985.

Shapiro, James. *Shakespeare and the Jews.* New York: Columbia UP, 1996.

This is a scholarly, detailed study of the interrelationship between the play and the history of the Jews in England before, during, and 150 years after the writing of *MV.*

Shell, Marc. "The Wether and the Ewe: Verbal Usury." *William Shakespeare's* The Merchant of Venice. Ed. Harold Bloom. New York: Chelsea House, 1986. 107–20.

Shell begins with the discussion of the pun as verbal usury—here, "use," "ewes," and "iews" (Jews)—and proceeds to a discussion of natural (sexual) and unnatural (monetary) exchange and generation.

Sinfield, Alan. "How to Read *The Merchant of Venice* Without Being Heterosexist." The Merchant of Venice: *William Shakespeare.* New Casebooks. New York: St. Martin's, 1998. 161–80.

Writing from the viewpoint of a gay man, Sinfield argues that like the culture of the sixteenth century, *MV* accepts same-sex relationships but only up to the point when offspring are required in the family.

Sinsheimer, Hermann. *Shylock: The History of a Character.* New York: Benjamin Blom, 1947. Benjamin Blom, New York:1963.

Sinsheimer presents historical, literary, and dramatic background for this most famous postbiblical Jewish figure, all of which aims to prove what John Middleton Murry states in the book's foreword: "The malignity of Shylock is more than motivated; it is justified."

Slights, Camille. "In Defense of Jessica: The Runaway Daughter in *The Merchant of Venice.*" *Shakespeare Quarterly* 31 (1980): 357–68.

> Slights's essay defends Jessica, who so often earns less sympathy from the audience than her father because of her seemingly thoughtless and selfish elopement; but Slights argues that her strength lies in her humility, flexibility, and receptivity to virtuous influences.

Smith, Bruce R. *Homosexual Desire in Shakespeare's England: A Cultural Poetics.* Chicago: U of Chicago P, 1991.

> This book focuses on homosexual desire and its interpretation in English Renaissance literature.

Stoll, E. E. "Shylock." *Shakespeare Studies: Historical and Comparative in Method.* 1927. New York: Frederick Ungar, 1960. 255–336.

> As a historicist, Stoll examines the play as a product of the Elizabethan world in which it was written and consequently finds the Jew Shylock, like Barabas in *The Jew of Malta,* a hated enemy.

Tennenhouse, Leonard. "The Counterfeit Order of *The Merchant of Venice.*" *Representing Shakespeare: New Psychoanalytic Essays.* Eds. Murray M. Schwartz and Coppélia Kahn. Baltimore: Johns Hopkins UP, 1980. 54–69.

> Tennenhouse uses a psychoanalytic approach in commenting on the play and focuses on issues of betrayal among the characters and the imperfect identity of wealth with love.

Tillyard, E. M. W. *The Elizabethan World Picture.* London: Chatto, 1943.

> Tillyard broadly outlines the concepts of the ordered hierarchy of the universe and the harmony of the natural world popular in the Renaissance.

———. *Shakespeare's Early Comedies.* New York: Barnes & Noble, 1965. 182–208.

> Tillyard agrees with what he calls the response to *MV* by the public who "have loved it" as a comedy and as a fairy tale complete with Portia as "princess" and Bassanio as "fairy prince."

Traversi, Derek A. "*The Merchant of Venice.*" *Shakespeare: The Early Comedies.* 1960. London: Longmans Green, 1964.

> This essay is a careful, New Critical reading of the play.

Wells, Stanley. *Shakespeare: A Life in Drama.* 1995. New York and London: Norton, 1997.

> Wells's book is a useful overview of Shakespeare's work. His analysis of *MV* (158–64), while brief, may serve as an introduction for readers new to the play.

———, ed. *The Cambridge Companion to Shakespeare Studies.* Cambridge: Cambridge UP, 1986.

> Wells gathers essays by scholars on a variety of subjects including genres, text history, performances, television productions, and theater productions.

Wells, Stanley, and Gary Taylor. *William Shakespeare: A Textual Companion.* Oxford: Clarendon, 1987.

> This volume contains extensive notes to the texts of the plays with notes on *MV* on pages 323–28.

Wheeler, Thomas, ed. The Merchant of Venice: *Critical Essays.* New York: Garland, 1991.

> This volume contains essays subdivided into three categories: the play as text, the character Shylock, and the play in performance.

Wilders, John, ed. *Shakespeare:* The Merchant of Venice: *A Casebook.* 1969. Nashville: Aurora, 1970.

> This casebook contains 22 excerpts of studies of *MV* from Nicholas Rowe in the eighteenth century through W. H. Auden in the mid-twentieth century.

Wilson, Thomas. *A Discourse Upon Usury.* 1572. Ed. R. H. Tawney. New York: Frank Cass, 1963.

> Wilson writes a traditional commentary on usury, a subject Tawney calls "the principal economic controversy of the sixteenth century," in the form of a dinner conversation among a preacher, a doctor, a merchant, and a lawyer. Tawney's 172-page introduction is insightful.

Yaffe, Martin W. *Shylock and the Jewish Question.* Baltimore and London: John Hopkins UP, 1997.

> Yaffe argues against Harold Bloom and other critics who hold that Shakespeare's play accepts the plausibility of anti-Semitism, and he further suggests that the play may even serve "as a helpful guide for the self-understanding of the modern Jew."

PERFORMANCE ASPECTS

Anderegg, Michael. *Orson Welles, Shakespeare, and Popular Culture.* New York: Columbia UP, 1999.

> This book offers information and commentary on a great deal of the art of Orson Welles and contains useful details concerning Welles's work with *MV.*

Baldwin, T. W. *The Organization and Personnel of the Shakespearean Company.* 1927. New York: Russell, 1961.

> This text contains a wealth of factual details concerning Elizabethan acting companies.

Ball, Robert Hamilton. *Shakespeare on Silent Film: A Strange Eventful History.* New York: Theater Arts, 1968.

> This book provides a detailed history, description, and evaluation of a number of selected silent films of Shakespeare's plays. Also included is a listing of all known productions and, in some cases, the entire text of some or all reels.

Barton, John. *Playing Shakespeare.* London: Methuen, 1984.

This 12-chapter text is an edited version of a series of conversations taped in 1982 and televised in 1984 concerning acting Shakespeare by a variety of well-known Shakespearean actors. Chapter 10 covers two productions of *MV.*

Bate, Jonathan, and Russell Jackson, eds. *Shakespeare: An Illustrated Stage History.* Oxford: Oxford UP, 1996.

This is a series of essays, written by various scholars in honor of Stanley Wells with 112 illustrations of Shakespearean actors and productions. It provides an excellent overview of stage productions and contains several references to *MV.*

Belasco, David. *A Comedy by William Shakespeare As Arranged for the Contemporary Stage by David Belasco.* New York: Privately printed, 1922.

This is a production script, highly edited and minutely detailed with stage directions.

Bulman, James C. *Shakespeare in Performance:* The Merchant of Venice. Manchester: Manchester UP, 1991.

Bulman provides detailed histories, descriptions, and analyses of six exceptional performances of *MV,* along with a background chapter, bibliography, and appendix.

Chambers, E. K. *The Elizabethan Stage.* 4 vols. 1923. Oxford: Clarendon, 1961.

Chambers' lengthy and accurate text remains the standard scholarly reference on Elizabethan theater.

Crowl, Samuel. *Shakespeare Observed: Studies in Performance on Stage and Screen.* Athens: Ohio UP, 1992.

Crowl examines a wide range of performances grouped according to director and includes some useful observations about performances on *MV.*

Cusack, Sinead. "Portia in *The Merchant of Venice.*" The Merchant of Venice: *Critical Essays.* Ed. Thomas Wheeler. New York: Garland, 1991, 339–50.

Cusack recalls her experience playing Portia with John Barton as director and David Suchet as Shylock in 1981.

Irving, Henry. *Impressions of America.* London: 1884.

Irving's observations of productions and their surroundings describe productions in America.

Jorgens, Jack L. *Shakespeare on Film.* Bloomington: Indiana UP, 1977.

Jorgens offers a thorough study and is limited only by his 1970s completion date.

Lelyveld, Toby. *Shylock on the Stage.* Cleveland: P of Western Reserve U, 1960.

A scrupulously detailed history of characterizations of Shylock and productions of *MV* through the mid-twentieth century.

Mazer, Cary M. *Shakespeare Refashioned: Elizabethan Plays on Edwardian Stages.* Ann Arbor: UMI Research P: 1980.

Mazer examines the variations in the Edwardian theater that characterize the transition from the actor-manager production to the Director's Theatre.

Odell, George. *Annals of the New York Stage.* Vol. I–XIV. New York: Columbia UP, 1927–1945.

Odell's detailed descriptions of theater in America are thorough and detailed.

————. *Shakespeare From Betterton to Irving.* 2 vols. 1920. New York: Benjamin Blom, 1963.

Odell examines the play's production history from *The Jew of Venice* through Beerbohm Tree's production covering at least 10 actor-manager productions.

Overton, Bill. The Merchant of Venice: *Text and Performance.* Atlantic Highlands: Humanities P International, 1987.

This brief and readable text (79 pages) includes five essays on textual topics and five essays on performance topics.

Shattuck, Charles H. *Shakespeare on the American Stage.* 2 vols. Washington, D.C.: Folger Library. 1987.

Shattuck's study of eighteenth- and nineteenth-century American productions of Shakespeare's plays is exceptionally thorough and includes material on *MV.*

Sprague, Arthur Colby. *Shakespeare and the Actors: The Stage Business in His Plays (1660–1905).* Cambridge: Harvard UP, 1948.

The text includes descriptions of performances with several mentions of *MV.*

Suchet, David, Patrick Stewart, and John Barton. "Exploring a Character." *Playing Shakespeare.* John Barton. London: Methuen, 1984. 169–79.

Suchet and Stewart, both of whom performed the role of Shylock under the direction of Barton, compare their interpretations.

Sullivan, Patrick J. "Strumpet Wind—The National Theatre's Merchant of Venice." The Merchant of Venice: *Critical Essays.* Ed. Thomas Wheeler. New York: Garland, 1991. 315–37.

This essay includes history and analysis of this most famous performance of *MV* in the second half of the twentieth century.

Trewin, J. C. *Going to Shakespeare.* London: George C. Allen, 1978.

The text offers easy-to-read observations on each play.

————. *Shakespeare on the English Stage 1900–1964: A Survey of Productions.* London: Barrie and Rockliff, 1964.

This volume presents more detailed descriptions of performances of the plays in the twentieth century.

Willis, Susan. *The BBC Shakespeare Plays: Making the Televised Canon.* Chapel Hill and London: U of North Carolina P, 1991.

This volume describes the history and production strategies of the 37-play series of Shakespeare's plays produced by the BBC between 1978 and 1985.

Winter, William. *Shakespeare on the Stage: First Series.* 1911. New York: Benjamin Blom, 1969.

This is a valuable history of performances, some of which Winter saw himself. The section on *MV* (129–231) covers performances by Richard Burbage through those of Ellen Terry.

INDEX

272
Index

Pope, Alexander, 18, 203
Portmanteau scenes, 55–56, 67
Post-Saussurean theory, 168, 177–78
Post-Structuralists, 183, 190
Prince of Wales Theatre, 217
Princess's Theatre, 62 (caption)
Promptbook, 5, 7
Proudfoot, Richard, Ann Thompson, and David Scott Kastan, 21
Psychoanalysis, 163
Psychoanalytic criticism, 163–64
Psychoanalytic theory, 161
Purchas, Samuel, 33–34
Puttenham, George, 115n, 189

Quarto 1 (Q1), 1, 9, 19, 14, 21. 22, 25n, 200
Quarto 2 (Q2), 2, 9,12
Quarto 3 (Q3), 2, 15–16
Queen Elizabeth, 27n, 32, 220
Queen's Master of the Revels, 3
Queen's Theatre, 228
Queer theory, 169, 190
Quiller-Couch, Arthur, 20, 27n, 154

Rabb, Ellis, 234
Rabkin, Norman, 84, 139
Redgrave, Michael, 230
Reed, Isaac, 19
Regisseur, 224, 226–27
Ribner, Irving, 106
Riddles, 69, 93, 189
Roberts, James, 2–8, 25n, 200
Rolfe, W. J., 20
Roman New Comedy, 54, 120, 145n
Romantic comedy, 120–21, 123–24, 172, 186
Romantics, 152–53
Rose, Paul, 230
Rowe, Nicholas, 17–18, 22, 27n, 55, 81n, 195n
Royal Lyceum Theatre, 211
Royal National Theatre, 245, 246 (caption)

Royal Shakespeare Company, 234, 237
Ruskin, John, 150, 152, 169
Ryan, Kiernan, 173–75

Saint Andrew, 1, 3
Saint Matthew, 1
San Andres, 1. See Saint Andrew
San Matias, 1. See Saint Matthew
Sandys, Sir Edwin, 34
Schwartz, Murray M. and Coppelia Kahn, 197n
Scott, George C., 231
Scribal copy, 9
Scrivener, 10
Second Folio, 16
Semiology (semiotics), 168
Seneca: De Beneficiis, 17, 138
Senecan melodrama, 172
Senex, 83, 220
Shaffer, Peter, 105
Shakespeare Festival, 221
Shakespeare, John, 32
Shakespeare, Memorial Theatre, 224
Shakespeare Society, 19
Shapiro, James, 34, 49n, 50n, 110, 132, 146n, 171, 176–77, 248n
Shell, Marc, 91, 97, 104, 115n, 147n
Sher, Anthony, 238
Sidney, Sir Philip, 32
Sinfield, Alan, 193–95, 197n
Sinsheimer, Hermann, 116n
Slights, Camille, 184
Smith, Bruce R., 190–92
Smith, Henry, 33
Sothern, Edward Hugh, 220–22
Sprezzatura, 133, 136
St. James Theatre, 228, 241
Star Theater, 212
Stationers' Company, 11
Stationers' Hall, 3, 5
Stationers' Register, 1, 3–5, 7, 11, 19, 50n
Staying entry, 4, 5. See blocking entry

About the Author

VICKI K. JANIK is Associate Professor of Humanities at the State University of New York at Farmingdale, where she has taught a variety of courses in Shakespeare, drama, and technical communications since 1987. Her previous books include *Modern British Women Writers: An A-to-Z Guide* (Greenwood, 2002) and *Fools and Jesters in Literature, Art, and History* (Greenwood, 1998).